A Kodansha Comics Trade Paperback Original.

Noragami: Stray God volume 20 copyright © 2019 Adachitoka
English translation copyright © 2019 Adachitoka

Published in the United States by Kodansha Comics, an imprint of Kodansha USA Publishing, LLC, New York.

Publication rights for this English edition arranged through Kodansha Ltd., Tokyo.

First published in Japan in 2019 by Kodansha Ltd., Tokyo.

ISBN 978-1-63236-504-0

Printed in the United States of America.

www.kodanshacomics.com

9 8 7 6 5 4 3 2 1

Translation: Alethea Nibley & Athena Nibley
Lettering: Lys Blakeslee
Editing: Haruko Hashimoto
Kodansha Comics edition cover design: Phil Balsman

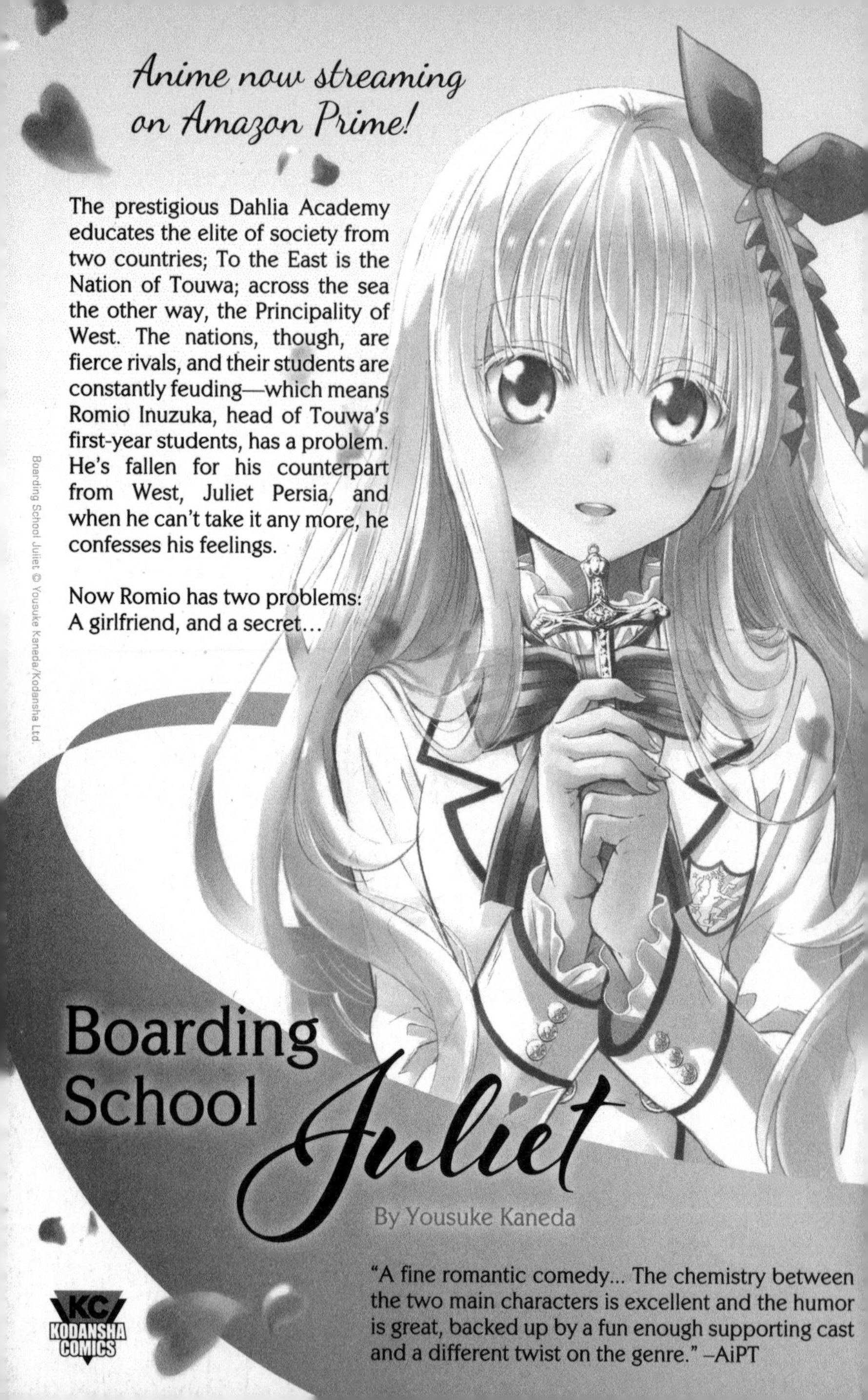
Anime now streaming on Amazon Prime!
The prestigious Dahlia Academy educates the elite of society from two countries; To the East is the Nation of Touwa; across the sea the other way, the Principality of West. The nations, though, are fierce rivals, and their students are constantly feuding—which means Romio Inuzuka, head of Touwa's first-year students, has a problem. He's fallen for his counterpart from West, Juliet Persia, and when he can't take it any more, he confesses his feelings.
Now Romio has two problems: A girlfriend, and a secret…
Boarding School Juliet © Yousuke Kaneda/Kodansha Ltd.
Boarding School Juliet
By Yousuke Kaneda
"A fine romantic comedy... The chemistry between the two main characters is excellent and the humor is great, backed up by a fun enough supporting cast and a different twist on the genre." –AiPT
KC KODANSHA COMICS

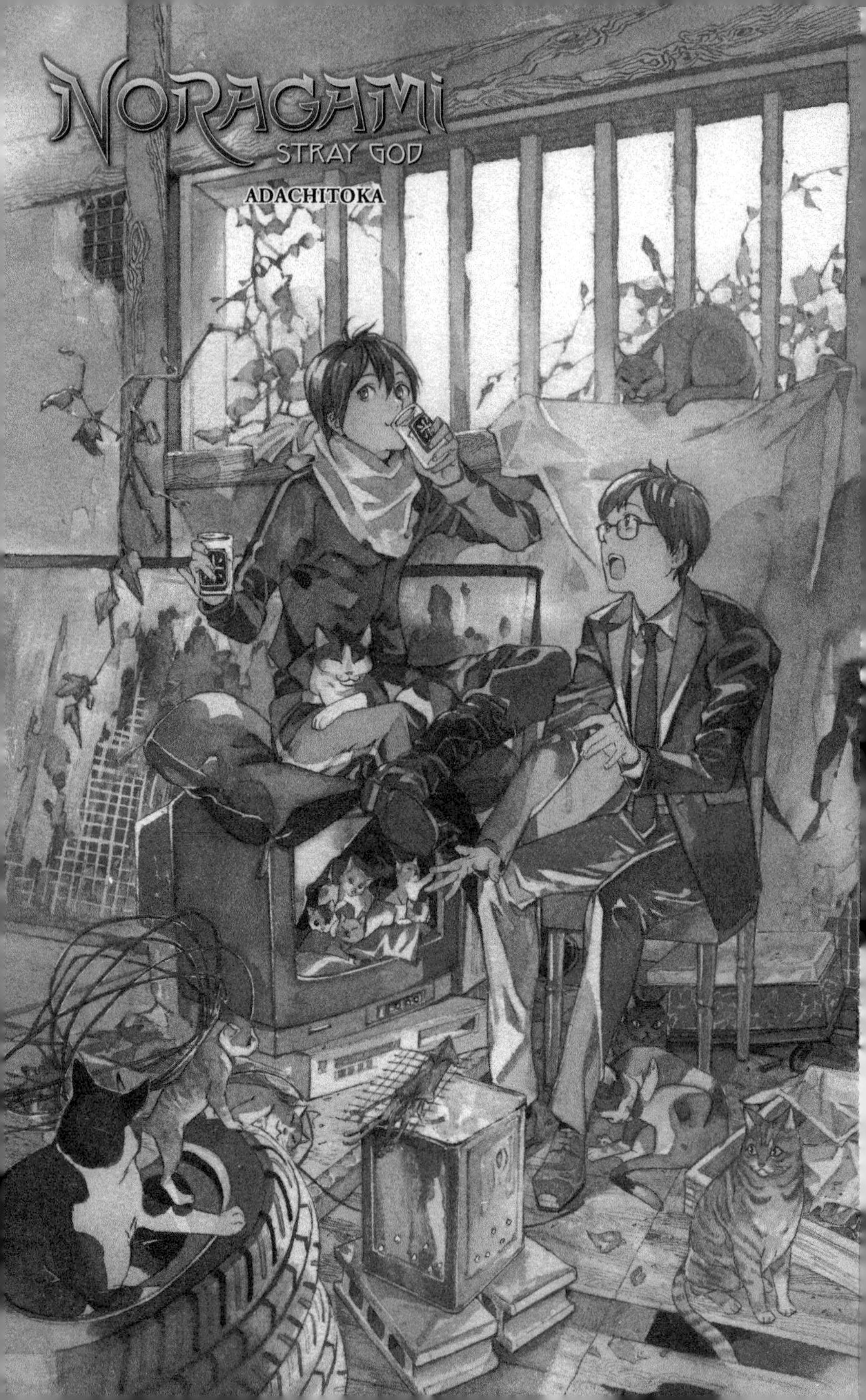
NORAGAMI
STRAY GOD
ADACHITOKA

characters

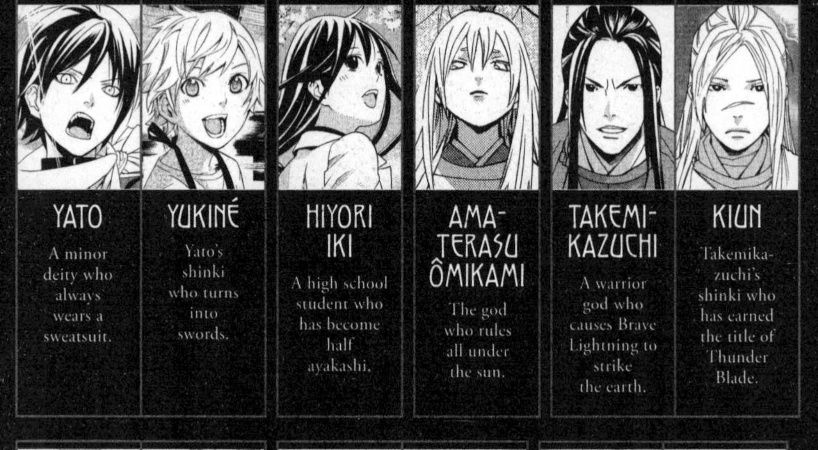

YATO
A minor deity who always wears a sweatsuit.

YUKINÉ
Yato's shinki who turns into swords.

HIYORI IKI
A high school student who has become half ayakashi.

AMA-TERASU ÔMIKAMI
The god who rules all under the sun.

TAKEMI-KAZUCHI
A warrior god who causes Brave Lightning to strike the earth.

KIUN
Takemika-zuchi's shinki who has earned the title of Thunder Blade.

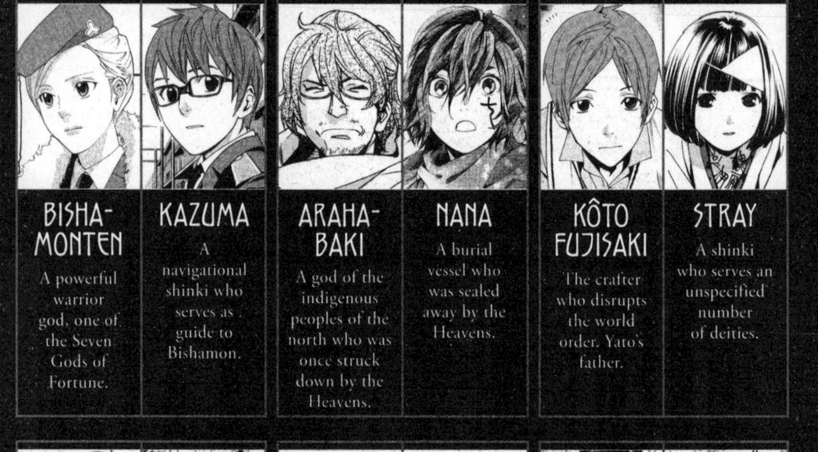

BISHA-MONTEN
A powerful warrior god, one of the Seven Gods of Fortune.

KAZUMA
A navigational shinki who serves as guide to Bishamon.

ARAHA-BAKI
A god of the indigenous peoples of the north who was once struck down by the Heavens.

NANA
A burial vessel who was sealed away by the Heavens.

KÔTO FUJISAKI
The crafter who disrupts the world order. Yato's father.

STRAY
A shinki who serves an unspecified number of deities.

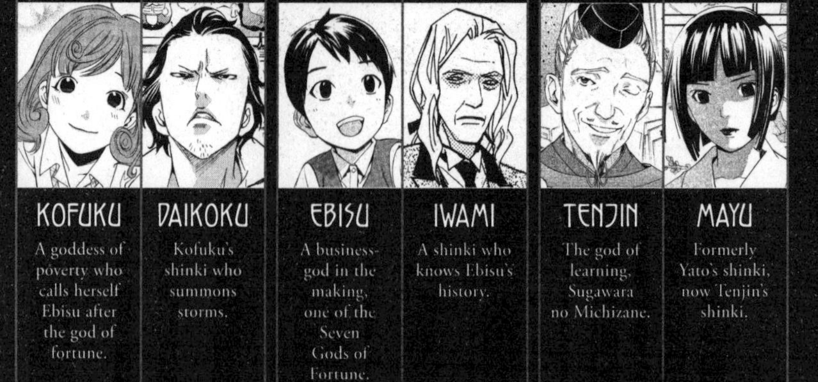

KOFUKU
A goddess of poverty who calls herself Ebisu after the god of fortune.

DAIKOKU
Kofuku's shinki who summons storms.

EBISU
A business-god in the making, one of the Seven Gods of Fortune.

IWAMI
A shinki who knows Ebisu's history.

TENJIN
The god of learning, Sugawara no Michizane.

MAYU
Formerly Yato's shinki, now Tenjin's shinki.

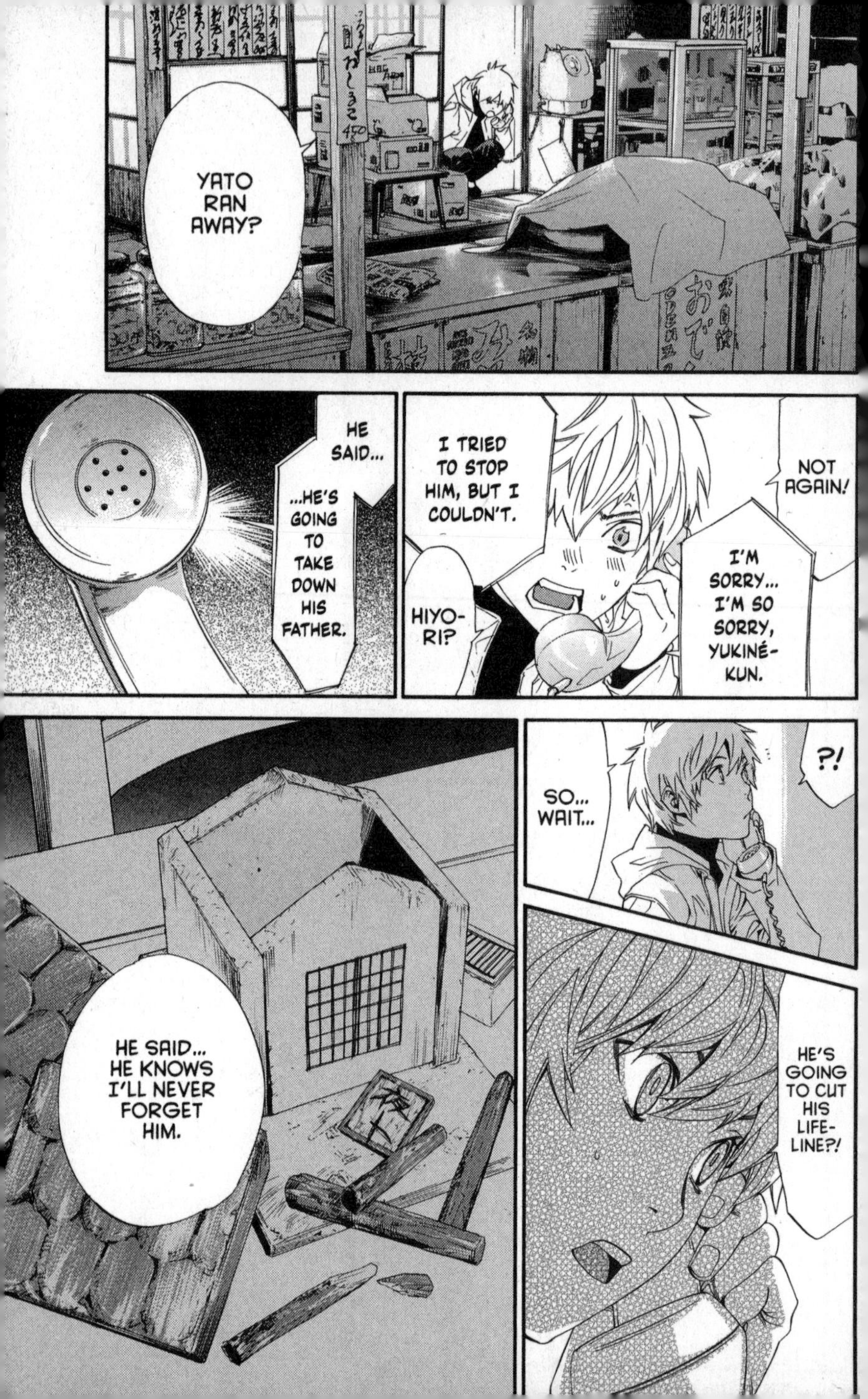
YATO RAN AWAY?
NOT AGAIN!
I TRIED TO STOP HIM, BUT I COULDN'T.
I'M SORRY... I'M SO SORRY, YUKINÉ-KUN.
HIYO-RI?
HE SAID...
...HE'S GOING TO TAKE DOWN HIS FATHER.
?!
SO... WAIT...
HE'S GOING TO CUT HIS LIFE-LINE?!
HE SAID... HE KNOWS I'LL NEVER FORGET HIM.

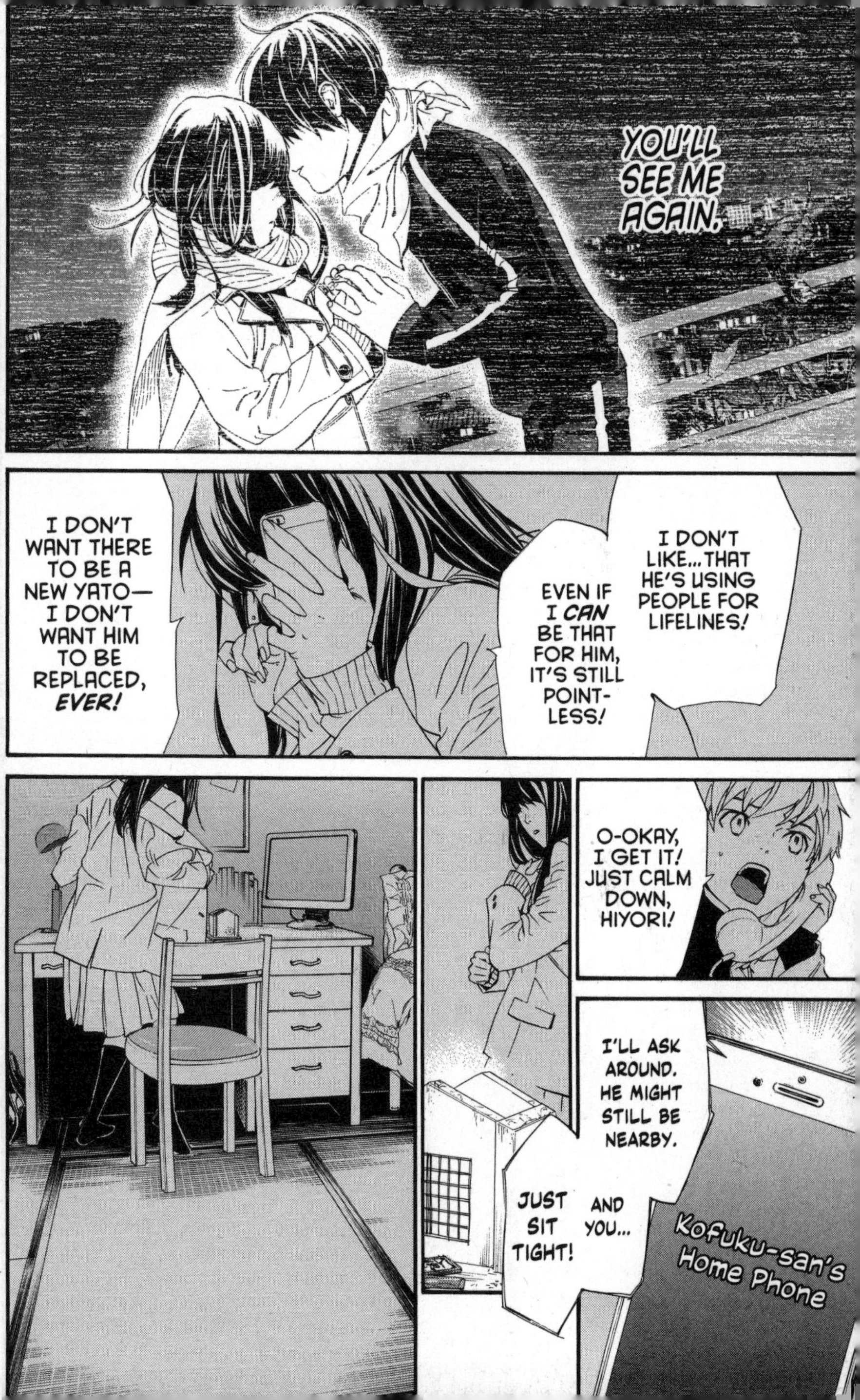
YOU'LL SEE ME AGAIN.
I DON'T LIKE... THAT HE'S USING PEOPLE FOR LIFELINES!
EVEN IF I CAN BE THAT FOR HIM, IT'S STILL POINTLESS!
I DON'T WANT THERE TO BE A NEW YATO— I DON'T WANT HIM TO BE REPLACED, EVER!
O-OKAY, I GET IT! JUST CALM DOWN, HIYORI!
I'LL ASK AROUND. HE MIGHT STILL BE NEARBY.
Kofuku-san's Home Phone
AND YOU...
JUST SIT TIGHT!

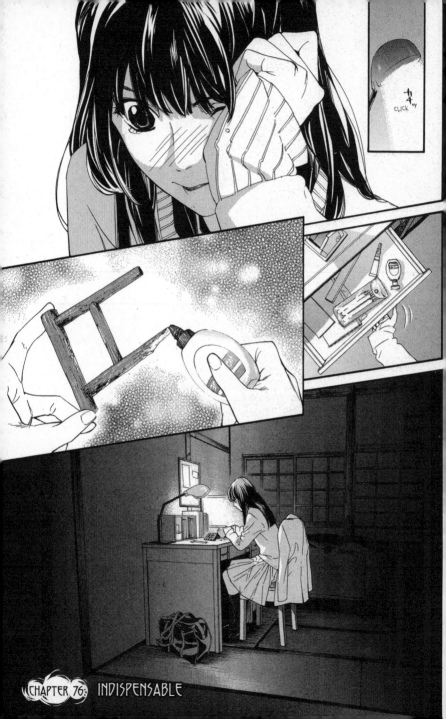

Chapter 76: INDISPENSABLE

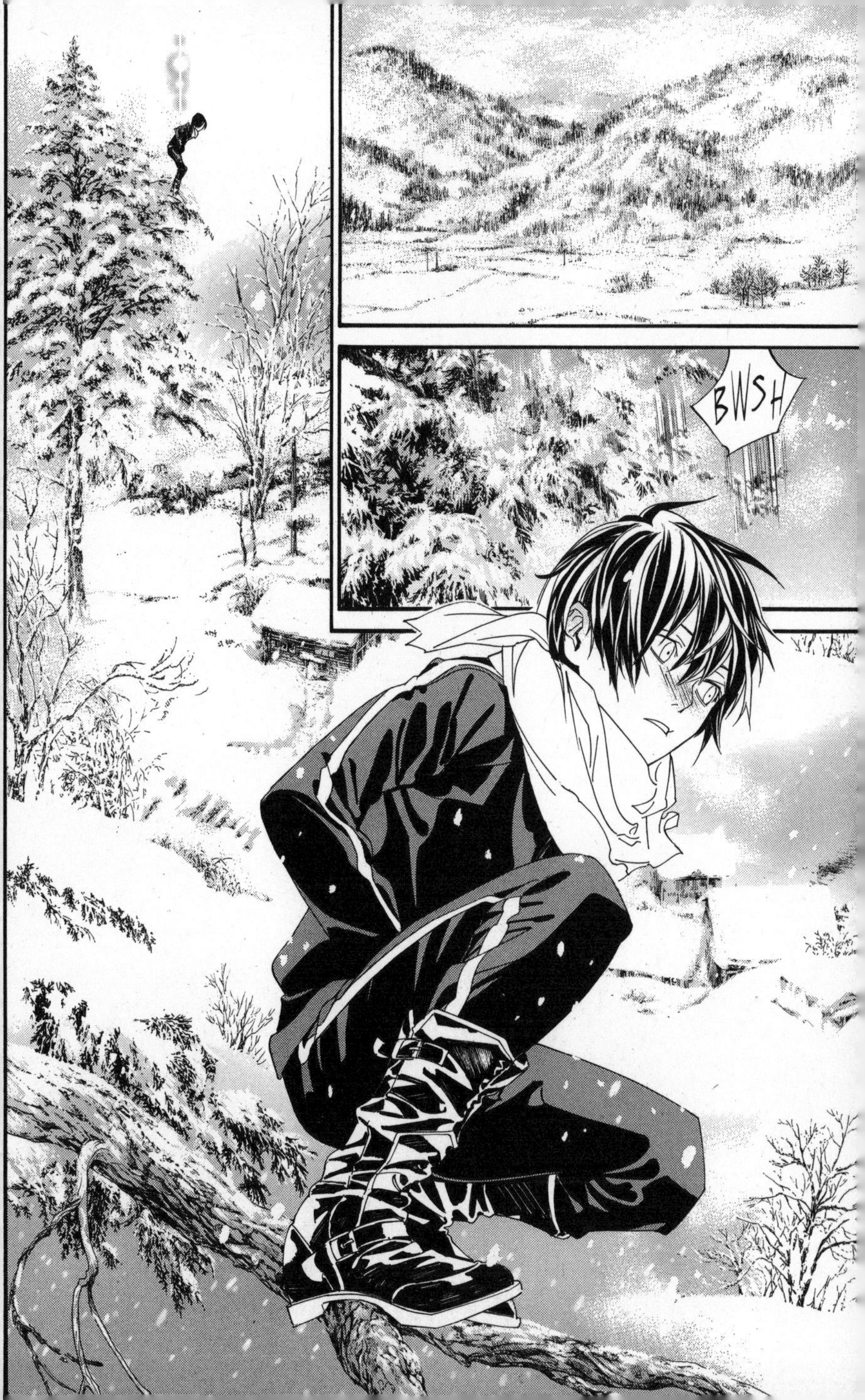
BWSH

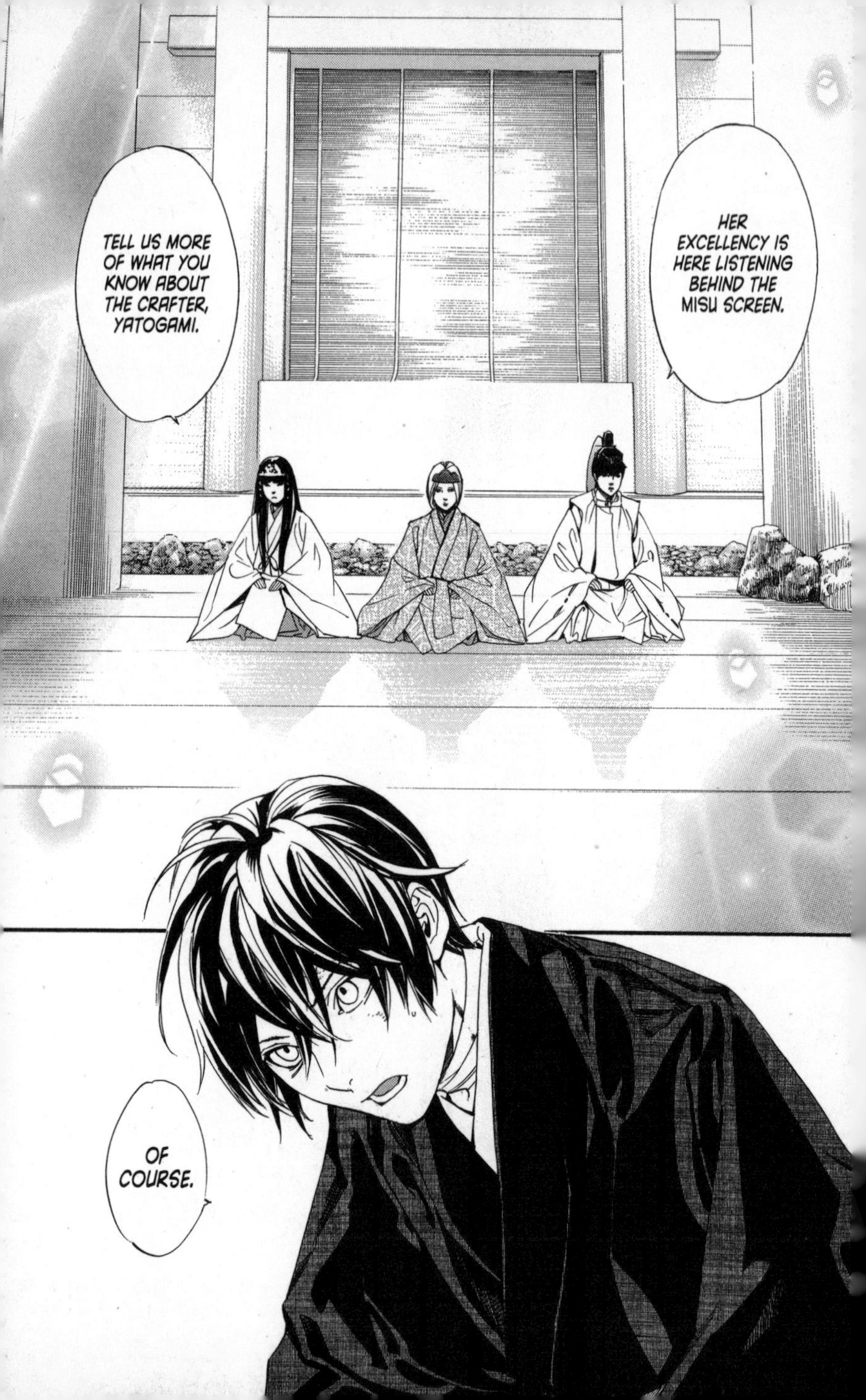
HER EXCELLENCY IS HERE LISTENING BEHIND THE MISU SCREEN.
TELL US MORE OF WHAT YOU KNOW ABOUT THE CRAFTER, YATOGAMI.
OF COURSE.

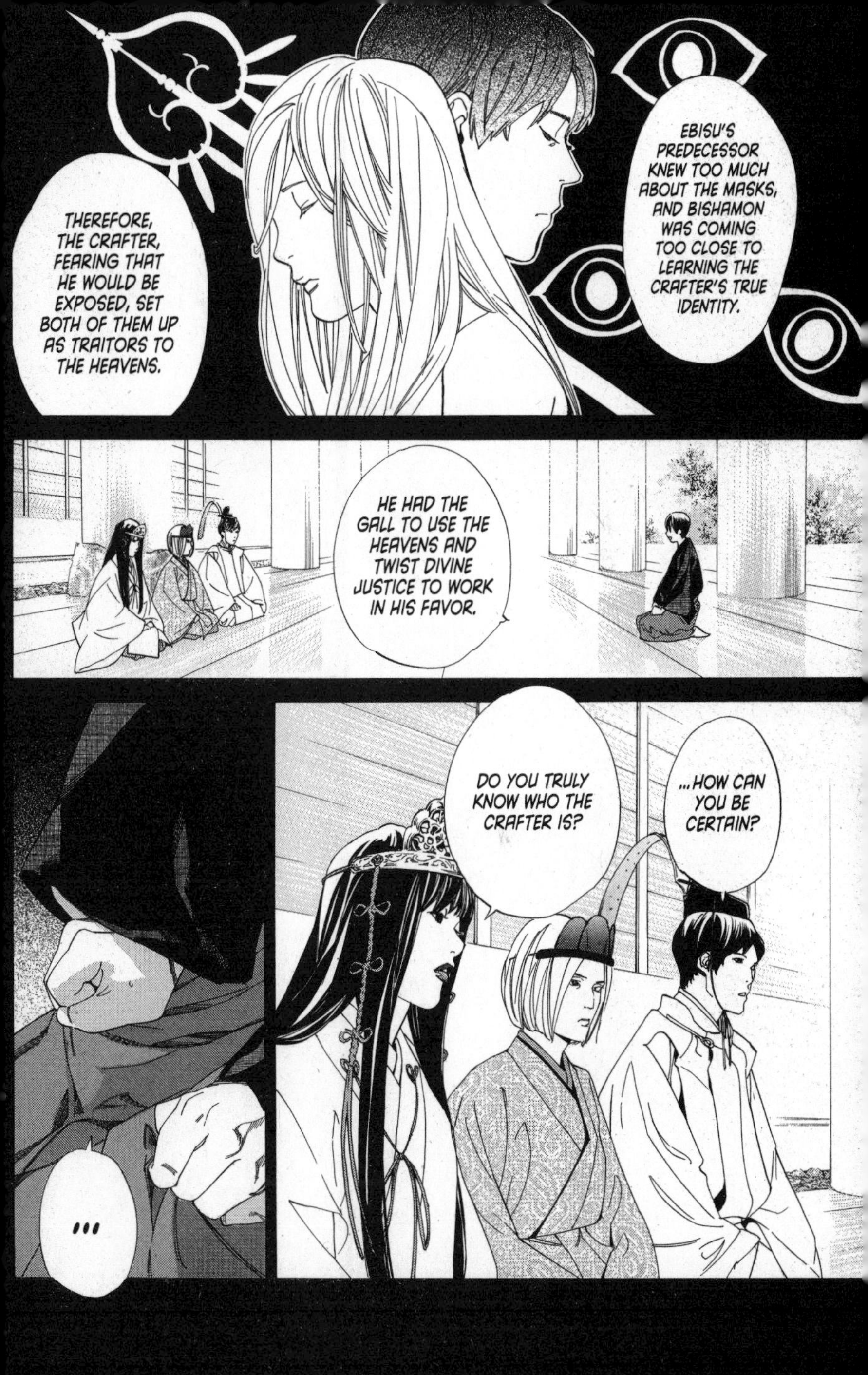
EBISU'S PREDECESSOR KNEW TOO MUCH ABOUT THE MASKS, AND BISHAMON WAS COMING TOO CLOSE TO LEARNING THE CRAFTER'S TRUE IDENTITY.
THEREFORE, THE CRAFTER, FEARING THAT HE WOULD BE EXPOSED, SET BOTH OF THEM UP AS TRAITORS TO THE HEAVENS.
HE HAD THE GALL TO USE THE HEAVENS AND TWIST DIVINE JUSTICE TO WORK IN HIS FAVOR.
...HOW CAN YOU BE CERTAIN?
DO YOU TRULY KNOW WHO THE CRAFTER IS?
...

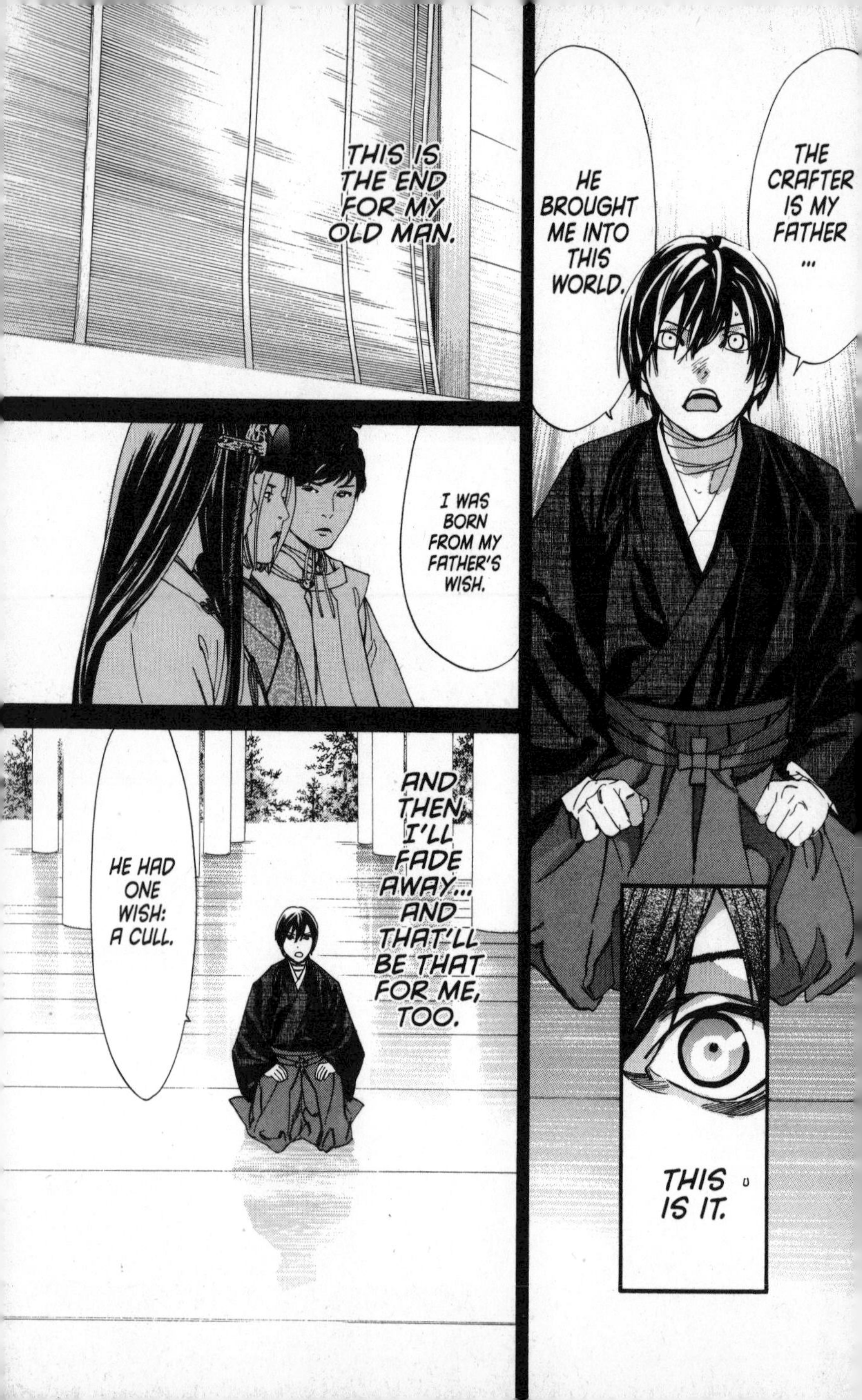
THE CRAFTER IS MY FATHER ...
HE BROUGHT ME INTO THIS WORLD.
THIS IS IT.
THIS IS THE END FOR MY OLD MAN.
I WAS BORN FROM MY FATHER'S WISH.
AND THEN, I'LL FADE AWAY... AND THAT'LL BE THAT FOR ME, TOO.
HE HAD ONE WISH: A CULL.

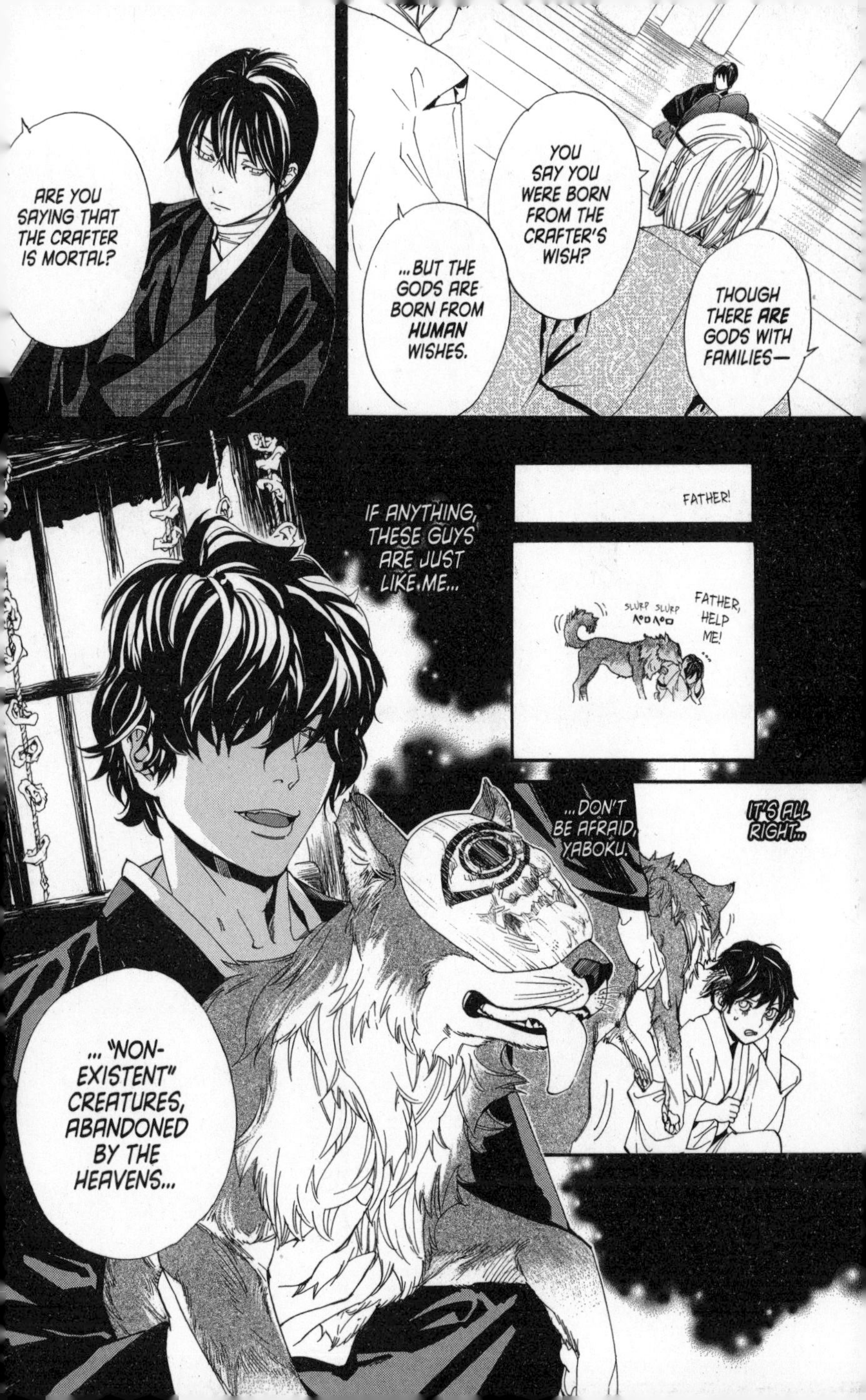
THOUGH THERE ARE GODS WITH FAMILIES—
...BUT THE GODS ARE BORN FROM HUMAN WISHES.
YOU SAY YOU WERE BORN FROM THE CRAFTER'S WISH?
ARE YOU SAYING THAT THE CRAFTER IS MORTAL?
FATHER!
FATHER, HELP ME!
SLURP SLURP
ペロペロ
IT'S ALL RIGHT...
...DON'T BE AFRAID, YABOKU.
IF ANYTHING, THESE GUYS ARE JUST LIKE ME...
... "NON-EXISTENT" CREATURES, ABANDONED BY THE HEAVENS...

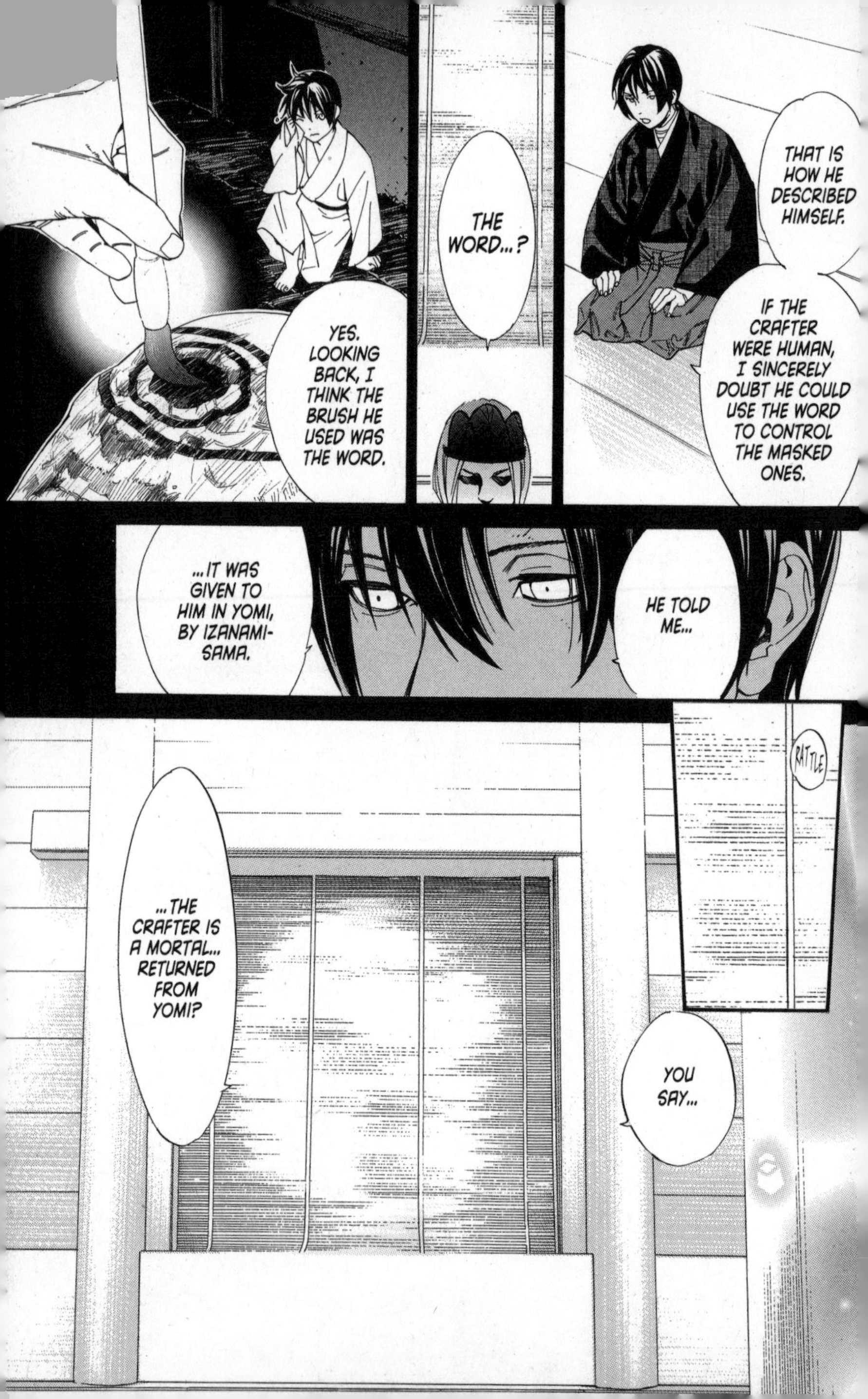
THAT IS HOW HE DESCRIBED HIMSELF.
IF THE CRAFTER WERE HUMAN, I SINCERELY DOUBT HE COULD USE THE WORD TO CONTROL THE MASKED ONES.
THE WORD...?
YES. LOOKING BACK, I THINK THE BRUSH HE USED WAS THE WORD.
HE TOLD ME...
...IT WAS GIVEN TO HIM IN YOMI, BY IZANAMI-SAMA.
RATTLE
...THE CRAFTER IS A MORTAL... RETURNED FROM YOMI?
YOU SAY...

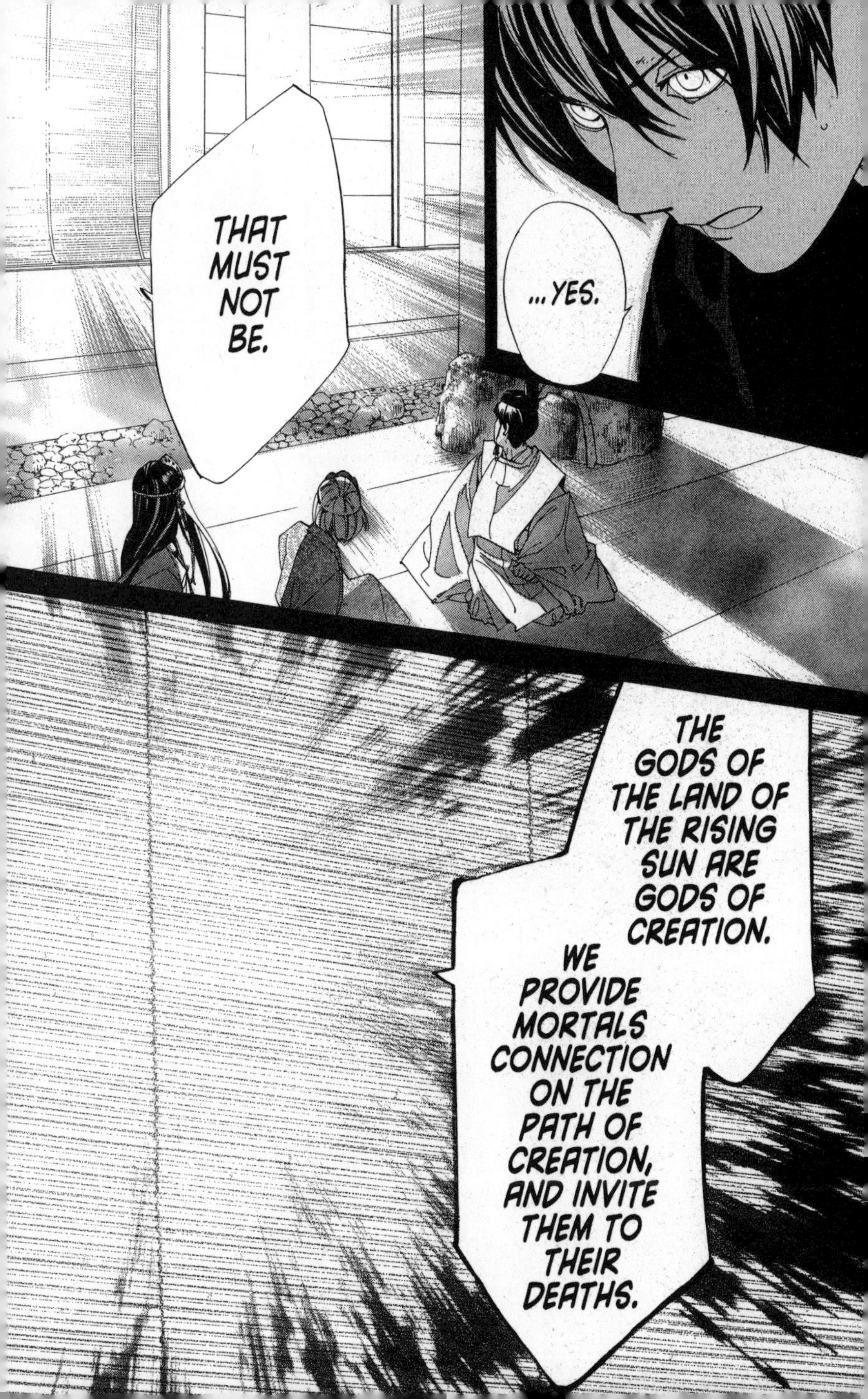
...YES.
THAT MUST NOT BE.
THE GODS OF THE LAND OF THE RISING SUN ARE GODS OF CREATION.
WE PROVIDE MORTALS CONNECTION ON THE PATH OF CREATION, AND INVITE THEM TO THEIR DEATHS.

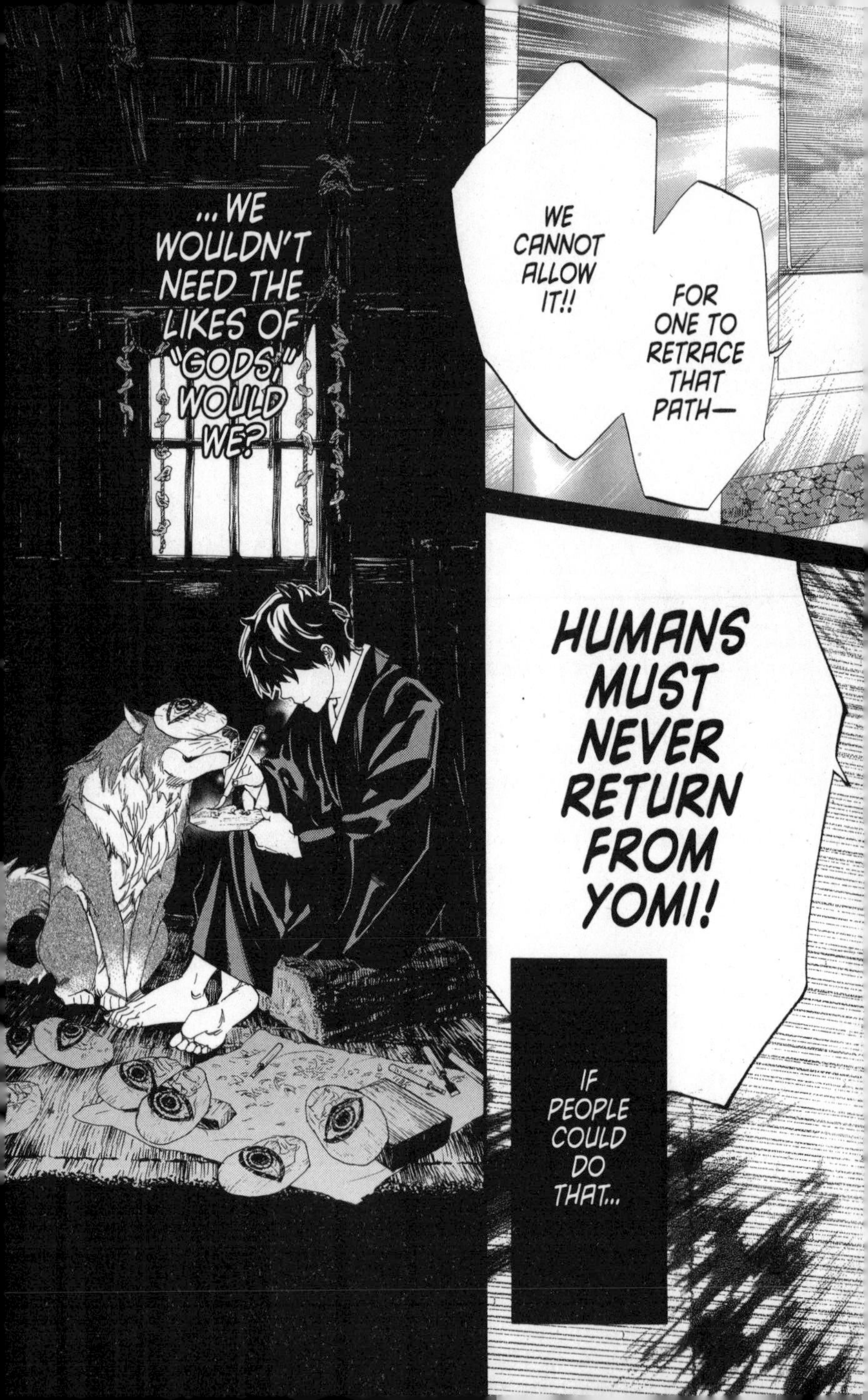
FOR ONE TO RETRACE THAT PATH—
WE CANNOT ALLOW IT!!
HUMANS MUST NEVER RETURN FROM YOMI!
IF PEOPLE COULD DO THAT...
...WE WOULDN'T NEED THE LIKES OF "GODS," WOULD WE?

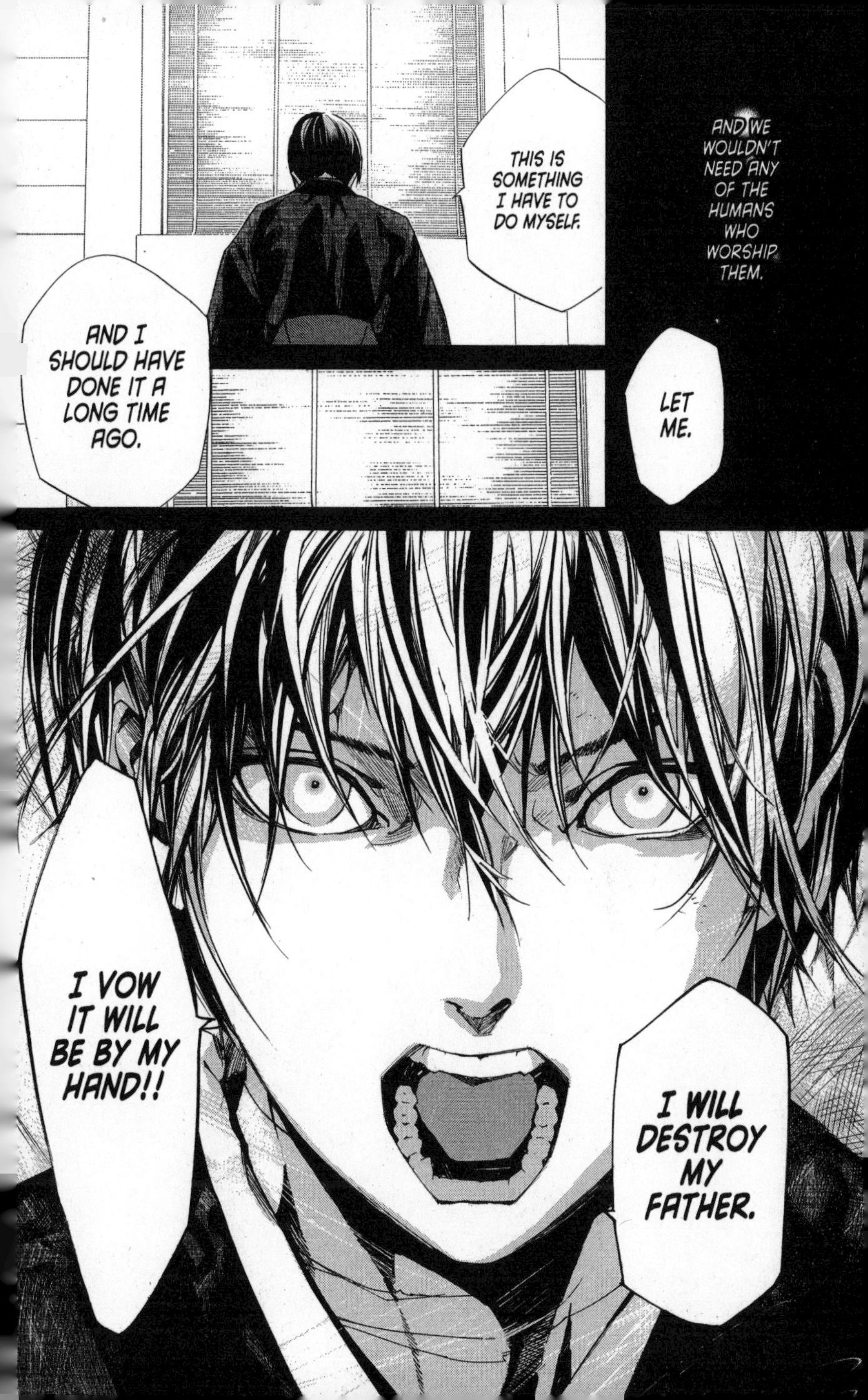
AND WE WOULDN'T NEED ANY OF THE HUMANS WHO WORSHIP THEM.
LET ME.
THIS IS SOMETHING I HAVE TO DO MYSELF.
AND I SHOULD HAVE DONE IT A LONG TIME AGO.
I WILL DESTROY MY FATHER.
I VOW IT WILL BE BY MY HAND!!

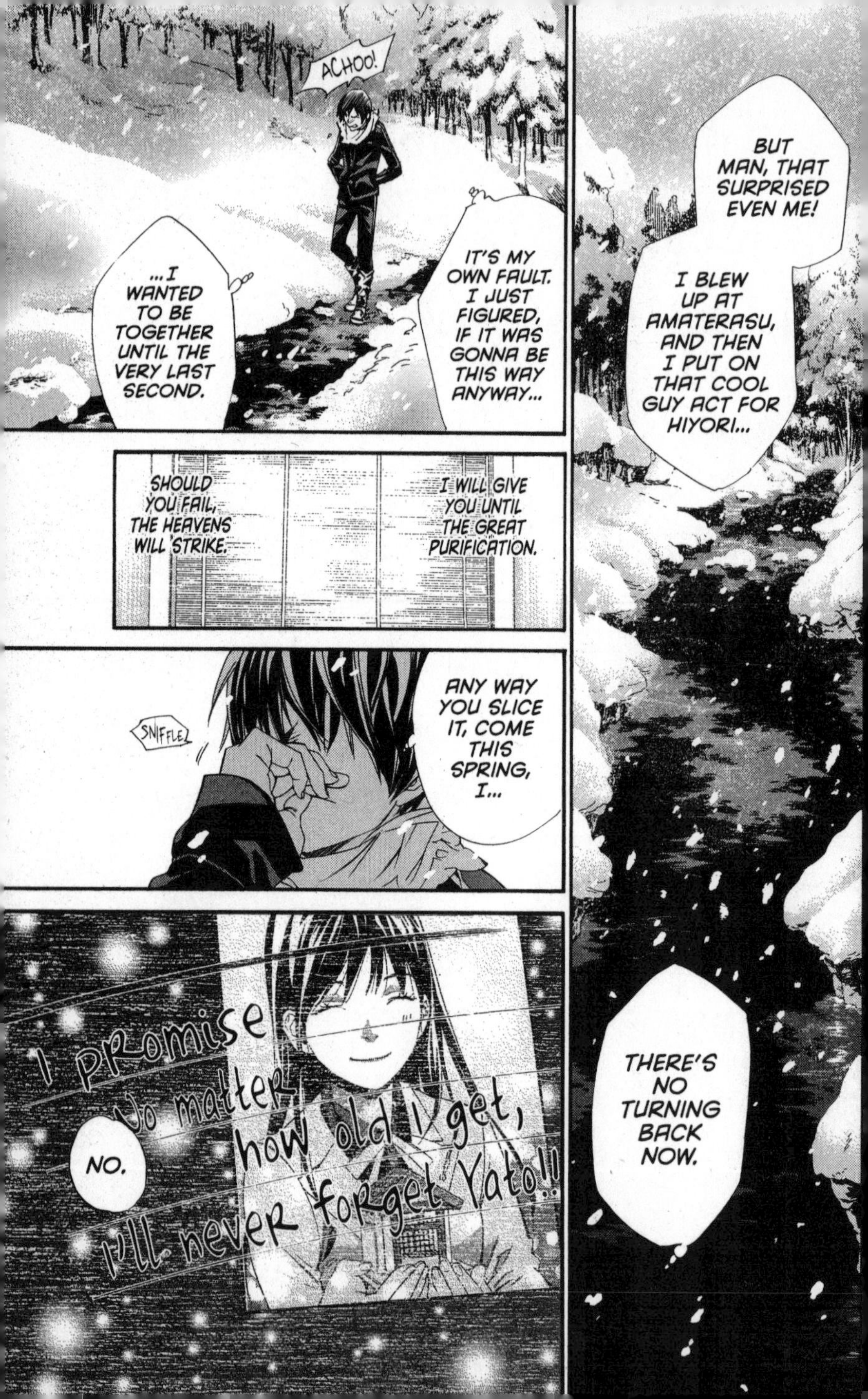
BUT MAN, THAT SURPRISED EVEN ME!
I BLEW UP AT AMATERASU, AND THEN I PUT ON THAT COOL GUY ACT FOR HIYORI...
THERE'S NO TURNING BACK NOW.
ACHOO!
IT'S MY OWN FAULT. I JUST FIGURED, IF IT WAS GONNA BE THIS WAY ANYWAY...
...I WANTED TO BE TOGETHER UNTIL THE VERY LAST SECOND.
I WILL GIVE YOU UNTIL THE GREAT PURIFICATION.
SHOULD YOU FAIL, THE HEAVENS WILL STRIKE.
ANY WAY YOU SLICE IT, COME THIS SPRING, I...
SNIFFLE
I promise No matter how old I get, I'll never forget Yato!!
NO.

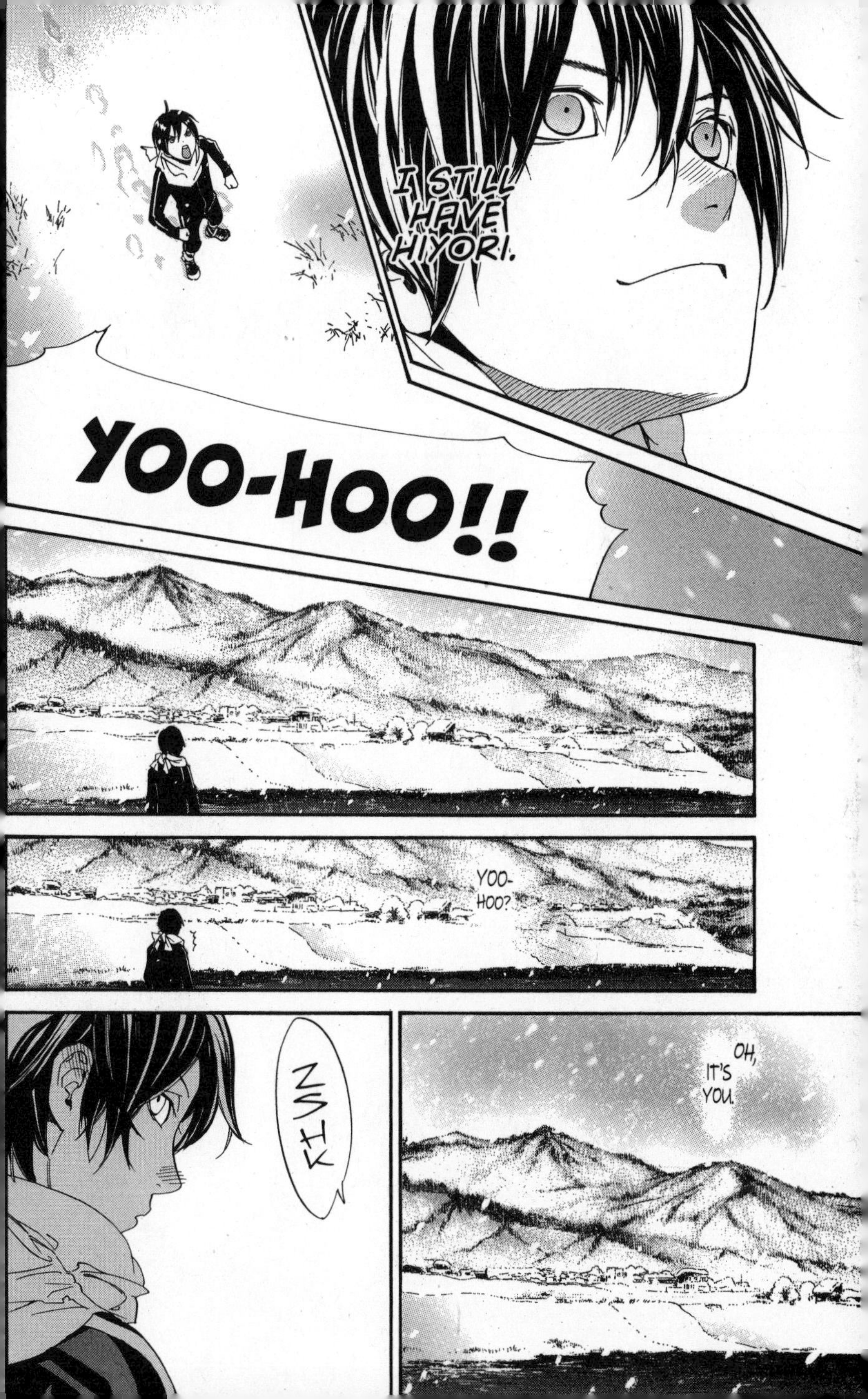
I STILL HAVE HIYORI.
YOO-HOO!!
YOO-HOO?
OH, IT'S YOU.
NSHK

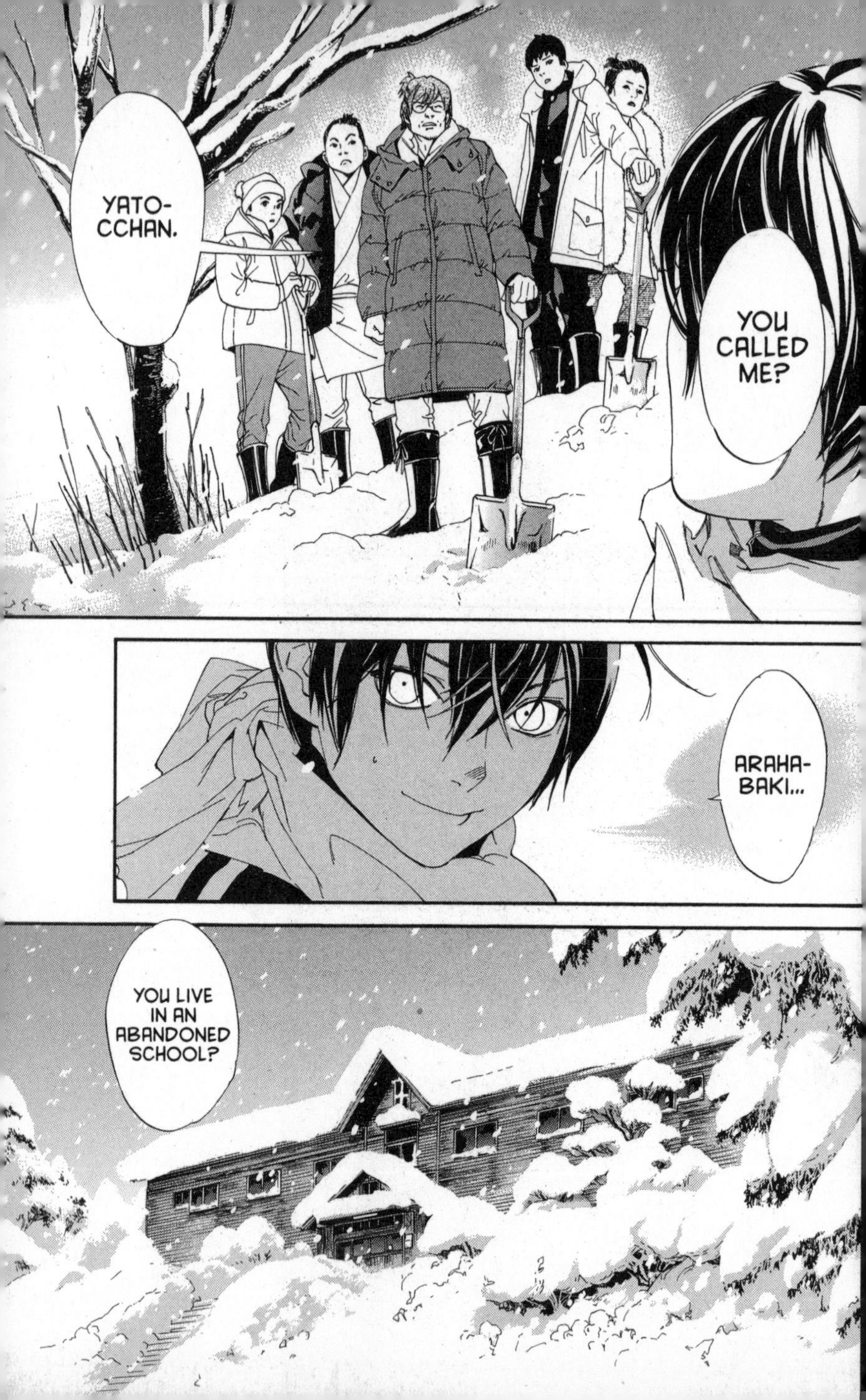
YATO-CCHAN.
YOU CALLED ME?
ARAHA-BAKI...
YOU LIVE IN AN ABANDONED SCHOOL?

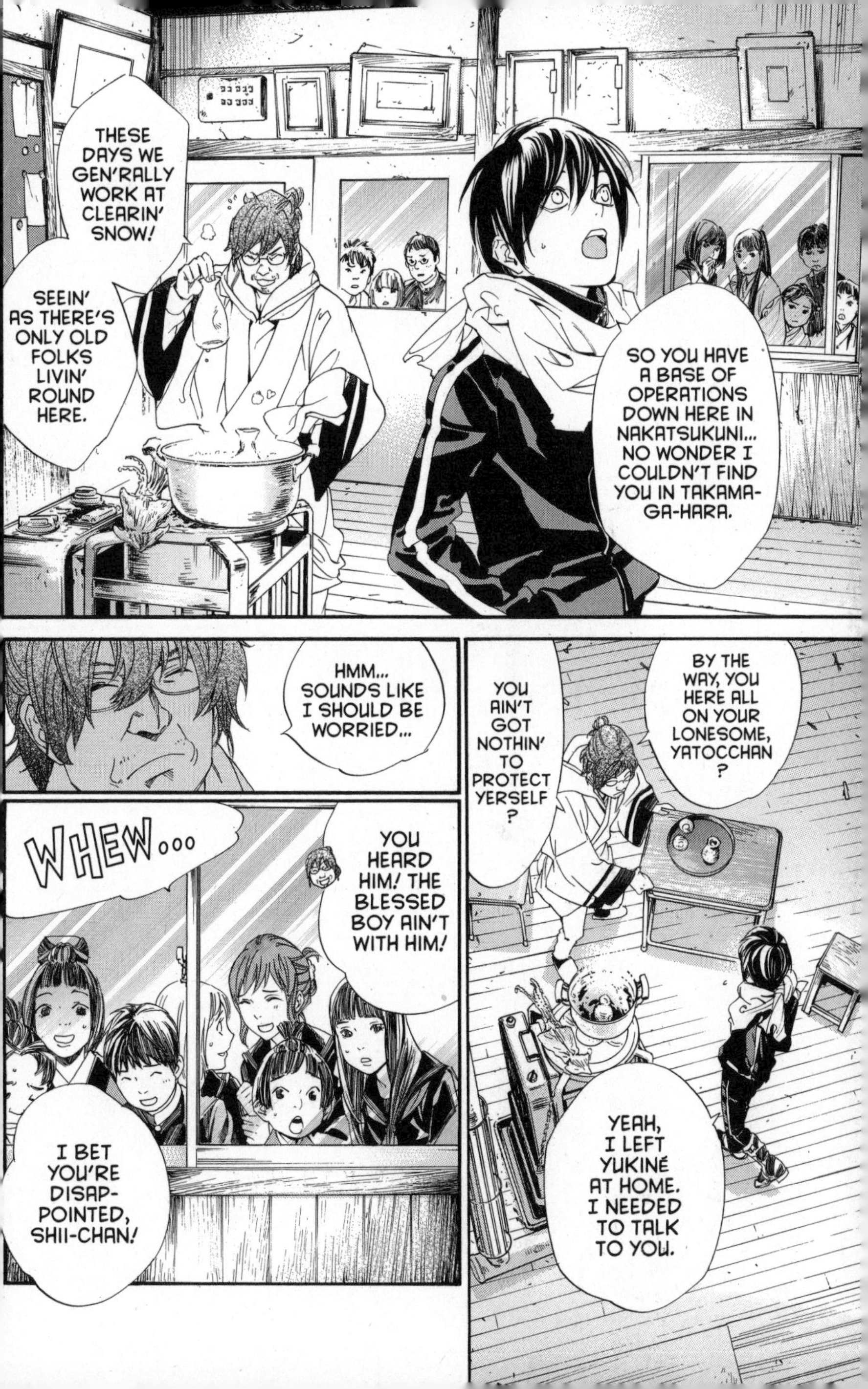
SO YOU HAVE A BASE OF OPERATIONS DOWN HERE IN NAKATSUKUNI... NO WONDER I COULDN'T FIND YOU IN TAKAMA-GA-HARA.
THESE DAYS WE GEN'RALLY WORK AT CLEARIN' SNOW!
SEEIN' AS THERE'S ONLY OLD FOLKS LIVIN' ROUND HERE.
BY THE WAY, YOU HERE ALL ON YOUR LONESOME, YATOCCHAN?
YOU AIN'T GOT NOTHIN' TO PROTECT YERSELF?
YEAH, I LEFT YUKINÉ AT HOME. I NEEDED TO TALK TO YOU.
HMM... SOUNDS LIKE I SHOULD BE WORRIED...
YOU HEARD HIM! THE BLESSED BOY AIN'T WITH HIM!
WHEW...
I BET YOU'RE DISAP-POINTED, SHII-CHAN!

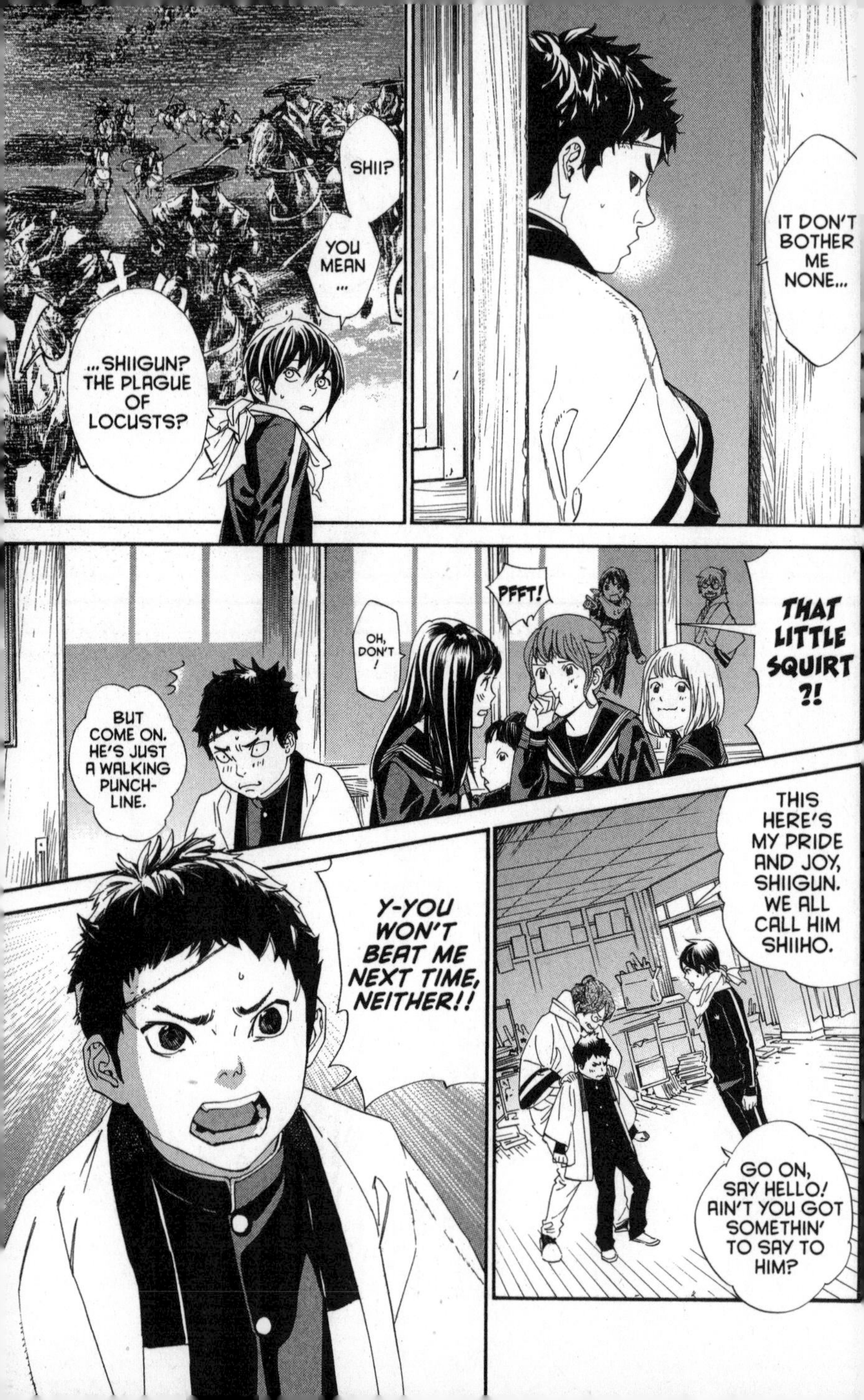
IT DON'T BOTHER ME NONE...
SHII?
YOU MEAN ...
...SHIIGUN? THE PLAGUE OF LOCUSTS?
THAT LITTLE SQUIRT?!
PFFT!
OH, DON'T!
BUT COME ON. HE'S JUST A WALKING PUNCH-LINE.
THIS HERE'S MY PRIDE AND JOY, SHIIGUN. WE ALL CALL HIM SHIIHO.
GO ON, SAY HELLO! AIN'T YOU GOT SOMETHIN' TO SAY TO HIM?
Y-YOU WON'T BEAT ME NEXT TIME, NEITHER!!

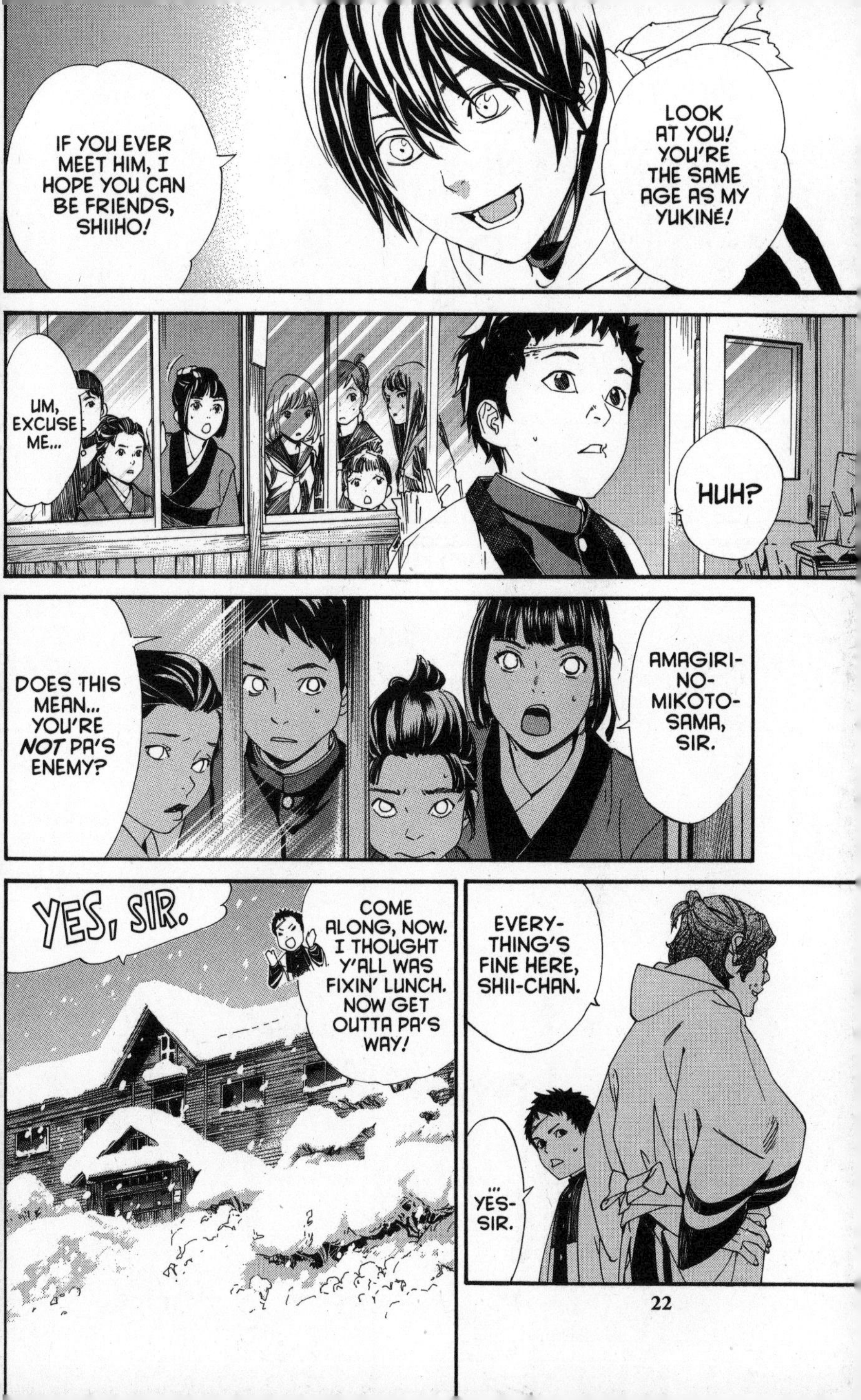
LOOK AT YOU! YOU'RE THE SAME AGE AS MY YUKINÉ!
IF YOU EVER MEET HIM, I HOPE YOU CAN BE FRIENDS, SHIIHO!
HUH?
UM, EXCUSE ME...
AMAGIRI-NO-MIKOTO-SAMA, SIR.
DOES THIS MEAN... YOU'RE *NOT* PA'S ENEMY?
EVERY-THING'S FINE HERE, SHII-CHAN.
...YES-SIR.
COME ALONG, NOW. I THOUGHT Y'ALL WAS FIXIN' LUNCH. NOW GET OUTTA PA'S WAY!
YES, SIR.

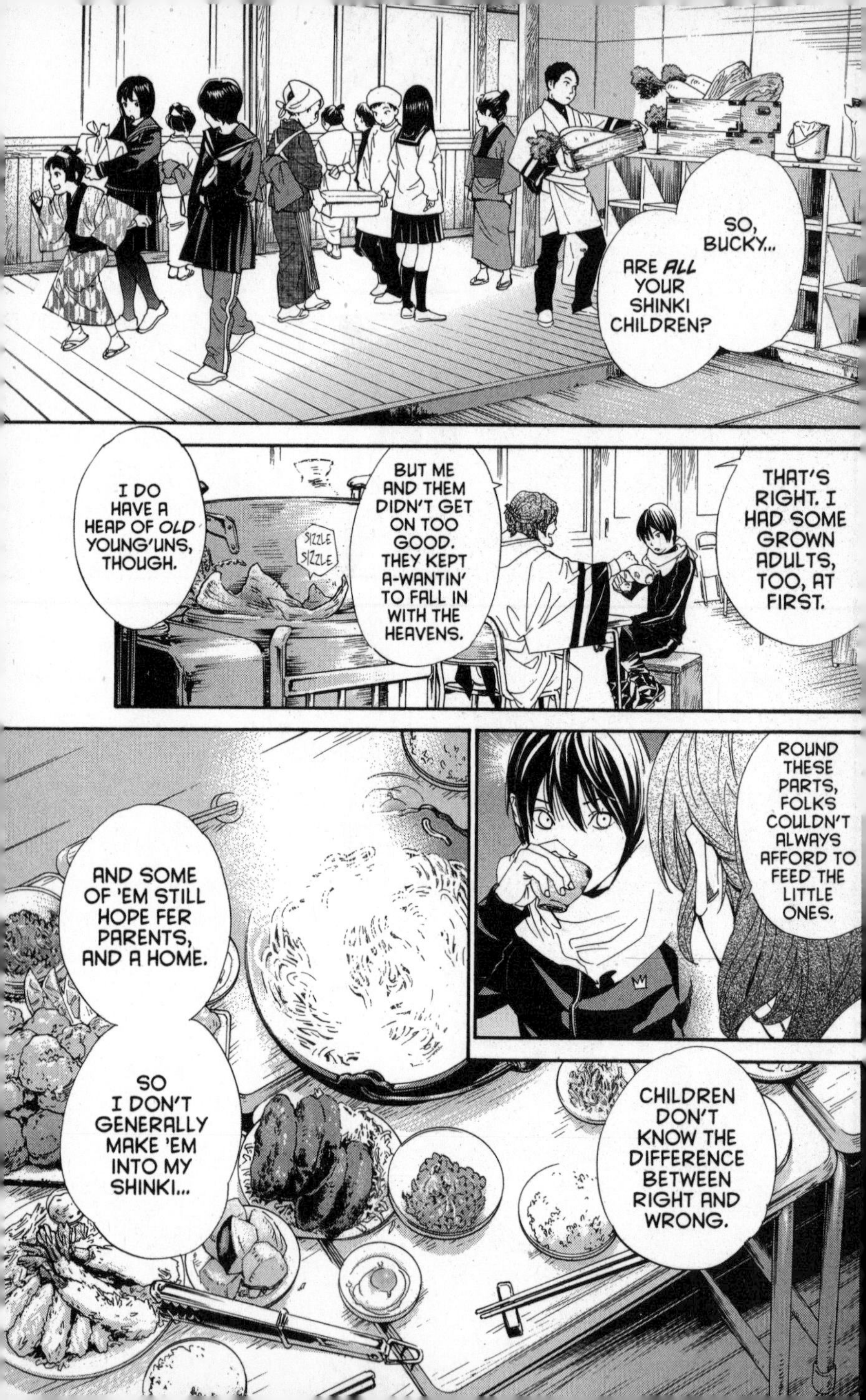

SO, BUCKY... ARE *ALL* YOUR SHINKI CHILDREN?
THAT'S RIGHT. I HAD SOME GROWN ADULTS, TOO, AT FIRST.
BUT ME AND THEM DIDN'T GET ON TOO GOOD. THEY KEPT A-WANTIN' TO FALL IN WITH THE HEAVENS.
SIZZLE SIZZLE
I DO HAVE A HEAP OF *OLD* YOUNG'UNS, THOUGH.
ROUND THESE PARTS, FOLKS COULDN'T ALWAYS AFFORD TO FEED THE LITTLE ONES.
CHILDREN DON'T KNOW THE DIFFERENCE BETWEEN RIGHT AND WRONG.
AND SOME OF 'EM STILL HOPE FER PARENTS, AND A HOME.
SO I DON'T GENERALLY MAKE 'EM INTO MY SHINKI...

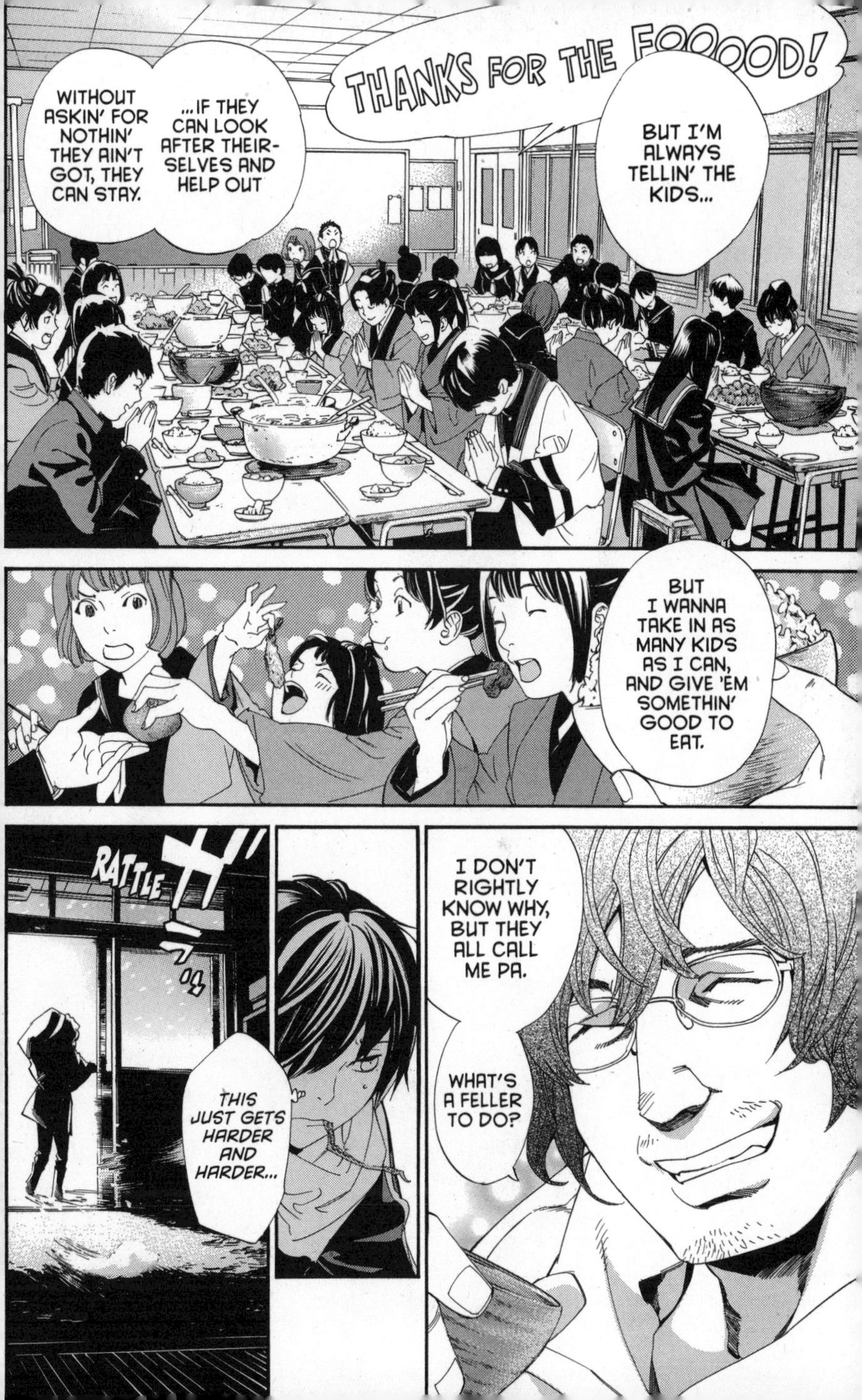
THANKS FOR THE FOOOOOD!
BUT I'M ALWAYS TELLIN' THE KIDS...
...IF THEY CAN LOOK AFTER THEIR-SELVES AND HELP OUT
WITHOUT ASKIN' FOR NOTHIN' THEY AIN'T GOT, THEY CAN STAY.
BUT I WANNA TAKE IN AS MANY KIDS AS I CAN, AND GIVE 'EM SOMETHIN' GOOD TO EAT.
I DON'T RIGHTLY KNOW WHY, BUT THEY ALL CALL ME PA.
WHAT'S A FELLER TO DO?
THIS JUST GETS HARDER AND HARDER...
RATTLE

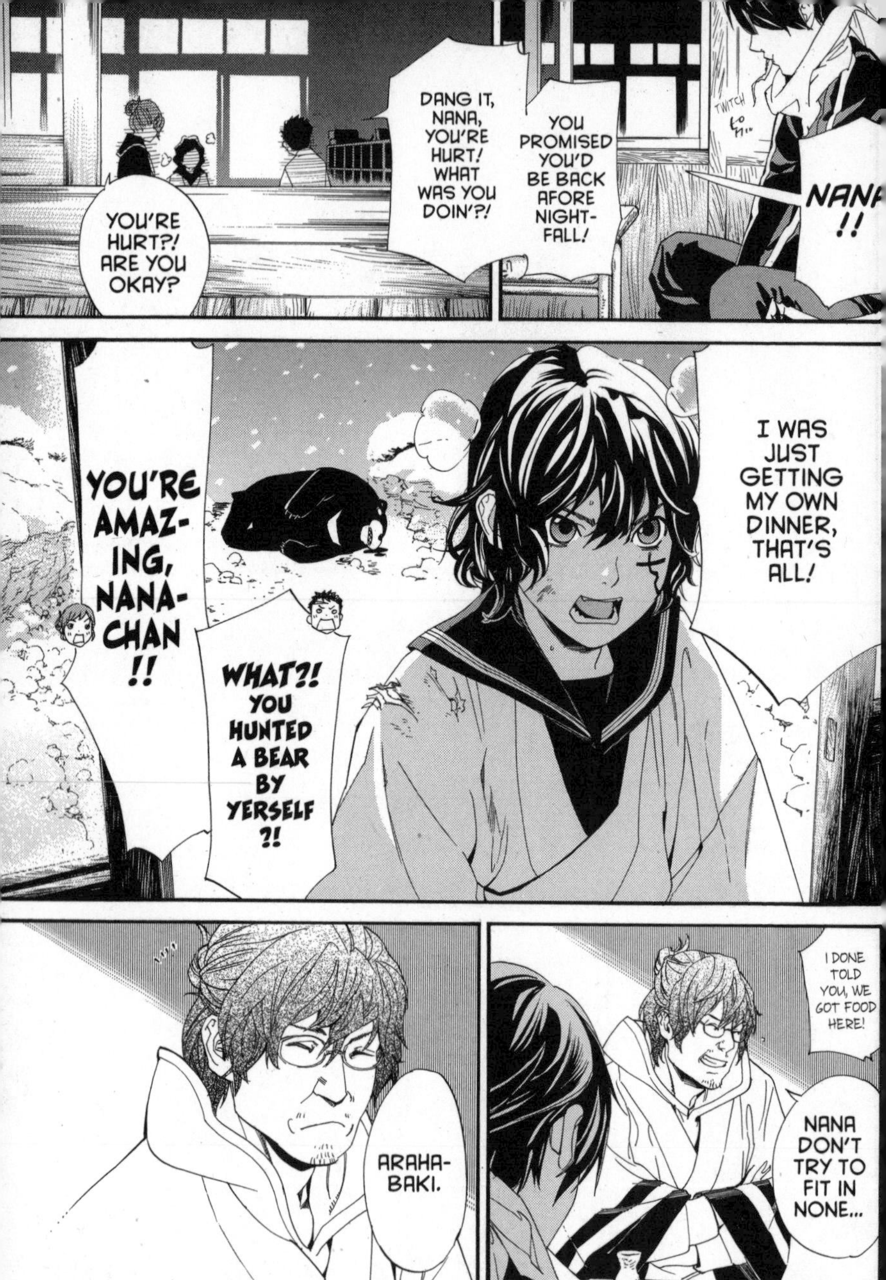
TWITCH
NANA!!
YOU PROMISED YOU'D BE BACK AFORE NIGHT-FALL!
DANG IT, NANA, YOU'RE HURT! WHAT WAS YOU DOIN'?!
YOU'RE HURT?! ARE YOU OKAY?
I WAS JUST GETTING MY OWN DINNER, THAT'S ALL!
WHAT?! YOU HUNTED A BEAR BY YERSELF?!
YOU'RE AMAZ-ING, NANA-CHAN!!
I DONE TOLD YOU, WE GOT FOOD HERE!
NANA DON'T TRY TO FIT IN NONE...
ARAHA-BAKI.

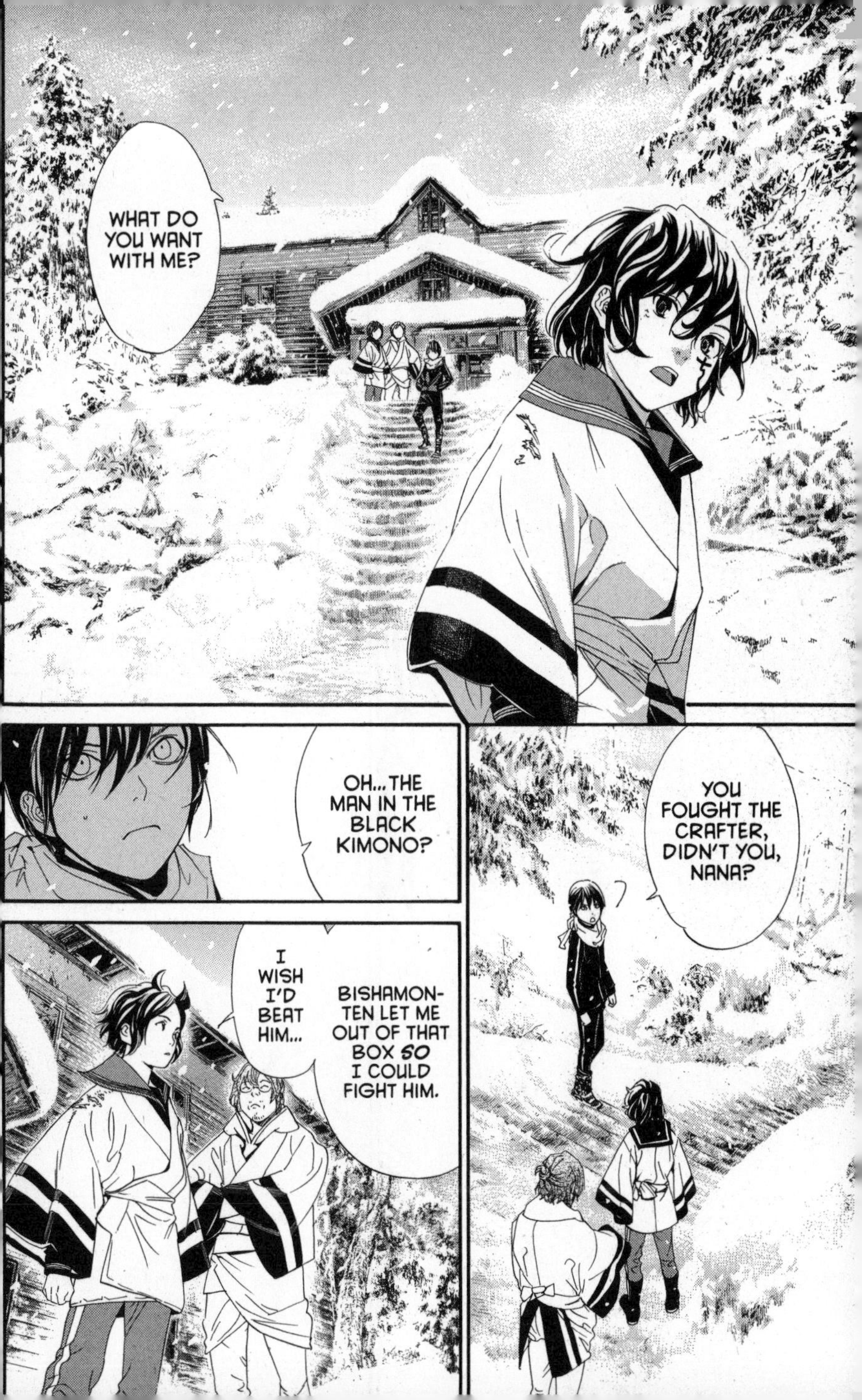
WHAT DO YOU WANT WITH ME?
YOU FOUGHT THE CRAFTER, DIDN'T YOU, NANA?
OH...THE MAN IN THE BLACK KIMONO?
BISHAMON-TEN LET ME OUT OF THAT BOX *SO* I COULD FIGHT HIM.
I WISH I'D BEAT HIM...

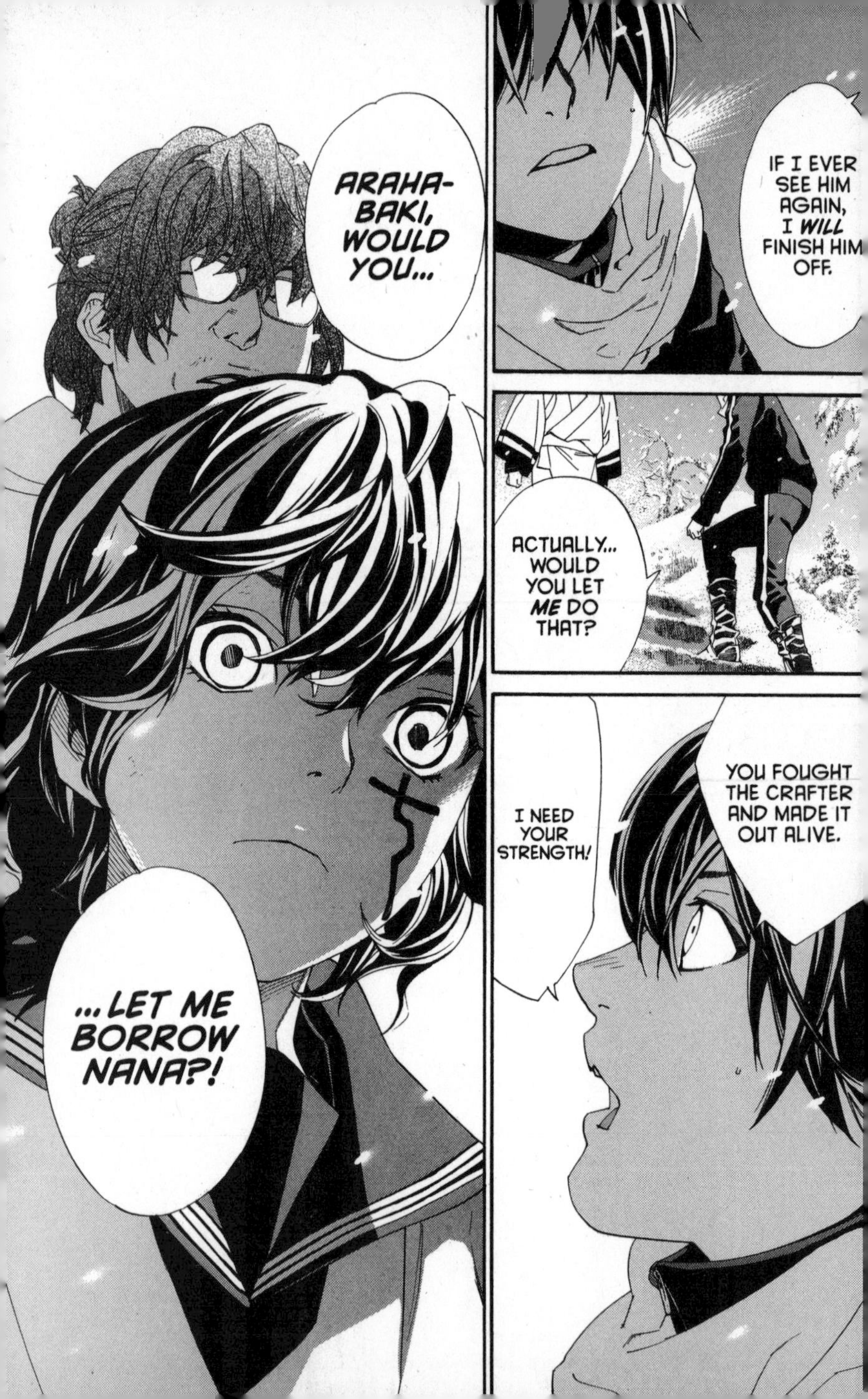
IF I EVER SEE HIM AGAIN, I WILL FINISH HIM OFF.
ACTUALLY... WOULD YOU LET ME DO THAT?
YOU FOUGHT THE CRAFTER AND MADE IT OUT ALIVE.
I NEED YOUR STRENGTH!
ARAHA-BAKI, WOULD YOU...
...LET ME BORROW NANA?!

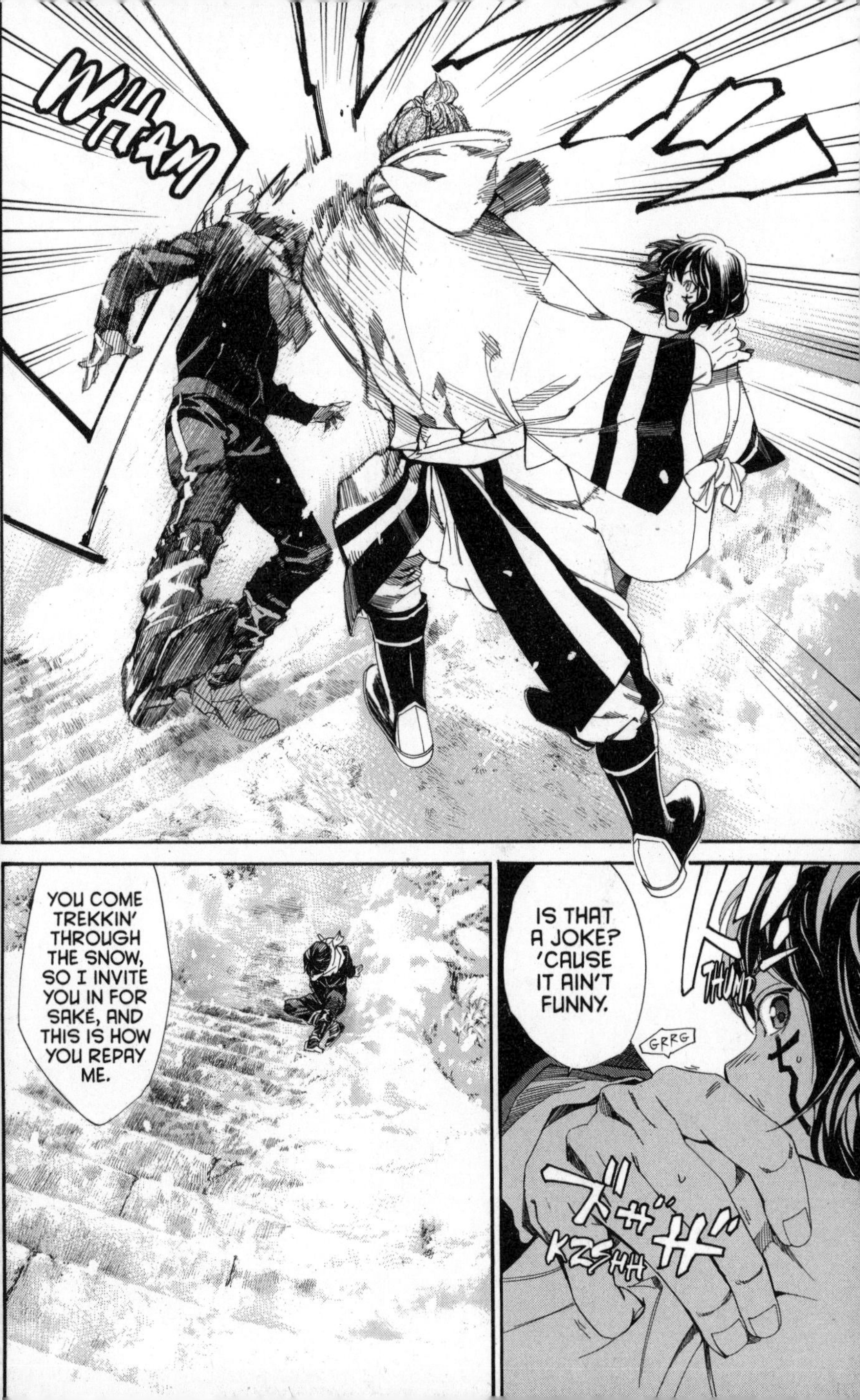

WHAM
IS THAT A JOKE? 'CAUSE IT AIN'T FUNNY.
THUMP
GRRG
ズザザ
KZSHH
YOU COME TREKKIN' THROUGH THE SNOW, SO I INVITE YOU IN FOR SAKÉ, AND THIS IS HOW YOU REPAY ME.

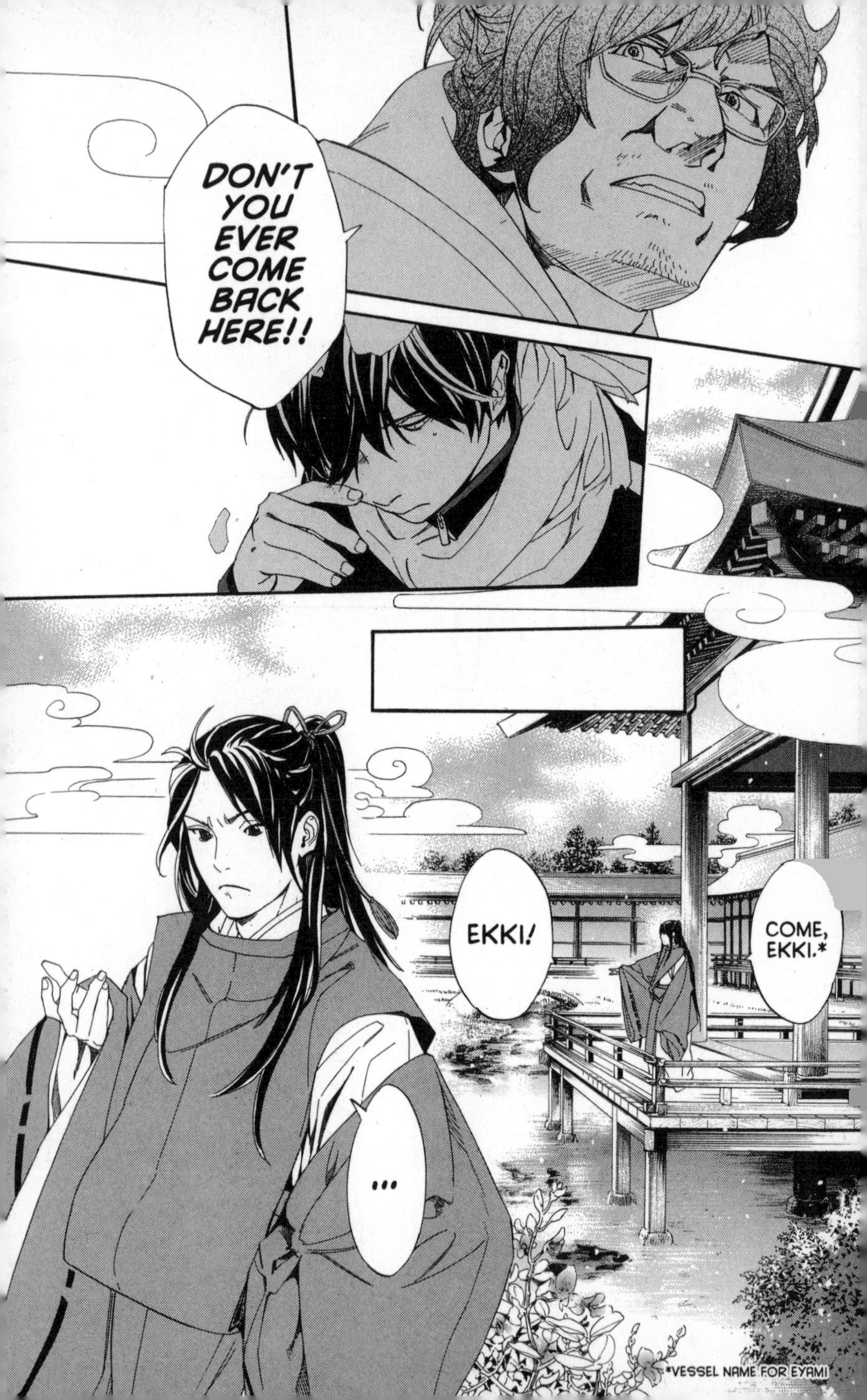
DON'T YOU EVER COME BACK HERE!!
COME, EKKI.*
EKKI!
...

*VESSEL NAME FOR EYAMI

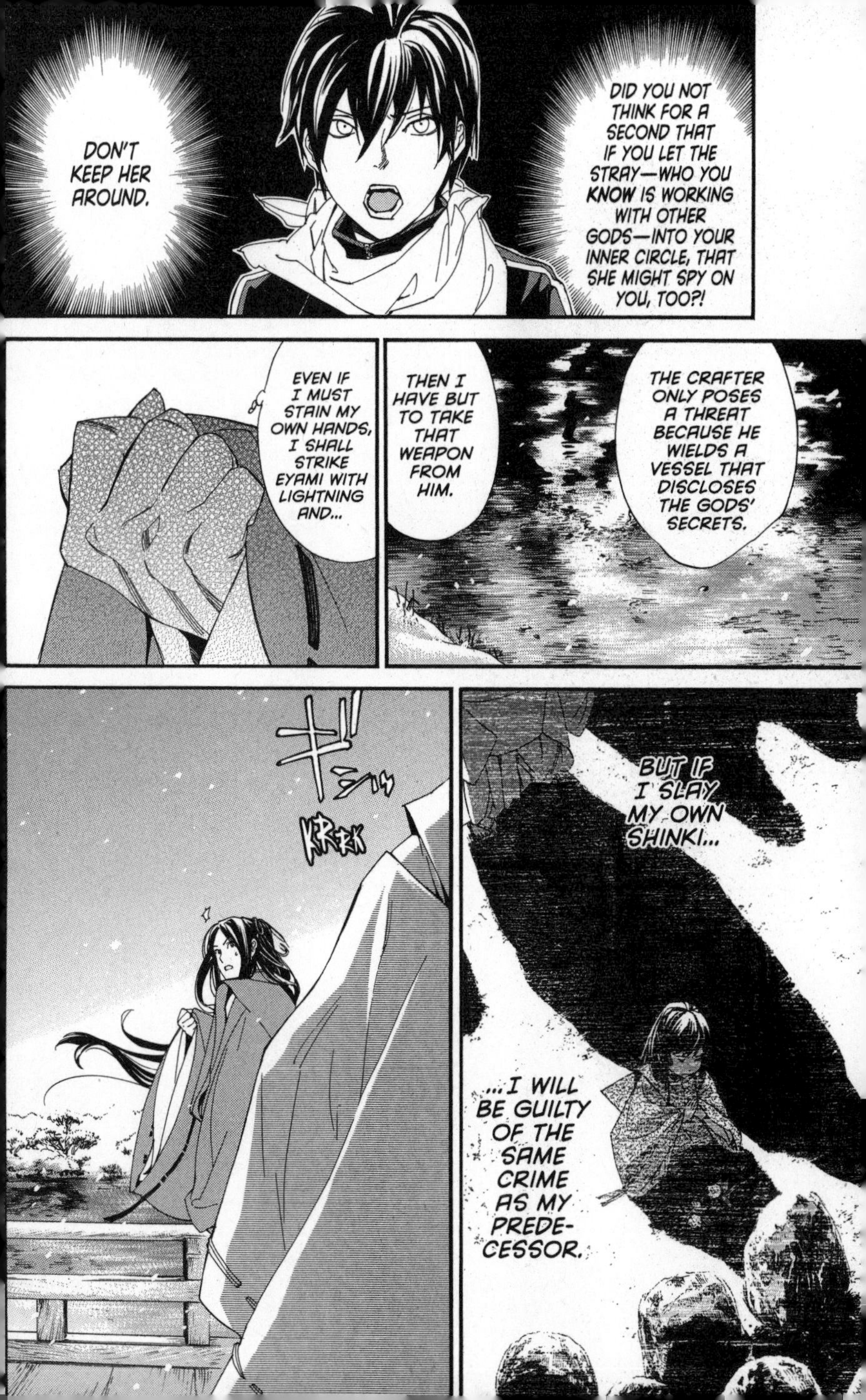
DID YOU NOT THINK FOR A SECOND THAT IF YOU LET THE STRAY—WHO YOU KNOW IS WORKING WITH OTHER GODS—INTO YOUR INNER CIRCLE, THAT SHE MIGHT SPY ON YOU, TOO?!
DON'T KEEP HER AROUND.
THE CRAFTER ONLY POSES A THREAT BECAUSE HE WIELDS A VESSEL THAT DISCLOSES THE GODS' SECRETS.
THEN I HAVE BUT TO TAKE THAT WEAPON FROM HIM.
EVEN IF I MUST STAIN MY OWN HANDS, I SHALL STRIKE EYAMI WITH LIGHTNING AND...
BUT IF I SLAY MY OWN SHINKI...
...I WILL BE GUILTY OF THE SAME CRIME AS MY PREDE-CESSOR.
KREK

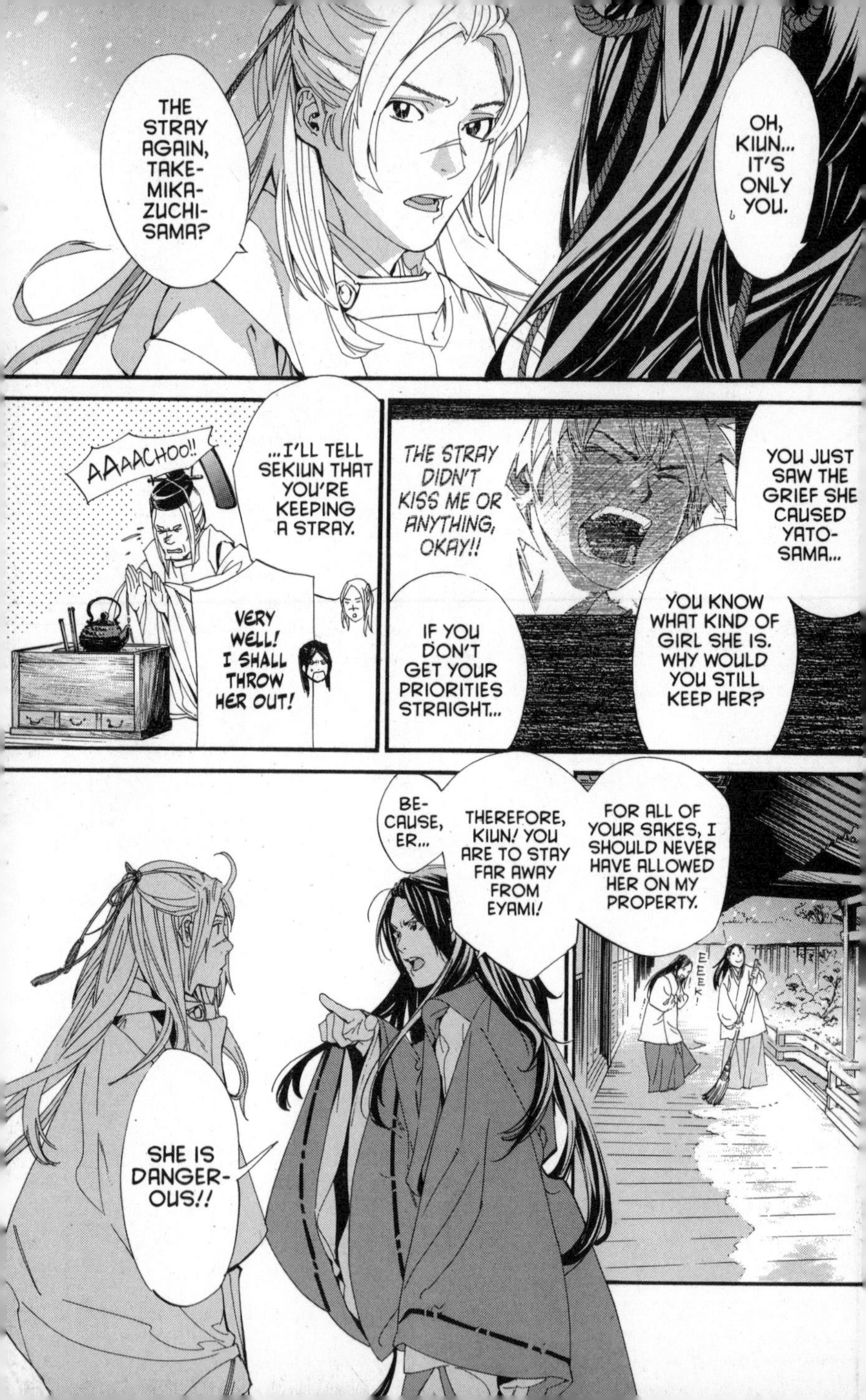
OH, KIUN... IT'S ONLY YOU.
THE STRAY AGAIN, TAKEMIKAZUCHI-SAMA?
YOU JUST SAW THE GRIEF SHE CAUSED YATO-SAMA...
YOU KNOW WHAT KIND OF GIRL SHE IS. WHY WOULD YOU STILL KEEP HER?
THE STRAY DIDN'T KISS ME OR ANYTHING, OKAY!!
IF YOU DON'T GET YOUR PRIORITIES STRAIGHT...
...I'LL TELL SEKIUN THAT YOU'RE KEEPING A STRAY.
AAAACHOO!!
VERY WELL! I SHALL THROW HER OUT!
FOR ALL OF YOUR SAKES, I SHOULD NEVER HAVE ALLOWED HER ON MY PROPERTY.
THEREFORE, KIUN! YOU ARE TO STAY FAR AWAY FROM EYAMI!
BECAUSE, ER...
EEEK!
SHE IS DANGEROUS!!

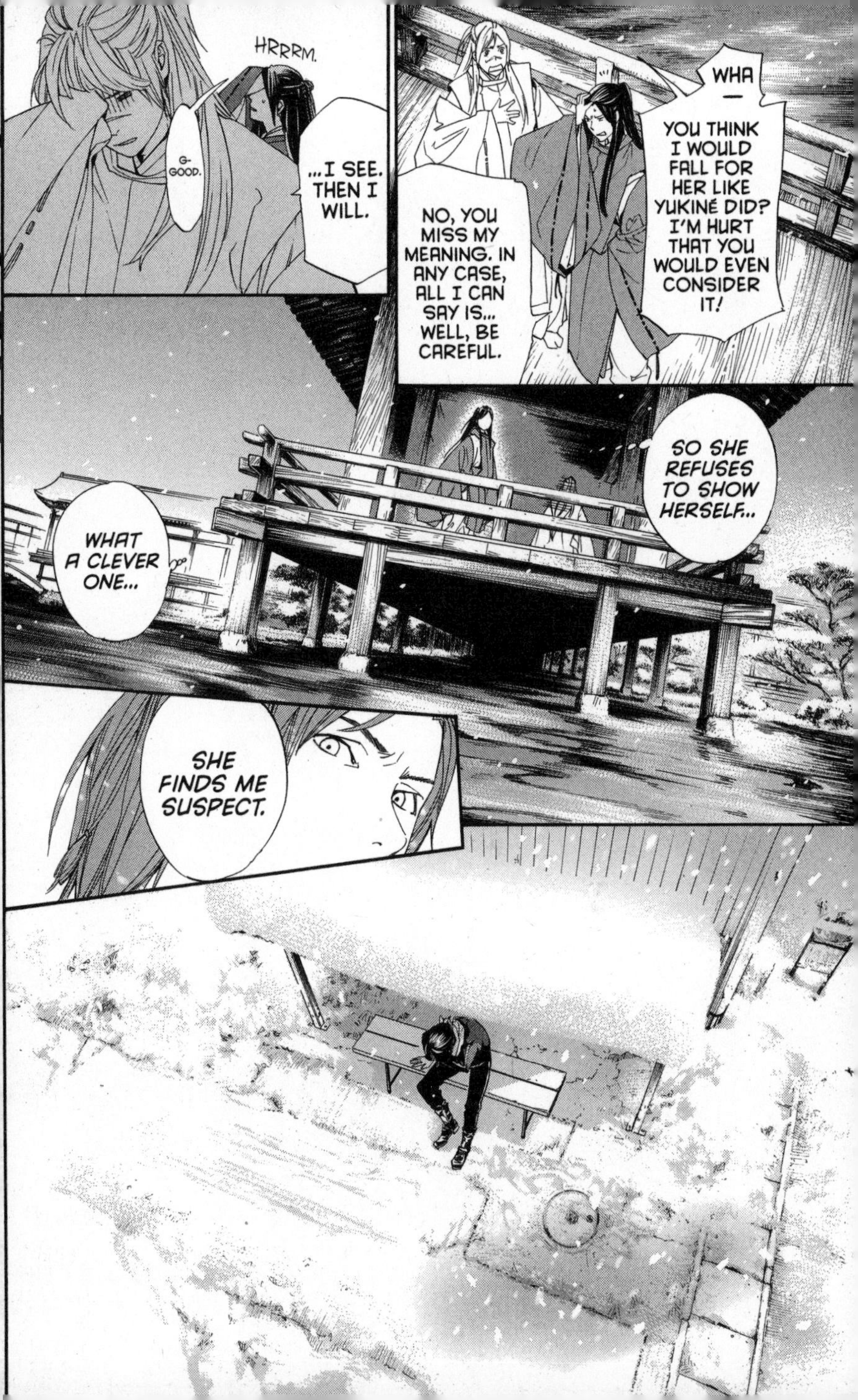
WHA —
YOU THINK I WOULD FALL FOR HER LIKE YUKINÉ DID? I'M HURT THAT YOU WOULD EVEN CONSIDER IT!
NO, YOU MISS MY MEANING. IN ANY CASE, ALL I CAN SAY IS... WELL, BE CAREFUL.
HRRRM.
...I SEE. THEN I WILL.
G-GOOD.
SO SHE REFUSES TO SHOW HERSELF...
WHAT A CLEVER ONE...
SHE FINDS ME SUSPECT.

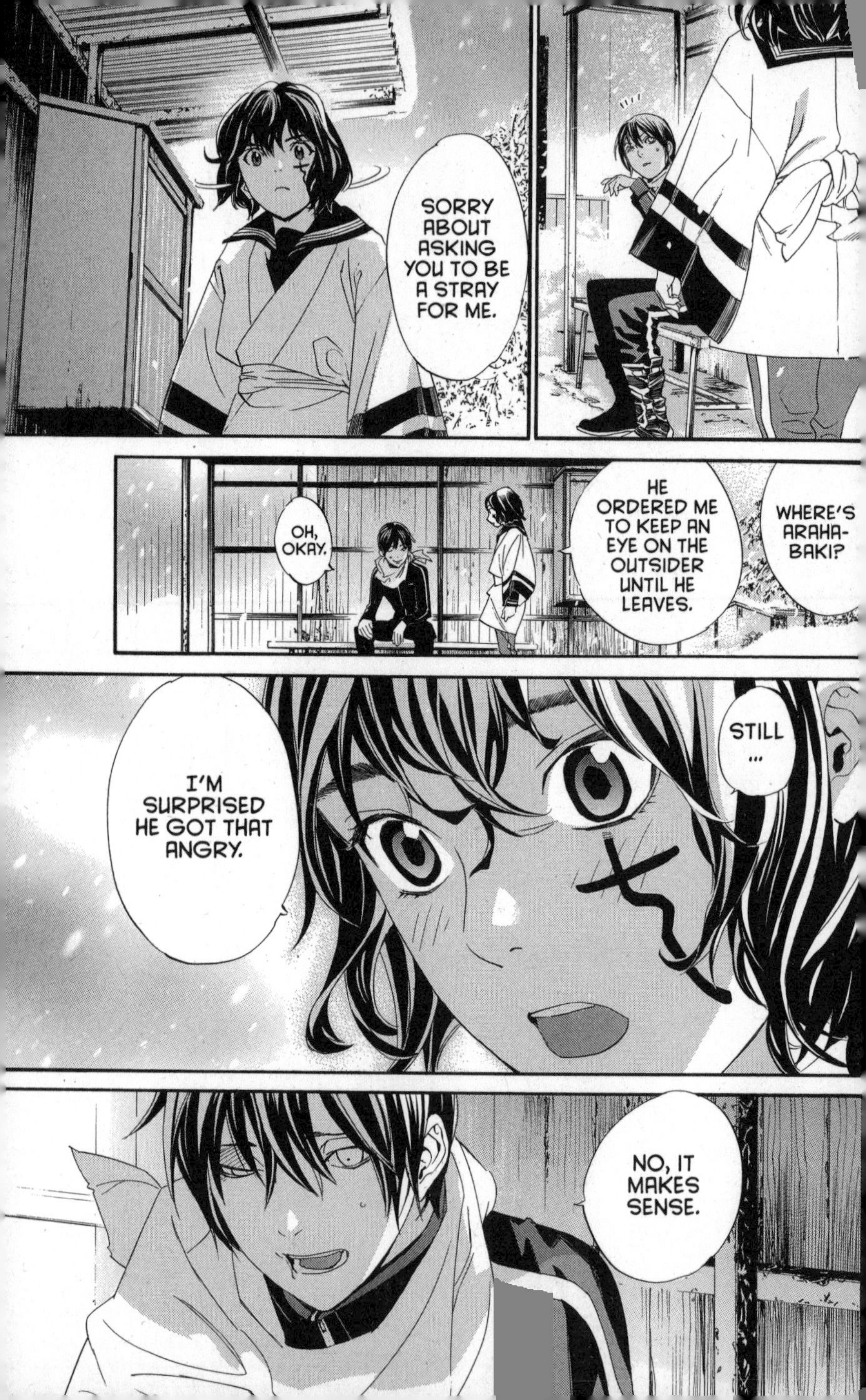
SORRY ABOUT ASKING YOU TO BE A STRAY FOR ME.
WHERE'S ARAHA-BAKI?
HE ORDERED ME TO KEEP AN EYE ON THE OUTSIDER UNTIL HE LEAVES.
OH, OKAY.
STILL ...
I'M SURPRISED HE GOT THAT ANGRY.
NO, IT MAKES SENSE.

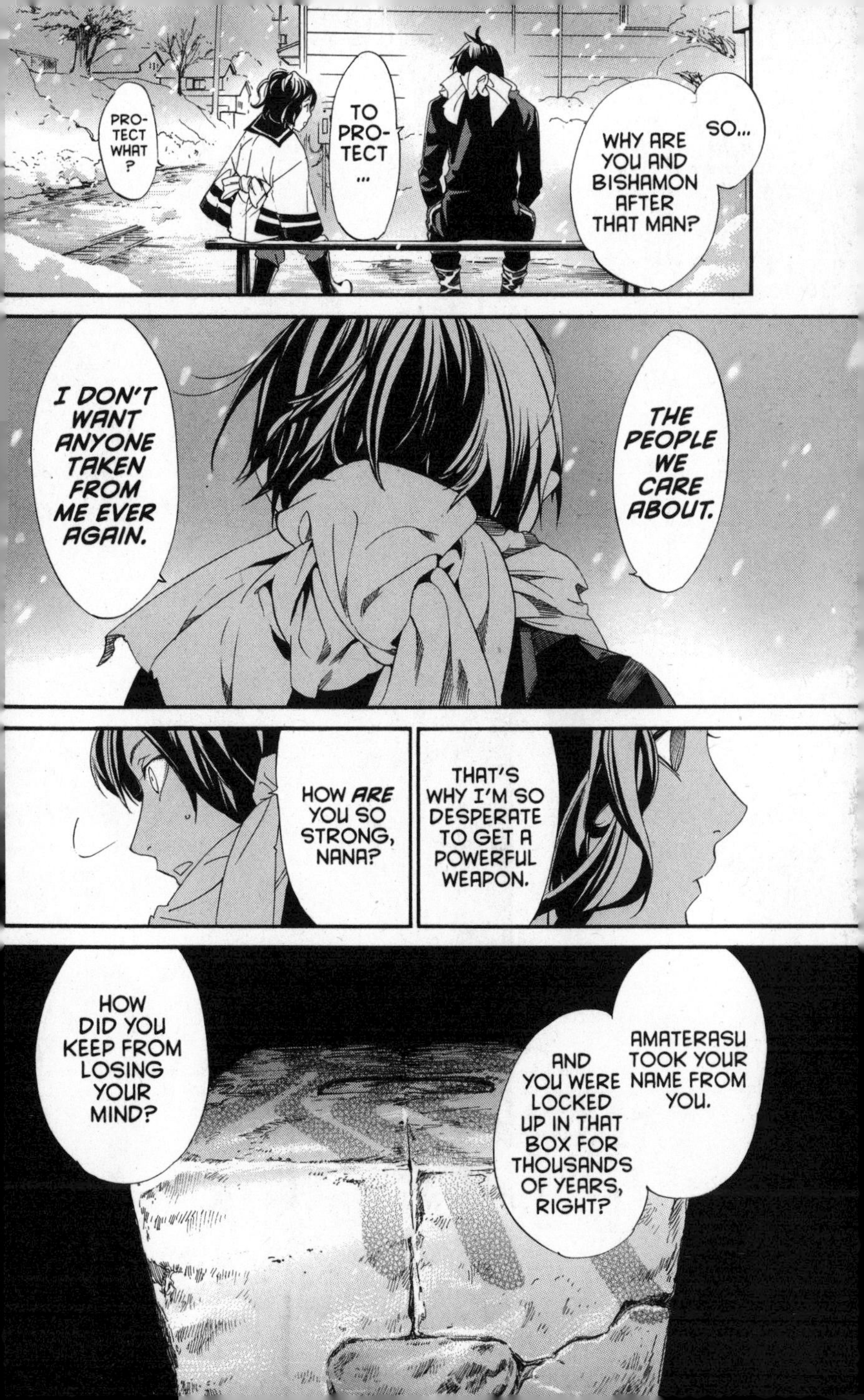
SO... WHY ARE YOU AND BISHAMON AFTER THAT MAN?
TO PROTECT...
PROTECT WHAT?
THE PEOPLE WE CARE ABOUT.
I DON'T WANT ANYONE TAKEN FROM ME EVER AGAIN.
THAT'S WHY I'M SO DESPERATE TO GET A POWERFUL WEAPON.
HOW *ARE* YOU SO STRONG, NANA?
AMATERASU TOOK YOUR NAME FROM YOU.
AND YOU WERE LOCKED UP IN THAT BOX FOR THOUSANDS OF YEARS, RIGHT?
HOW DID YOU KEEP FROM LOSING YOUR MIND?

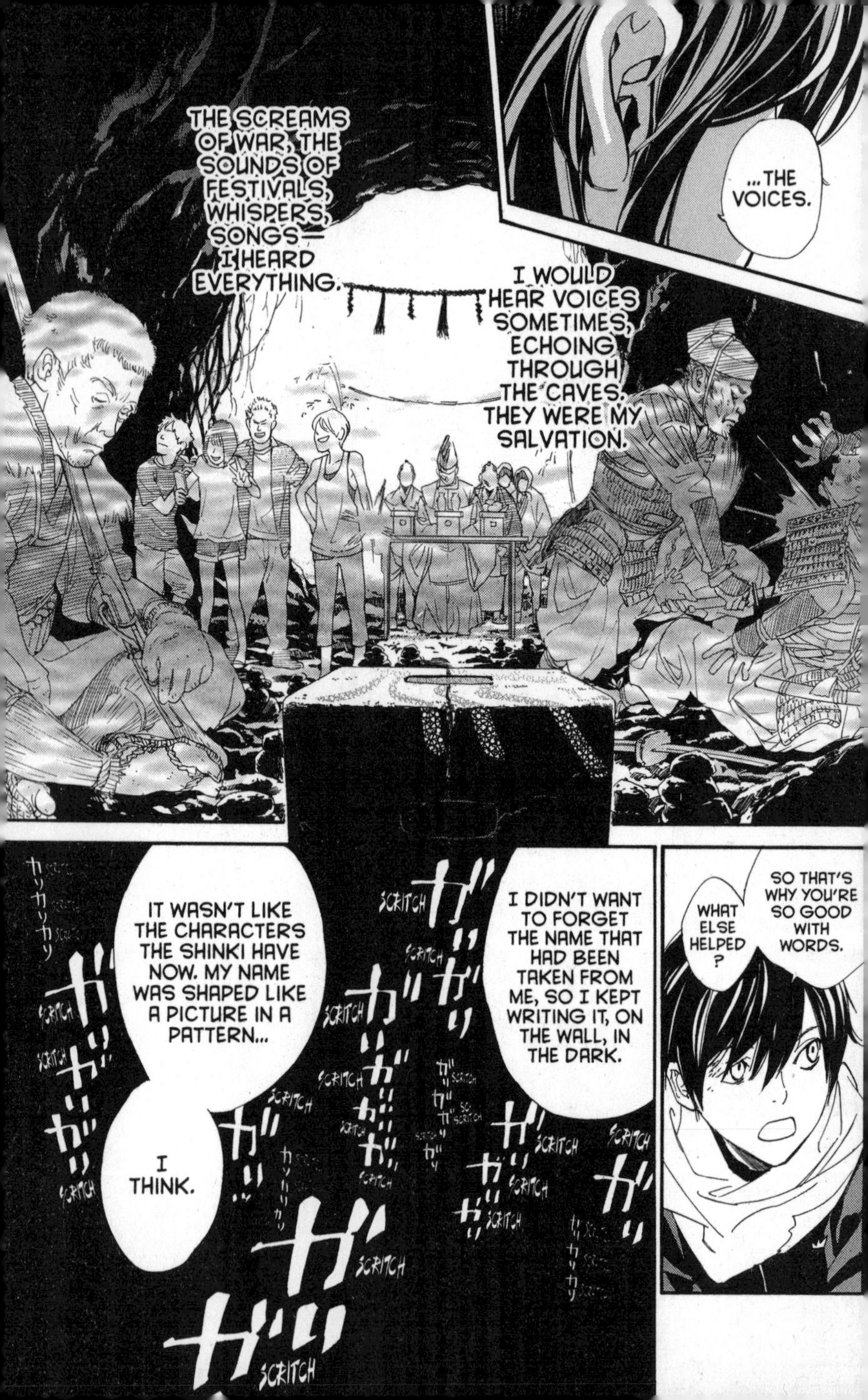
...THE VOICES.
I WOULD HEAR VOICES SOMETIMES, ECHOING THROUGH THE CAVES. THEY WERE MY SALVATION.
THE SCREAMS OF WAR, THE SOUNDS OF FESTIVALS, WHISPERS, SONGS— I HEARD EVERYTHING.
SO THAT'S WHY YOU'RE SO GOOD WITH WORDS.
WHAT ELSE HELPED?
I DIDN'T WANT TO FORGET THE NAME THAT HAD BEEN TAKEN FROM ME, SO I KEPT WRITING IT, ON THE WALL, IN THE DARK.
SCRITCH
SCRITCH
IT WASN'T LIKE THE CHARACTERS THE SHINKI HAVE NOW. MY NAME WAS SHAPED LIKE A PICTURE IN A PATTERN...
I THINK.
SCRITCH
SCRITCH

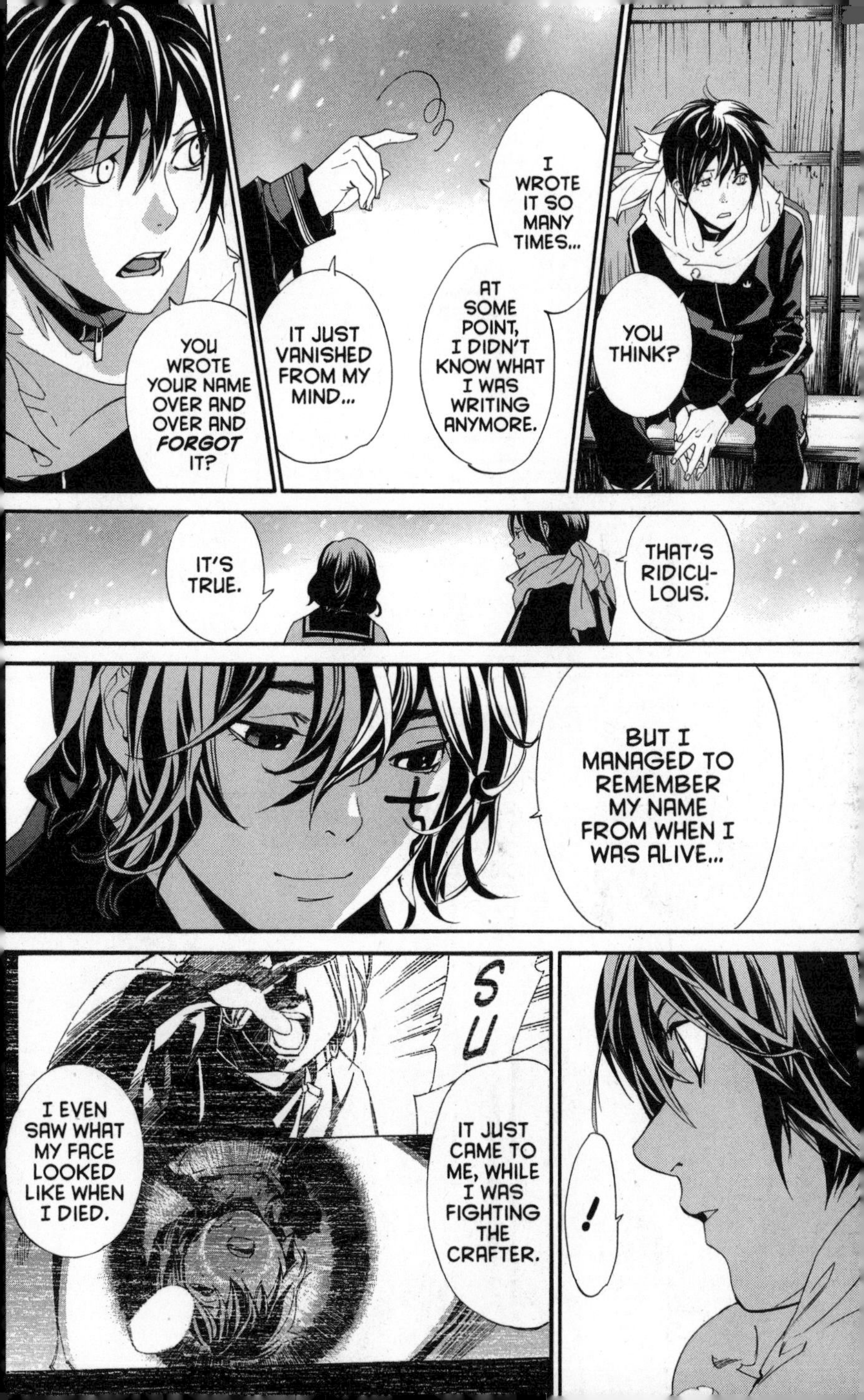
YOU THINK?
I WROTE IT SO MANY TIMES...
AT SOME POINT, I DIDN'T KNOW WHAT I WAS WRITING ANYMORE.
IT JUST VANISHED FROM MY MIND...
YOU WROTE YOUR NAME OVER AND OVER AND *FORGOT* IT?
THAT'S RIDICU-LOUS.
IT'S TRUE.
BUT I MANAGED TO REMEMBER MY NAME FROM WHEN I WAS ALIVE...
!
SU
IT JUST CAME TO ME, WHILE I WAS FIGHTING THE CRAFTER.
I EVEN SAW WHAT MY FACE LOOKED LIKE WHEN I DIED.

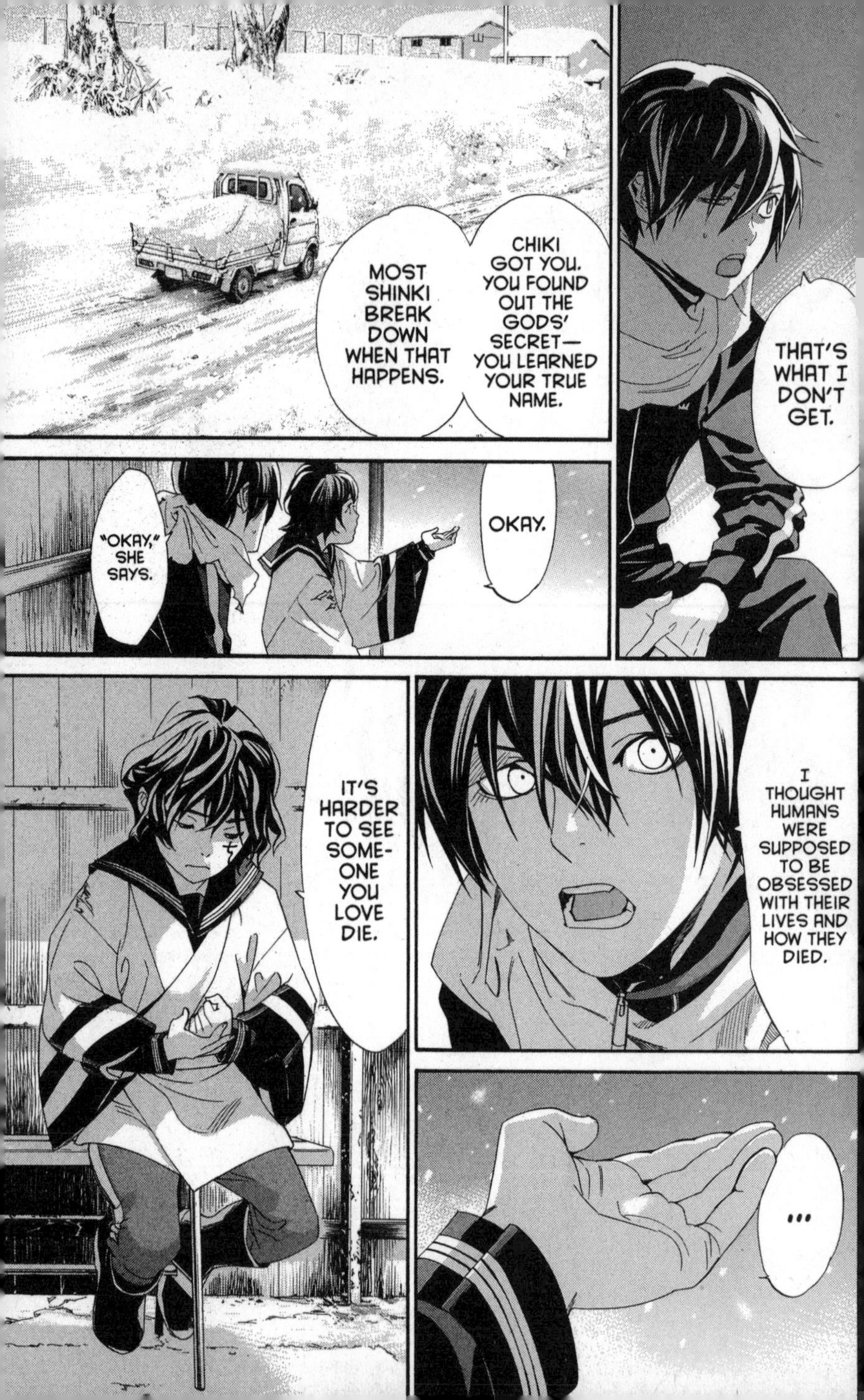
THAT'S WHAT I DON'T GET.
CHIKI GOT YOU. YOU FOUND OUT THE GODS' SECRET—YOU LEARNED YOUR TRUE NAME.
MOST SHINKI BREAK DOWN WHEN THAT HAPPENS.
OKAY.
"OKAY," SHE SAYS.
I THOUGHT HUMANS WERE SUPPOSED TO BE OBSESSED WITH THEIR LIVES AND HOW THEY DIED.
...
IT'S HARDER TO SEE SOME-ONE YOU LOVE DIE.

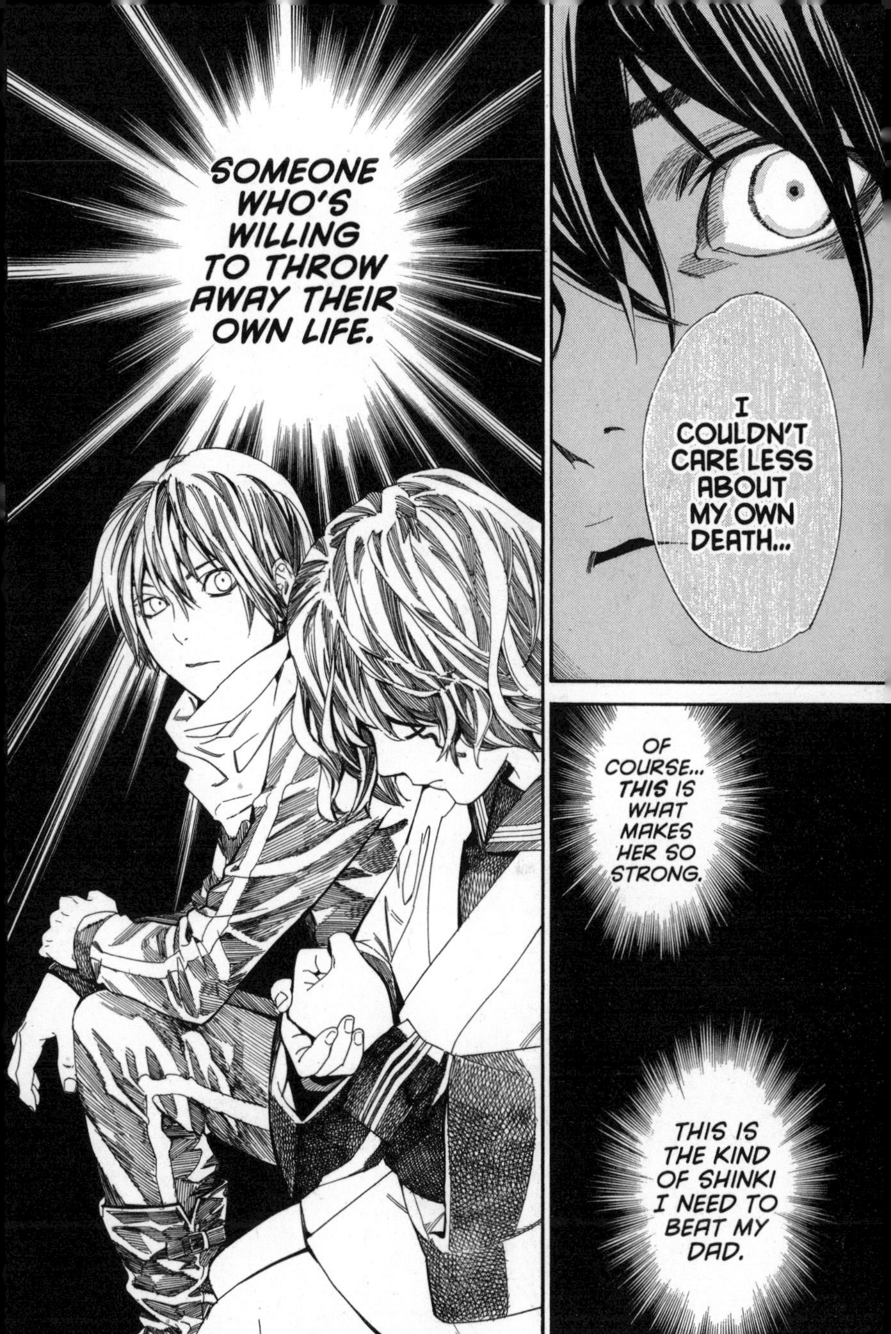
I COULDN'T CARE LESS ABOUT MY OWN DEATH...
OF COURSE... *THIS* IS WHAT MAKES HER SO STRONG.
THIS IS THE KIND OF SHINKI I NEED TO BEAT MY DAD.
SOMEONE WHO'S WILLING TO THROW AWAY THEIR OWN LIFE.

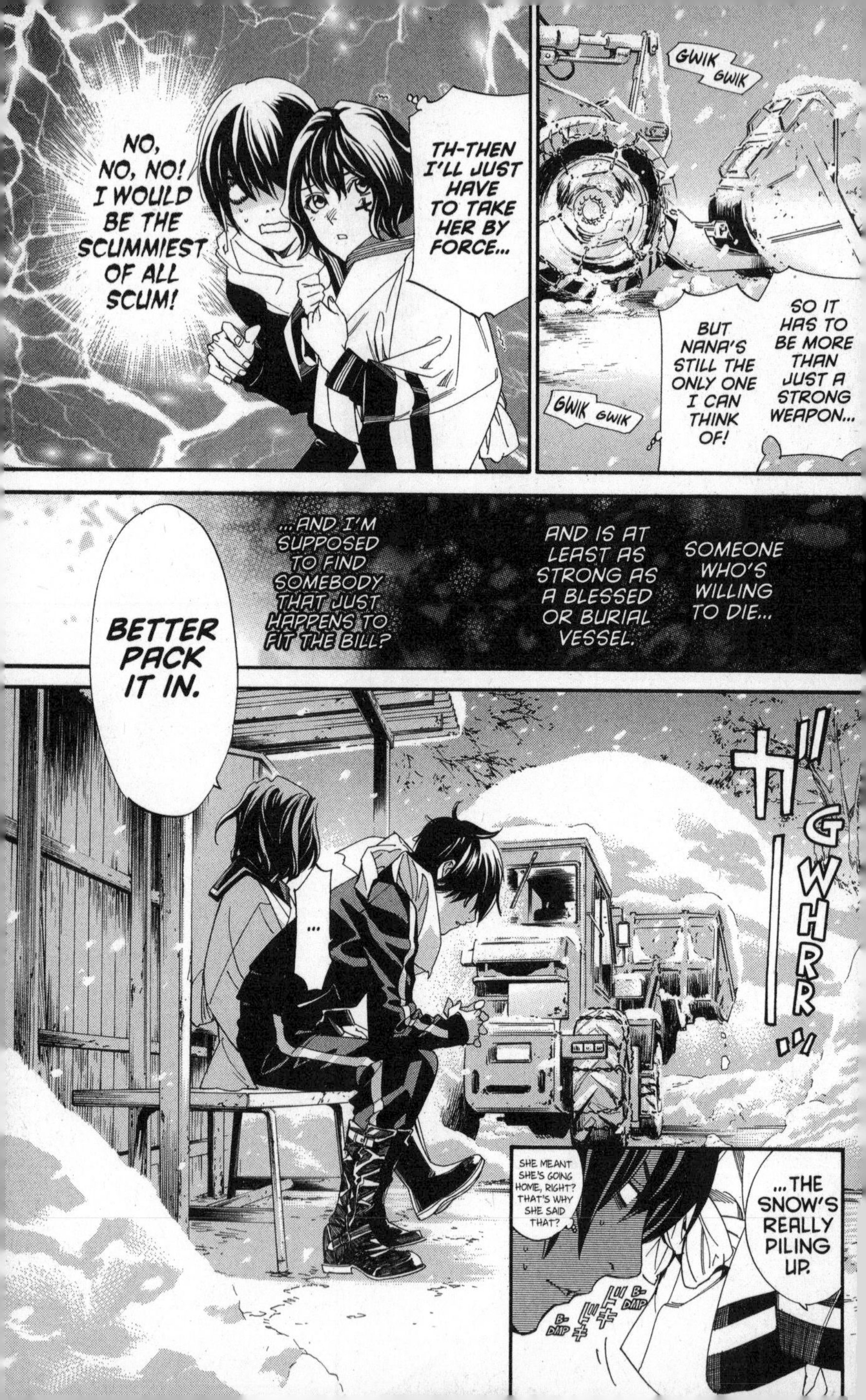
GWIK GWIK
SO IT HAS TO BE MORE THAN JUST A STRONG WEAPON...
BUT NANA'S STILL THE ONLY ONE I CAN THINK OF!
GWIK GWIK
TH-THEN I'LL JUST HAVE TO TAKE HER BY FORCE...
NO, NO, NO! I WOULD BE THE SCUMMIEST OF ALL SCUM!
SOMEONE WHO'S WILLING TO DIE...
AND IS AT LEAST AS STRONG AS A BLESSED OR BURIAL VESSEL.
...AND I'M SUPPOSED TO FIND SOMEBODY THAT JUST HAPPENS TO FIT THE BILL?
BETTER PACK IT IN.
GWHRR
...
...THE SNOW'S REALLY PILING UP.
SHE MEANT SHE'S GOING HOME, RIGHT? THAT'S WHY SHE SAID THAT?
B-DMP
B-DMP

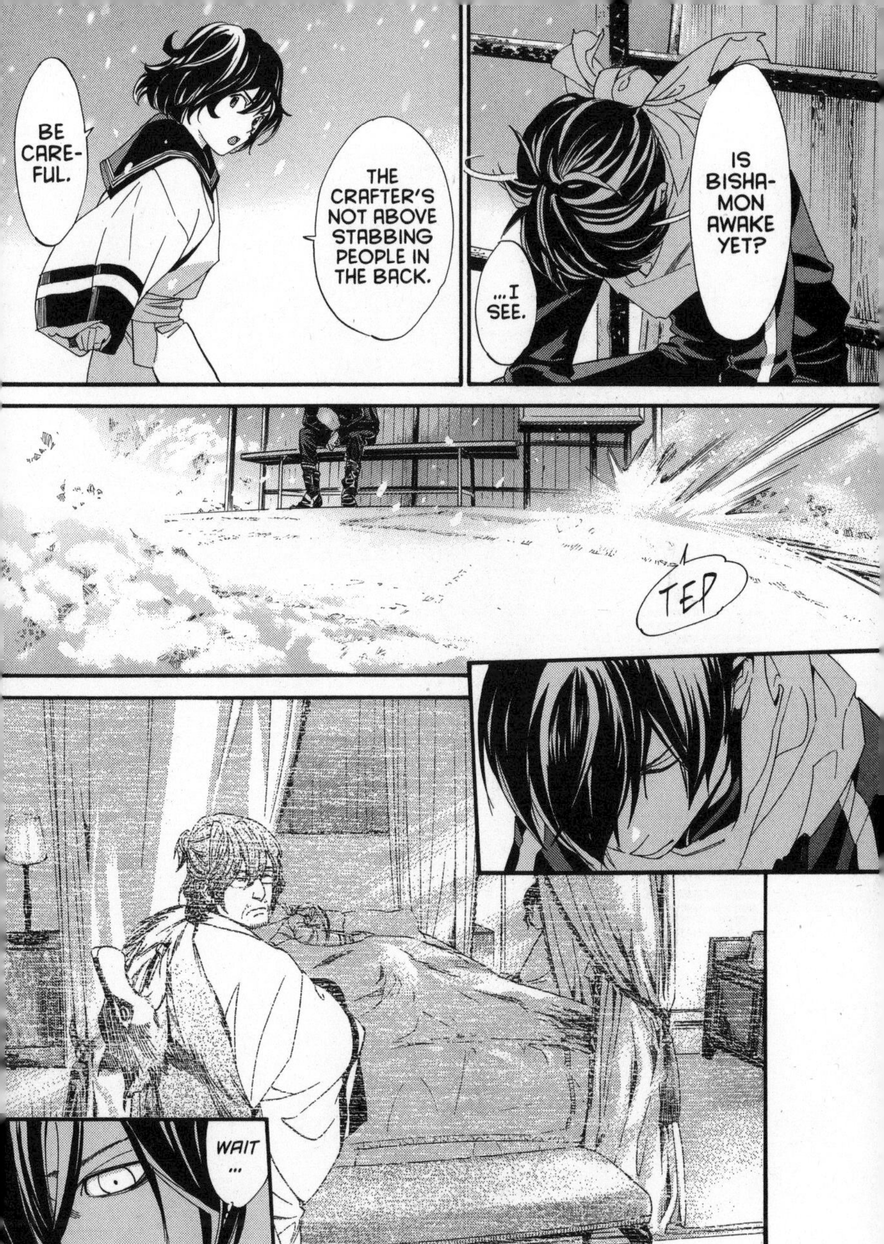
IS BISHA-MON AWAKE YET?
...I SEE.
BE CARE-FUL.
THE CRAFTER'S NOT ABOVE STABBING PEOPLE IN THE BACK.
TEP
WAIT ...

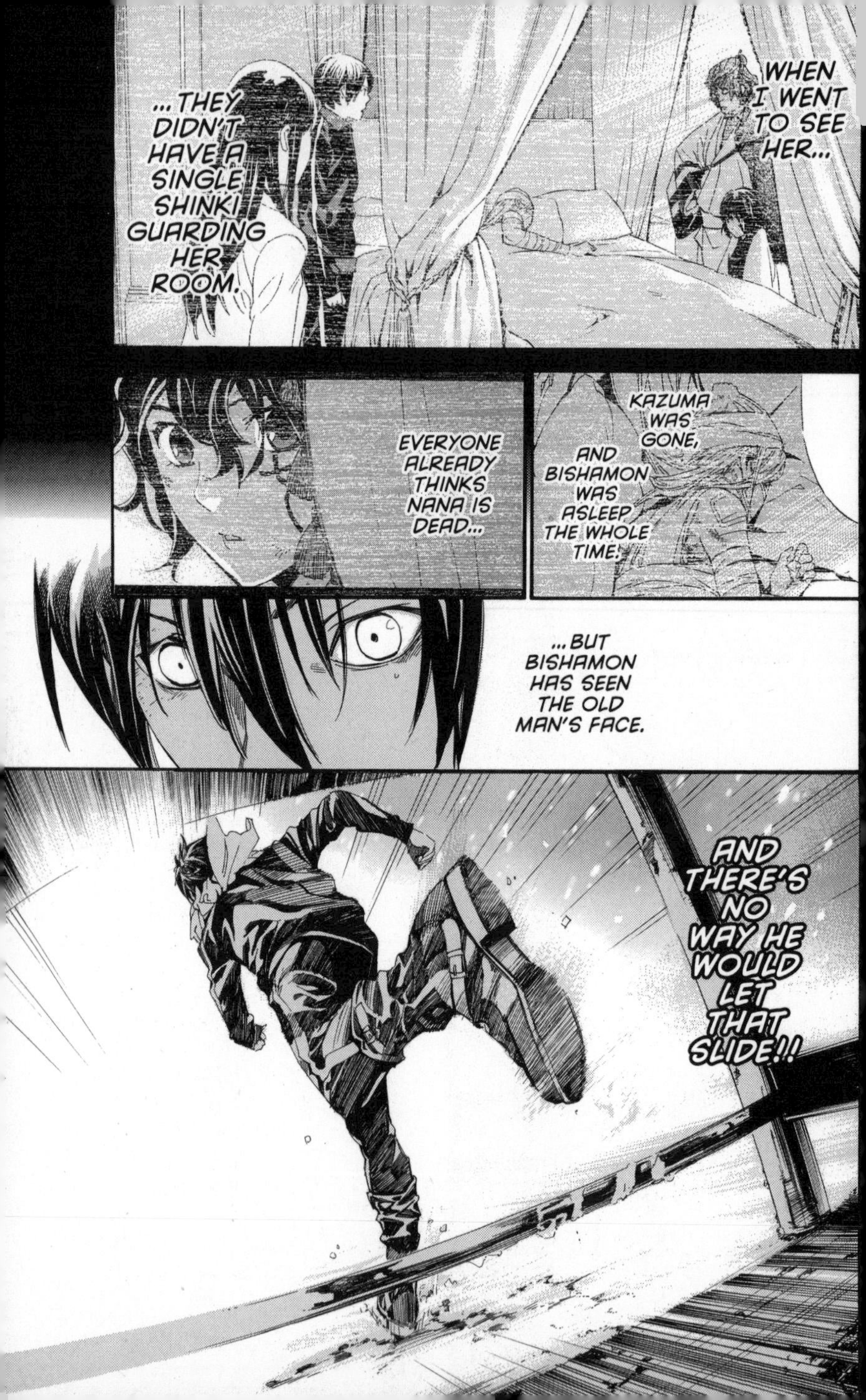
WHEN I WENT TO SEE HER...
...THEY DIDN'T HAVE A SINGLE SHINKI GUARDING HER ROOM.
KAZUMA WAS GONE,
AND BISHAMON WAS ASLEEP THE WHOLE TIME.
EVERYONE ALREADY THINKS NANA IS DEAD...
...BUT BISHAMON HAS SEEN THE OLD MAN'S FACE.
AND THERE'S NO WAY HE WOULD LET THAT SLIDE!!

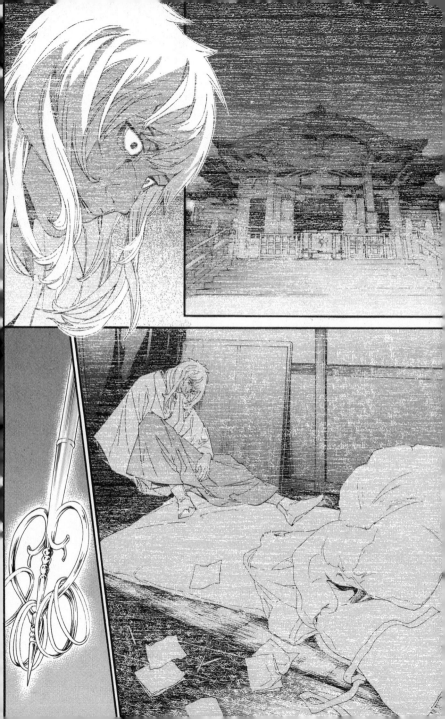

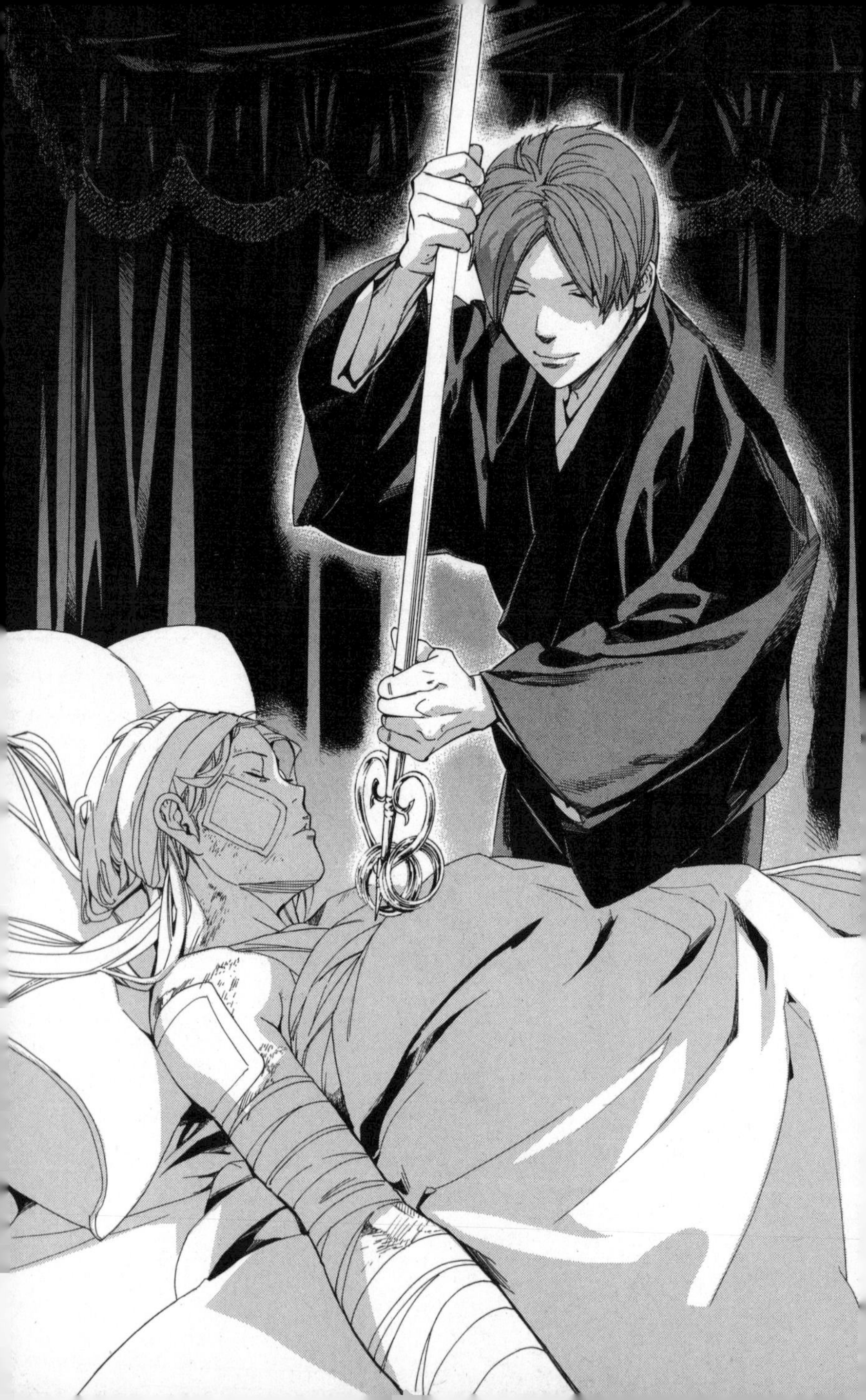

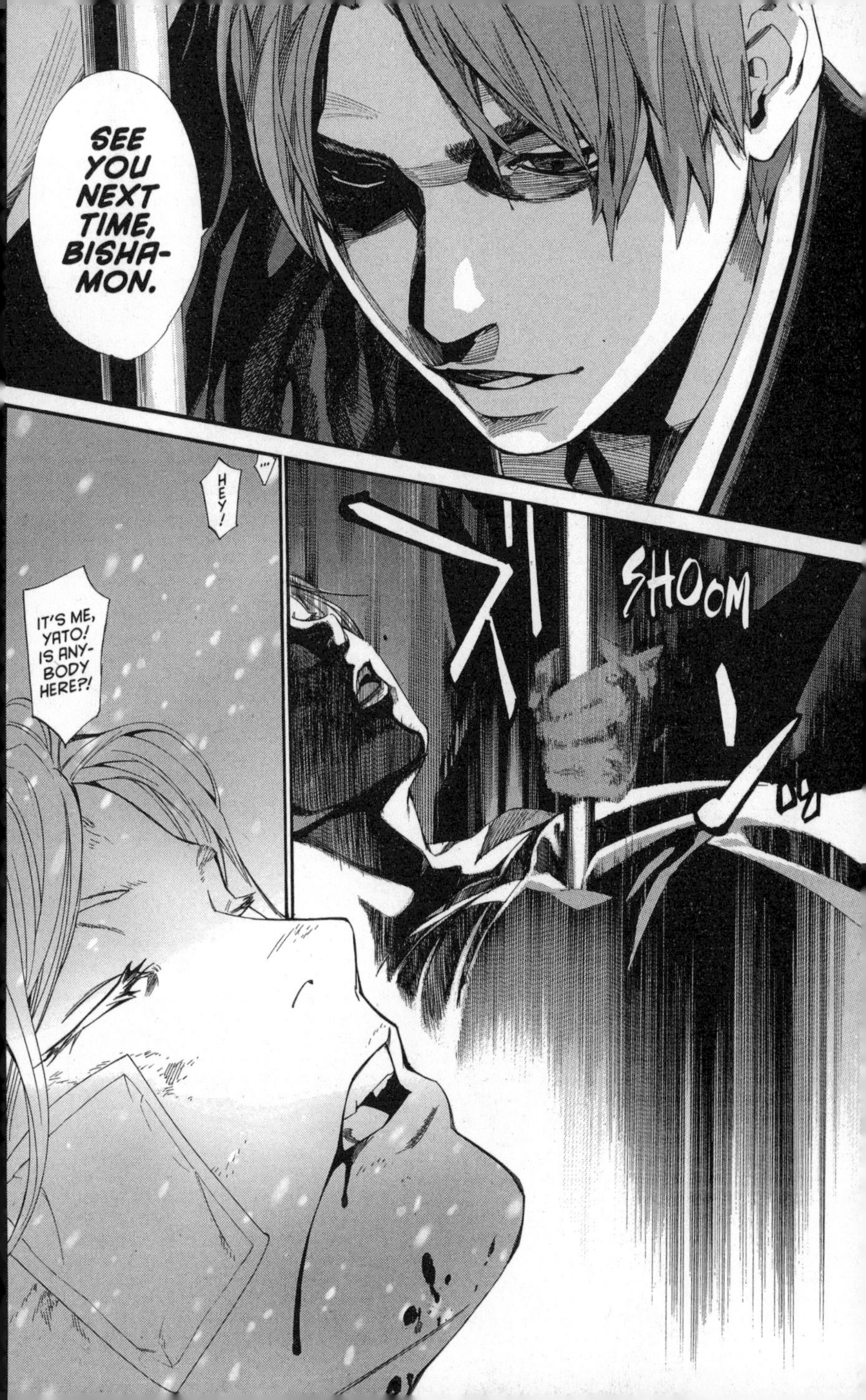
SEE YOU NEXT TIME, BISHA-MON.
SHOOM
...
HEY!
IT'S ME, YATO! IS ANY-BODY HERE?!

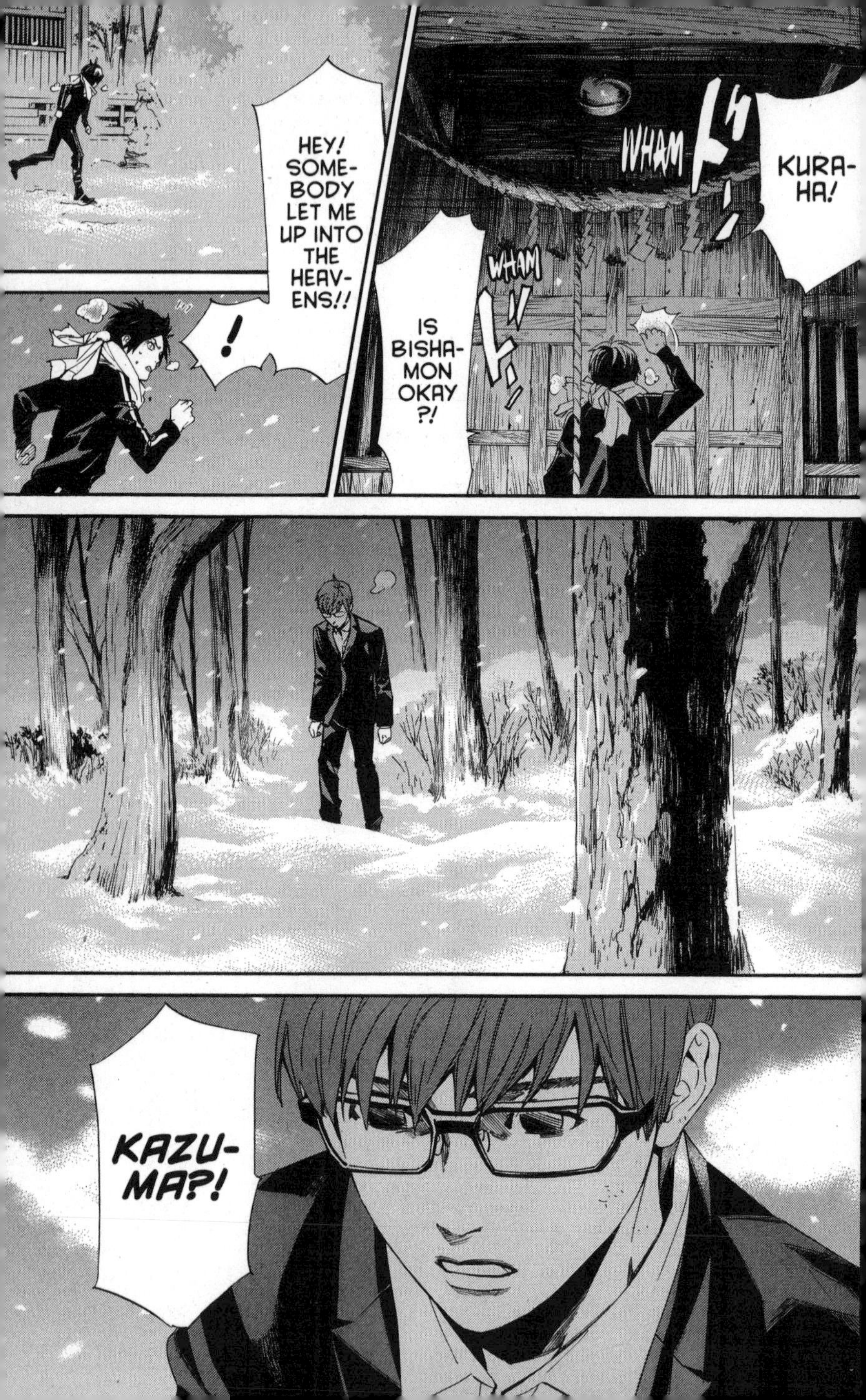
KURA-HA!
WHAM
WHAM
IS BISHA-MON OKAY?!
HEY! SOME-BODY LET ME UP INTO THE HEAV-ENS!!
!
KAZU-MA?!

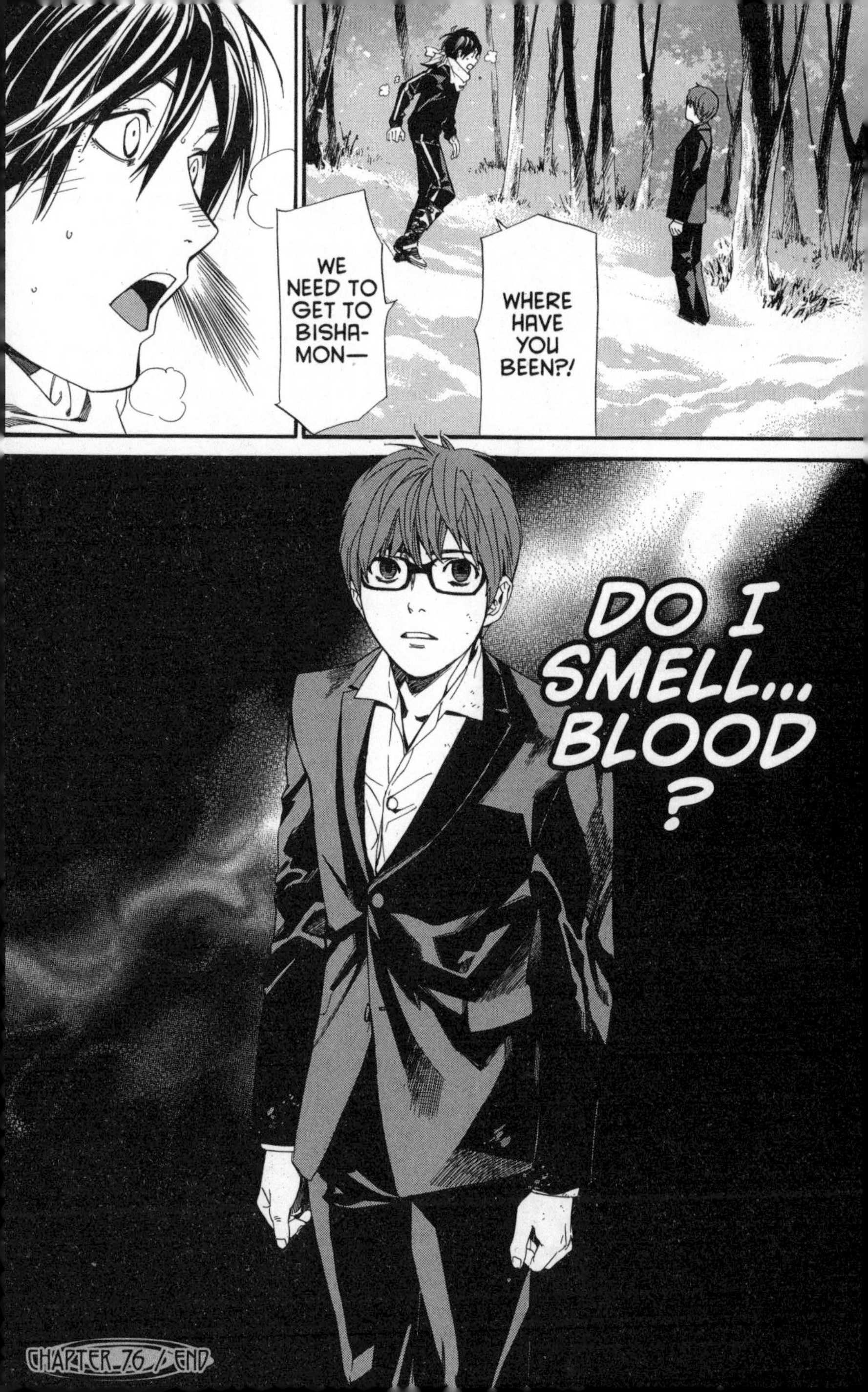
WHERE HAVE YOU BEEN?!
WE NEED TO GET TO BISHAMON—
DO I SMELL... BLOOD?
CHAPTER 76 / END

野

曼

神

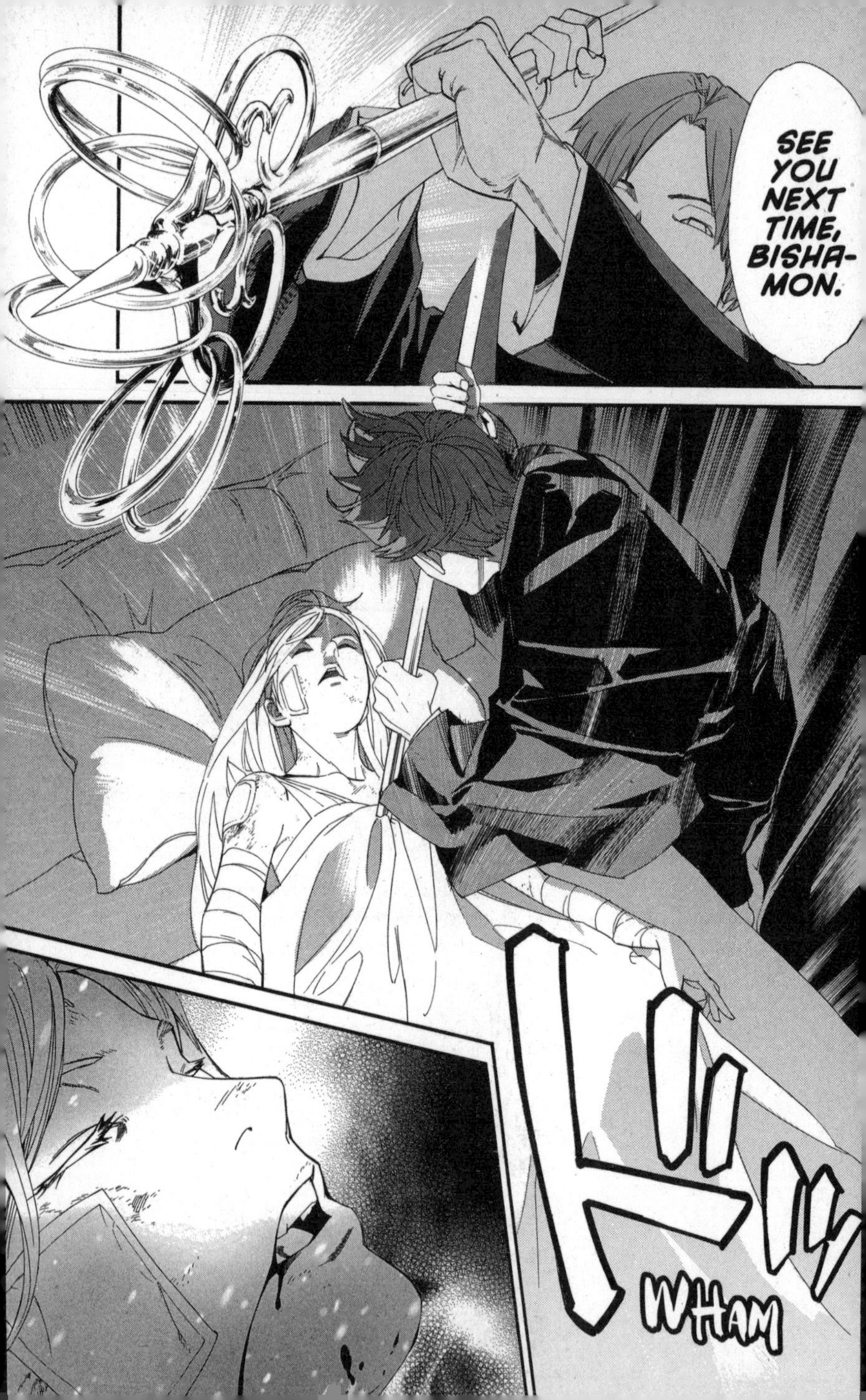
SEE YOU NEXT TIME, BISHAMON.
WHAM

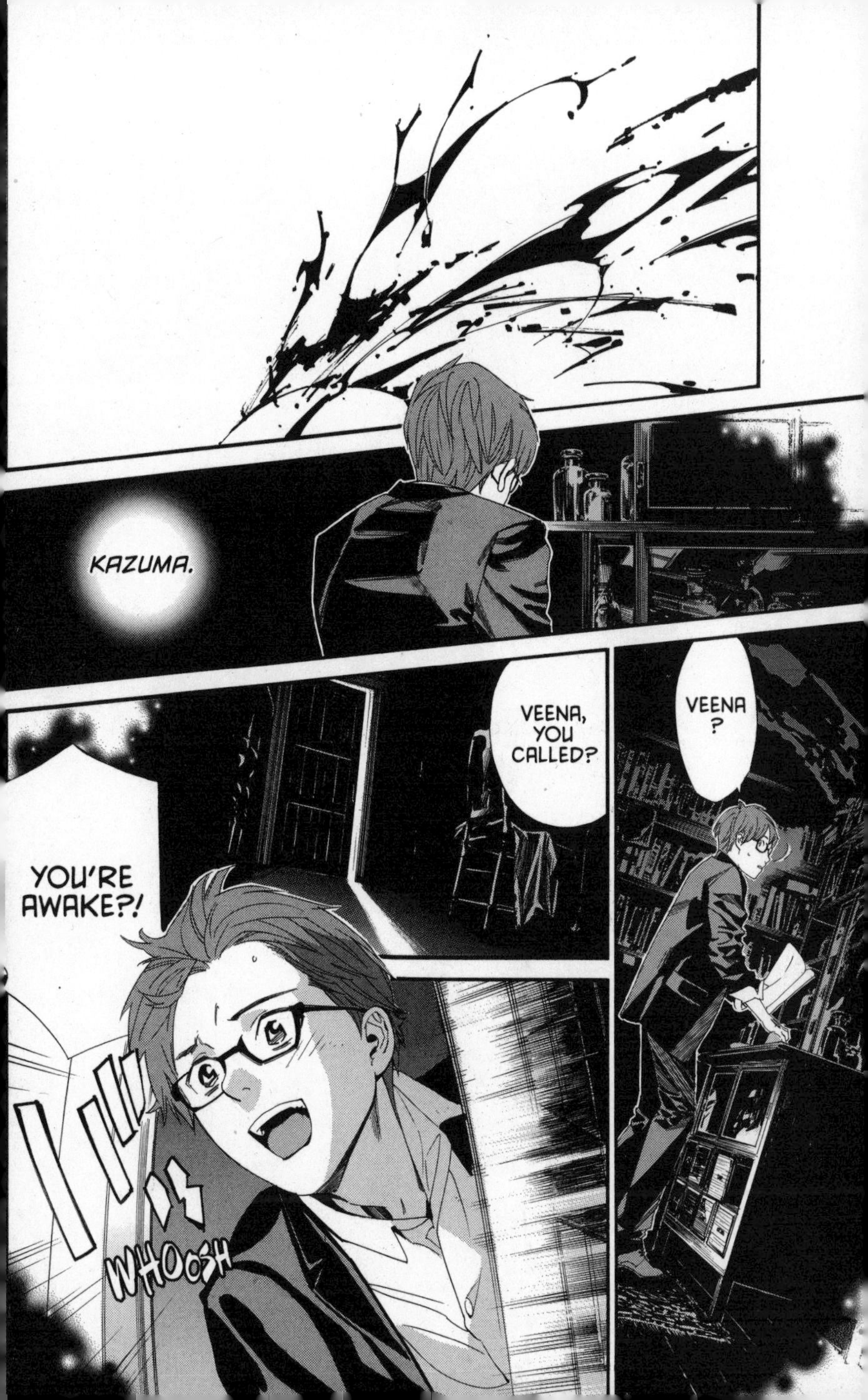
KAZUMA.
VEENA?
VEENA, YOU CALLED?
YOU'RE AWAKE?!
WHOOSH

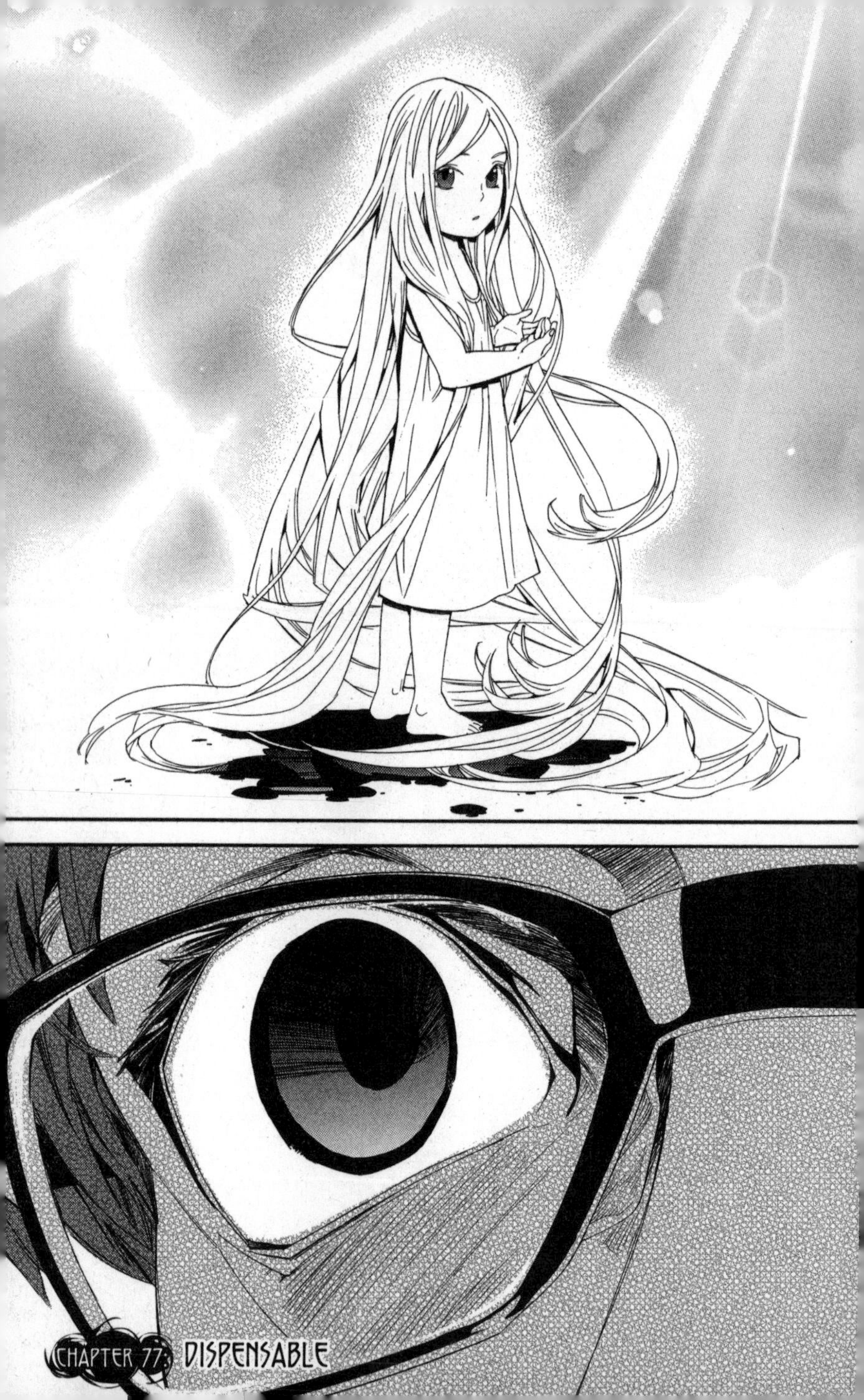
CHAPTER 77: DISPENSABLE

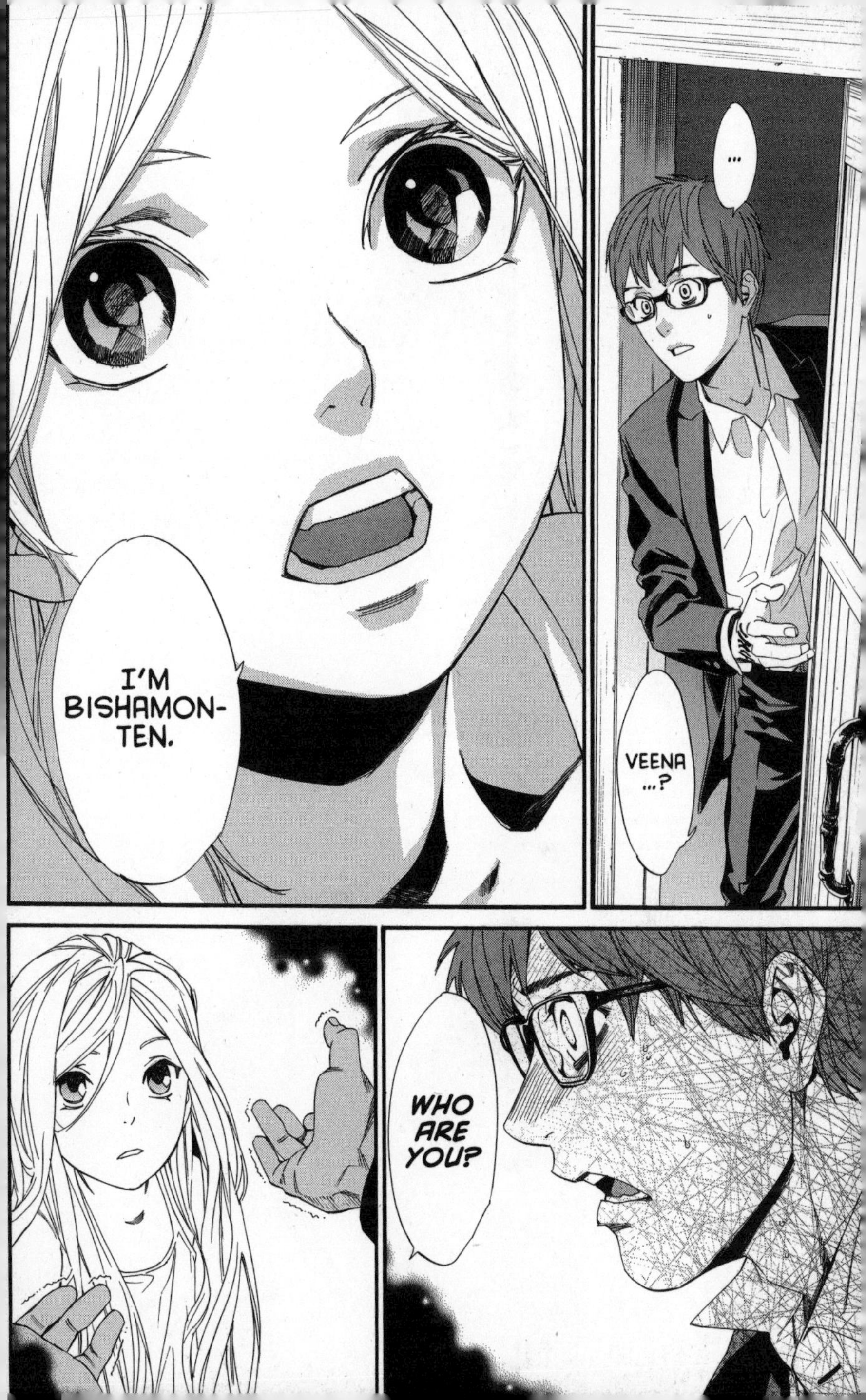
...
VEENA ...?
I'M BISHAMON-TEN.
WHO ARE YOU?

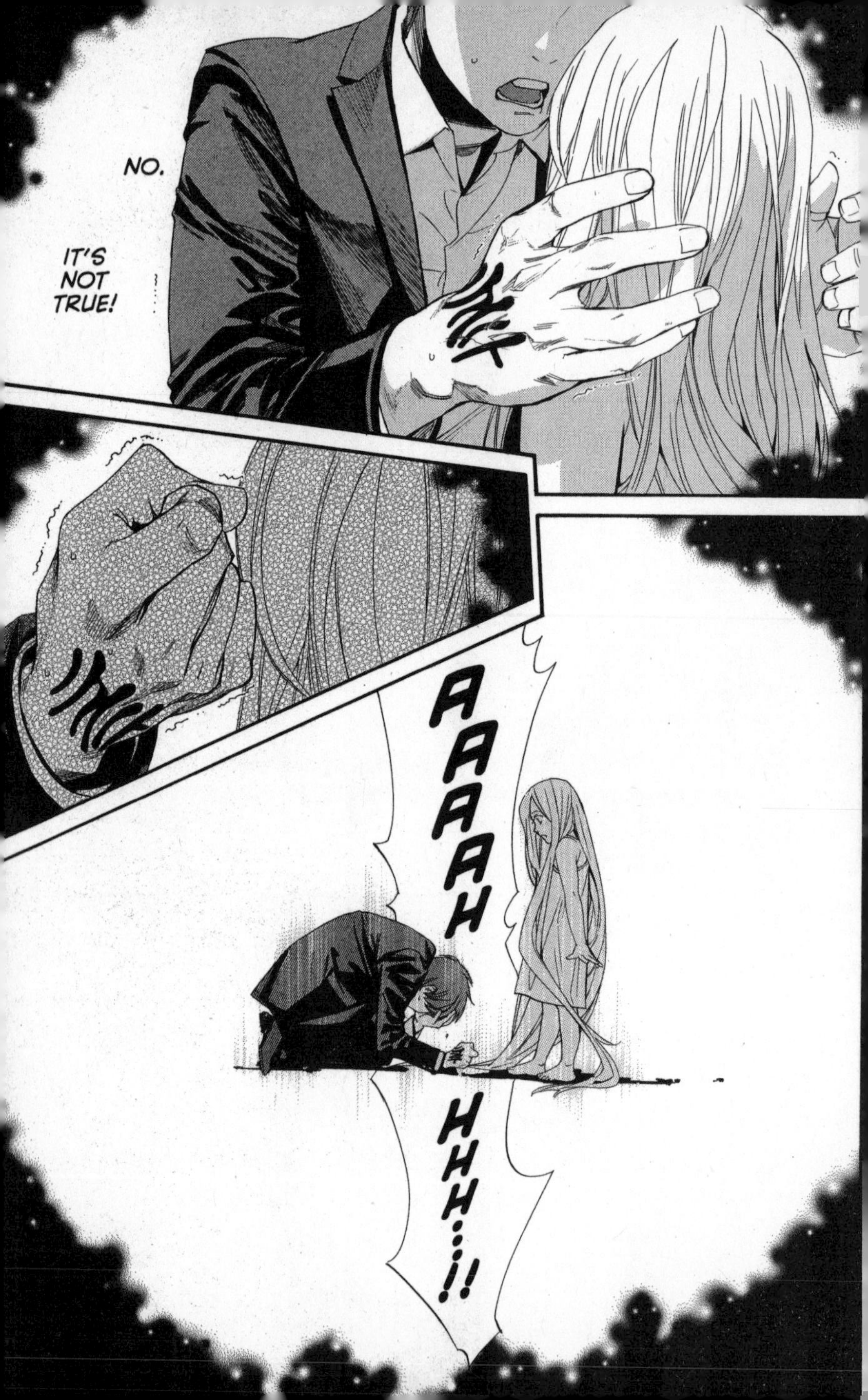
NO.
IT'S NOT TRUE!
AAAAAH HHHH...!!

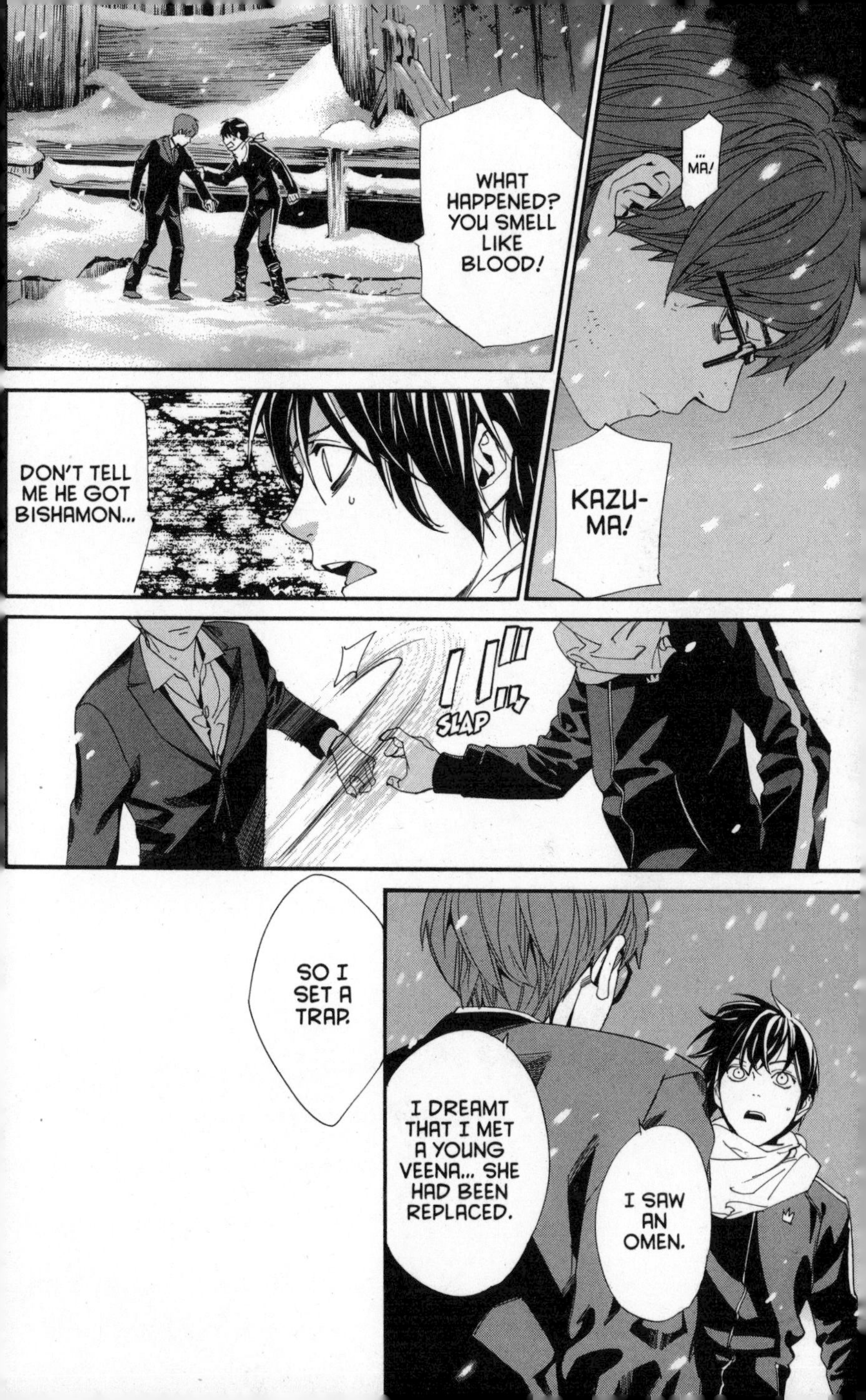
...MA!
KAZU-MA!
WHAT HAPPENED? YOU SMELL LIKE BLOOD!
DON'T TELL ME HE GOT BISHAMON...
SLAP
I SAW AN OMEN.
I DREAMT THAT I MET A YOUNG VEENA... SHE HAD BEEN REPLACED.
SO I SET A TRAP.

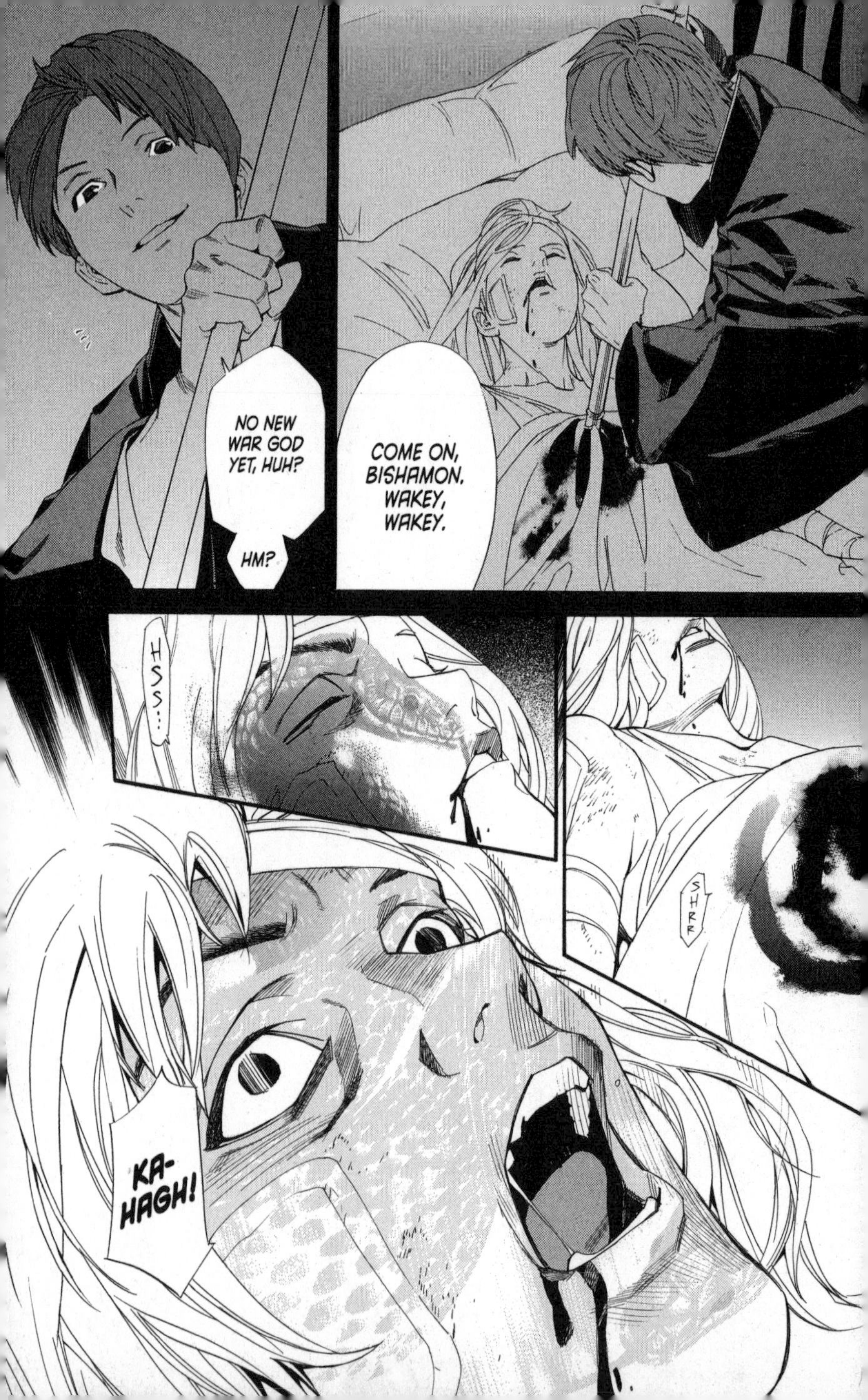
COME ON, BISHAMON. WAKEY, WAKEY.
NO NEW WAR GOD YET, HUH?
HM?
SHRR
HSS...
KA-HAGH!

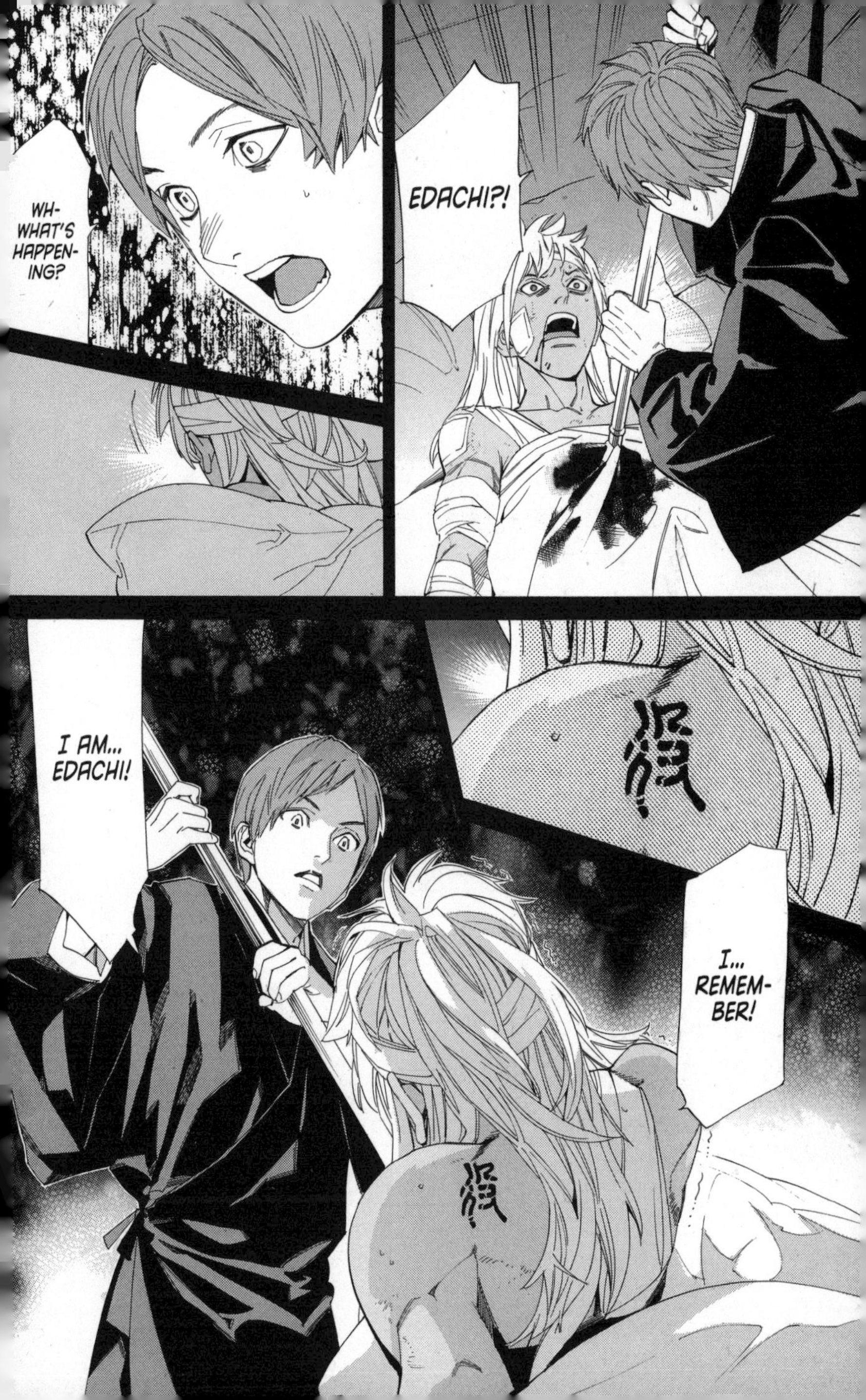
EDACHI?!
WH- WHAT'S HAPPEN- ING?
I... REMEM- BER!
I AM... EDACHI!

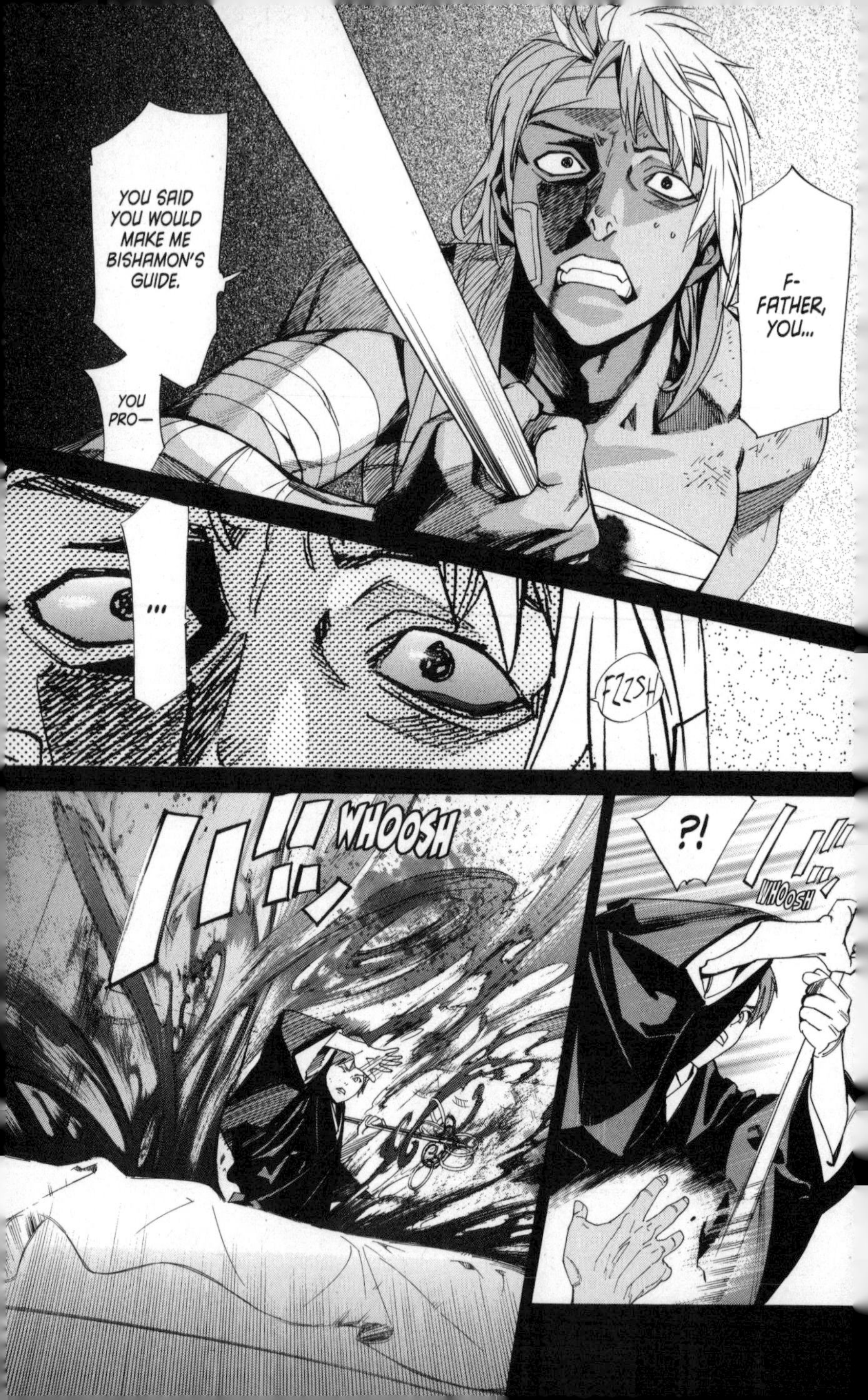
F-
FATHER,
YOU...
YOU SAID YOU WOULD MAKE ME BISHAMON'S GUIDE.
YOU PRO—
...
FZZSH
?!
WHOOSH
WHOOSH

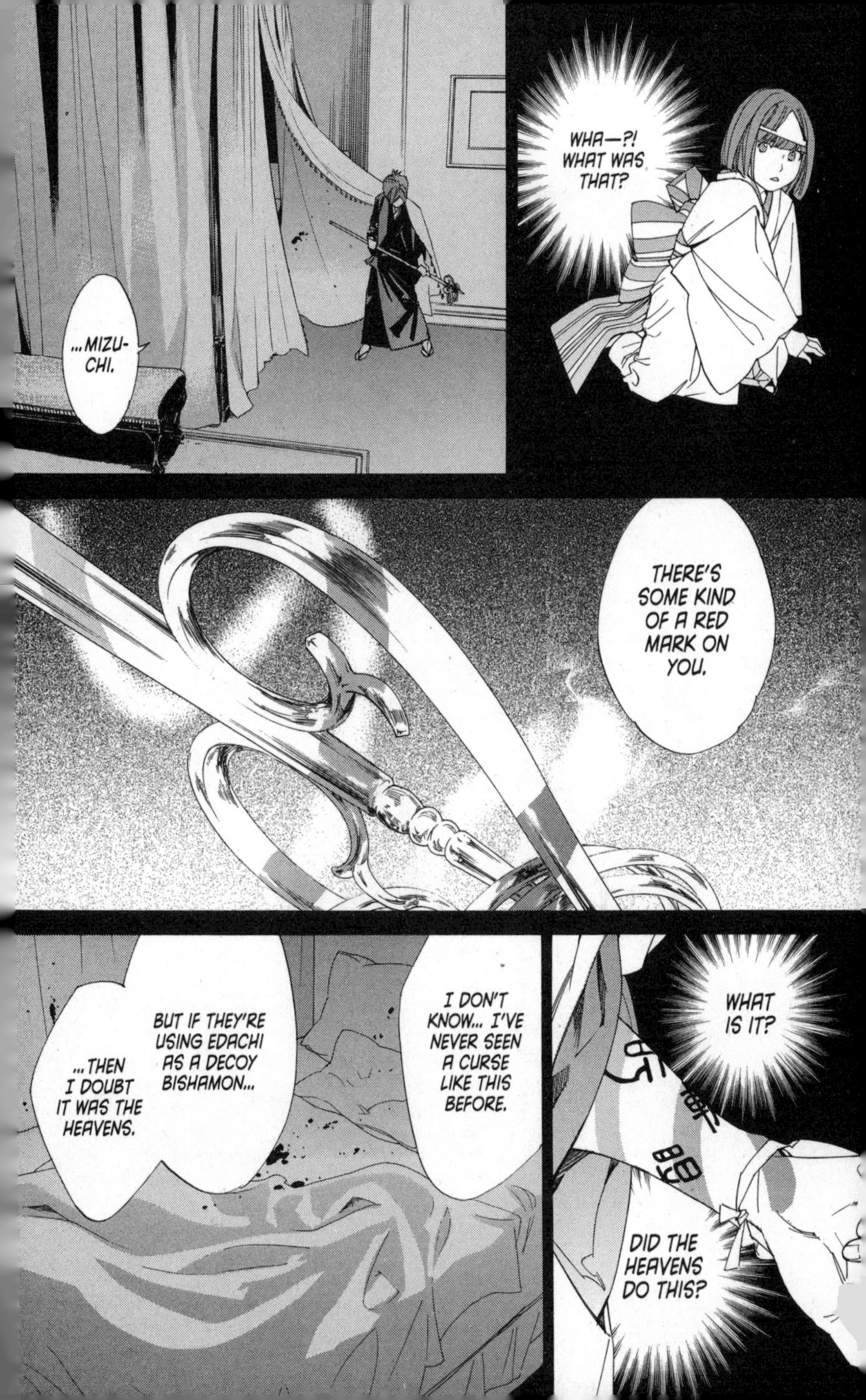
WHA—?! WHAT WAS THAT?
...MIZU-CHI.
THERE'S SOME KIND OF A RED MARK ON YOU.
WHAT IS IT?
DID THE HEAVENS DO THIS?
I DON'T KNOW... I'VE NEVER SEEN A CURSE LIKE THIS BEFORE.
BUT IF THEY'RE USING EDACHI AS A DECOY BISHAMON...
...THEN I DOUBT IT WAS THE HEAVENS.

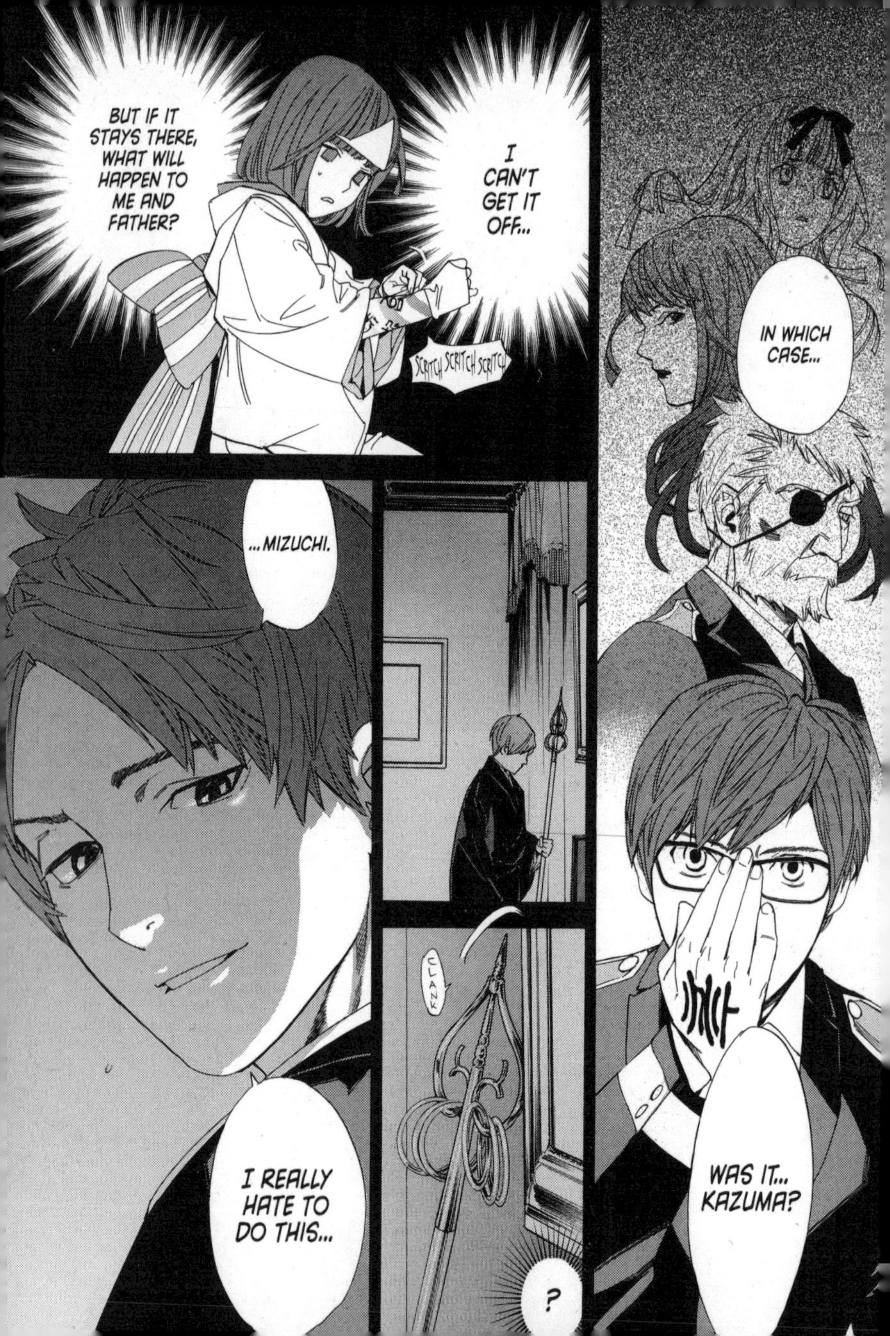
IN WHICH CASE...
WAS IT... KAZUMA?
I CAN'T GET IT OFF...
BUT IF IT STAYS THERE, WHAT WILL HAPPEN TO ME AND FATHER?
SCRITCH SCRITCH SCRITCH
CLANK
?
...MIZUCHI.
I REALLY HATE TO DO THIS...

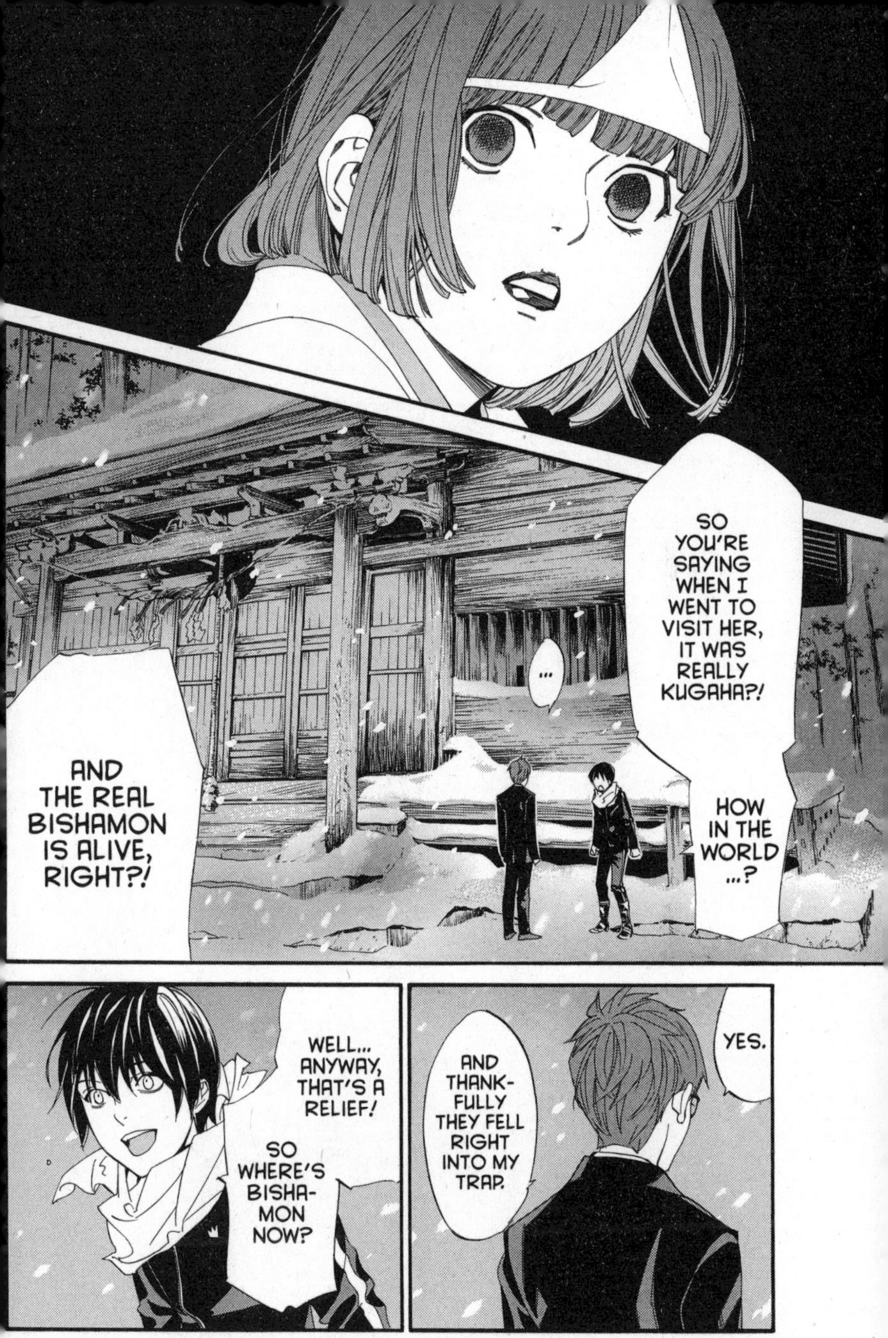
SO YOU'RE SAYING WHEN I WENT TO VISIT HER, IT WAS REALLY KUGAHA?!
HOW IN THE WORLD ...?
...
AND THE REAL BISHAMON IS ALIVE, RIGHT?!
YES.
AND THANK-FULLY THEY FELL RIGHT INTO MY TRAP.
WELL... ANYWAY, THAT'S A RELIEF!
SO WHERE'S BISHA-MON NOW?

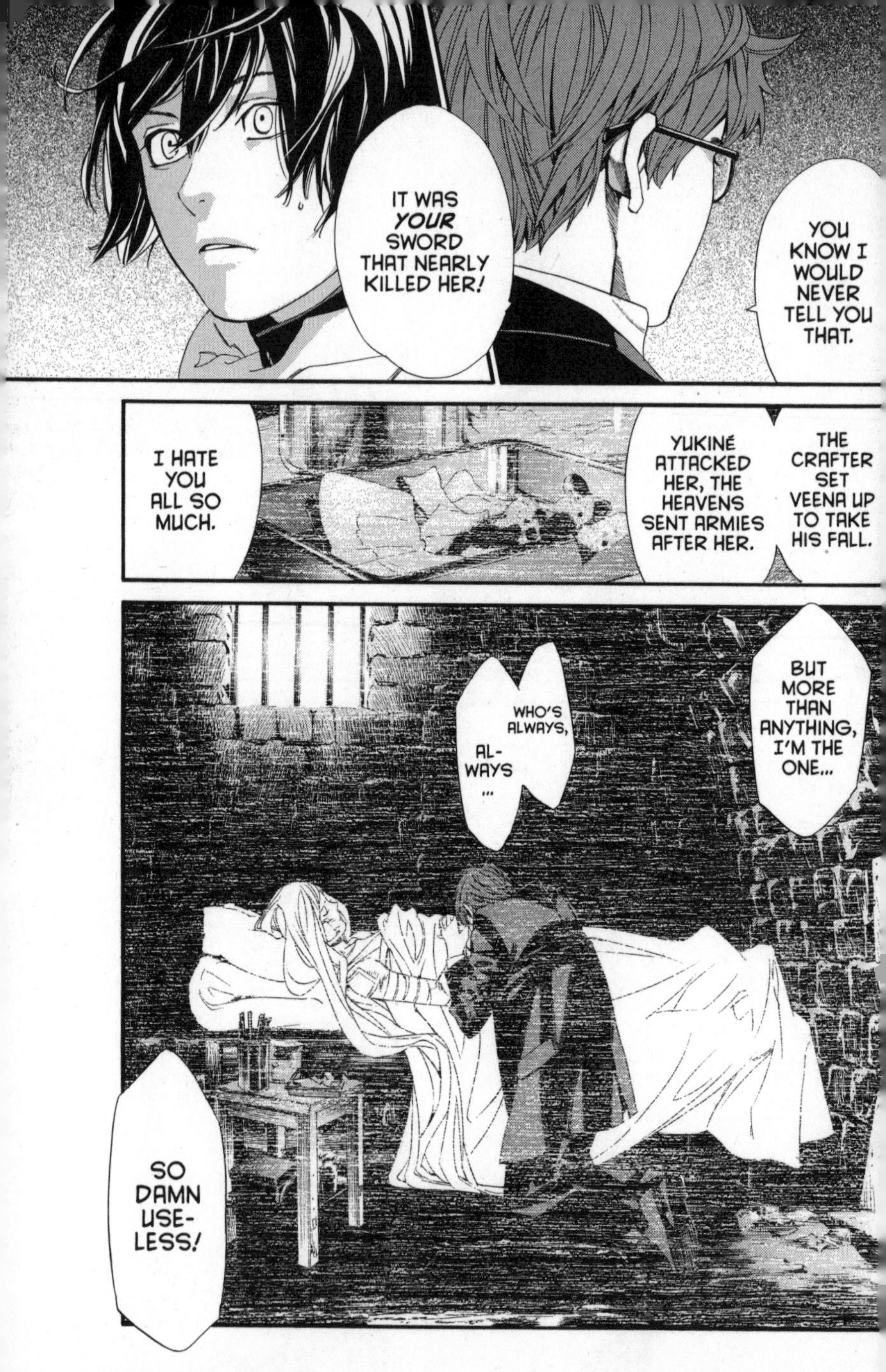
YOU KNOW I WOULD NEVER TELL YOU THAT.
IT WAS *YOUR* SWORD THAT NEARLY KILLED HER!
THE CRAFTER SET VEENA UP TO TAKE HIS FALL.
YUKINÉ ATTACKED HER, THE HEAVENS SENT ARMIES AFTER HER.
I HATE YOU ALL SO MUCH.
BUT MORE THAN ANYTHING, I'M THE ONE...
WHO'S ALWAYS,
AL-WAYS...
SO DAMN USE-LESS!

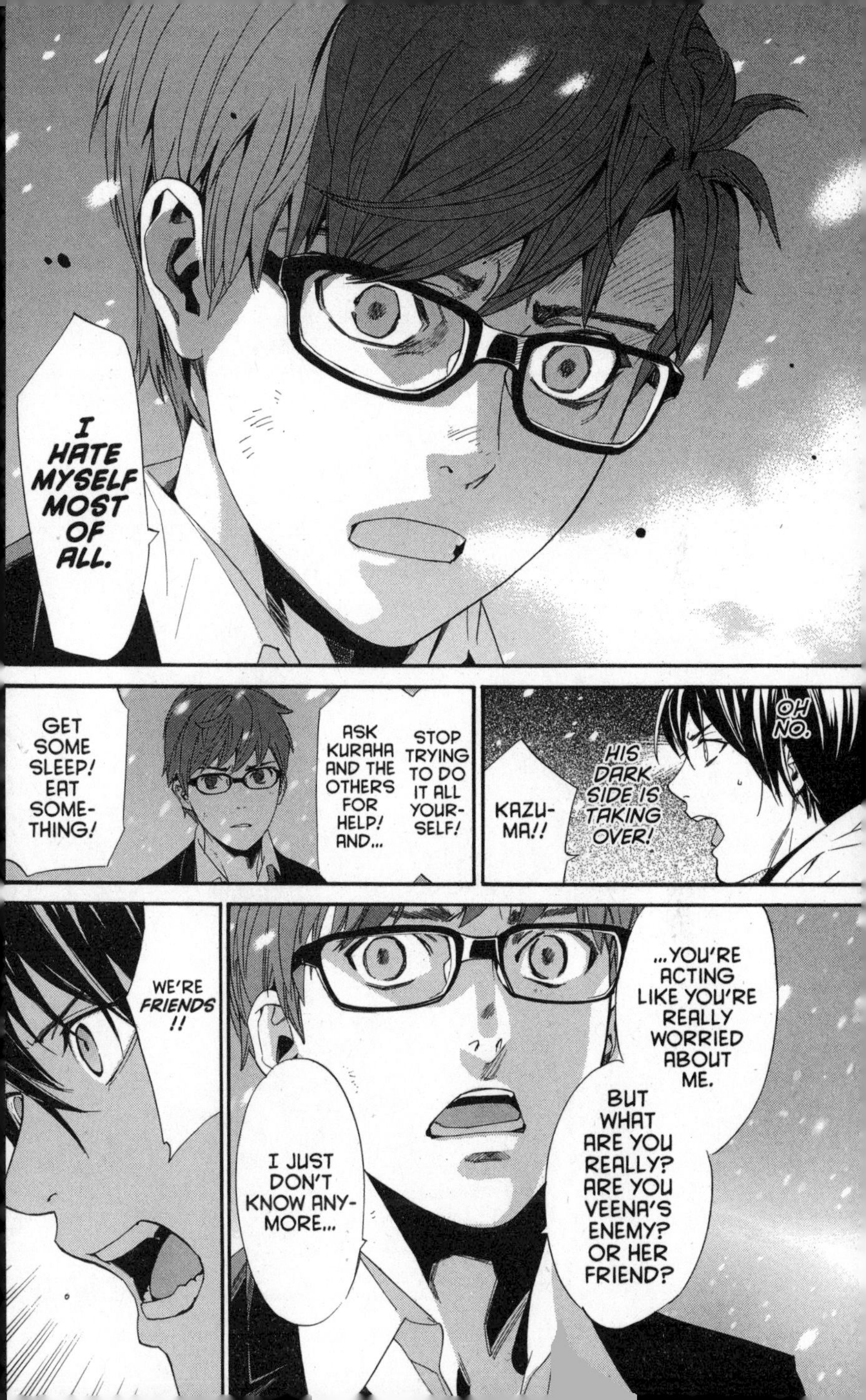
I HATE MYSELF MOST OF ALL.
OH NO.
HIS DARK SIDE IS TAKING OVER!
KAZUMA!!
STOP TRYING TO DO IT ALL YOURSELF!
ASK KURAHA AND THE OTHERS FOR HELP! AND...
GET SOME SLEEP! EAT SOMETHING!
...YOU'RE ACTING LIKE YOU'RE REALLY WORRIED ABOUT ME.
BUT WHAT ARE YOU REALLY? ARE YOU VEENA'S ENEMY? OR HER FRIEND?
I JUST DON'T KNOW ANYMORE...
WE'RE *FRIENDS* !!

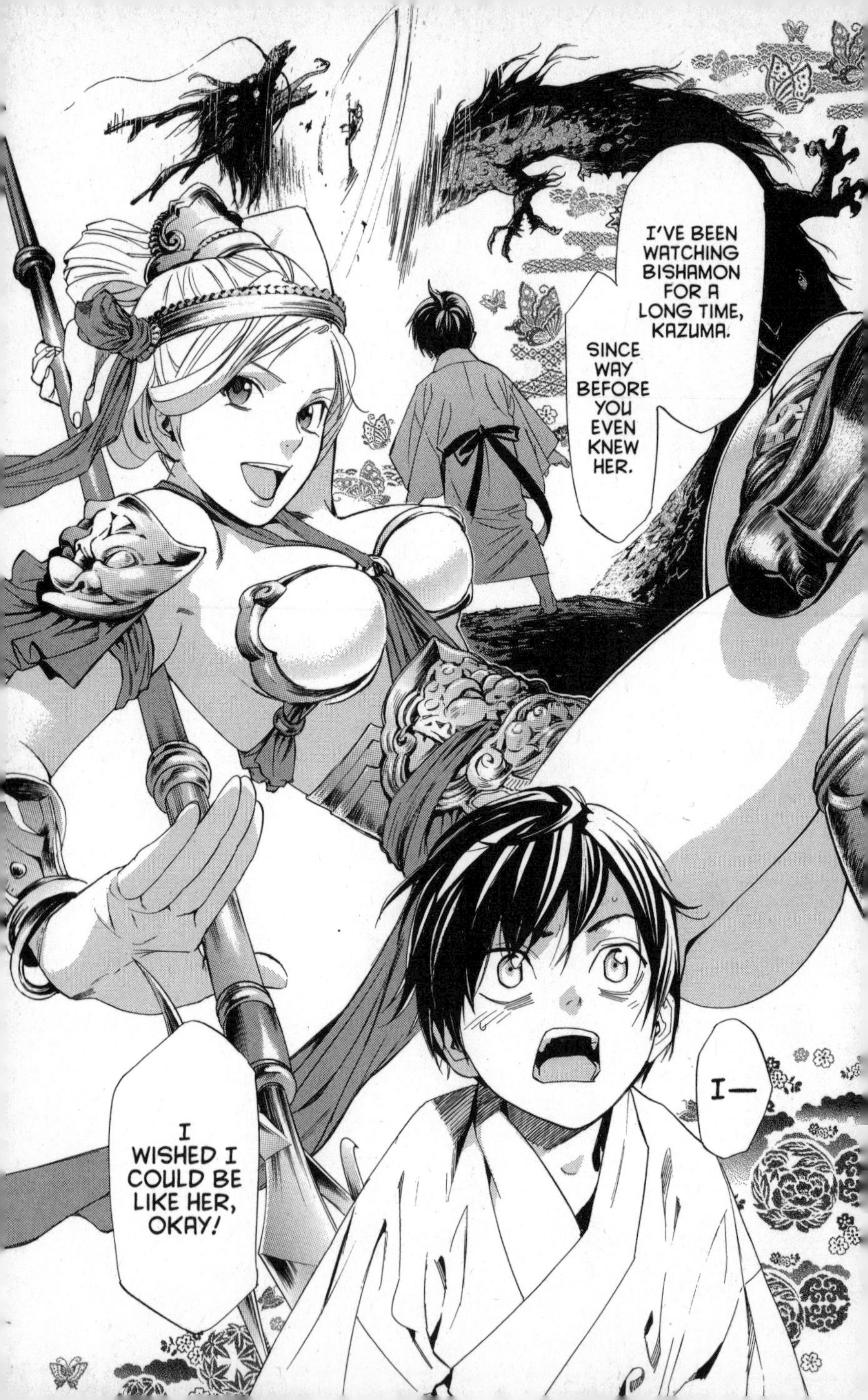
I'VE BEEN WATCHING BISHAMON FOR A LONG TIME, KAZUMA.
SINCE WAY BEFORE YOU EVEN KNEW HER.
I—
I WISHED I COULD BE LIKE HER, OKAY!

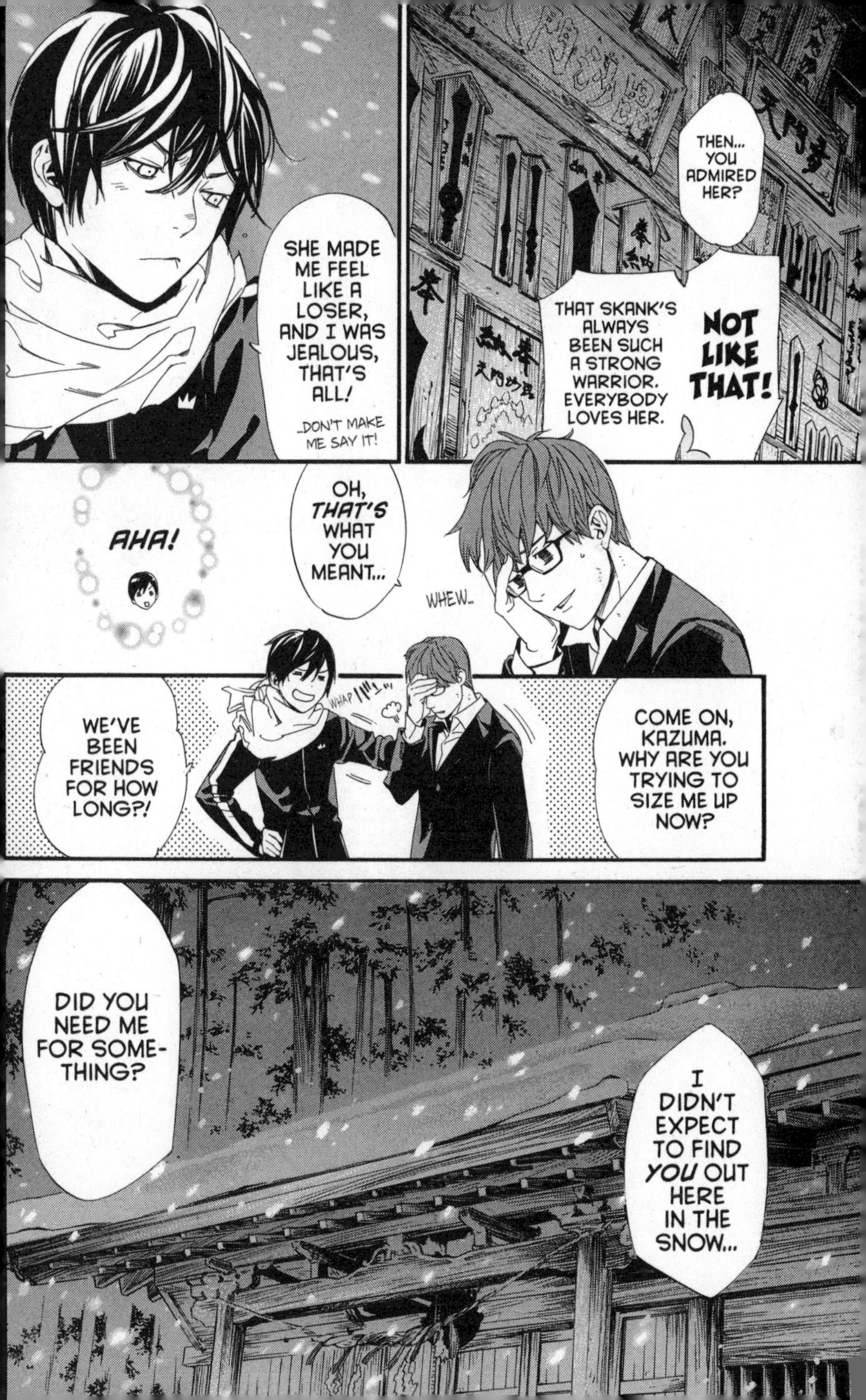
THEN... YOU ADMIRED HER?
NOT LIKE THAT!
THAT SKANK'S ALWAYS BEEN SUCH A STRONG WARRIOR. EVERYBODY LOVES HER.
SHE MADE ME FEEL LIKE A LOSER, AND I WAS JEALOUS, THAT'S ALL!
...DON'T MAKE ME SAY IT!
OH, *THAT'S* WHAT YOU MEANT...
WHEW...
AHA!
COME ON, KAZUMA. WHY ARE YOU TRYING TO SIZE ME UP NOW?
WHAP
WE'VE BEEN FRIENDS FOR HOW LONG?!
I DIDN'T EXPECT TO FIND *YOU* OUT HERE IN THE SNOW...
DID YOU NEED ME FOR SOME-THING?

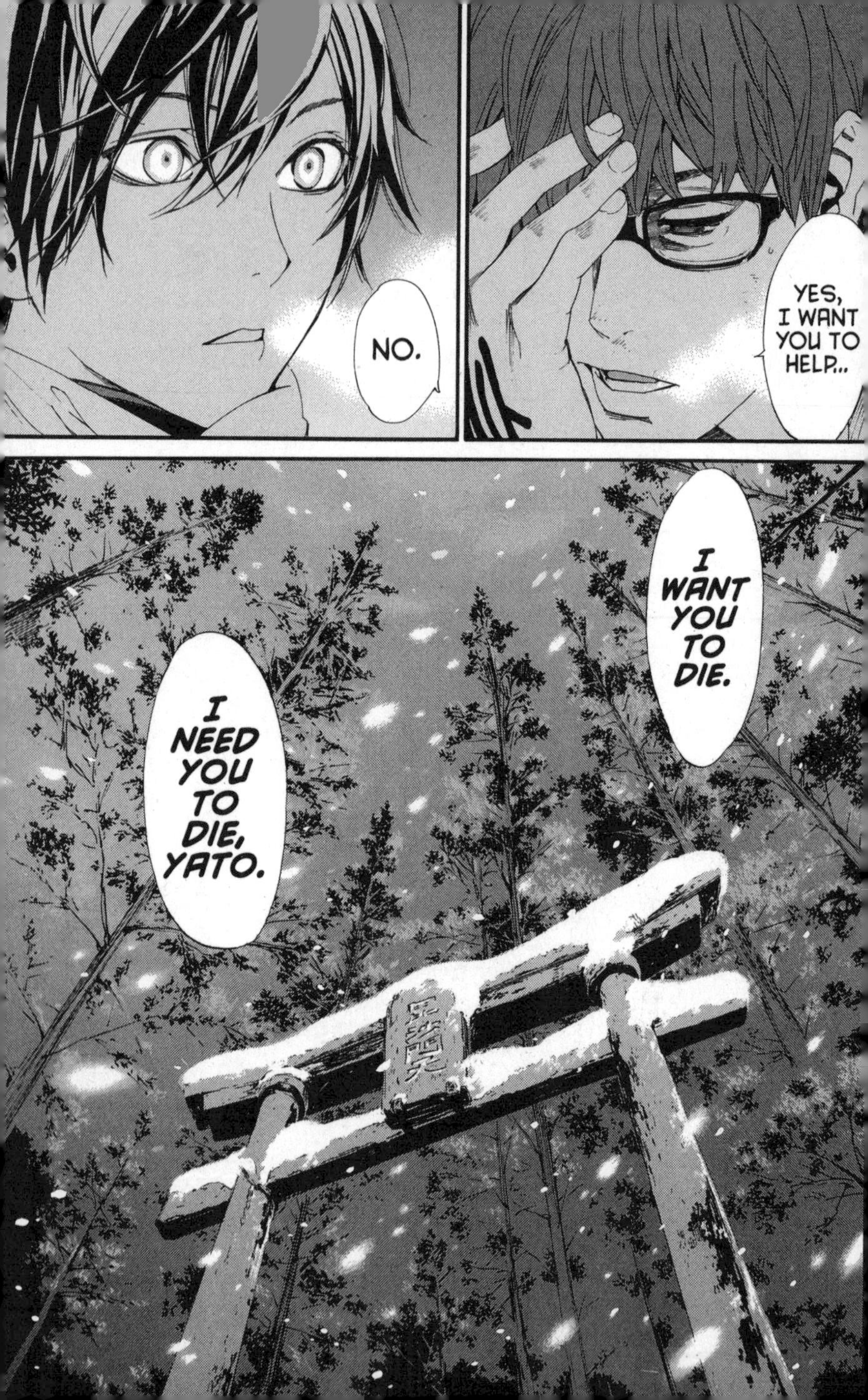
YES, I WANT YOU TO HELP...
NO.
I WANT YOU TO DIE.
I NEED YOU TO DIE, YATO.

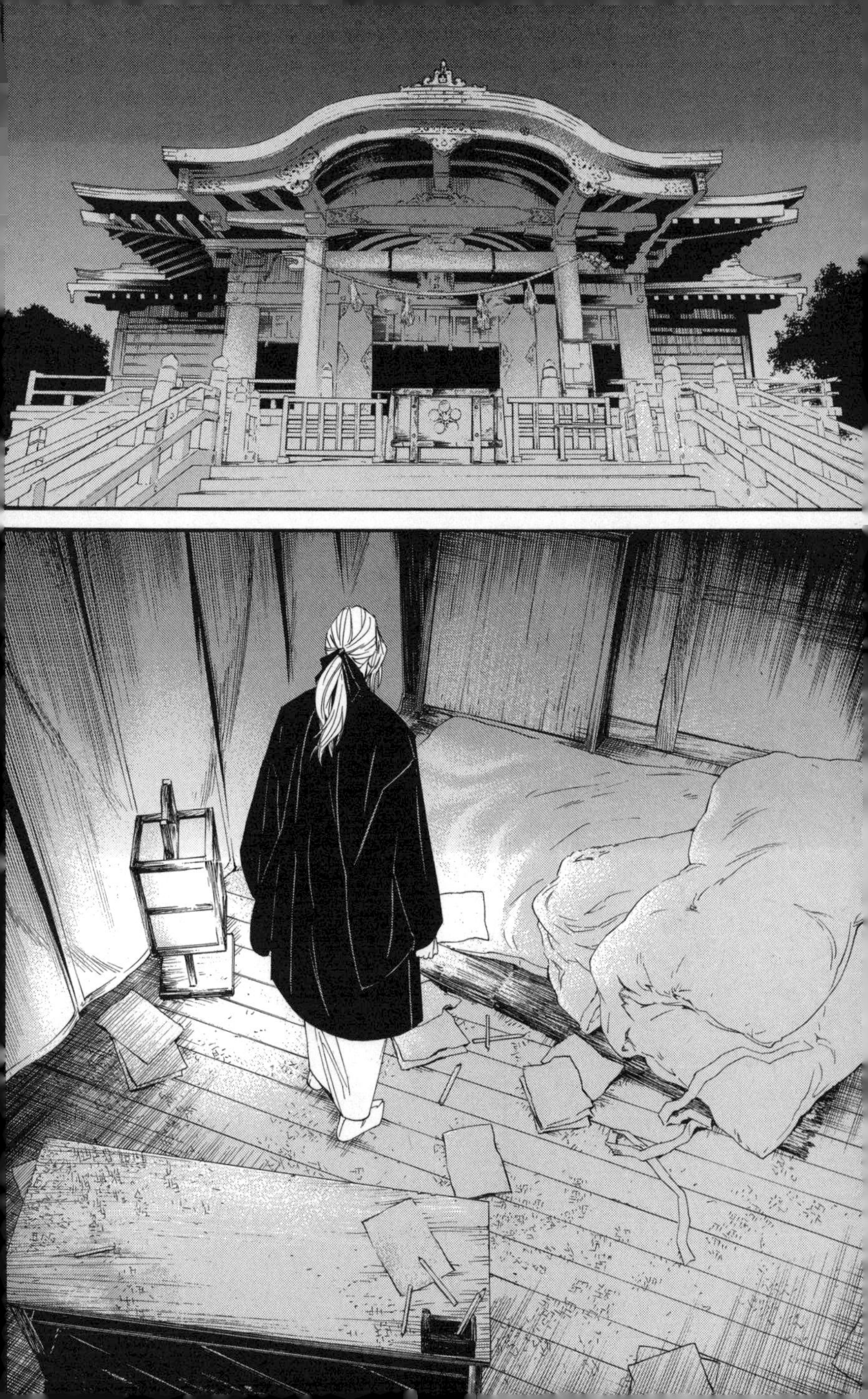

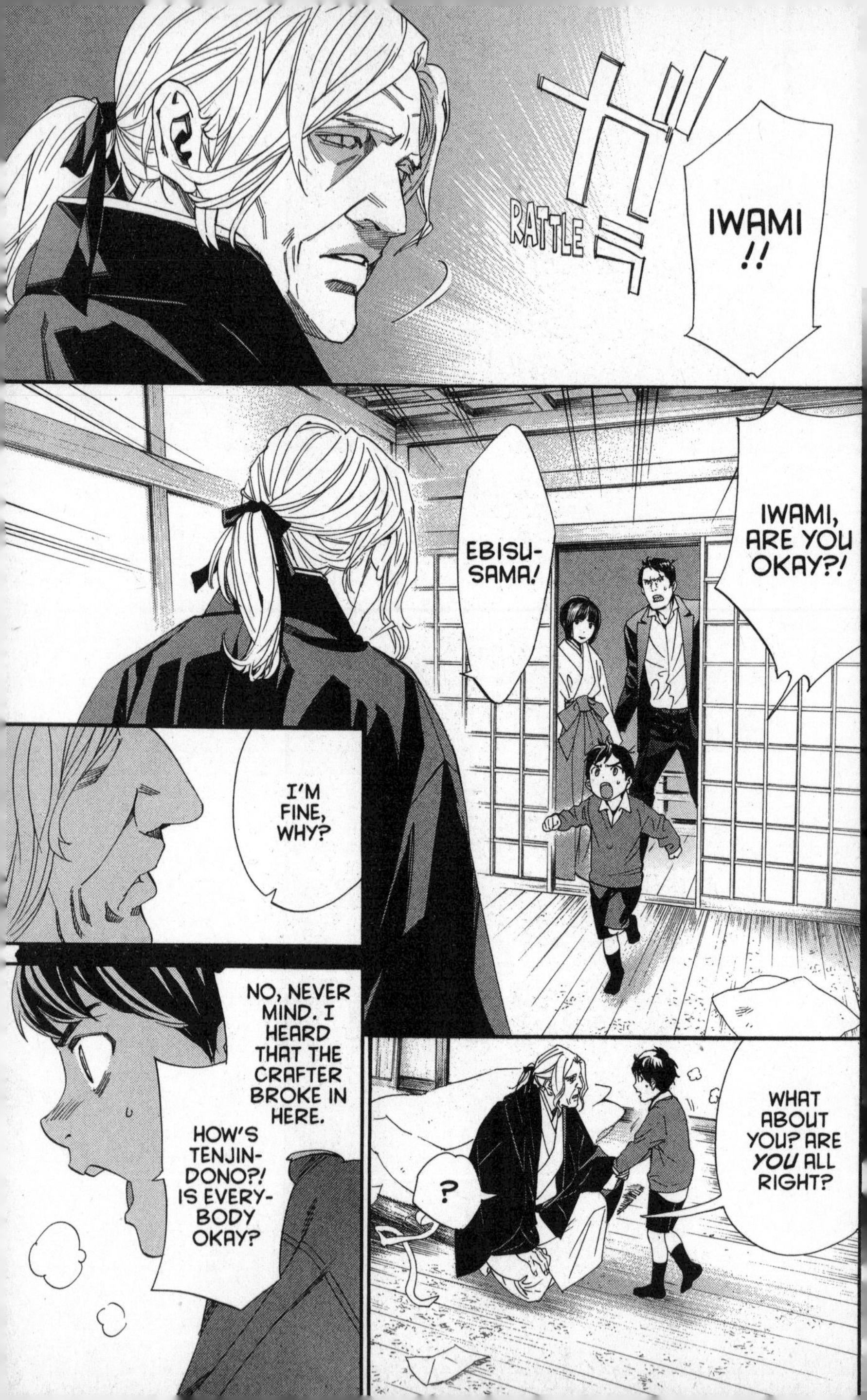
IWAMI !!
RATTLE
IWAMI, ARE YOU OKAY?!
EBISU-SAMA!
I'M FINE, WHY?
WHAT ABOUT YOU? ARE *YOU* ALL RIGHT?
?
NO, NEVER MIND. I HEARD THAT THE CRAFTER BROKE IN HERE.
HOW'S TENJIN-DONO?! IS EVERYBODY OKAY?

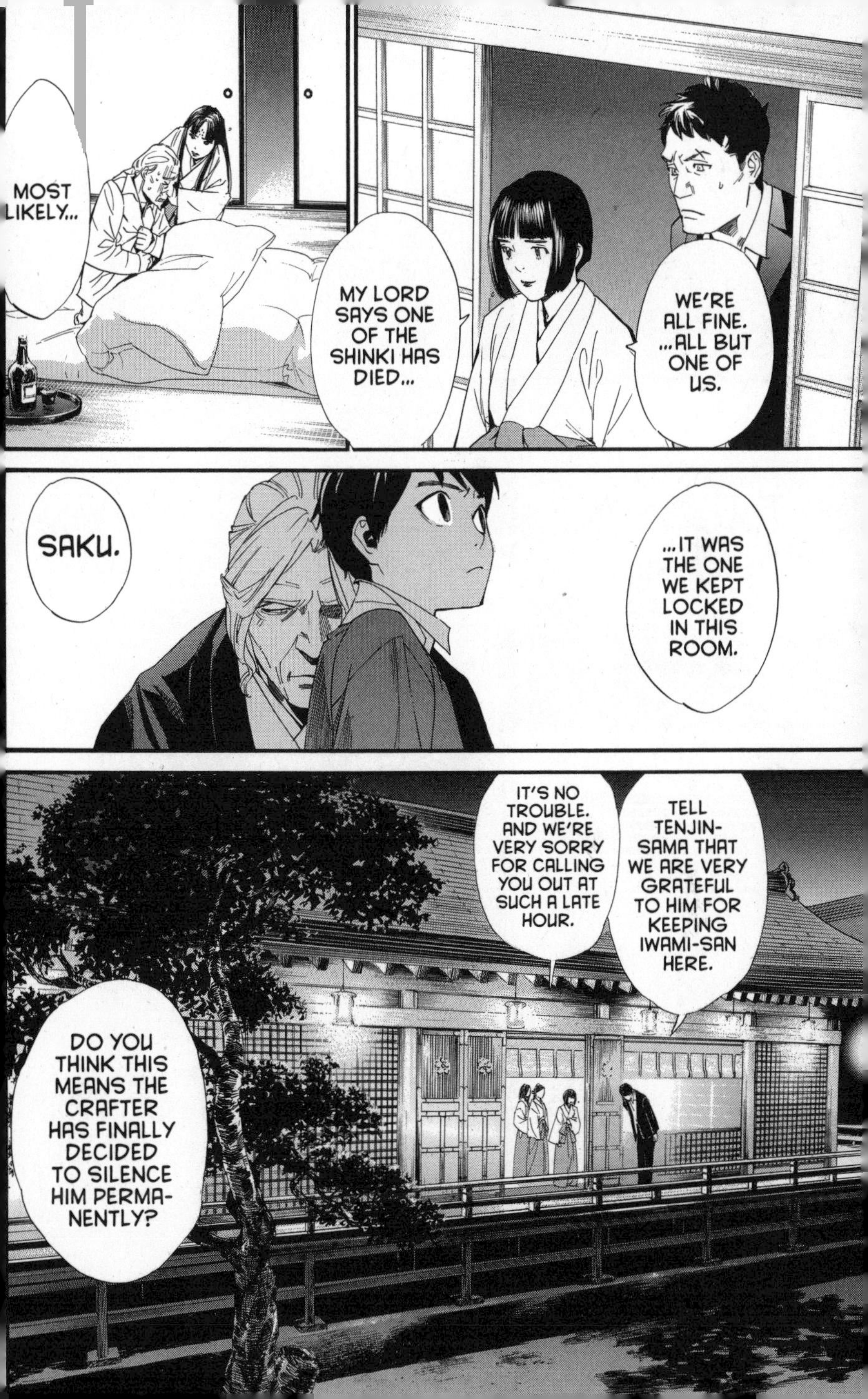
WE'RE ALL FINE. ...ALL BUT ONE OF US.
MY LORD SAYS ONE OF THE SHINKI HAS DIED...
MOST LIKELY...
...IT WAS THE ONE WE KEPT LOCKED IN THIS ROOM.
SAKU.
TELL TENJIN-SAMA THAT WE ARE VERY GRATEFUL TO HIM FOR KEEPING IWAMI-SAN HERE.
IT'S NO TROUBLE. AND WE'RE VERY SORRY FOR CALLING YOU OUT AT SUCH A LATE HOUR.
DO YOU THINK THIS MEANS THE CRAFTER HAS FINALLY DECIDED TO SILENCE HIM PERMA-NENTLY?

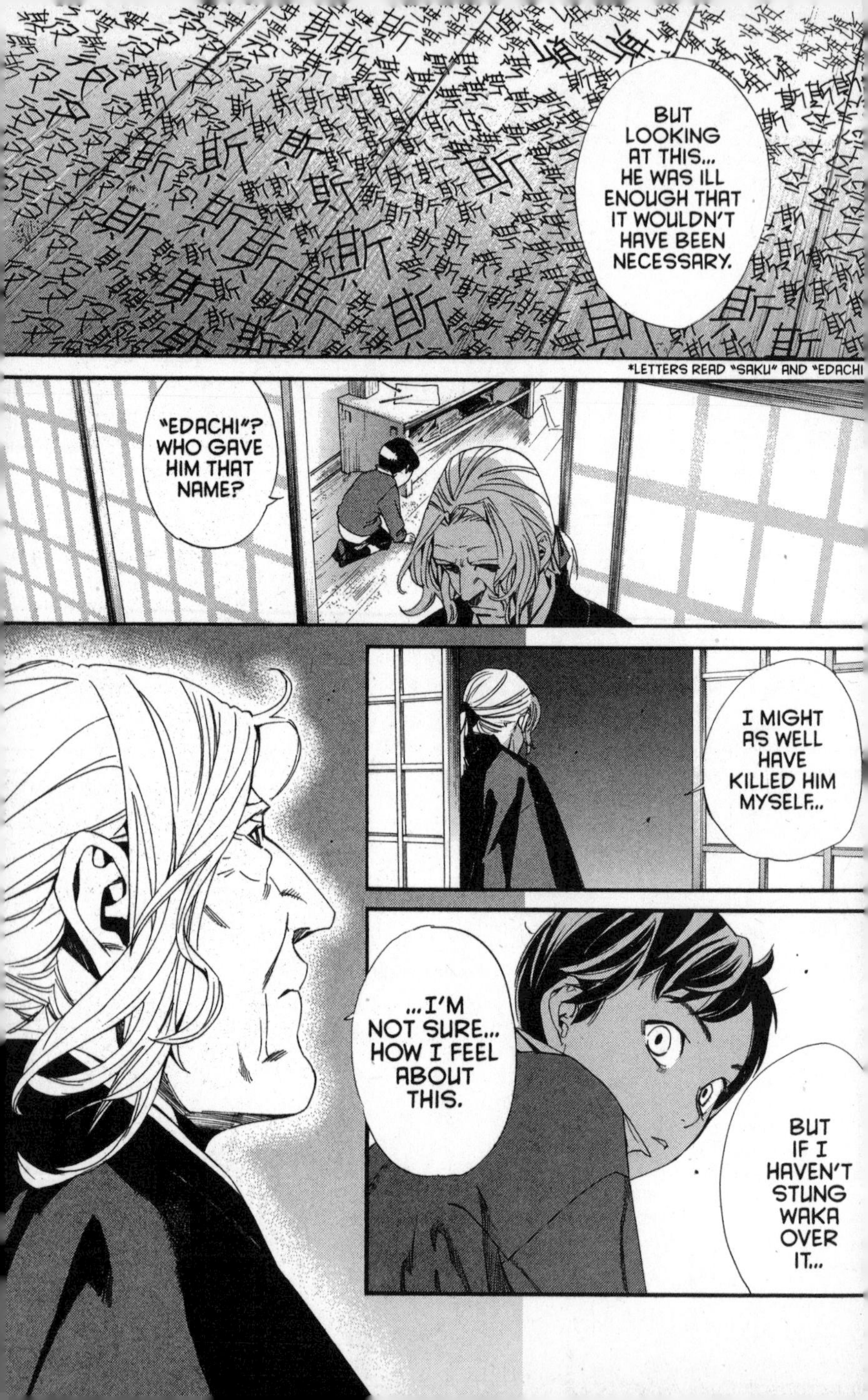
BUT LOOKING AT THIS... HE WAS ILL ENOUGH THAT IT WOULDN'T HAVE BEEN NECESSARY.
*LETTERS READ "SAKU" AND "EDACHI
"EDACHI"? WHO GAVE HIM THAT NAME?
I MIGHT AS WELL HAVE KILLED HIM MYSELF...
...I'M NOT SURE... HOW I FEEL ABOUT THIS.
BUT IF I HAVEN'T STUNG WAKA OVER IT...

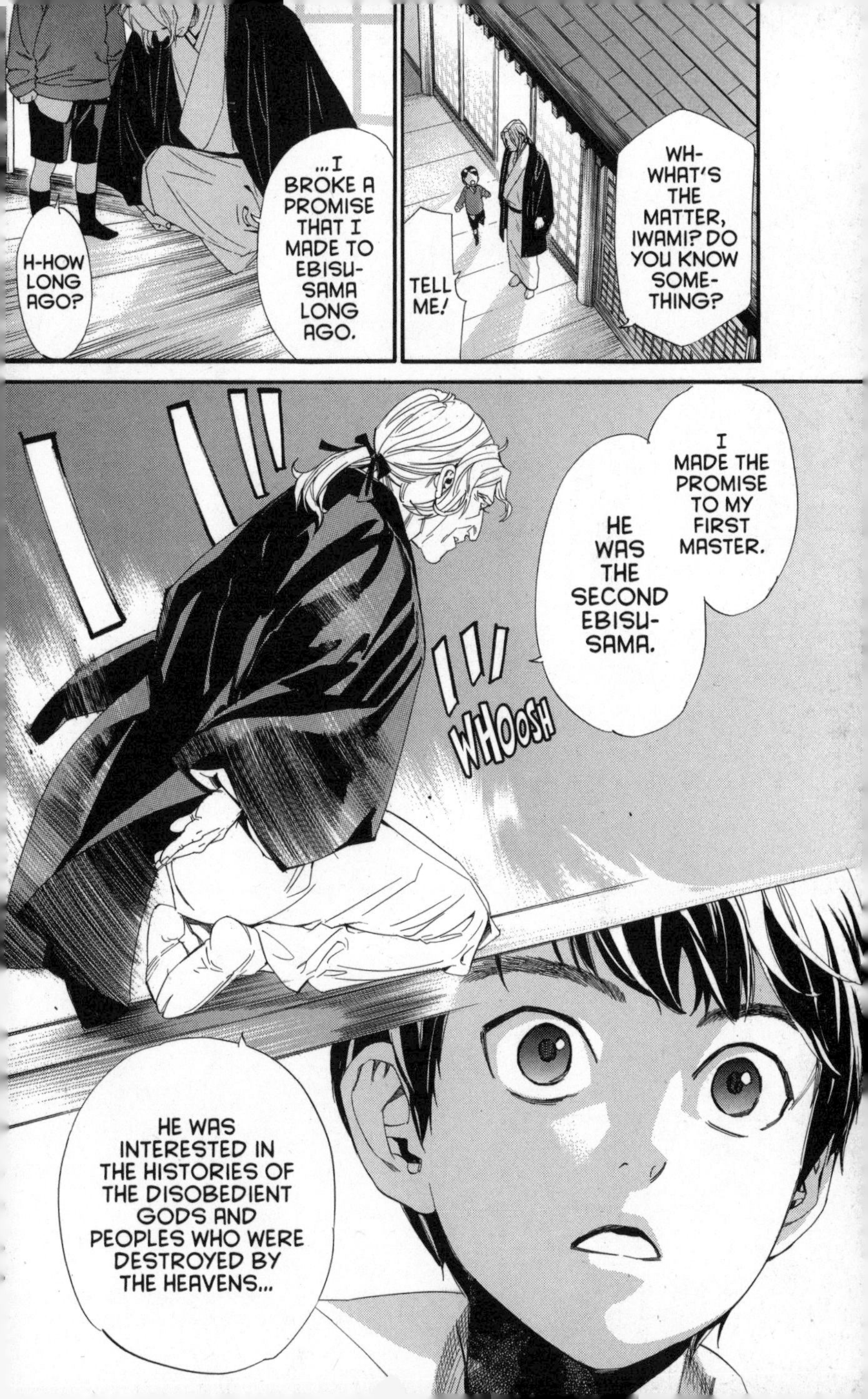
WH-WHAT'S THE MATTER, IWAMI? DO YOU KNOW SOME-THING?
TELL ME!
...I BROKE A PROMISE THAT I MADE TO EBISU-SAMA LONG AGO.
H-HOW LONG AGO?
I MADE THE PROMISE TO MY FIRST MASTER.
HE WAS THE SECOND EBISU-SAMA.
WHOOSH
HE WAS INTERESTED IN THE HISTORIES OF THE DISOBEDIENT GODS AND PEOPLES WHO WERE DESTROYED BY THE HEAVENS...

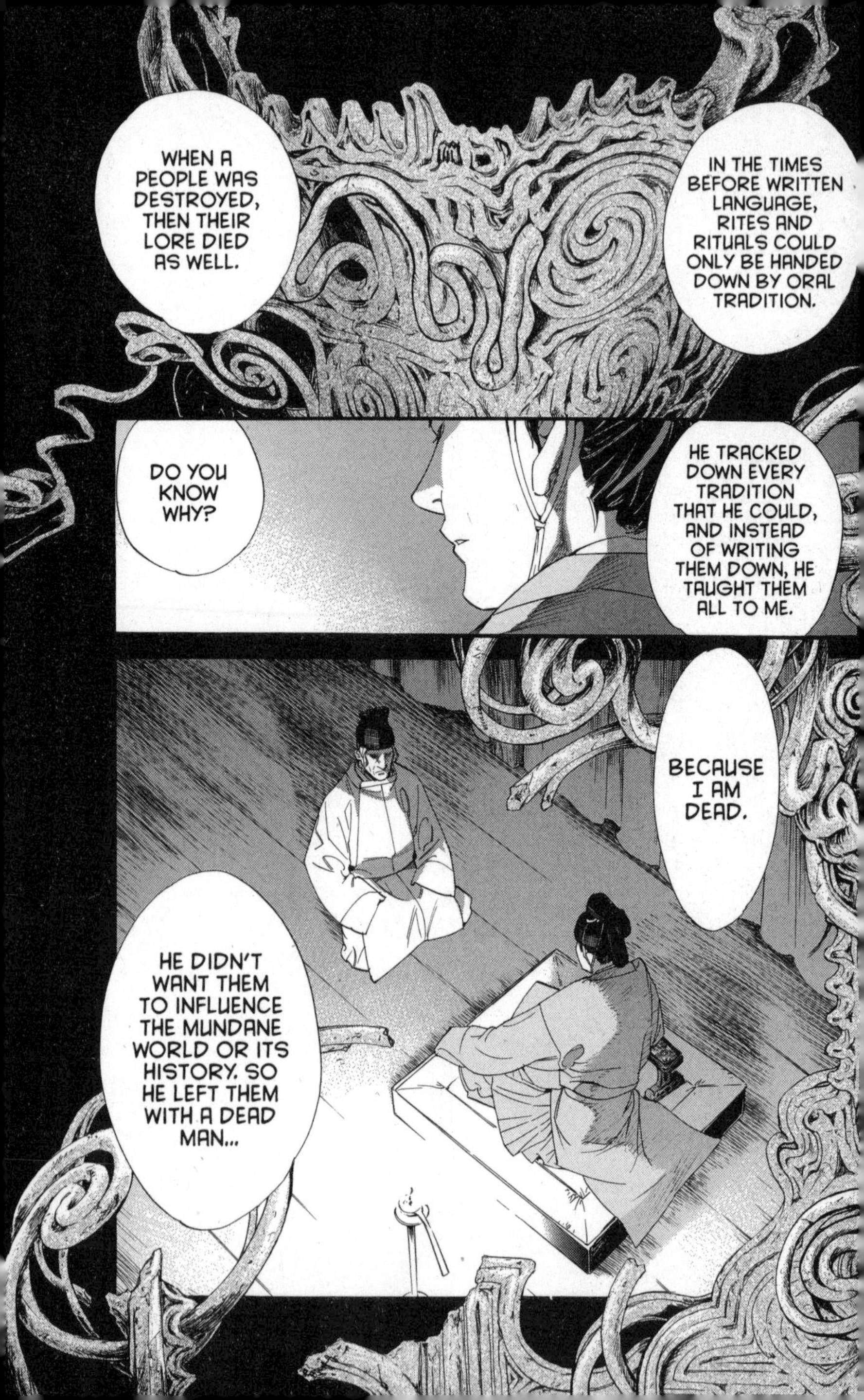
IN THE TIMES BEFORE WRITTEN LANGUAGE, RITES AND RITUALS COULD ONLY BE HANDED DOWN BY ORAL TRADITION.
WHEN A PEOPLE WAS DESTROYED, THEN THEIR LORE DIED AS WELL.
HE TRACKED DOWN EVERY TRADITION THAT HE COULD, AND INSTEAD OF WRITING THEM DOWN, HE TAUGHT THEM ALL TO ME.
DO YOU KNOW WHY?
BECAUSE I AM DEAD.
HE DIDN'T WANT THEM TO INFLUENCE THE MUNDANE WORLD OR ITS HISTORY. SO HE LEFT THEM WITH A DEAD MAN...

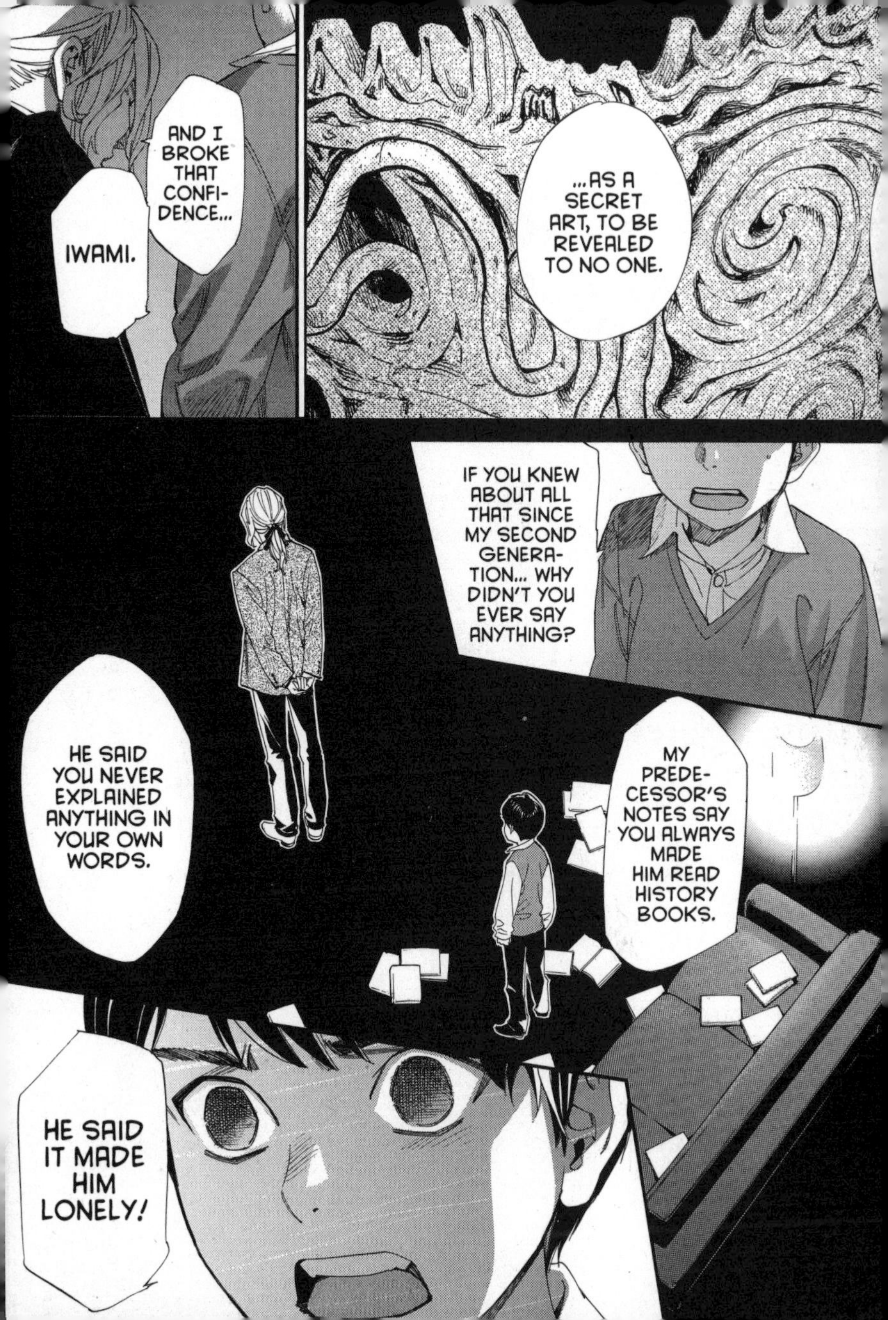
...AS A SECRET ART, TO BE REVEALED TO NO ONE.
AND I BROKE THAT CONFIDENCE...
IWAMI.
IF YOU KNEW ABOUT ALL THAT SINCE MY SECOND GENERATION... WHY DIDN'T YOU EVER SAY ANYTHING?
MY PREDECESSOR'S NOTES SAY YOU ALWAYS MADE HIM READ HISTORY BOOKS.
HE SAID YOU NEVER EXPLAINED ANYTHING IN YOUR OWN WORDS.
HE SAID IT MADE HIM LONELY!

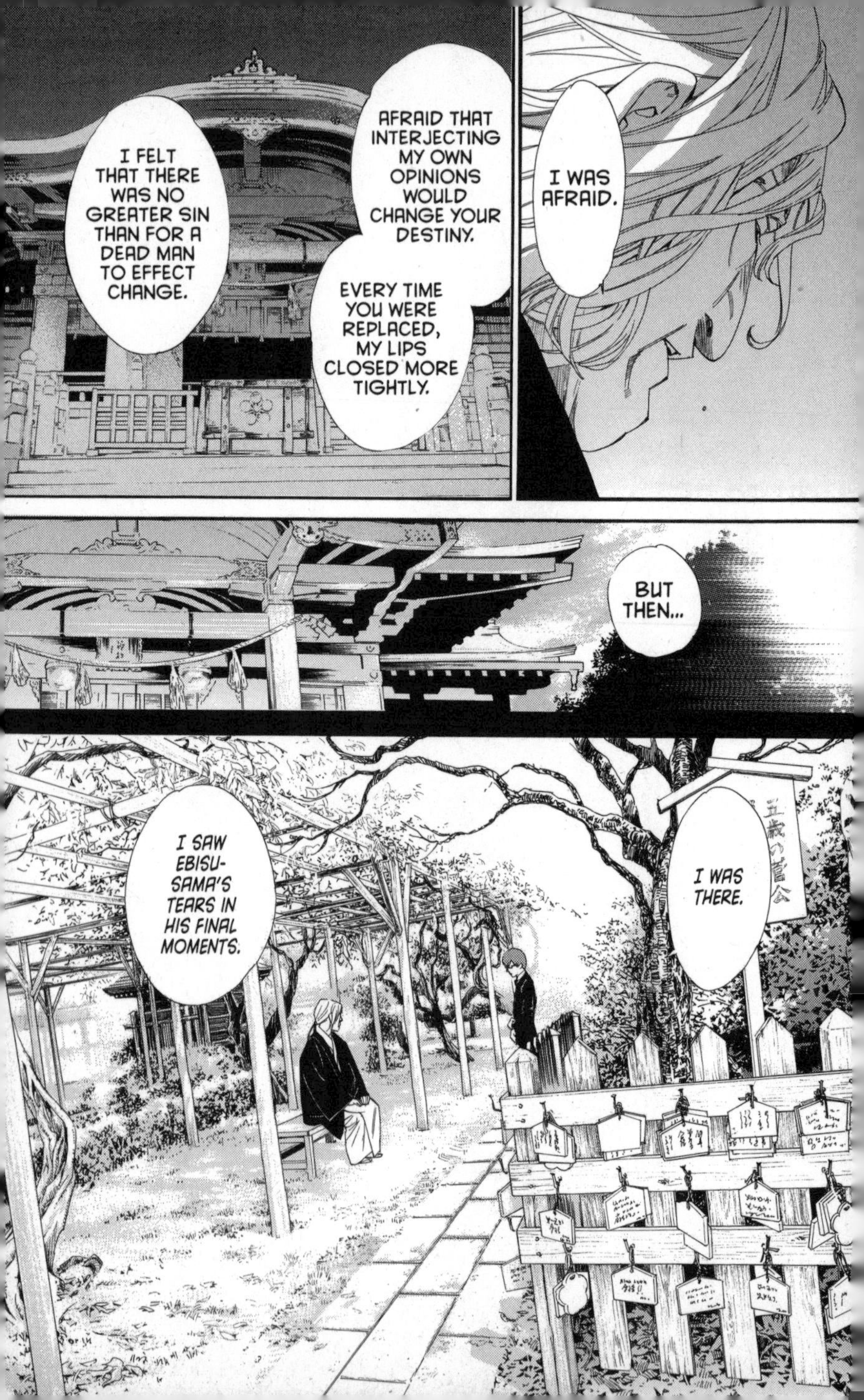
I WAS AFRAID.
AFRAID THAT INTERJECTING MY OWN OPINIONS WOULD CHANGE YOUR DESTINY.
EVERY TIME YOU WERE REPLACED, MY LIPS CLOSED MORE TIGHTLY.
I FELT THAT THERE WAS NO GREATER SIN THAN FOR A DEAD MAN TO EFFECT CHANGE.
BUT THEN...
I WAS THERE.
I SAW EBISU-SAMA'S TEARS IN HIS FINAL MOMENTS.

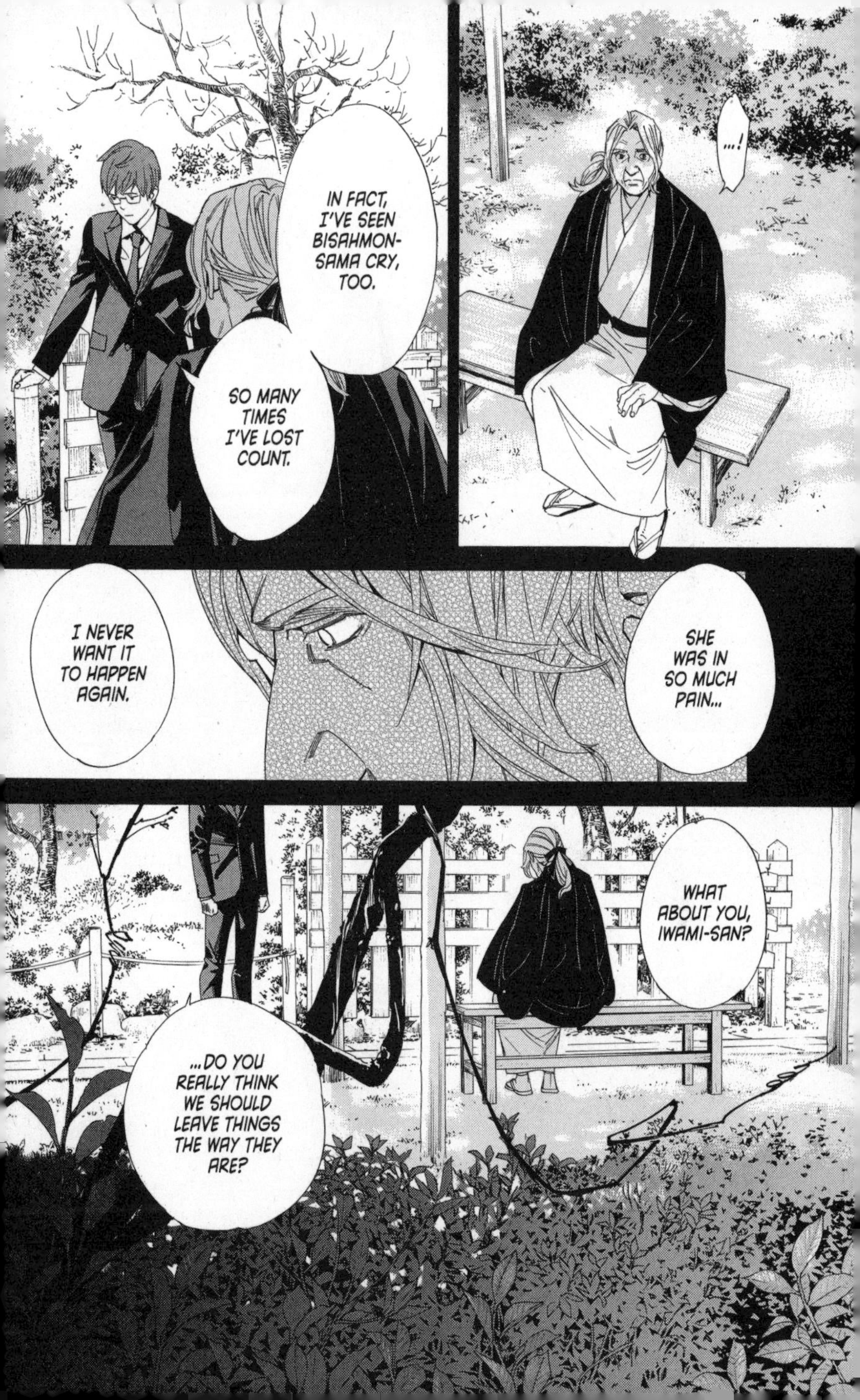
...!
IN FACT, I'VE SEEN BISAHMON-SAMA CRY, TOO.
SO MANY TIMES I'VE LOST COUNT.
SHE WAS IN SO MUCH PAIN...
I NEVER WANT IT TO HAPPEN AGAIN.
WHAT ABOUT YOU, IWAMI-SAN?
...DO YOU REALLY THINK WE SHOULD LEAVE THINGS THE WAY THEY ARE?

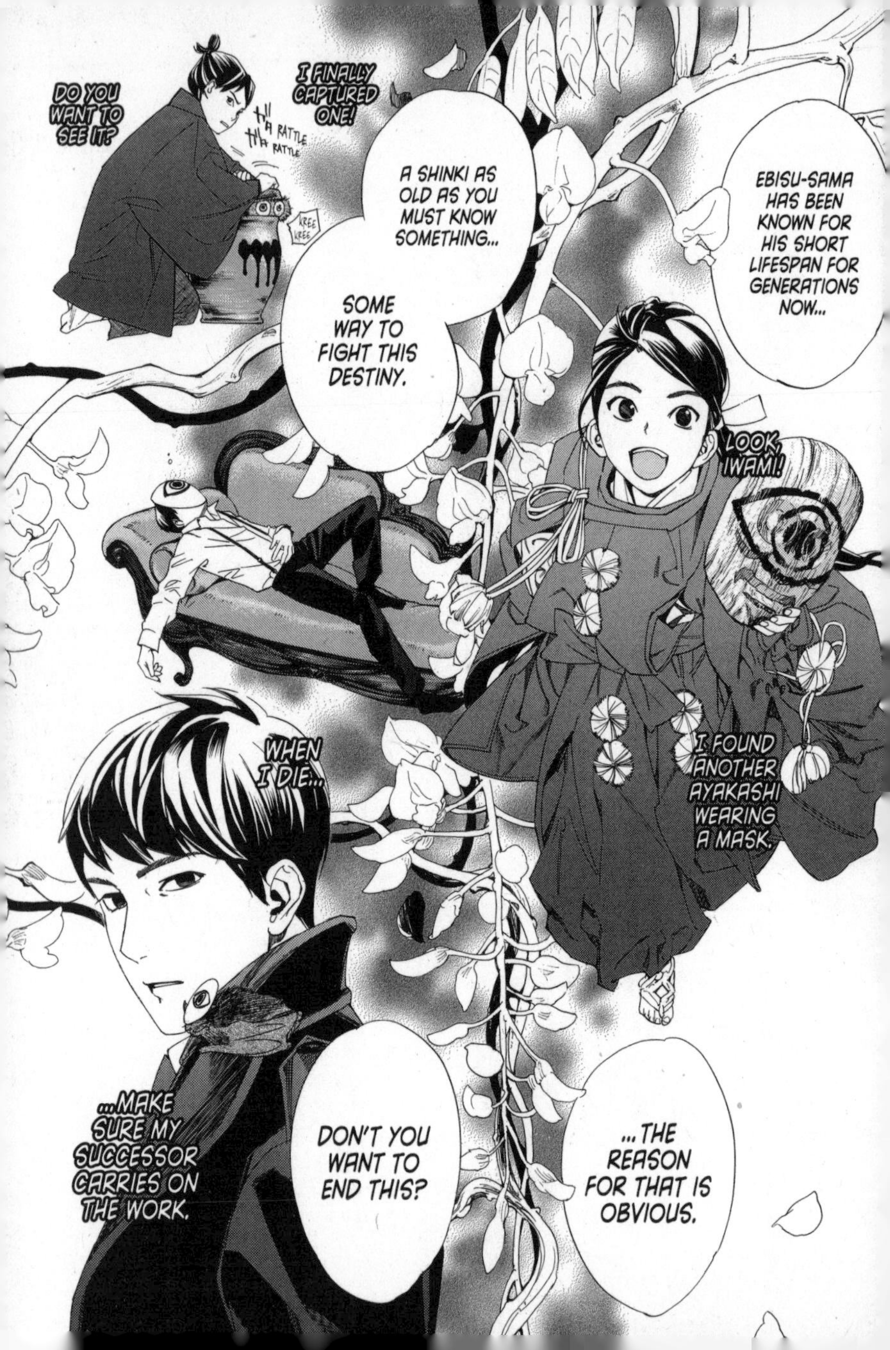
EBISU-SAMA HAS BEEN KNOWN FOR HIS SHORT LIFESPAN FOR GENERATIONS NOW...
A SHINKI AS OLD AS YOU MUST KNOW SOMETHING...
SOME WAY TO FIGHT THIS DESTINY.
I FINALLY CAPTURED ONE!
DO YOU WANT TO SEE IT?
RATTLE RATTLE
KREE KREE
LOOK, IWAMI!
I FOUND ANOTHER AYAKASHI WEARING A MASK.
WHEN I DIE...
...MAKE SURE MY SUCCESSOR CARRIES ON THE WORK.
...THE REASON FOR THAT IS OBVIOUS.
DON'T YOU WANT TO END THIS?

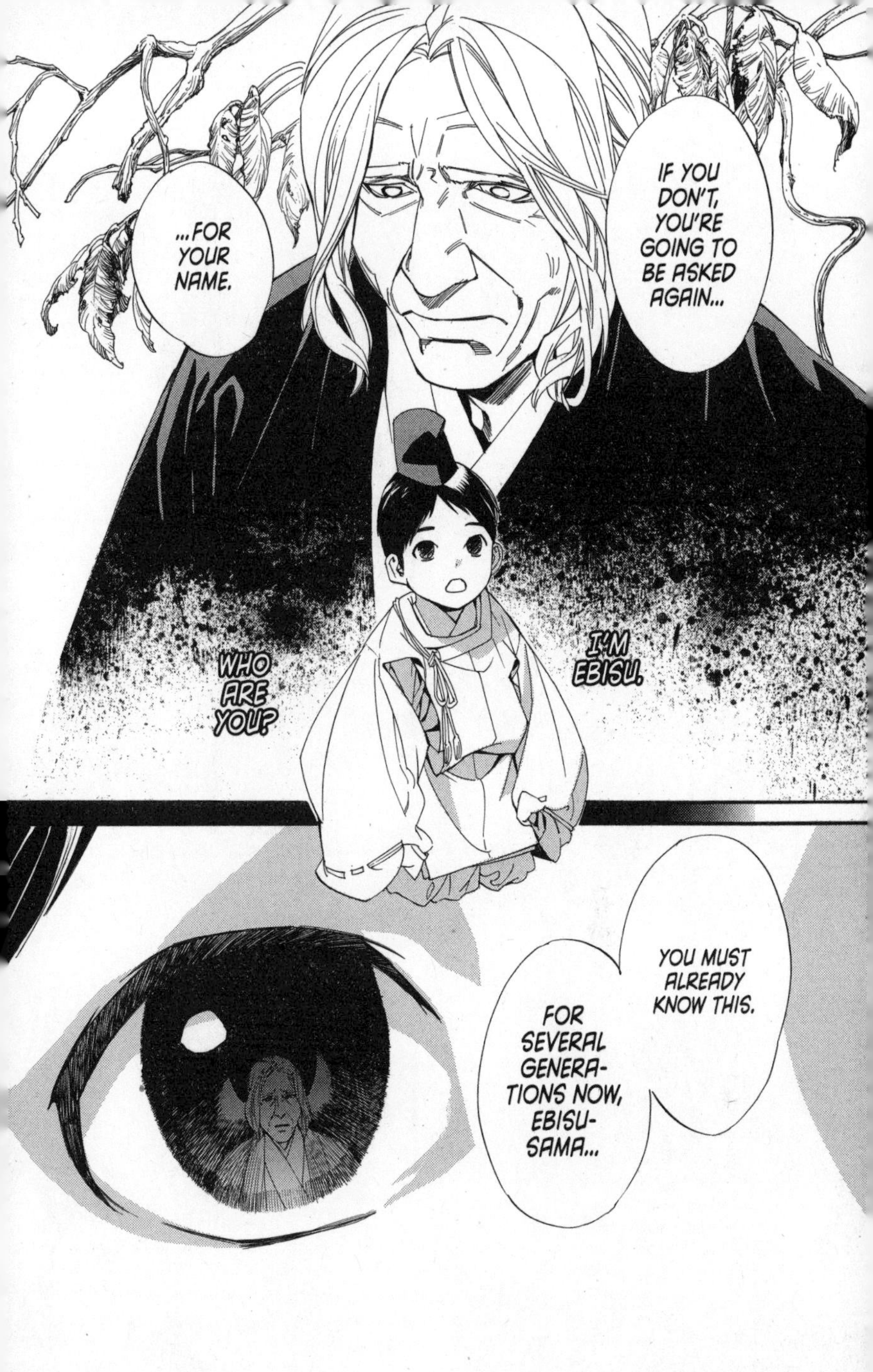
IF YOU DON'T, YOU'RE GOING TO BE ASKED AGAIN...
...FOR YOUR NAME.
I'M EBISU.
WHO ARE YOU?
YOU MUST ALREADY KNOW THIS.
FOR SEVERAL GENERATIONS NOW, EBISU-SAMA...

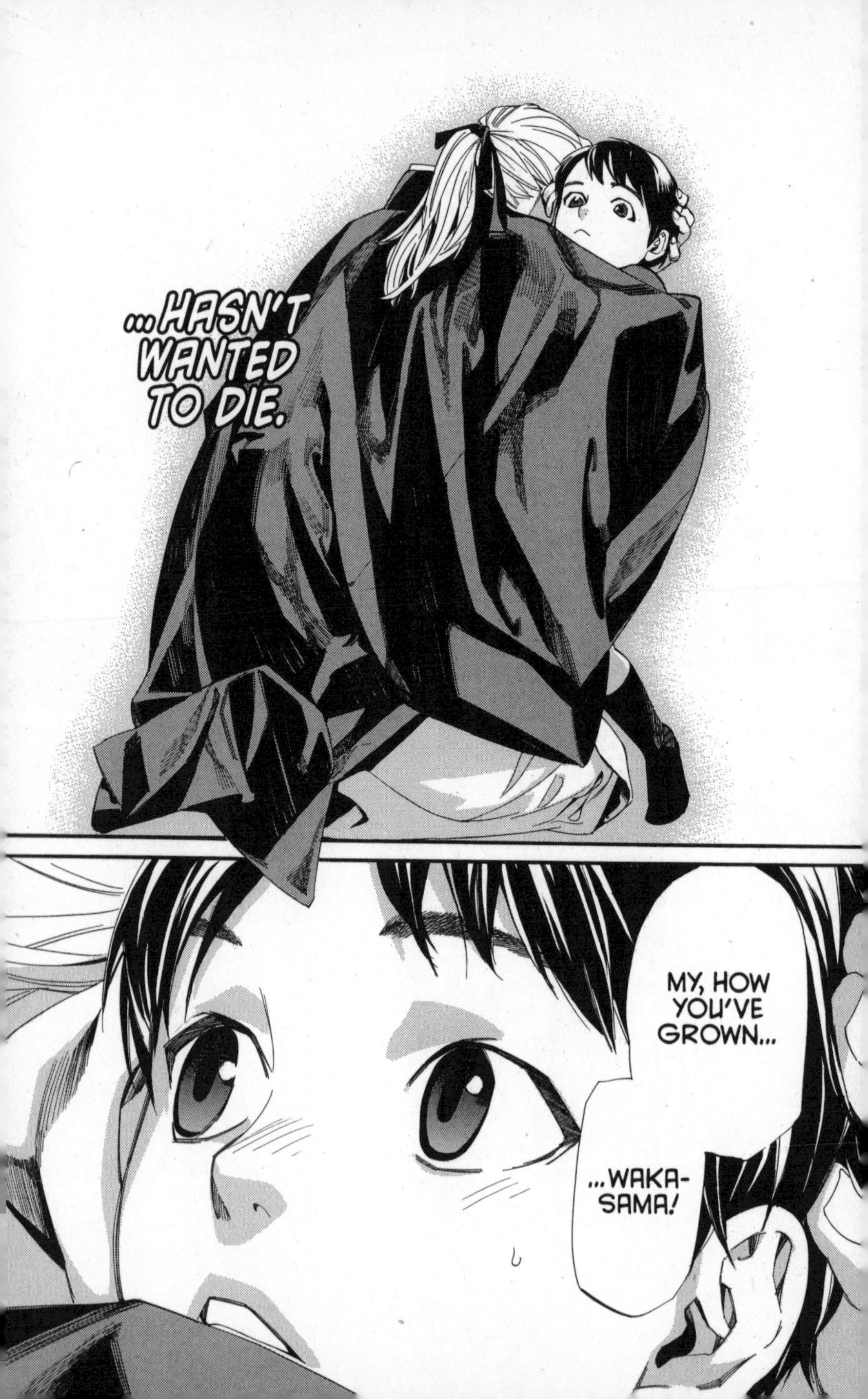
...HASN'T WANTED TO DIE.
MY, HOW YOU'VE GROWN...
...WAKA-SAMA!

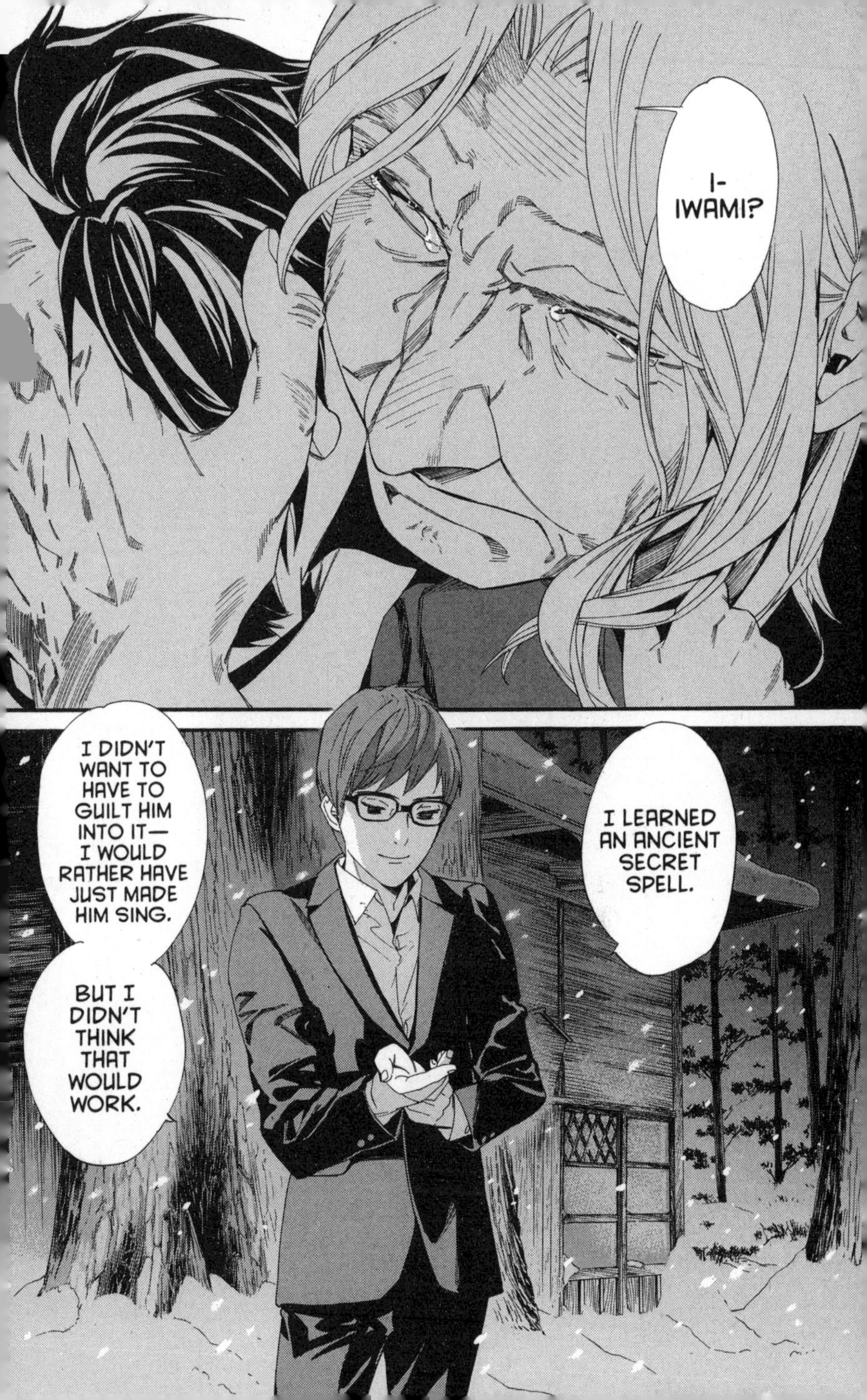
I- IWAMI?
I LEARNED AN ANCIENT SECRET SPELL.
I DIDN'T WANT TO HAVE TO GUILT HIM INTO IT— I WOULD RATHER HAVE JUST MADE HIM SING.
BUT I DIDN'T THINK THAT WOULD WORK.

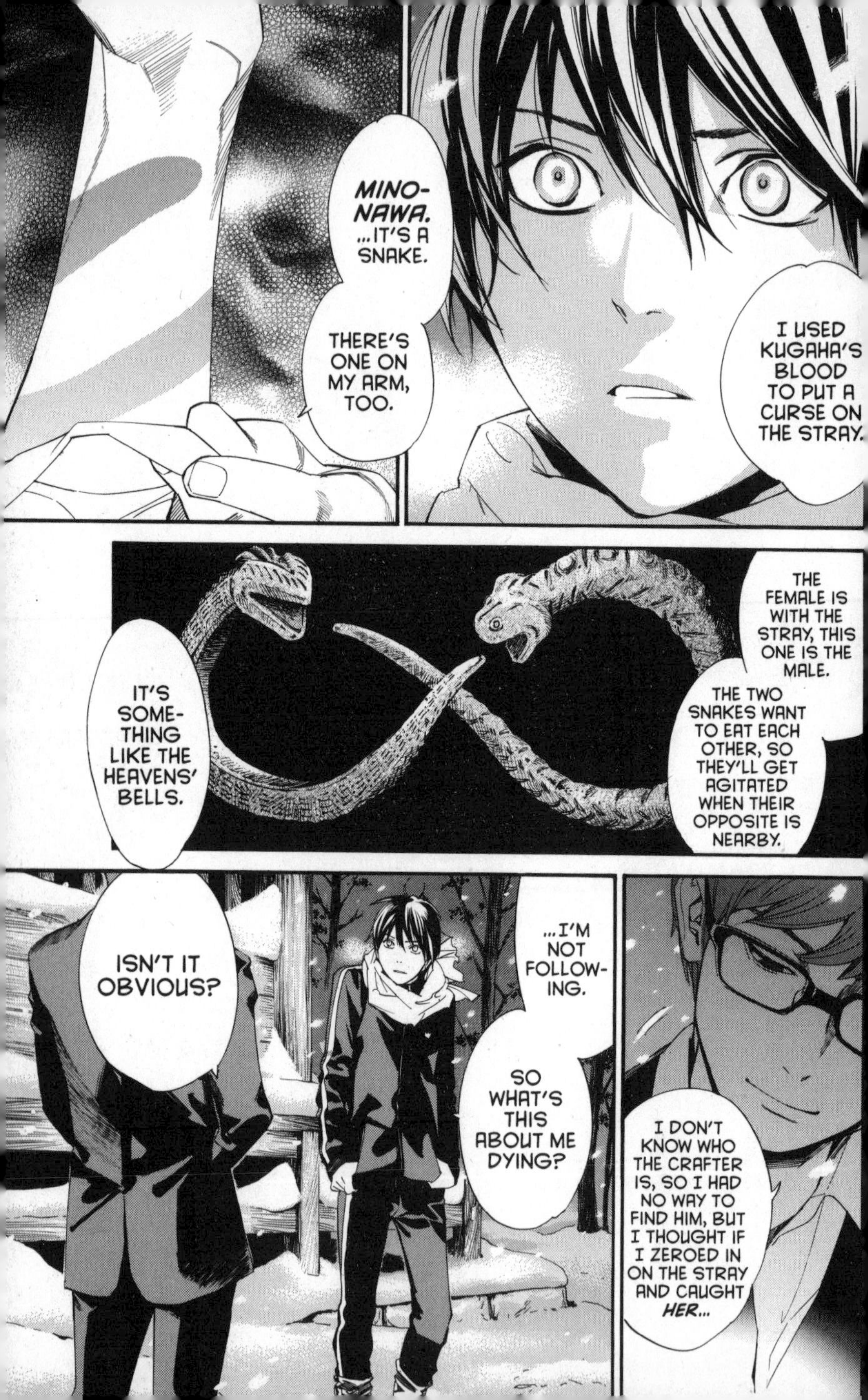
I USED KUGAHA'S BLOOD TO PUT A CURSE ON THE STRAY.
MINO-NAWA. ...IT'S A SNAKE.
THERE'S ONE ON MY ARM, TOO.
THE FEMALE IS WITH THE STRAY, THIS ONE IS THE MALE.
THE TWO SNAKES WANT TO EAT EACH OTHER, SO THEY'LL GET AGITATED WHEN THEIR OPPOSITE IS NEARBY.
IT'S SOME-THING LIKE THE HEAVENS' BELLS.
I DON'T KNOW WHO THE CRAFTER IS, SO I HAD NO WAY TO FIND HIM, BUT I THOUGHT IF I ZEROED IN ON THE STRAY AND CAUGHT ***HER***...
...I'M NOT FOLLOW-ING.
SO WHAT'S THIS ABOUT ME DYING?
ISN'T IT OBVIOUS?

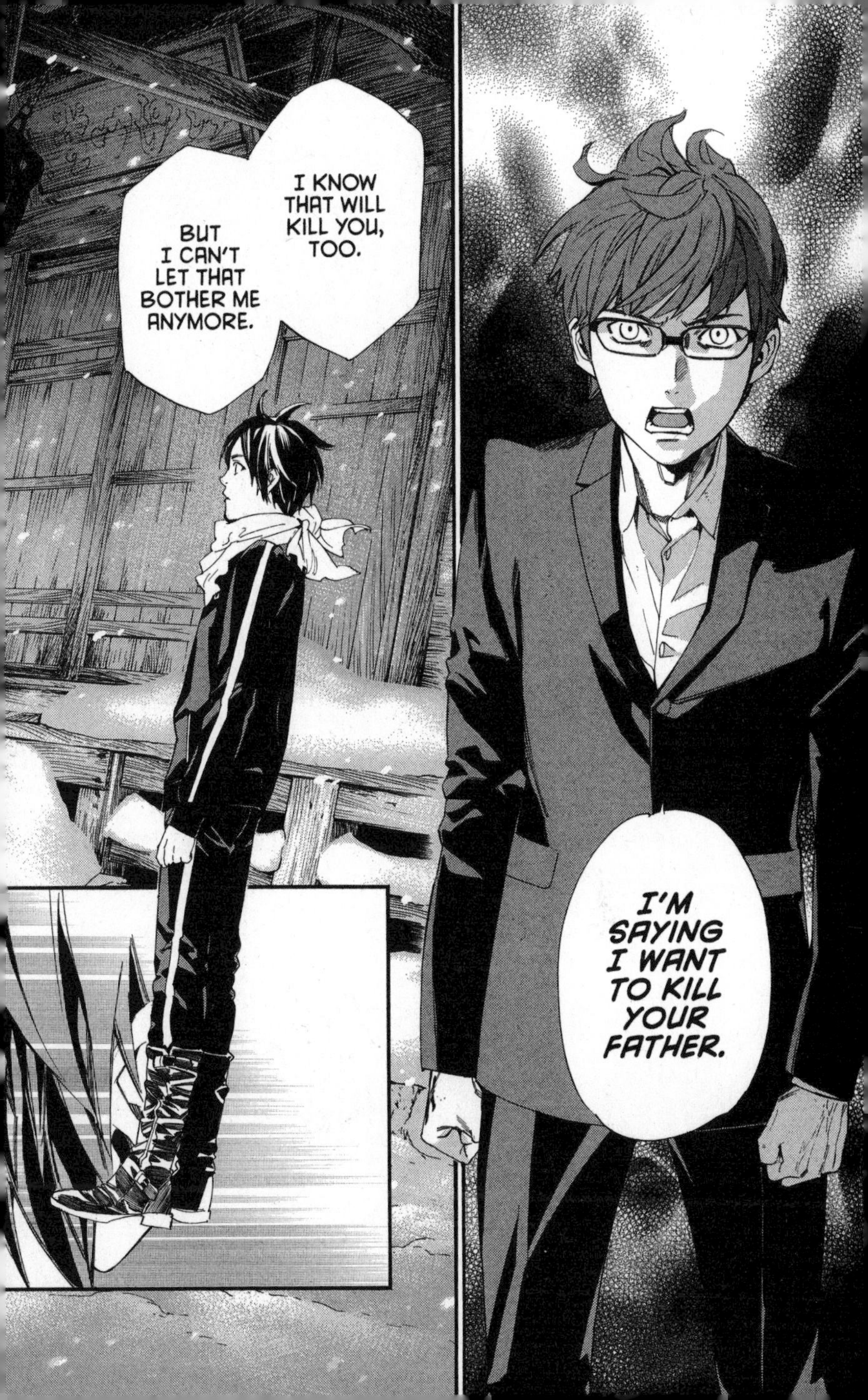
I'M SAYING I WANT TO KILL YOUR FATHER.
I KNOW THAT WILL KILL YOU, TOO.
BUT I CAN'T LET THAT BOTHER ME ANYMORE.

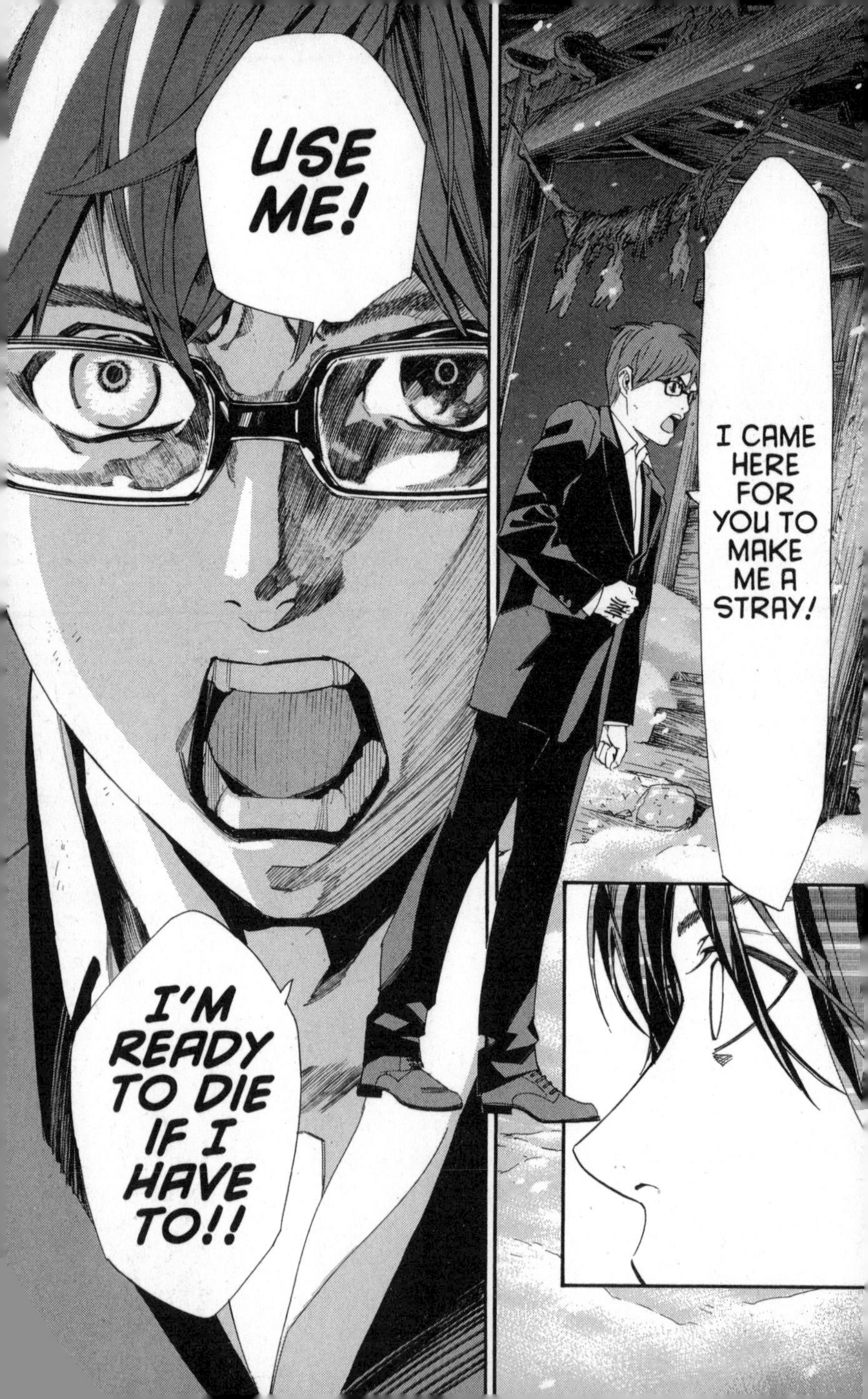
I CAME HERE FOR YOU TO MAKE ME A STRAY!
USE ME!
I'M READY TO DIE IF I HAVE TO!!

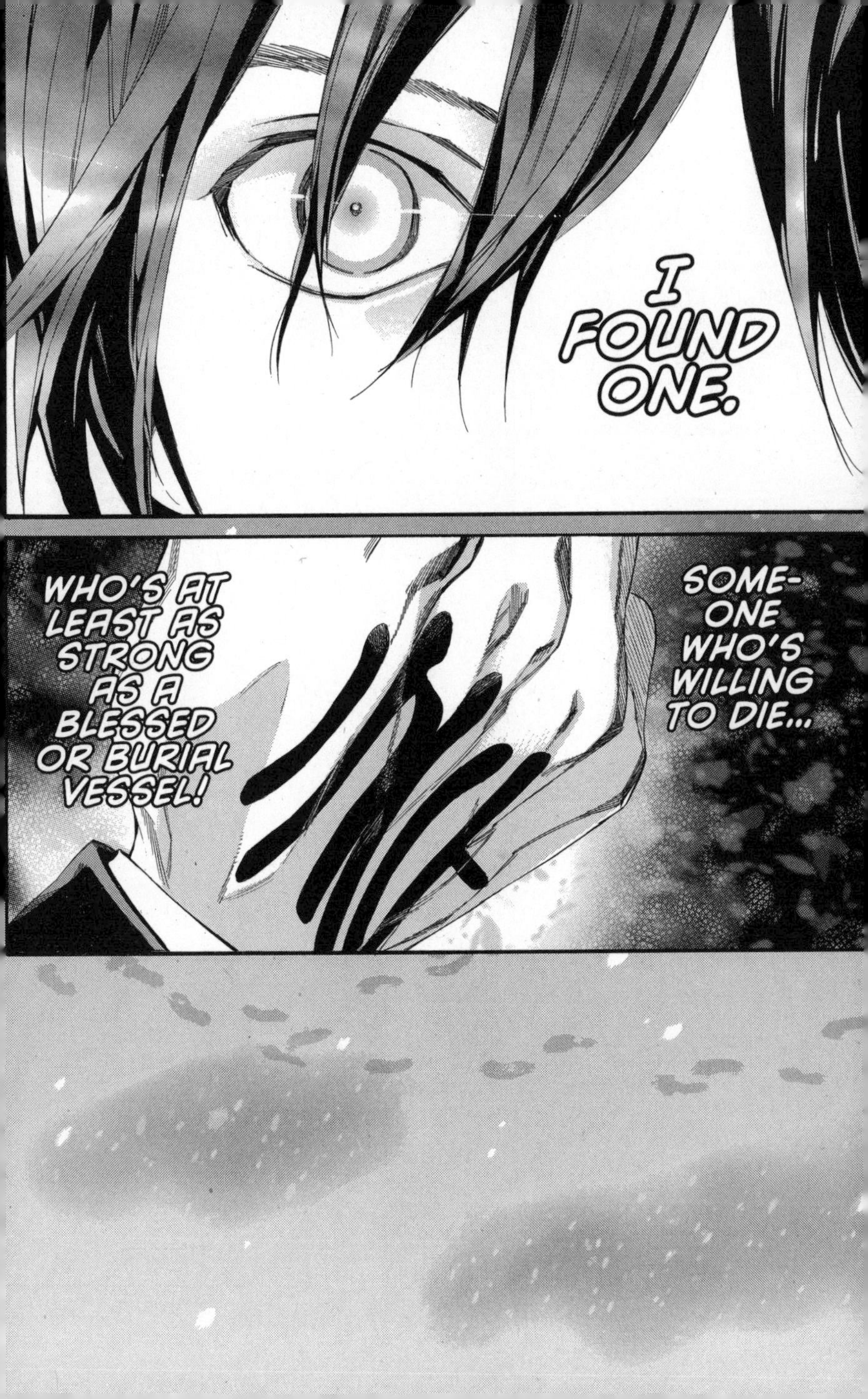
I FOUND ONE.
SOME-ONE WHO'S WILLING TO DIE...
WHO'S AT LEAST AS STRONG AS A BLESSED OR BURIAL VESSEL!

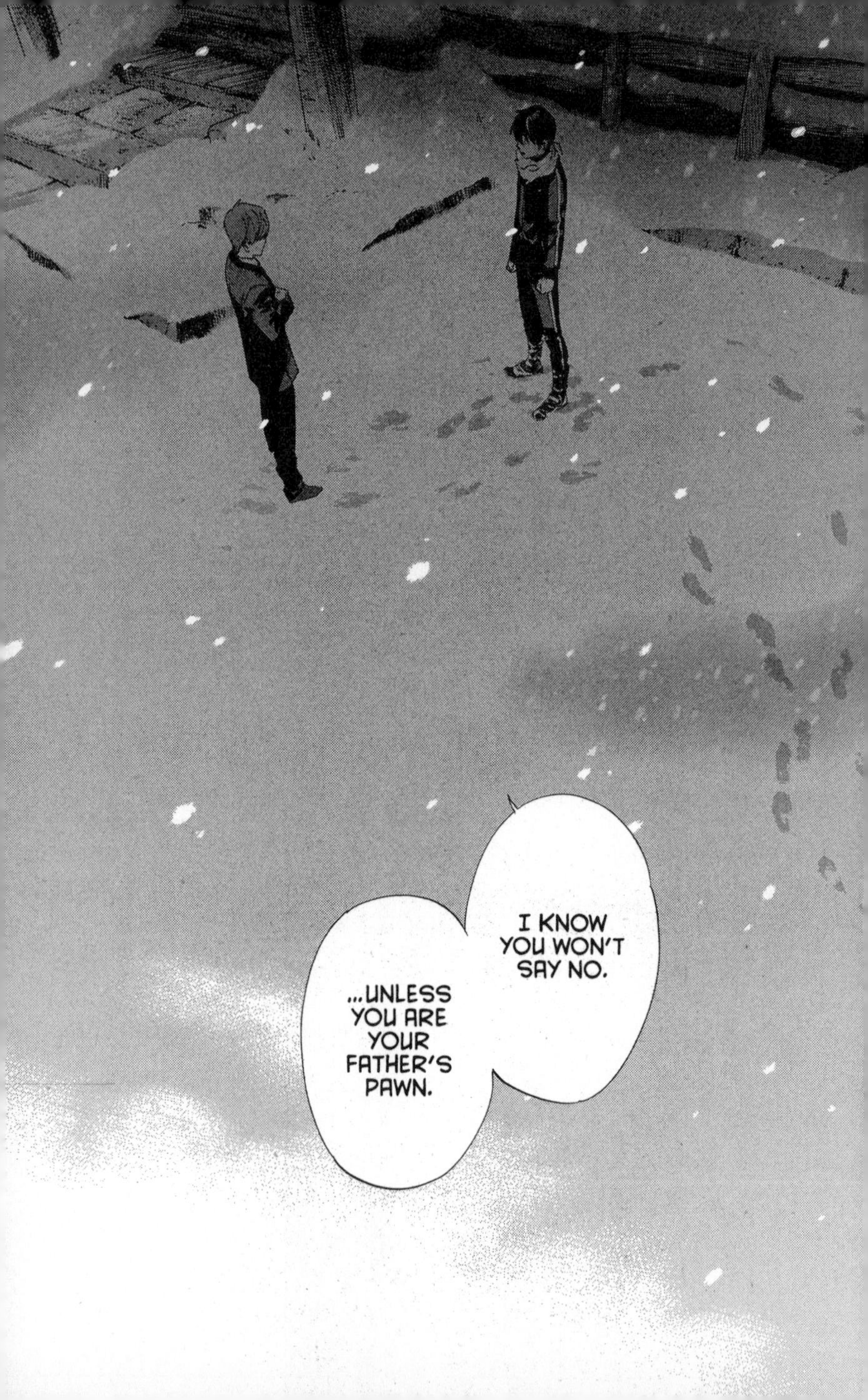
I KNOW YOU WON'T SAY NO.
...UNLESS YOU ARE YOUR FATHER'S PAWN.

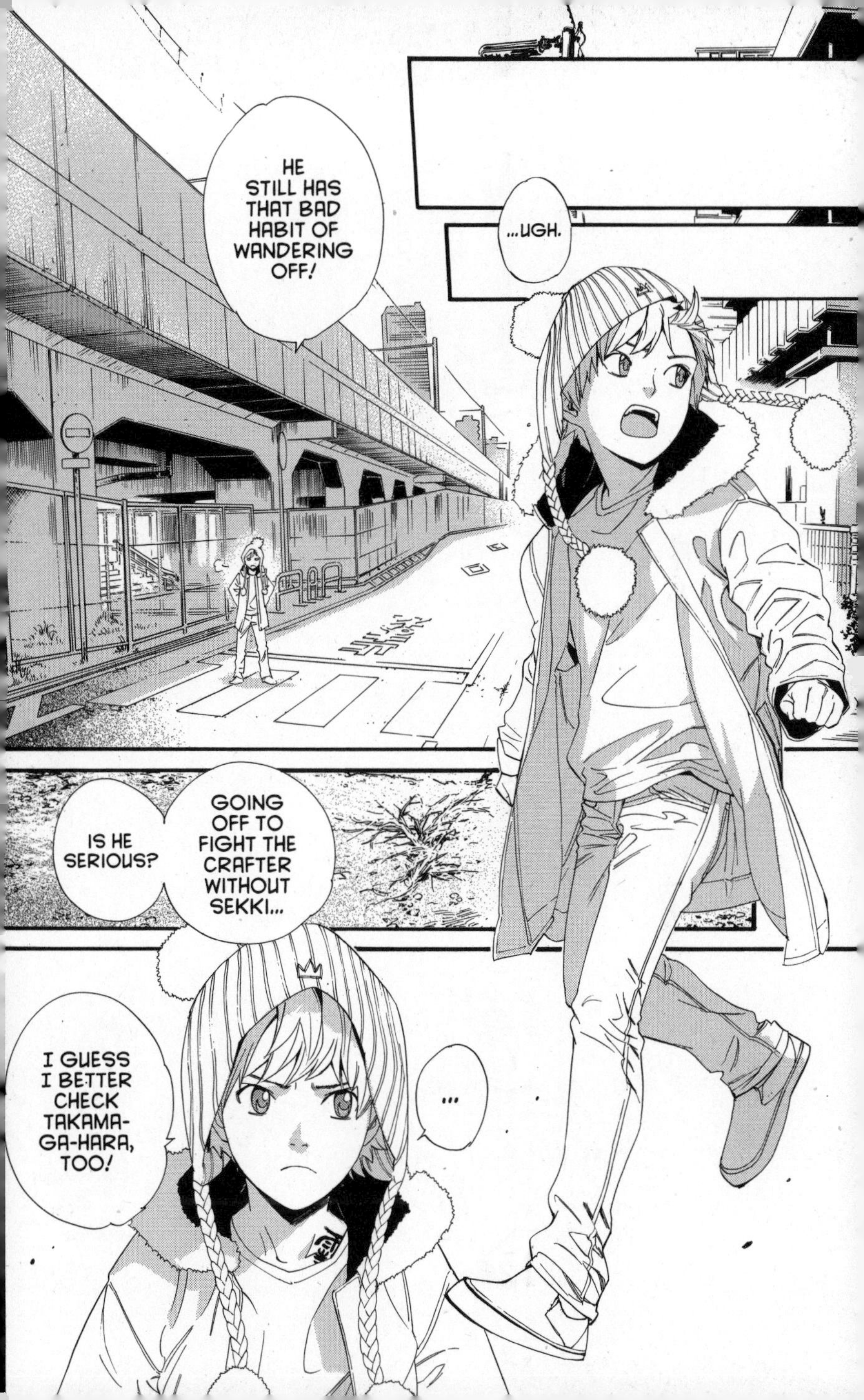
...UGH.
HE STILL HAS THAT BAD HABIT OF WANDERING OFF!
GOING OFF TO FIGHT THE CRAFTER WITHOUT SEKKI...
IS HE SERIOUS?
...
I GUESS I BETTER CHECK TAKAMA-GA-HARA, TOO!

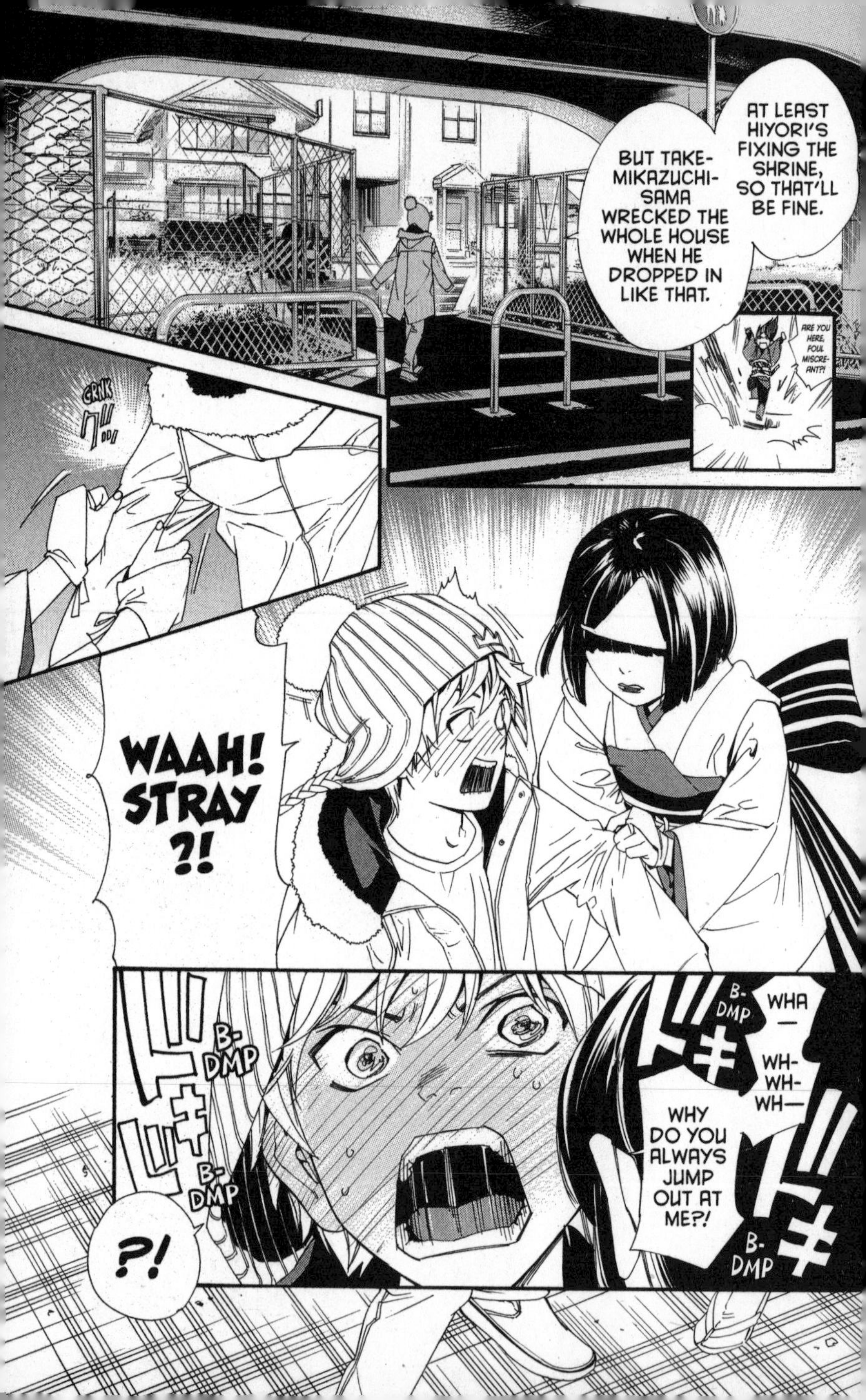
AT LEAST HIYORI'S FIXING THE SHRINE, SO THAT'LL BE FINE.
BUT TAKE-MIKAZUCHI-SAMA WRECKED THE WHOLE HOUSE WHEN HE DROPPED IN LIKE THAT.
ARE YOU HERE, FOUL MISCRE-ANT?!
GRNK
WAAH! STRAY ?!
B-DMP
WHA—
WH-WH-WH—
WHY DO YOU ALWAYS JUMP OUT AT ME?!
B-DMP
B-DMP
B-DMP
?!

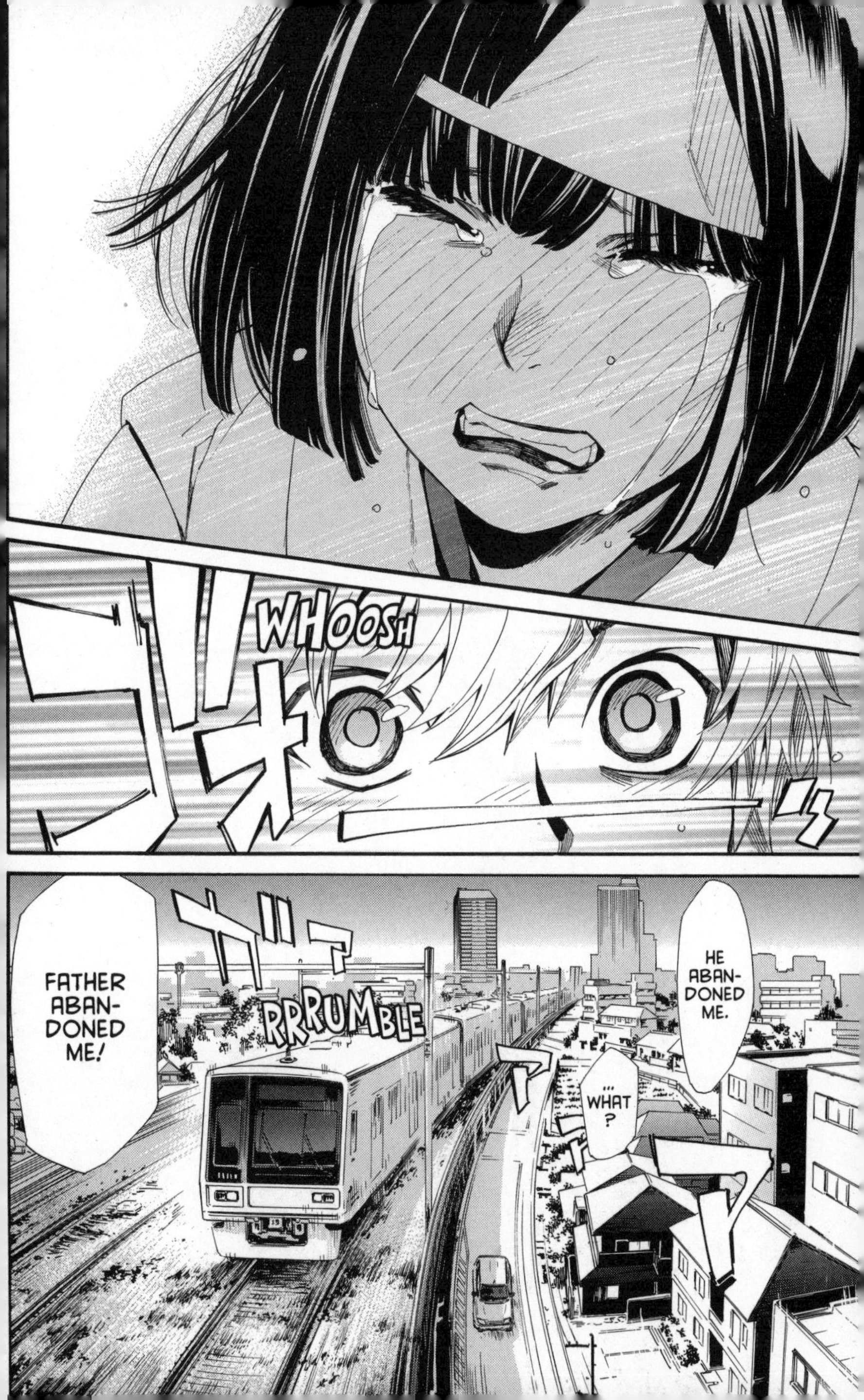
WHOOSH
HE ABANDONED ME.
...WHAT?
FATHER ABANDONED ME!
RRRUMBLE

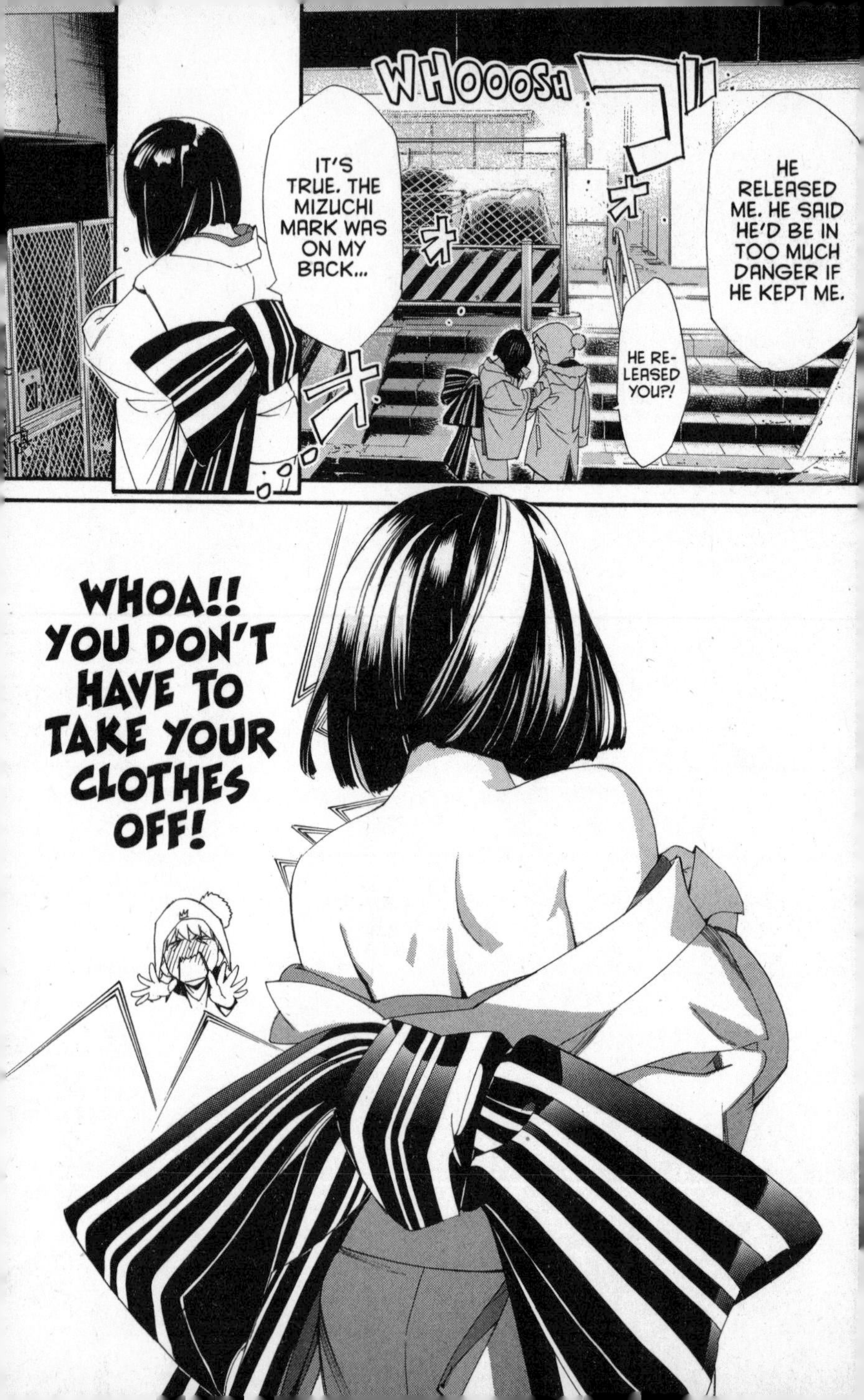
WHOOOSH
HE RELEASED ME. HE SAID HE'D BE IN TOO MUCH DANGER IF HE KEPT ME.
HE RE-LEASED YOU?!
IT'S TRUE. THE MIZUCHI MARK WAS ON MY BACK...
WHOA!! YOU DON'T HAVE TO TAKE YOUR CLOTHES OFF!

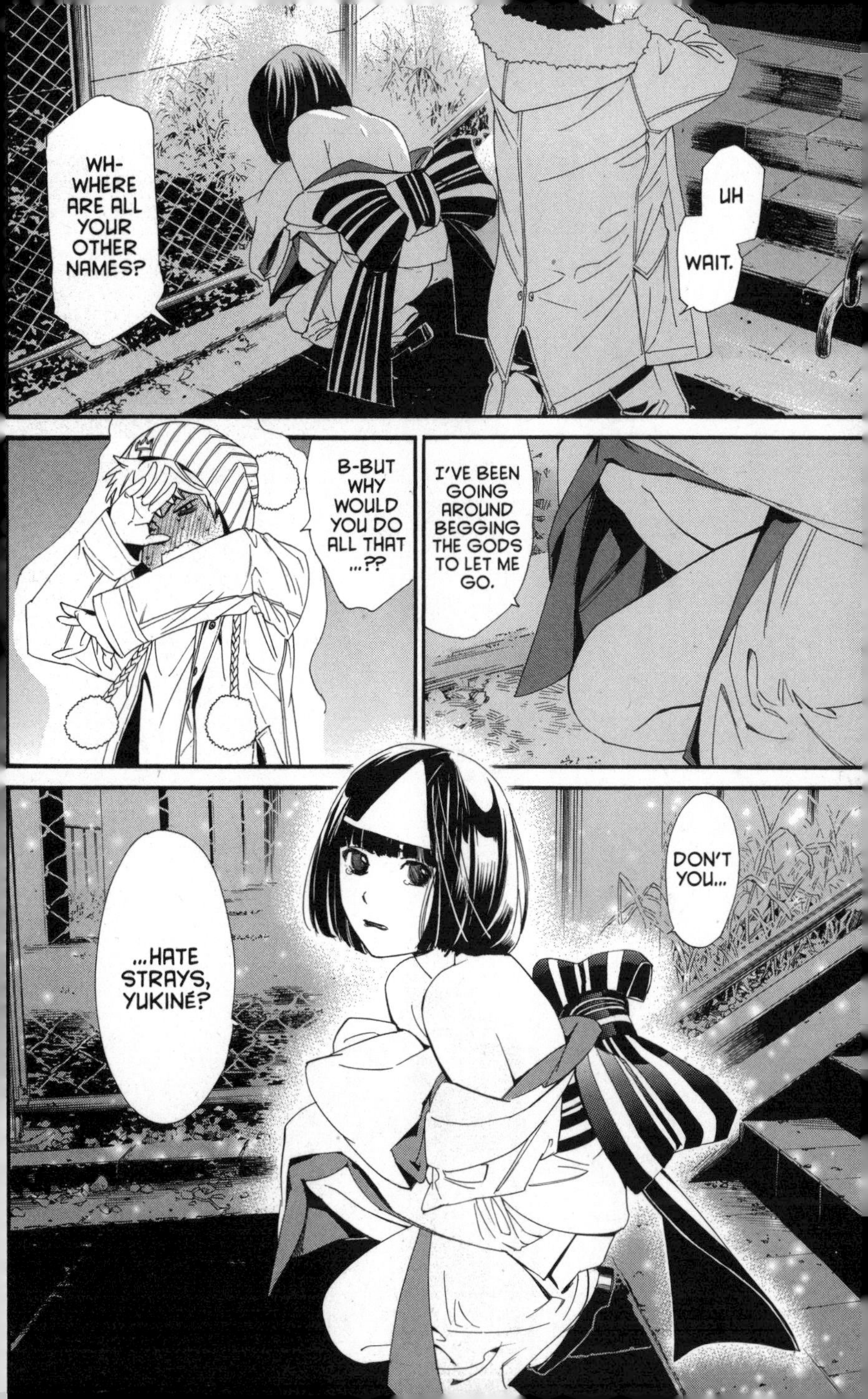
UH
WAIT.
WH-WHERE ARE ALL YOUR OTHER NAMES?
I'VE BEEN GOING AROUND BEGGING THE GODS TO LET ME GO.
B-BUT WHY WOULD YOU DO ALL THAT ...??
DON'T YOU...
...HATE STRAYS, YUKINÉ?

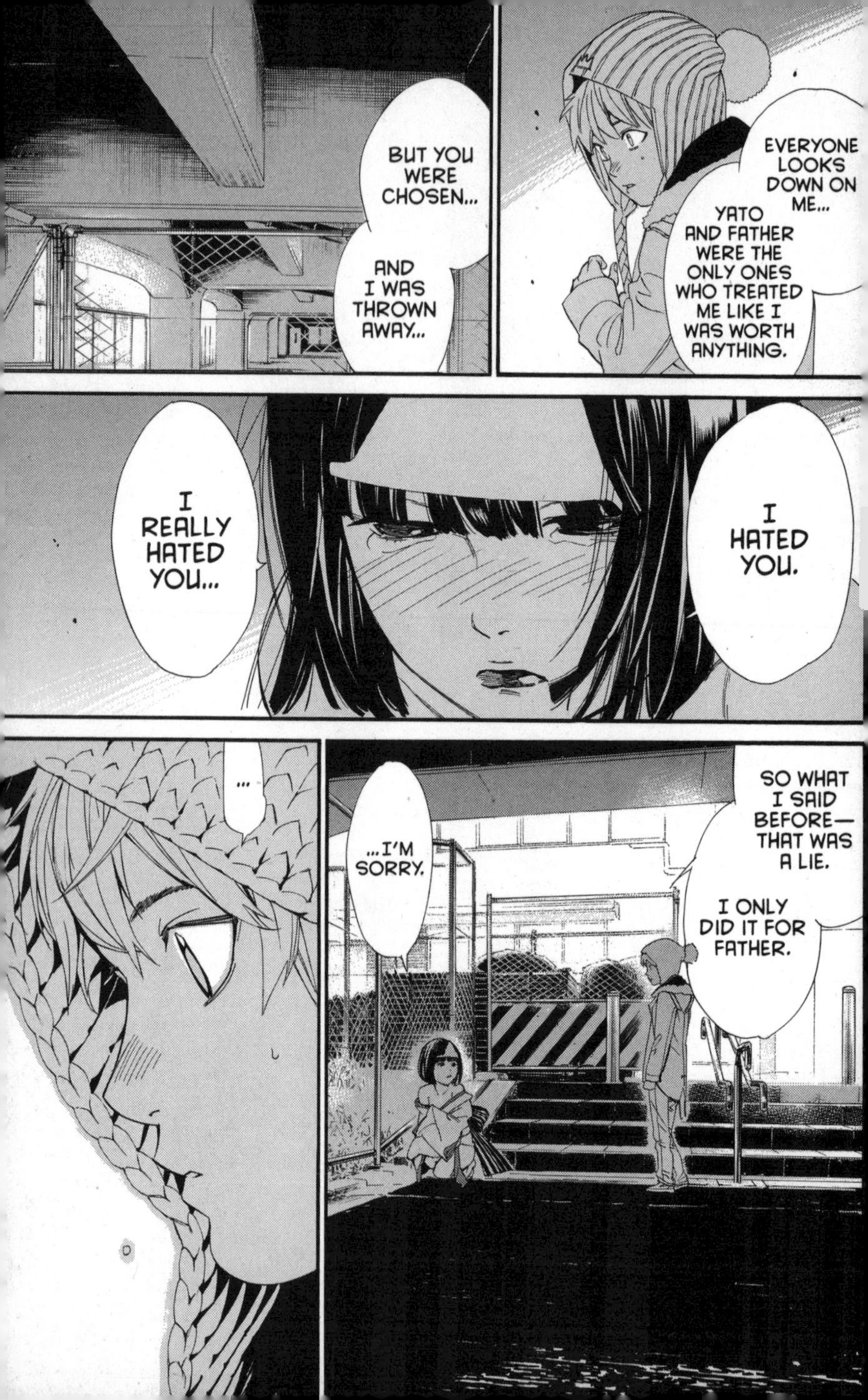
EVERYONE LOOKS DOWN ON ME...
YATO AND FATHER WERE THE ONLY ONES WHO TREATED ME LIKE I WAS WORTH ANYTHING.
BUT YOU WERE CHOSEN...
AND I WAS THROWN AWAY...
I HATED YOU.
I REALLY HATED YOU...
SO WHAT I SAID BEFORE—THAT WAS A LIE.
I ONLY DID IT FOR FATHER.
...I'M SORRY.
...

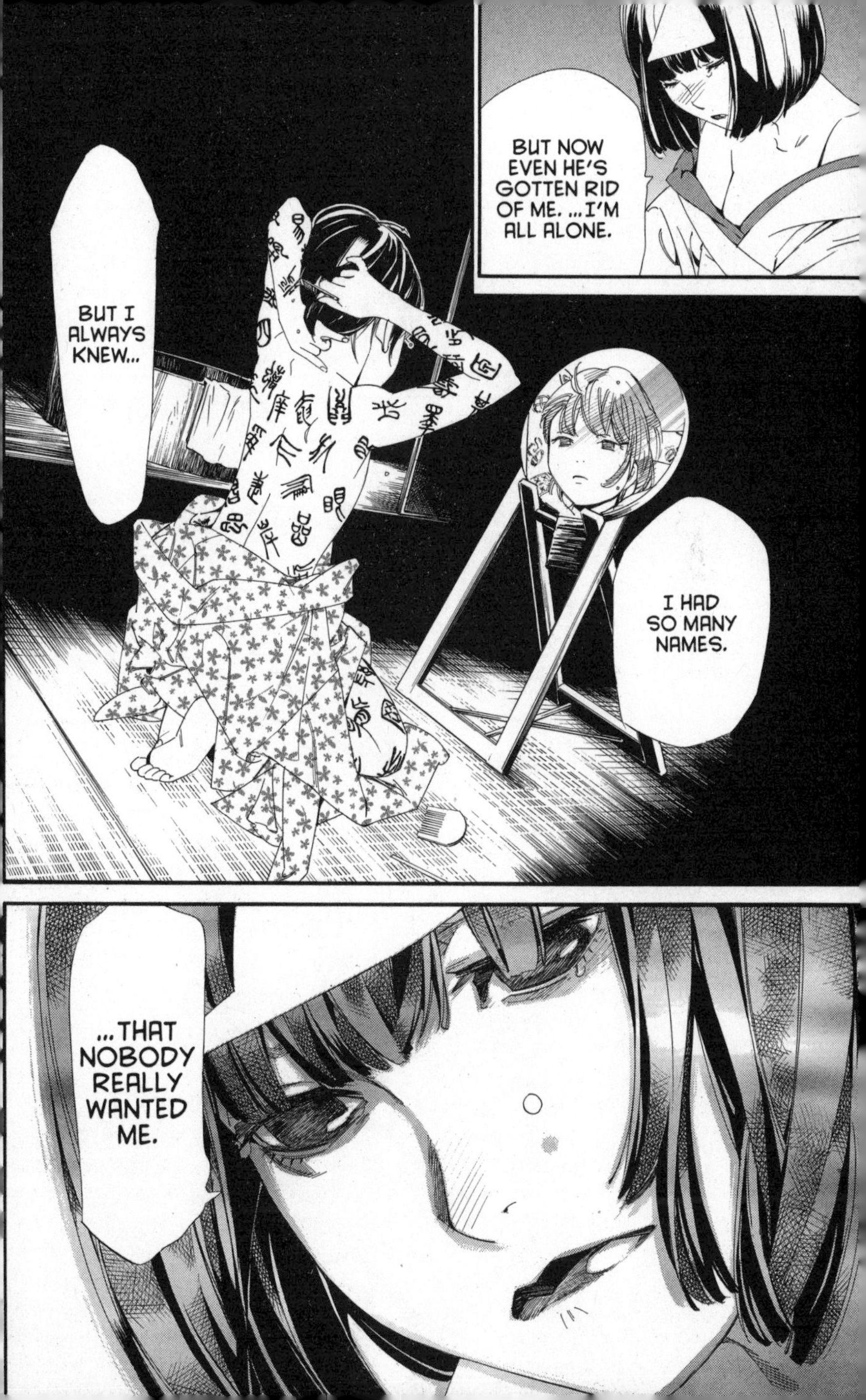
BUT NOW EVEN HE'S GOTTEN RID OF ME. ...I'M ALL ALONE.
I HAD SO MANY NAMES.
BUT I ALWAYS KNEW...
...THAT NOBODY REALLY WANTED ME.

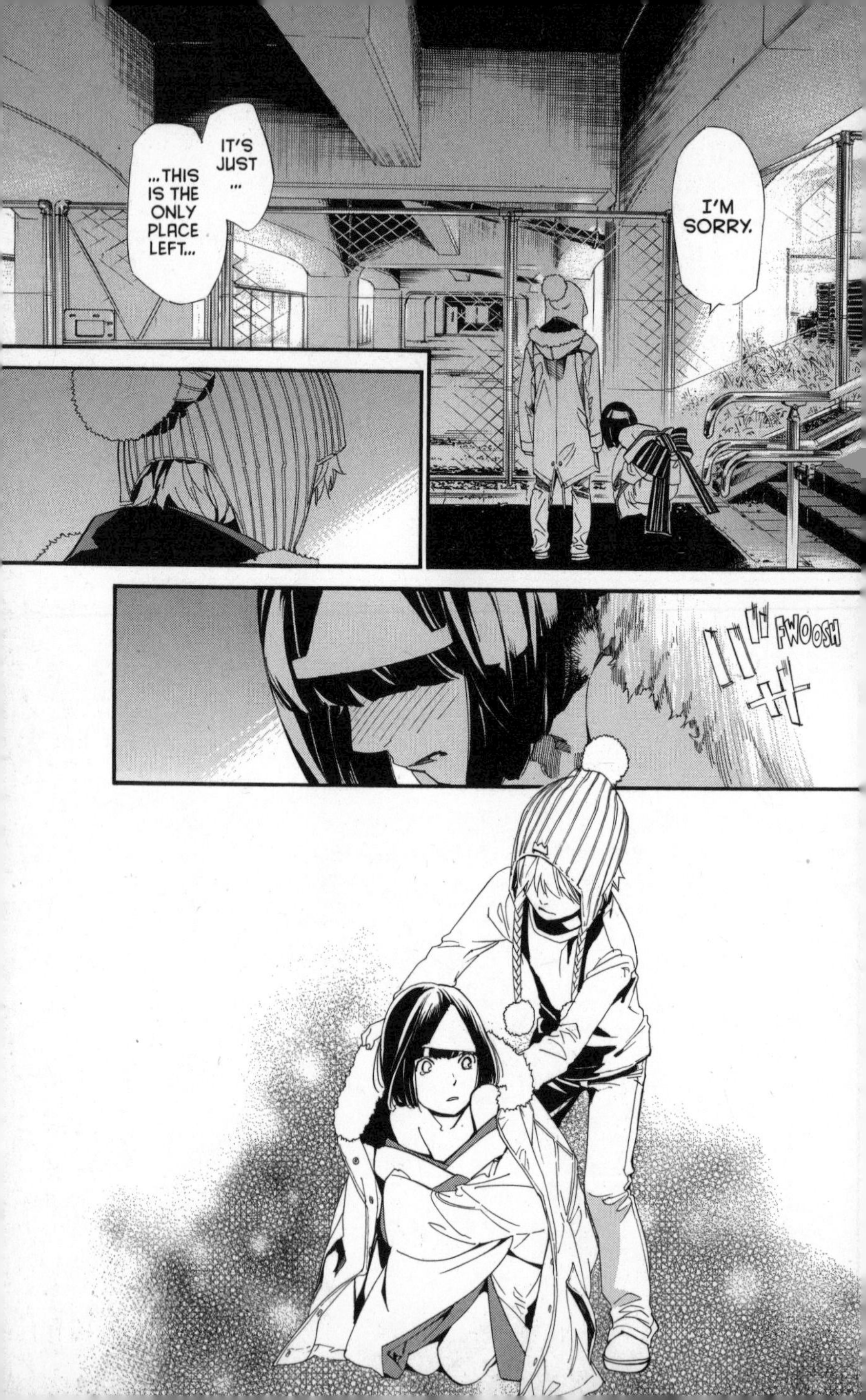
I'M SORRY.
IT'S JUST ...
...THIS IS THE ONLY PLACE LEFT...
FWOOSH

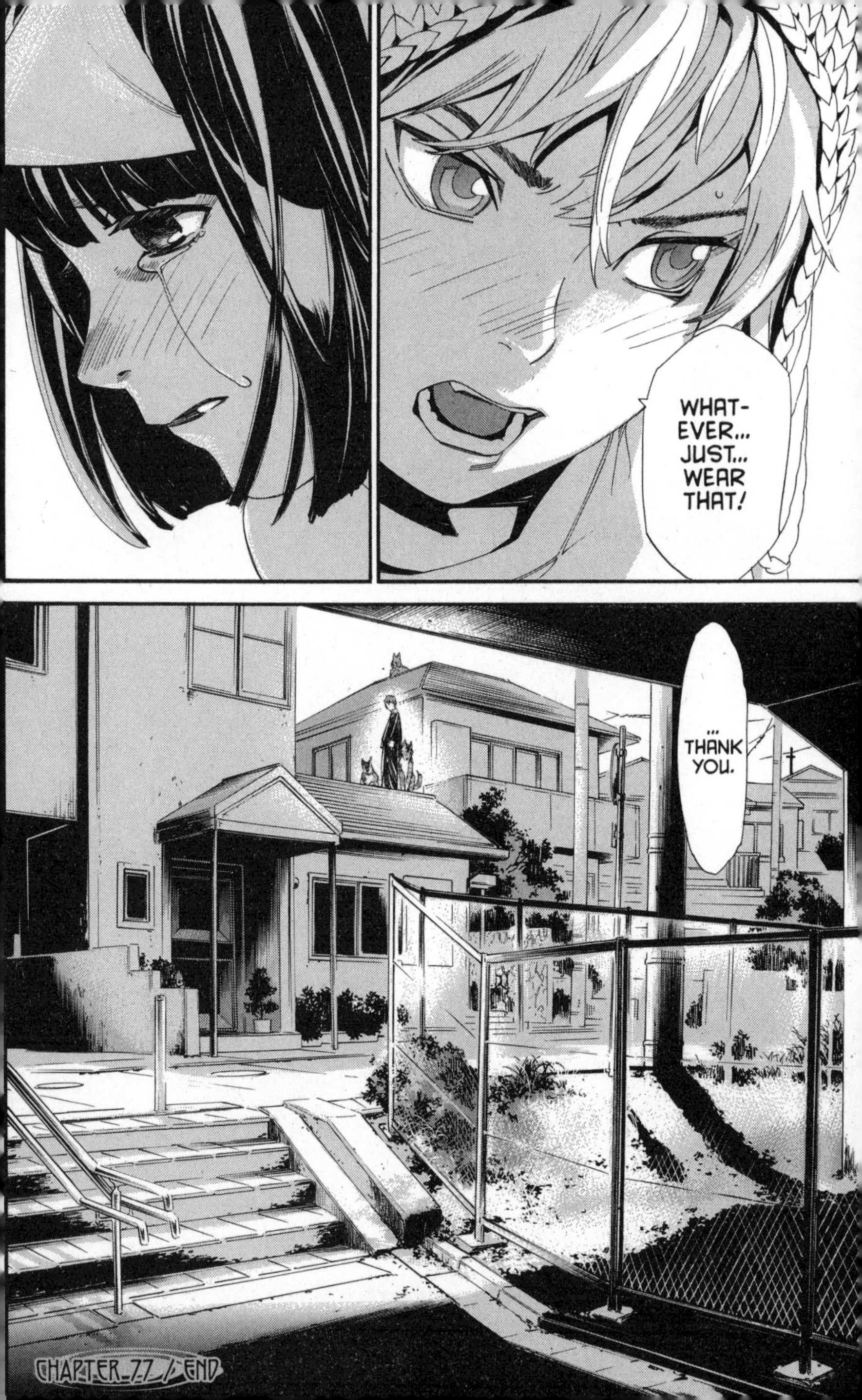
WHAT-EVER... JUST... WEAR THAT!
...THANK YOU.
CHAPTER 77 / END

野

㝢

神

野

身

師

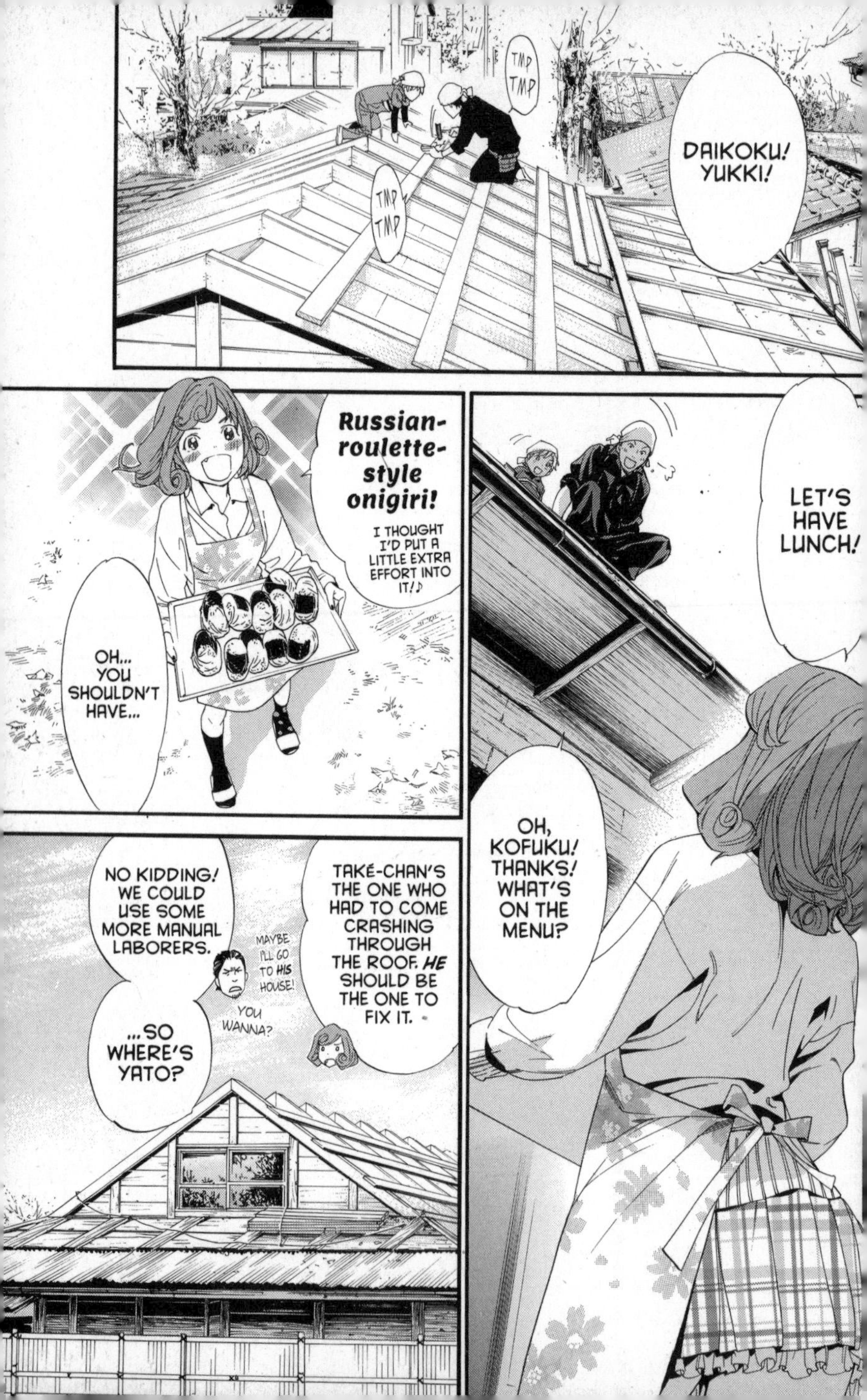
DAIKOKU! YUKKI!
TMP TMP
TMP TMP
LET'S HAVE LUNCH!
OH, KOFUKU! THANKS! WHAT'S ON THE MENU?
Russian-roulette-style onigiri!
I THOUGHT I'D PUT A LITTLE EXTRA EFFORT INTO IT!♪
OH... YOU SHOULDN'T HAVE...
TAKÉ-CHAN'S THE ONE WHO HAD TO COME CRASHING THROUGH THE ROOF. *HE* SHOULD BE THE ONE TO FIX IT.
NO KIDDING! WE COULD USE SOME MORE MANUAL LABORERS.
MAYBE I'LL GO TO *HIS* HOUSE!
YOU WANNA?
...SO WHERE'S YATO?

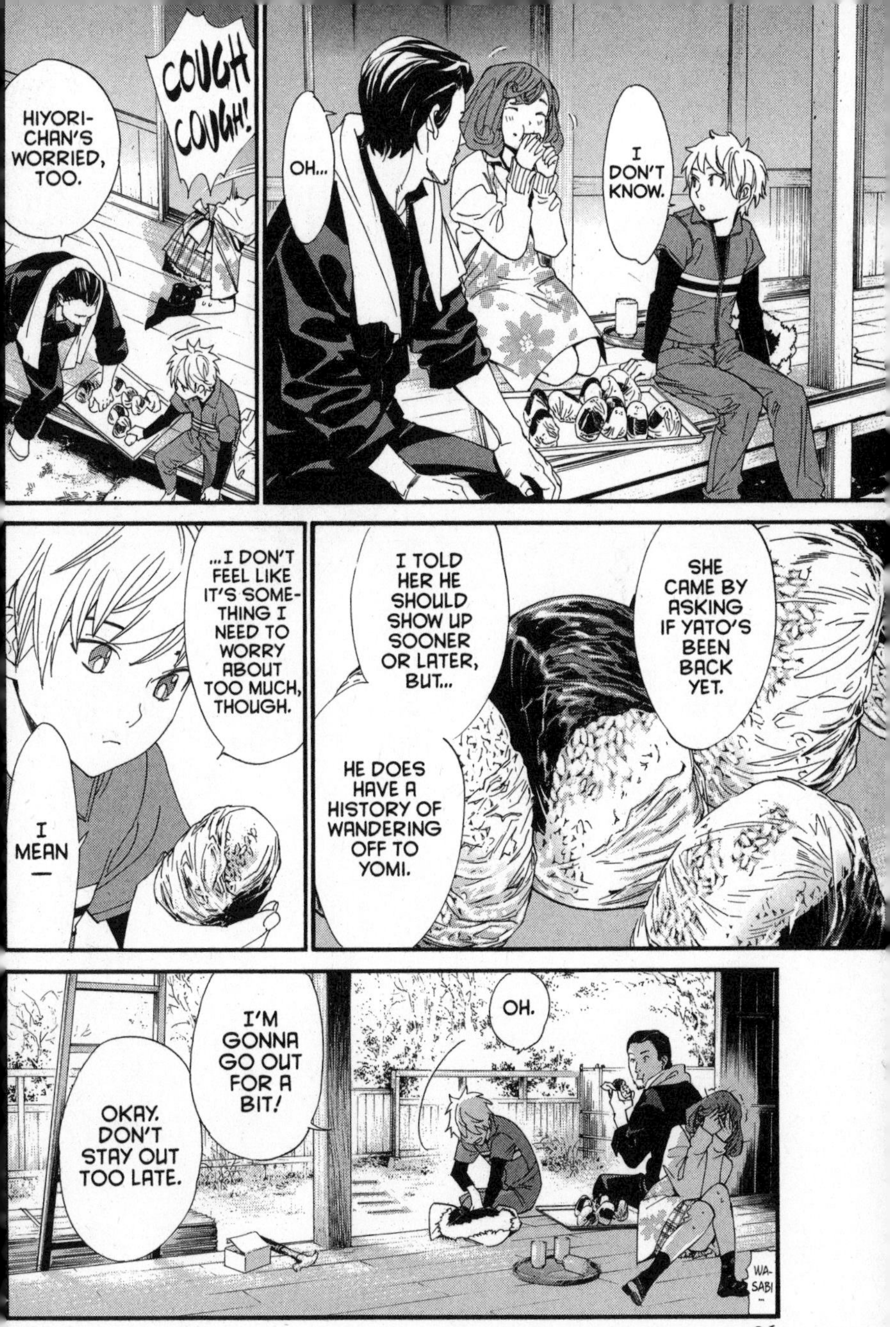
I DON'T KNOW.
OH...
COUGH COUGH!
HIYORI-CHAN'S WORRIED, TOO.
SHE CAME BY ASKING IF YATO'S BEEN BACK YET.
I TOLD HER HE SHOULD SHOW UP SOONER OR LATER, BUT...
HE DOES HAVE A HISTORY OF WANDERING OFF TO YOMI.
...I DON'T FEEL LIKE IT'S SOMETHING I NEED TO WORRY ABOUT TOO MUCH, THOUGH.
I MEAN—
OH.
WASABI...
I'M GONNA GO OUT FOR A BIT!
OKAY. DON'T STAY OUT TOO LATE.

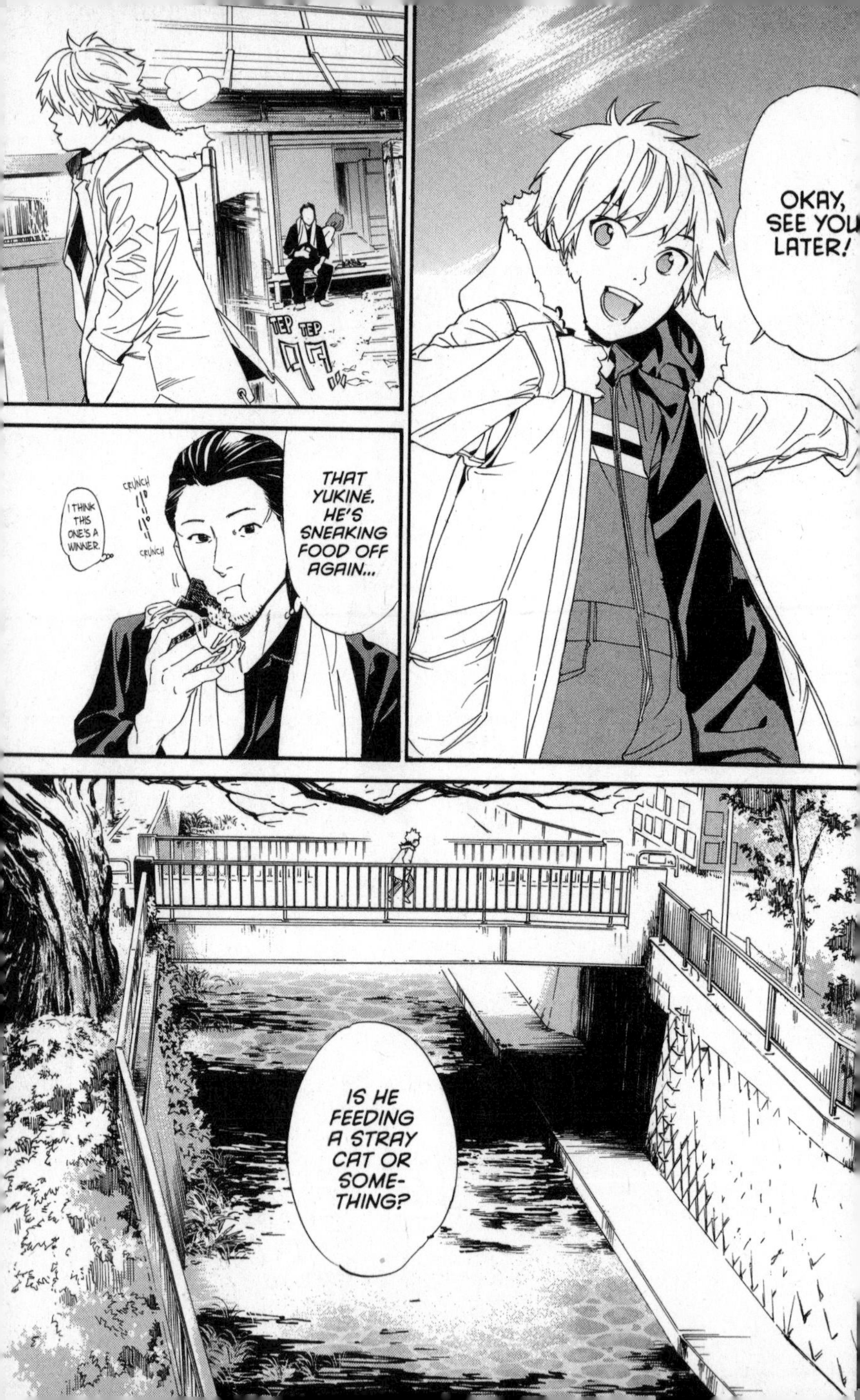
OKAY, SEE YOU LATER!
TEP TEP
THAT YUKINÉ. HE'S SNEAKING FOOD OFF AGAIN...
CRUNCH
CRUNCH
I THINK THIS ONE'S A WINNER.
IS HE FEEDING A STRAY CAT OR SOME-THING?

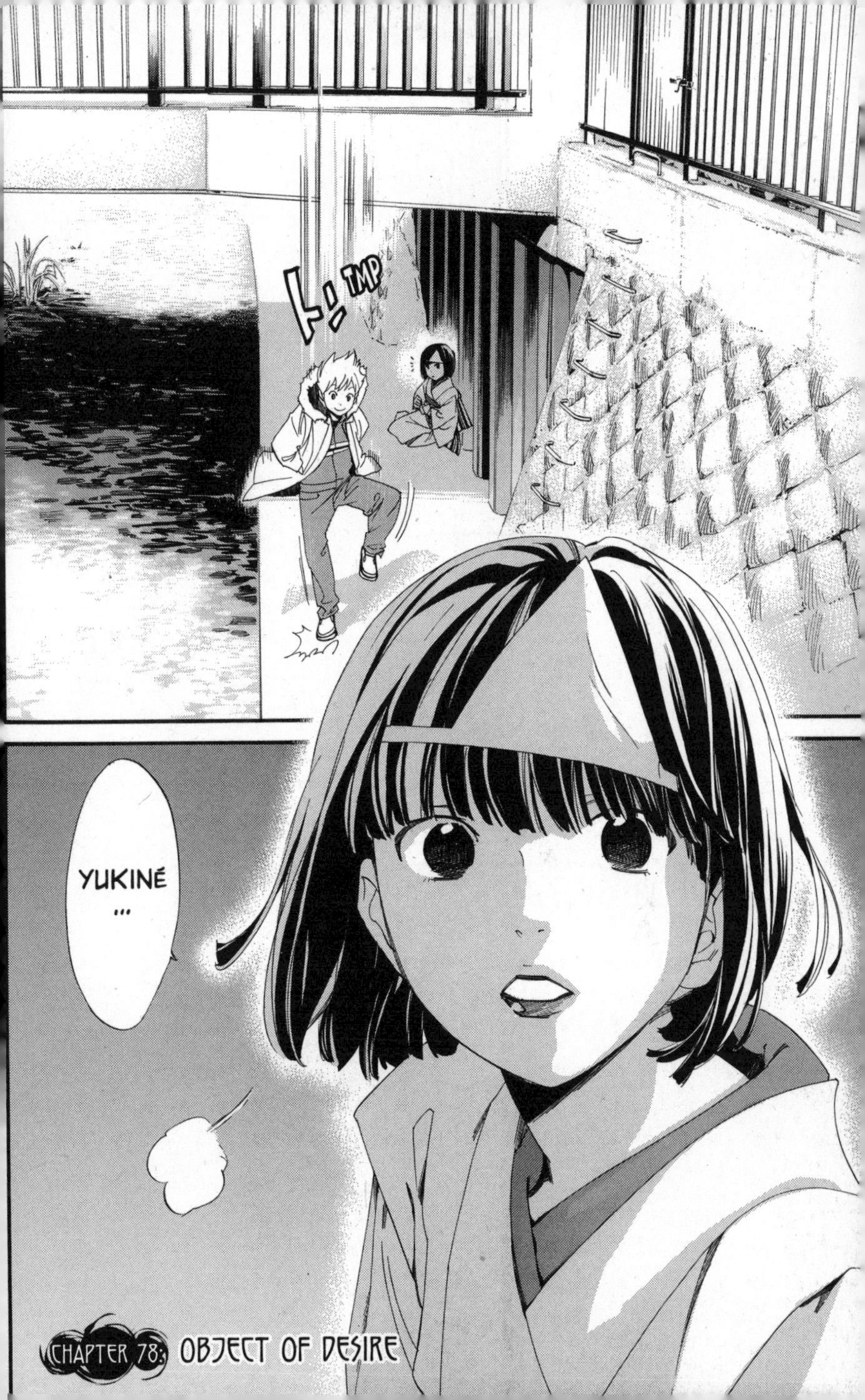
TMP
YUKINÉ ...
CHAPTER 78: OBJECT OF DESIRE

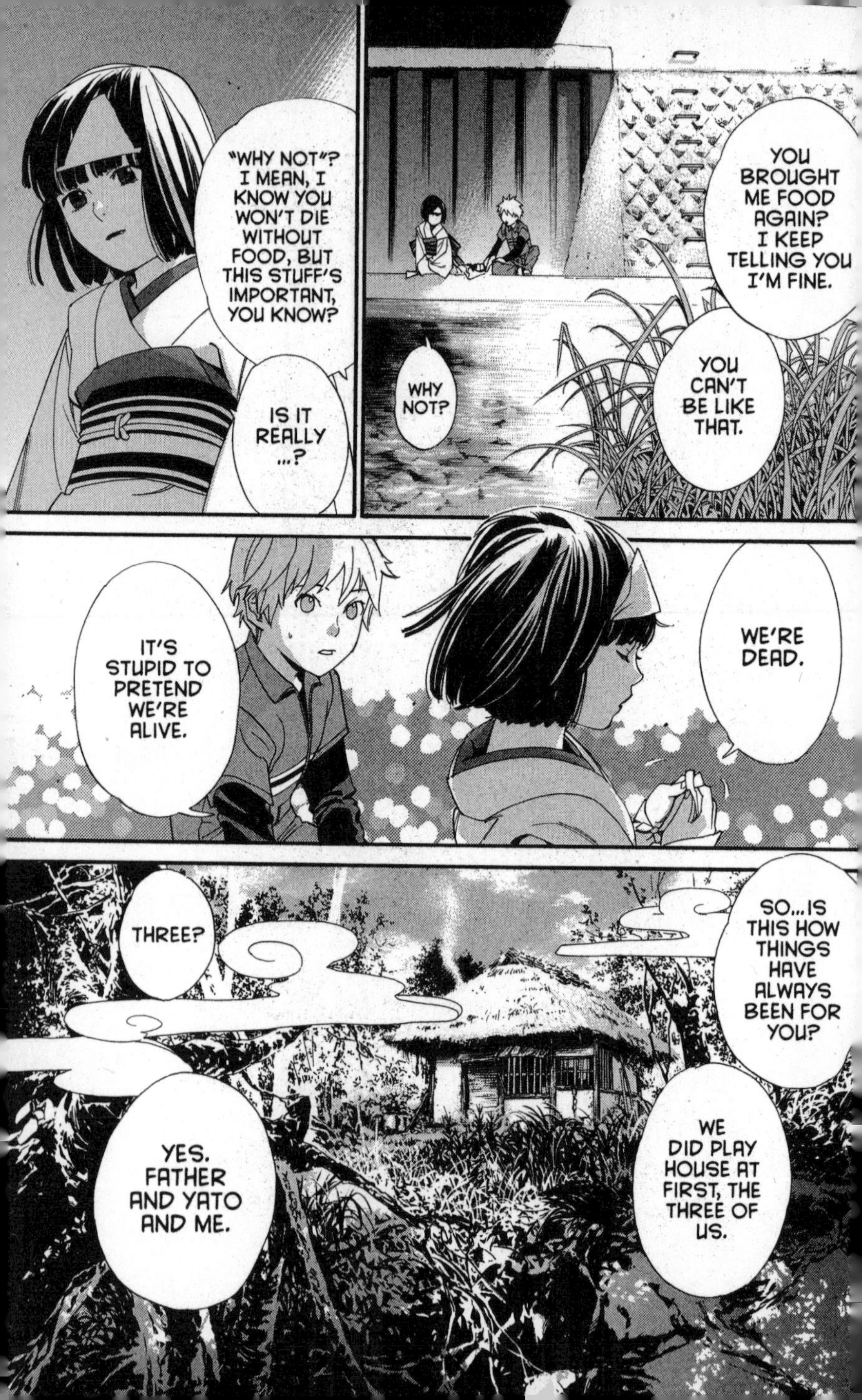
YOU BROUGHT ME FOOD AGAIN? I KEEP TELLING YOU I'M FINE.
YOU CAN'T BE LIKE THAT.
WHY NOT?
"WHY NOT"? I MEAN, I KNOW YOU WON'T DIE WITHOUT FOOD, BUT THIS STUFF'S IMPORTANT, YOU KNOW?
IS IT REALLY ...?
WE'RE DEAD.
IT'S STUPID TO PRETEND WE'RE ALIVE.
SO...IS THIS HOW THINGS HAVE ALWAYS BEEN FOR YOU?
WE DID PLAY HOUSE AT FIRST, THE THREE OF US.
THREE?
YES. FATHER AND YATO AND ME.

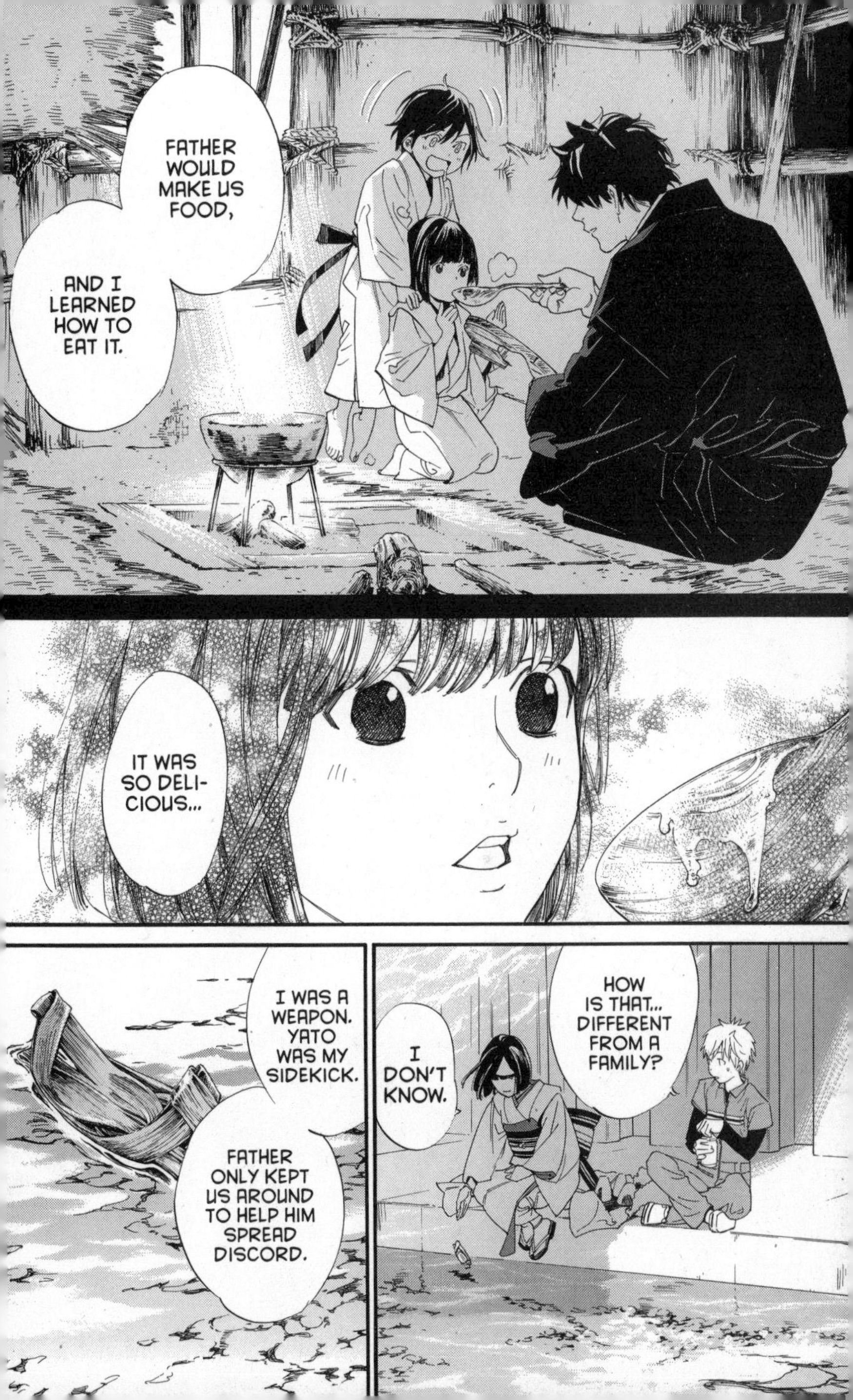
FATHER WOULD MAKE US FOOD,
AND I LEARNED HOW TO EAT IT.
IT WAS SO DELI-CIOUS...
HOW IS THAT... DIFFERENT FROM A FAMILY?
I DON'T KNOW.
I WAS A WEAPON. YATO WAS MY SIDEKICK.
FATHER ONLY KEPT US AROUND TO HELP HIM SPREAD DISCORD.

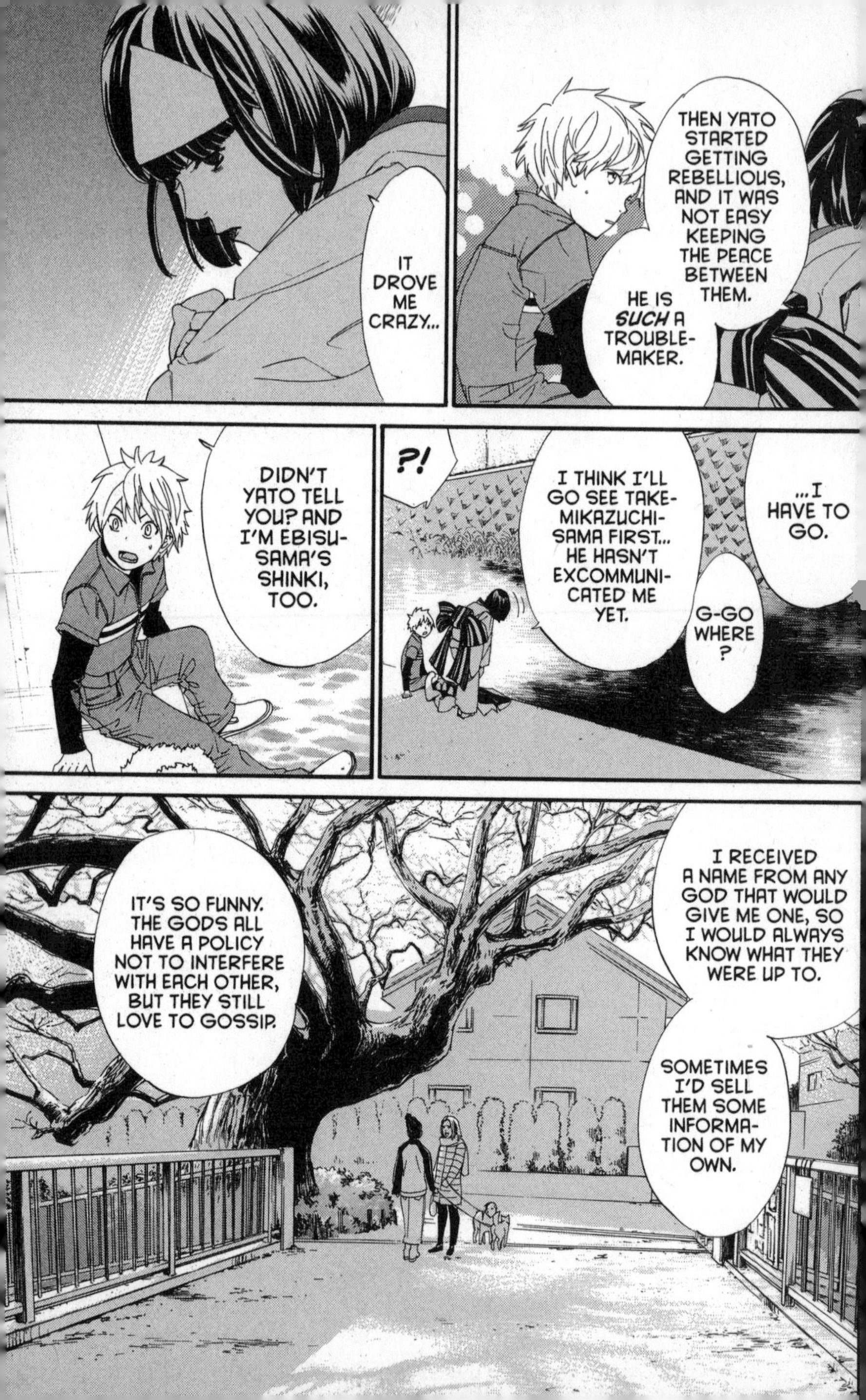
THEN YATO STARTED GETTING REBELLIOUS, AND IT WAS NOT EASY KEEPING THE PEACE BETWEEN THEM.
HE IS *SUCH* A TROUBLE-MAKER.
IT DROVE ME CRAZY...
...I HAVE TO GO.
G-GO WHERE?
I THINK I'LL GO SEE TAKE-MIKAZUCHI-SAMA FIRST... HE HASN'T EXCOMMUNICATED ME YET.
?!
DIDN'T YATO TELL YOU? AND I'M EBISU-SAMA'S SHINKI, TOO.
I RECEIVED A NAME FROM ANY GOD THAT WOULD GIVE ME ONE, SO I WOULD ALWAYS KNOW WHAT THEY WERE UP TO.
SOMETIMES I'D SELL THEM SOME INFORMATION OF MY OWN.
IT'S SO FUNNY. THE GODS ALL HAVE A POLICY NOT TO INTERFERE WITH EACH OTHER, BUT THEY STILL LOVE TO GOSSIP.

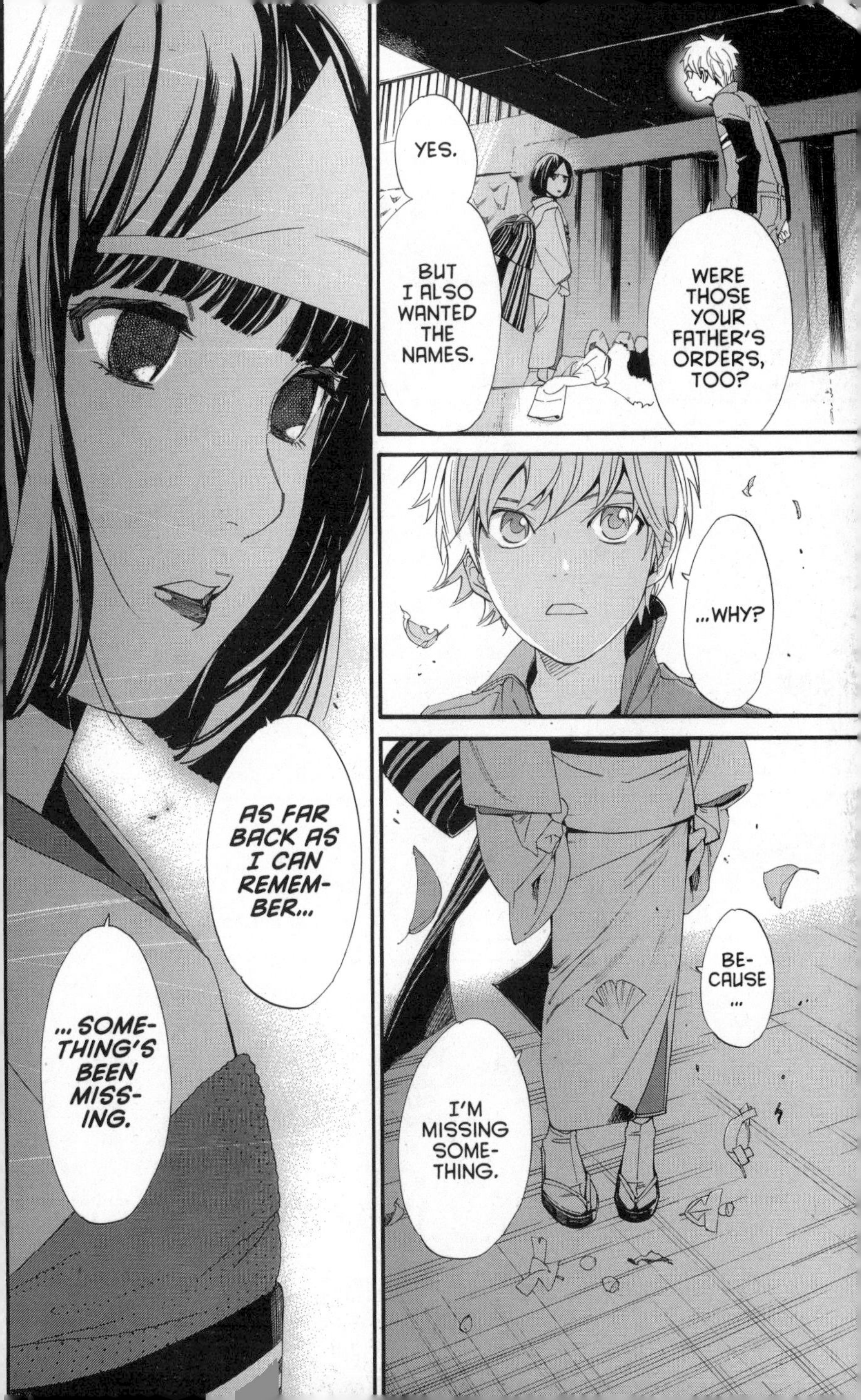
WERE THOSE YOUR FATHER'S ORDERS, TOO?
YES.
BUT I ALSO WANTED THE NAMES.
...WHY?
BE-CAUSE...
I'M MISSING SOME-THING.
AS FAR BACK AS I CAN REMEM-BER...
...SOME-THING'S BEEN MISS-ING.

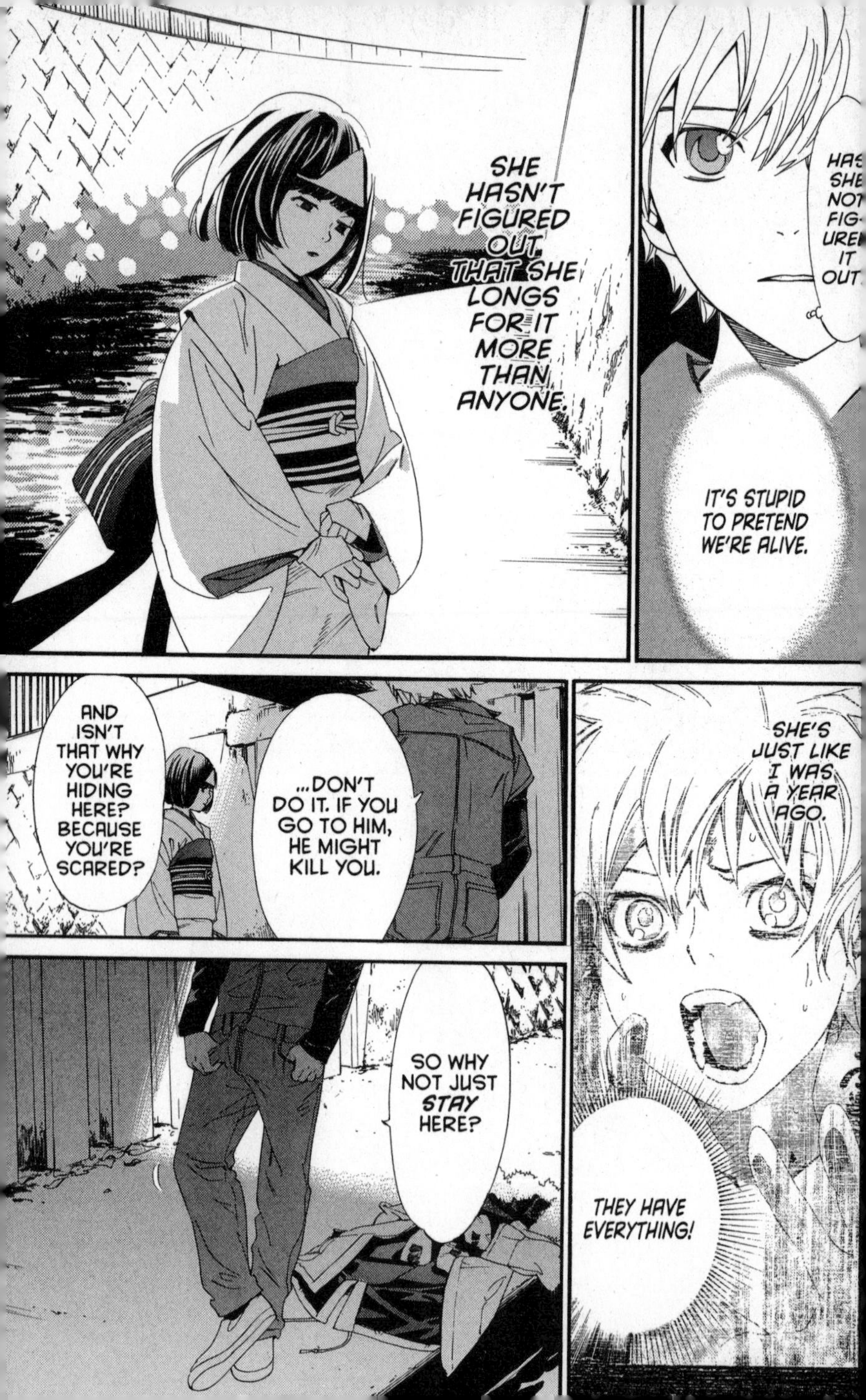
HAS SHE NOT FIG-URED IT OUT
IT'S STUPID TO PRETEND WE'RE ALIVE.
SHE HASN'T FIGURED OUT THAT SHE LONGS FOR IT MORE THAN ANYONE.
SHE'S JUST LIKE I WAS A YEAR AGO.
THEY HAVE EVERYTHING!
...DON'T DO IT. IF YOU GO TO HIM, HE MIGHT KILL YOU.
AND ISN'T THAT WHY YOU'RE HIDING HERE? BECAUSE YOU'RE SCARED?
SO WHY NOT JUST *STAY* HERE?

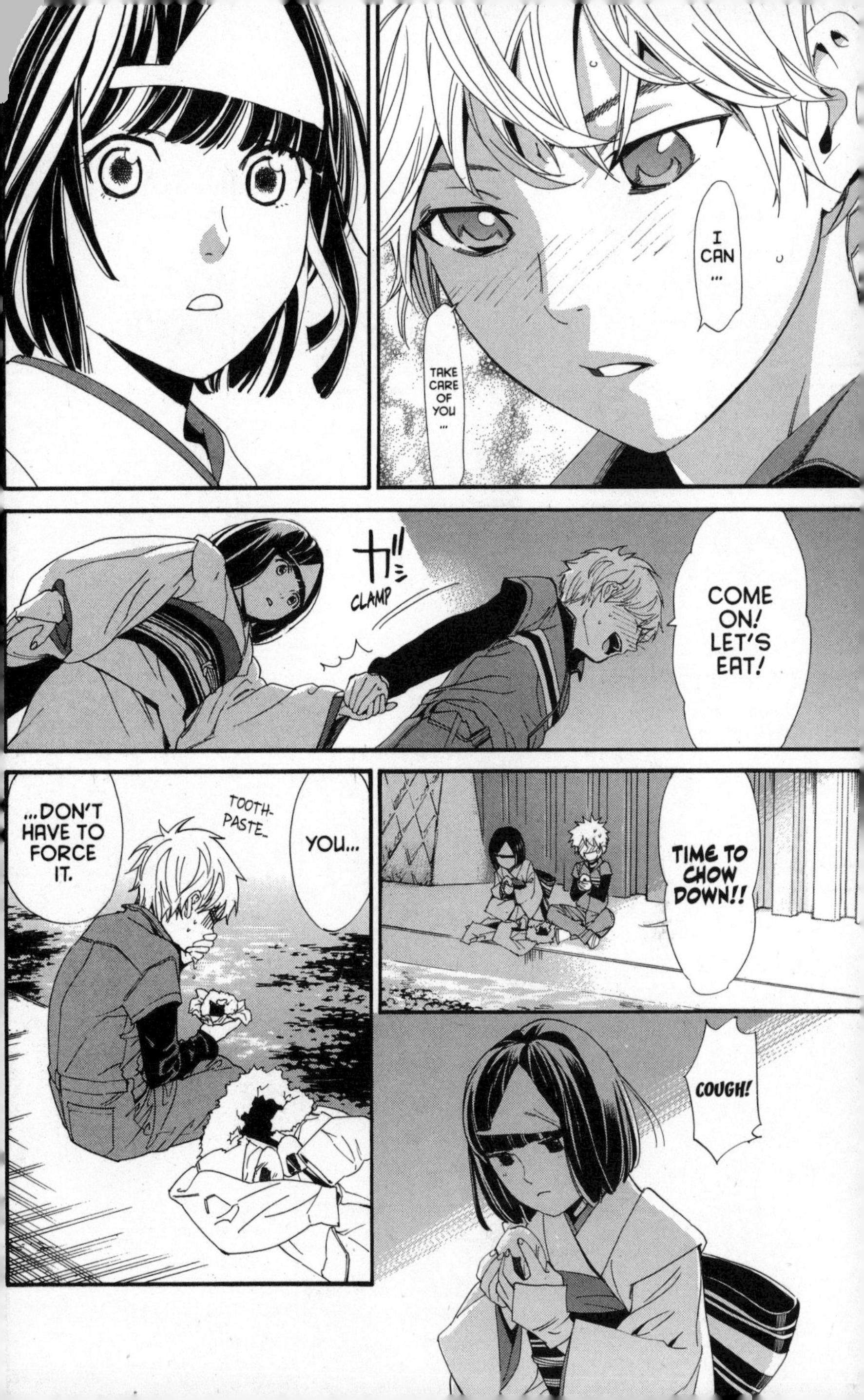

I CAN...
TAKE CARE OF YOU...
COME ON! LET'S EAT!
CLAMP
TIME TO CHOW DOWN!!
COUGH!
YOU...
TOOTH-PASTE...
...DON'T HAVE TO FORCE IT.

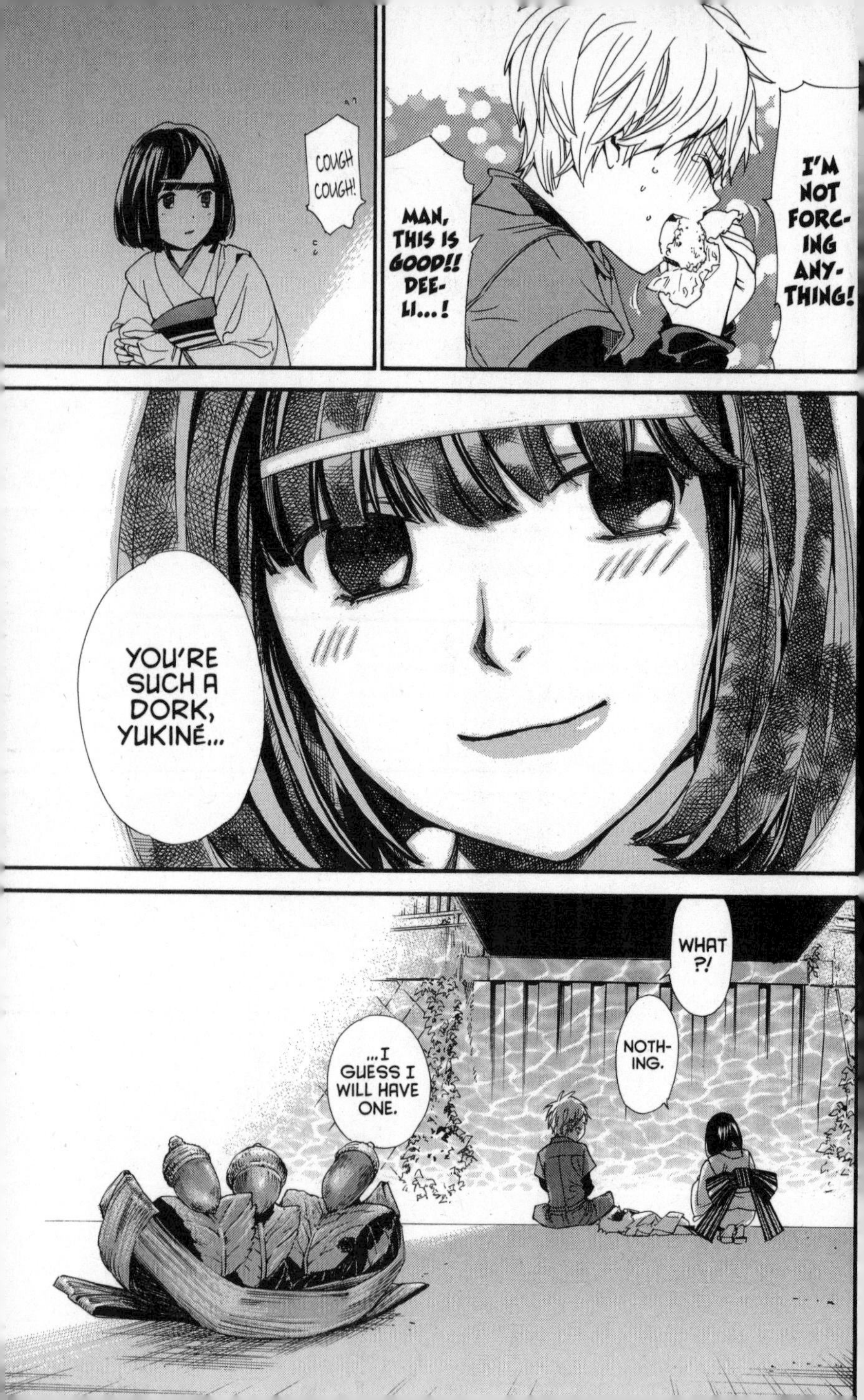

I'M NOT FORC-ING ANY-THING!
MAN, THIS IS GOOD!! DEE-LI...!
COUGH COUGH!
YOU'RE SUCH A DORK, YUKINÉ...
WHAT?!
NOTH-ING.
...I GUESS I WILL HAVE ONE.

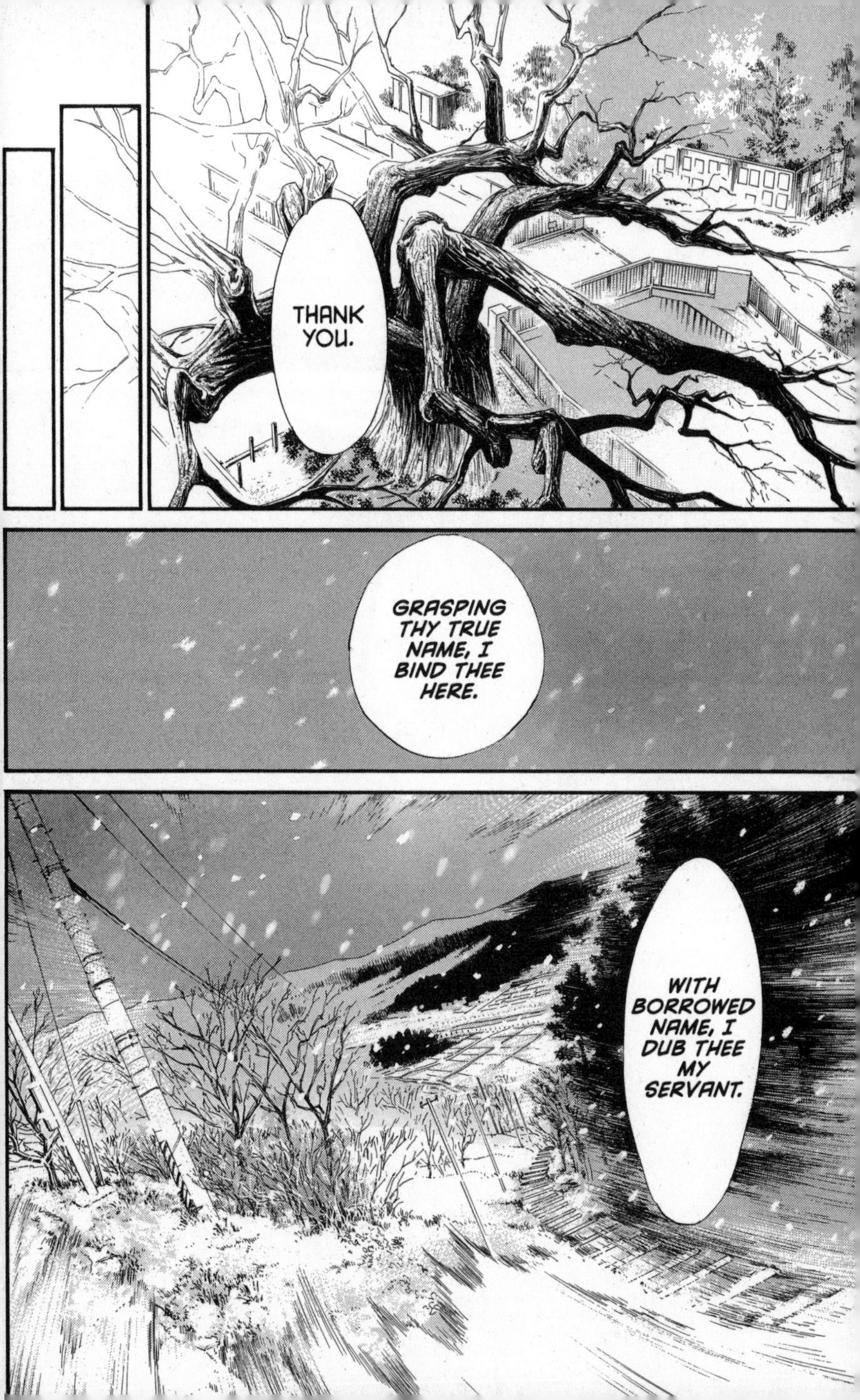
THANK YOU.
GRASPING THY TRUE NAME, I BIND THEE HERE.
WITH BORROWED NAME, I DUB THEE MY SERVANT.

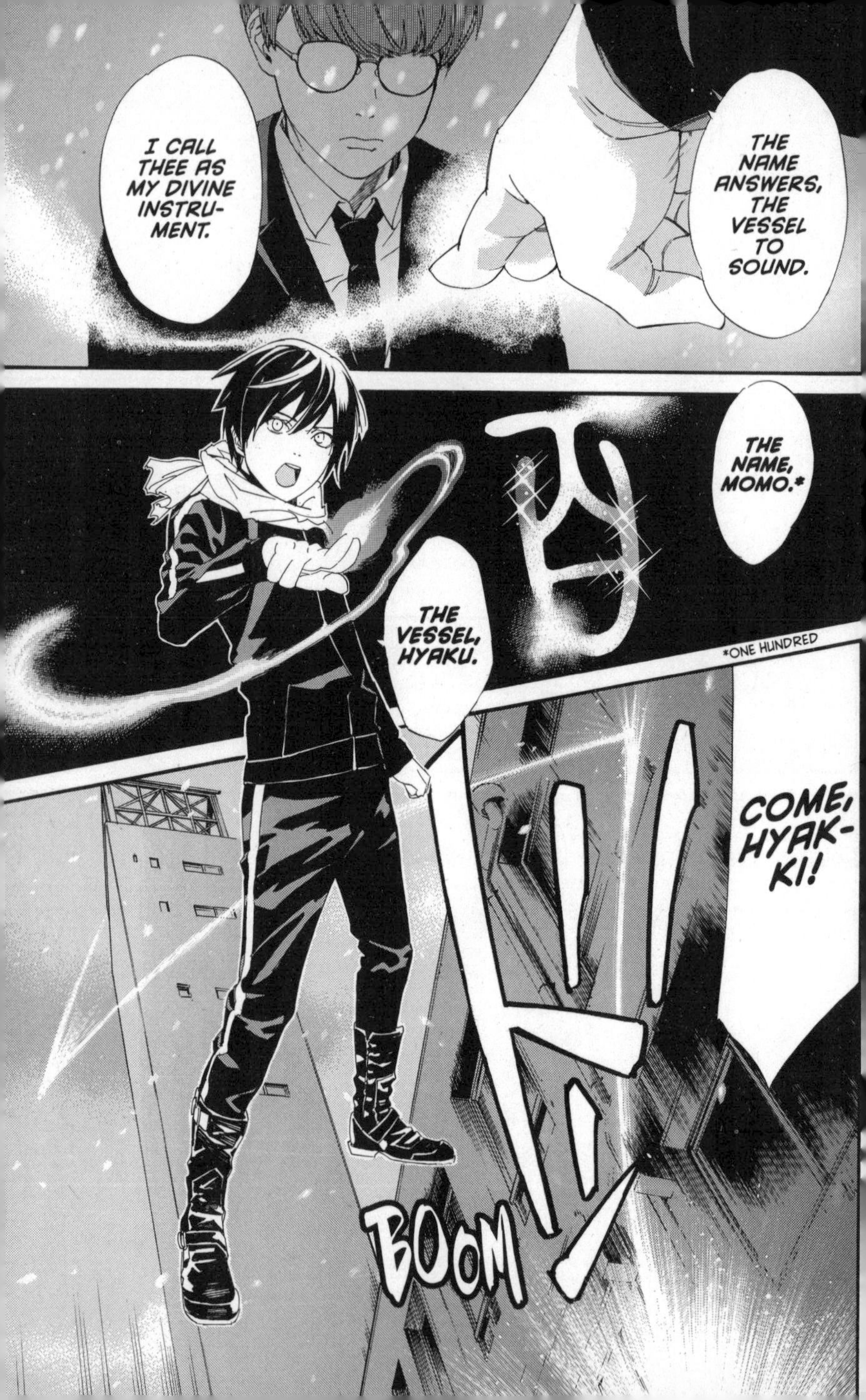
THE NAME ANSWERS, THE VESSEL TO SOUND.
I CALL THEE AS MY DIVINE INSTRUMENT.
THE NAME, MOMO.*
百
THE VESSEL, HYAKU.
*ONE HUNDRED
COME, HYAKKI!
BOOM

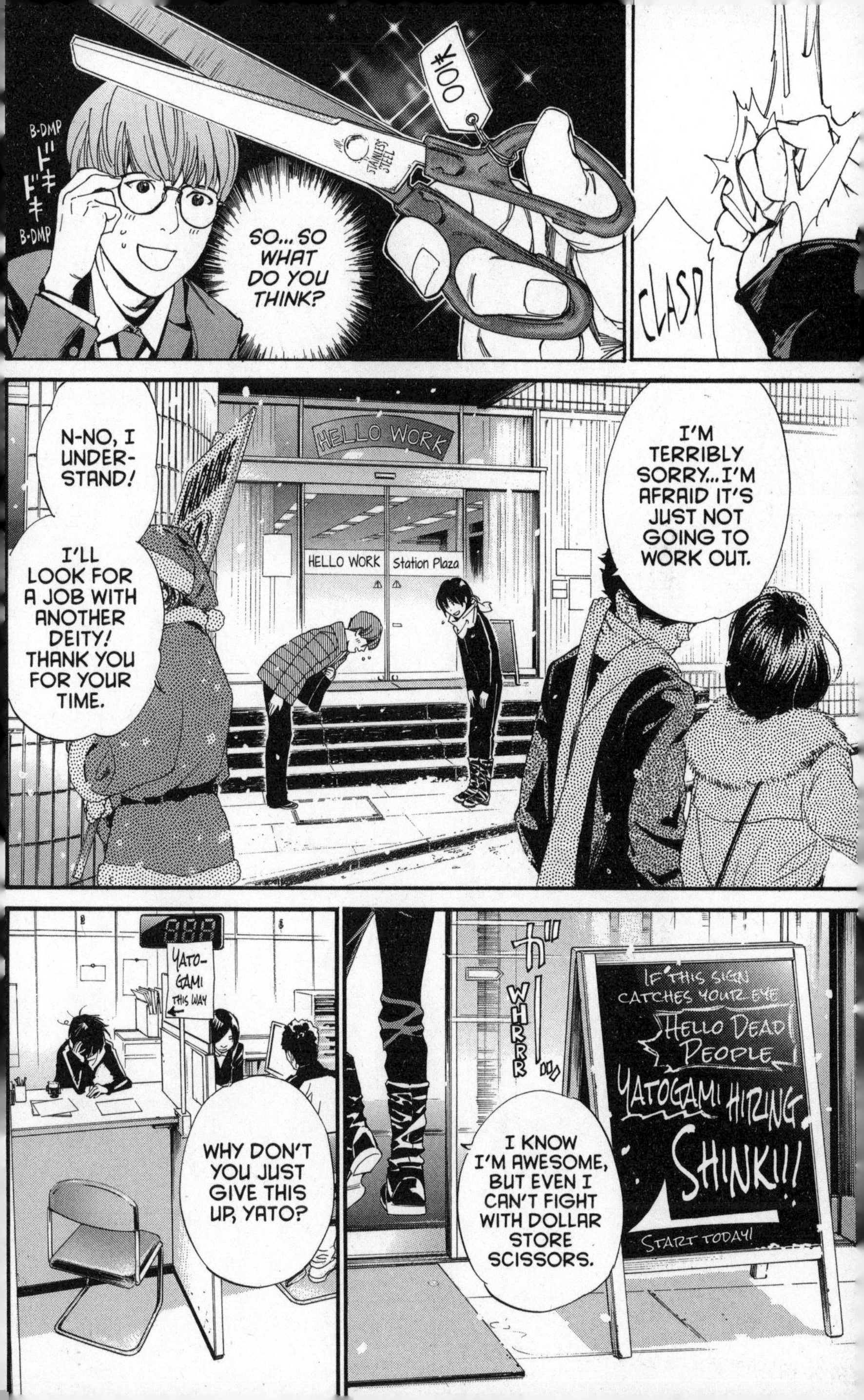
CLASP
¥100
STAINLESS STEEL
SO... SO WHAT DO YOU THINK?
B-DMP ドキドキ B-DMP
I'M TERRIBLY SORRY...I'M AFRAID IT'S JUST NOT GOING TO WORK OUT.
HELLO WORK
HELLO WORK Station Plaza
N-NO, I UNDER-STAND!
I'LL LOOK FOR A JOB WITH ANOTHER DEITY! THANK YOU FOR YOUR TIME.
IF THIS SIGN CATCHES YOUR EYE
HELLO DEAD PEOPLE
YATOGAMI HIRING SHINKI!!
START TODAY!
ガー WHRRR
I KNOW I'M AWESOME, BUT EVEN I CAN'T FIGHT WITH DOLLAR STORE SCISSORS.
YATO-GAMI THIS WAY
WHY DON'T YOU JUST GIVE THIS UP, YATO?

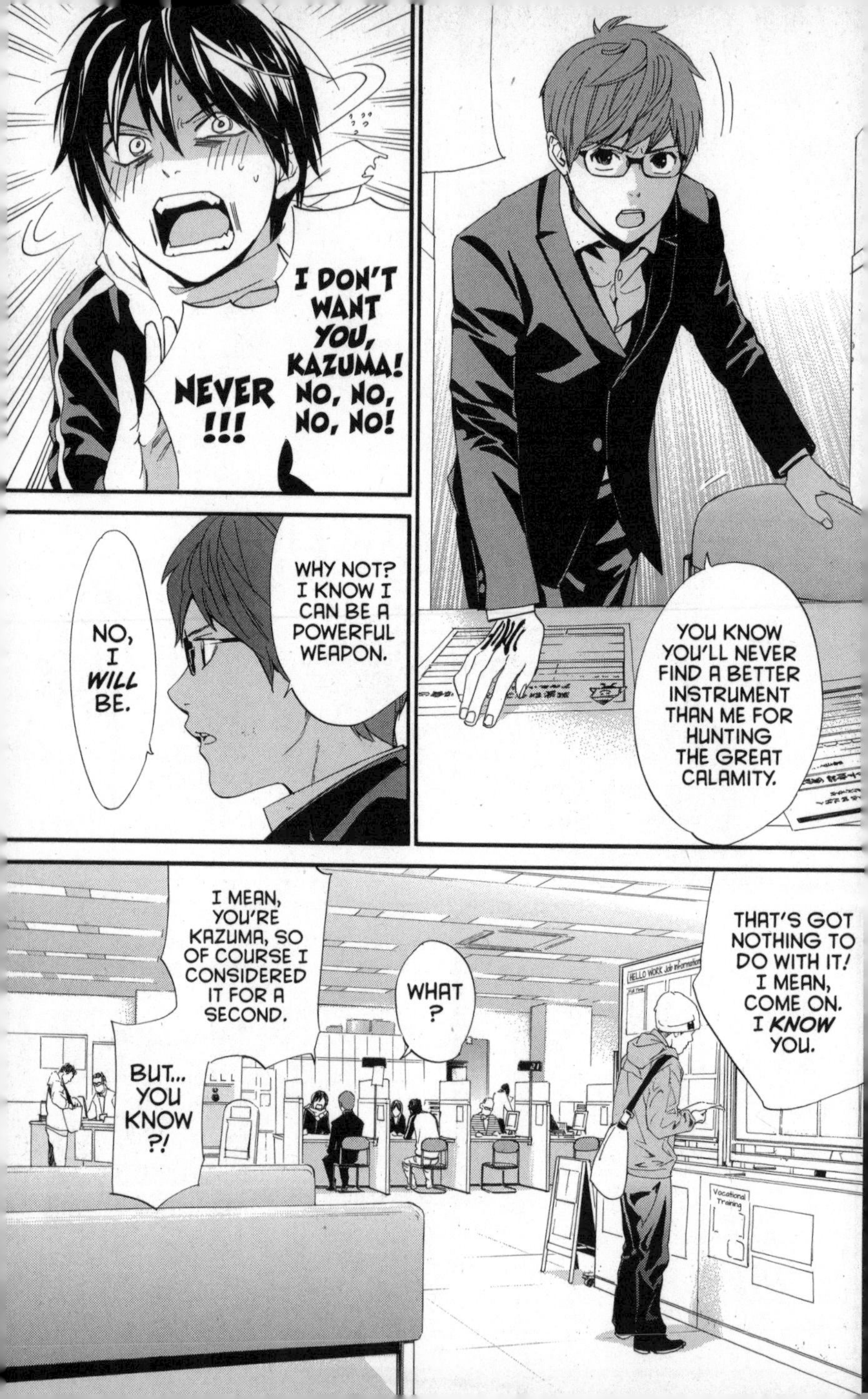
YOU KNOW YOU'LL NEVER FIND A BETTER INSTRUMENT THAN ME FOR HUNTING THE GREAT CALAMITY.
I DON'T WANT *YOU*, KAZUMA! NO, NO, NO, NO!
NEVER!!!
WHY NOT? I KNOW I CAN BE A POWERFUL WEAPON.
NO, I *WILL* BE.
THAT'S GOT NOTHING TO DO WITH IT! I MEAN, COME ON. I *KNOW* YOU.
WHAT?
I MEAN, YOU'RE KAZUMA, SO OF COURSE I CONSIDERED IT FOR A SECOND.
BUT... YOU KNOW?!
HELLO WORK Job Information
Vocational Training

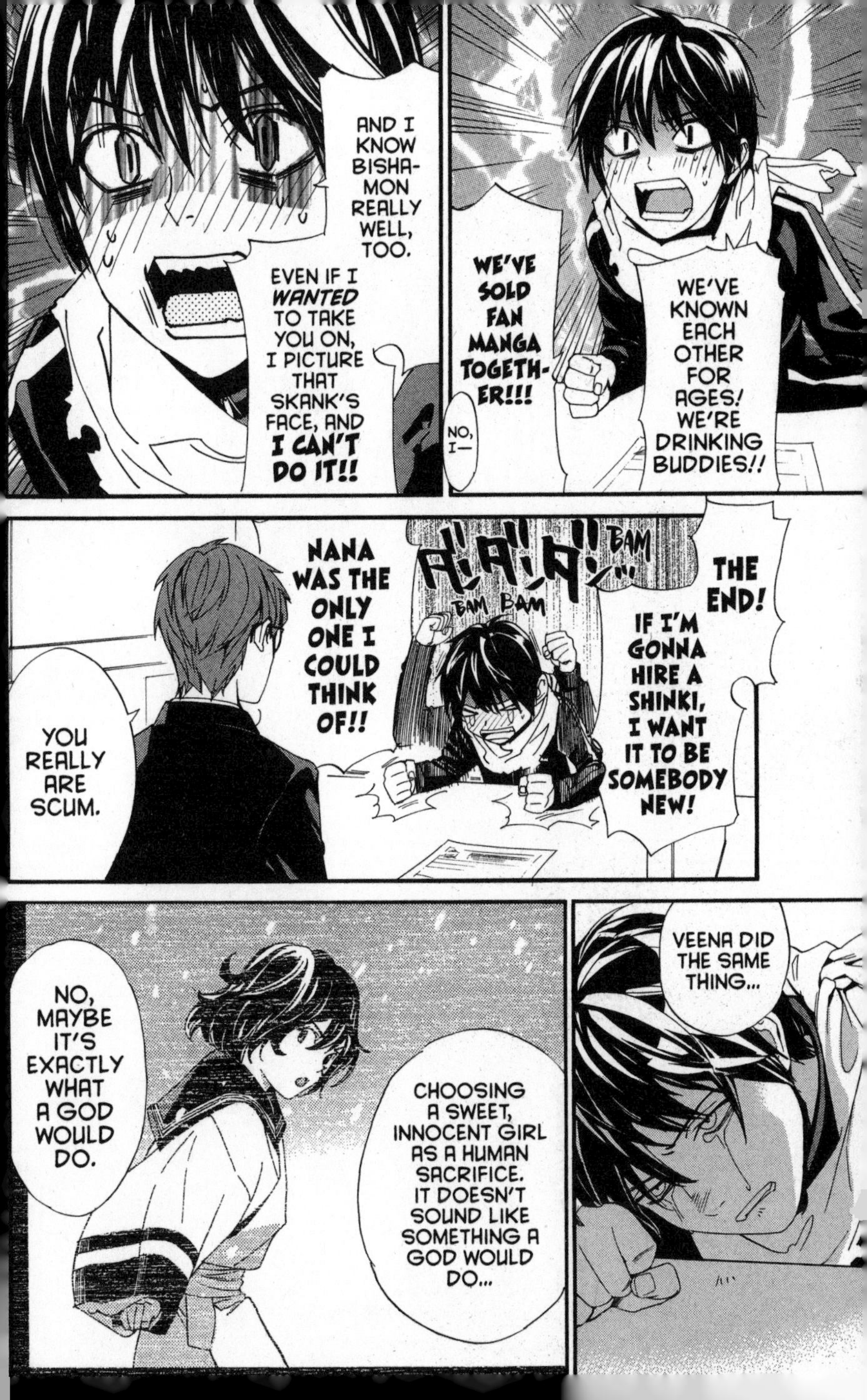
WE'VE KNOWN EACH OTHER FOR AGES! WE'RE DRINKING BUDDIES!!
WE'VE SOLD FAN MANGA TOGETHER!!!
NO, I—
AND I KNOW BISHAMON REALLY WELL, TOO.
EVEN IF I *WANTED* TO TAKE YOU ON, I PICTURE THAT SKANK'S FACE, AND **I CAN'T DO IT!!**
THE END! IF I'M GONNA HIRE A SHINKI, I WANT IT TO BE SOMEBODY NEW!
BAM
BAM BAM
NANA WAS THE ONLY ONE I COULD THINK OF!!
YOU REALLY ARE SCUM.
VEENA DID THE SAME THING...
CHOOSING A SWEET, INNOCENT GIRL AS A HUMAN SACRIFICE. IT DOESN'T SOUND LIKE SOMETHING A GOD WOULD DO...
NO, MAYBE IT'S EXACTLY WHAT A GOD WOULD DO.

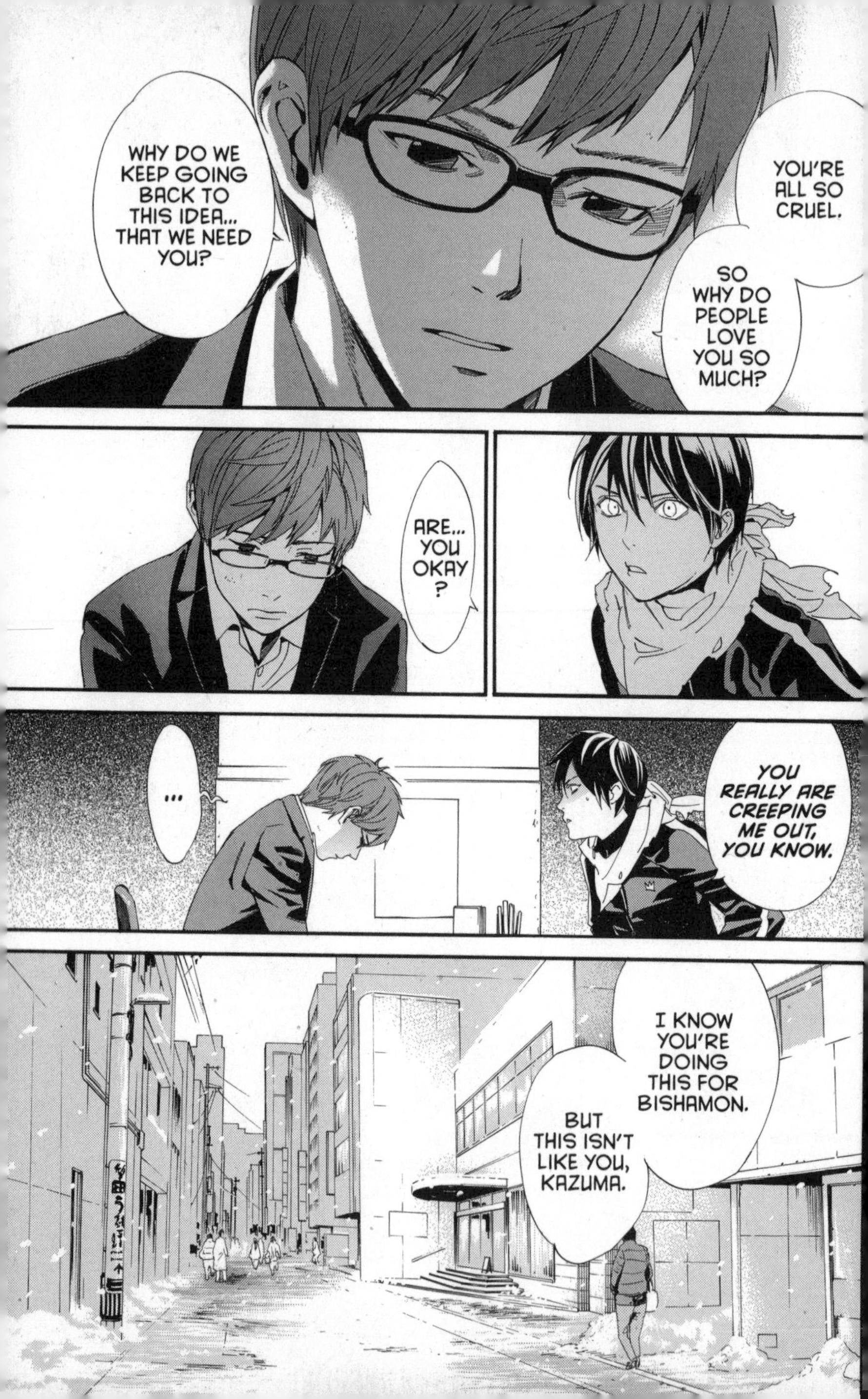
YOU'RE ALL SO CRUEL.
SO WHY DO PEOPLE LOVE YOU SO MUCH?
WHY DO WE KEEP GOING BACK TO THIS IDEA... THAT WE NEED YOU?
ARE... YOU OKAY?
YOU REALLY ARE CREEPING ME OUT, YOU KNOW.
...
I KNOW YOU'RE DOING THIS FOR BISHAMON.
BUT THIS ISN'T LIKE YOU, KAZUMA.

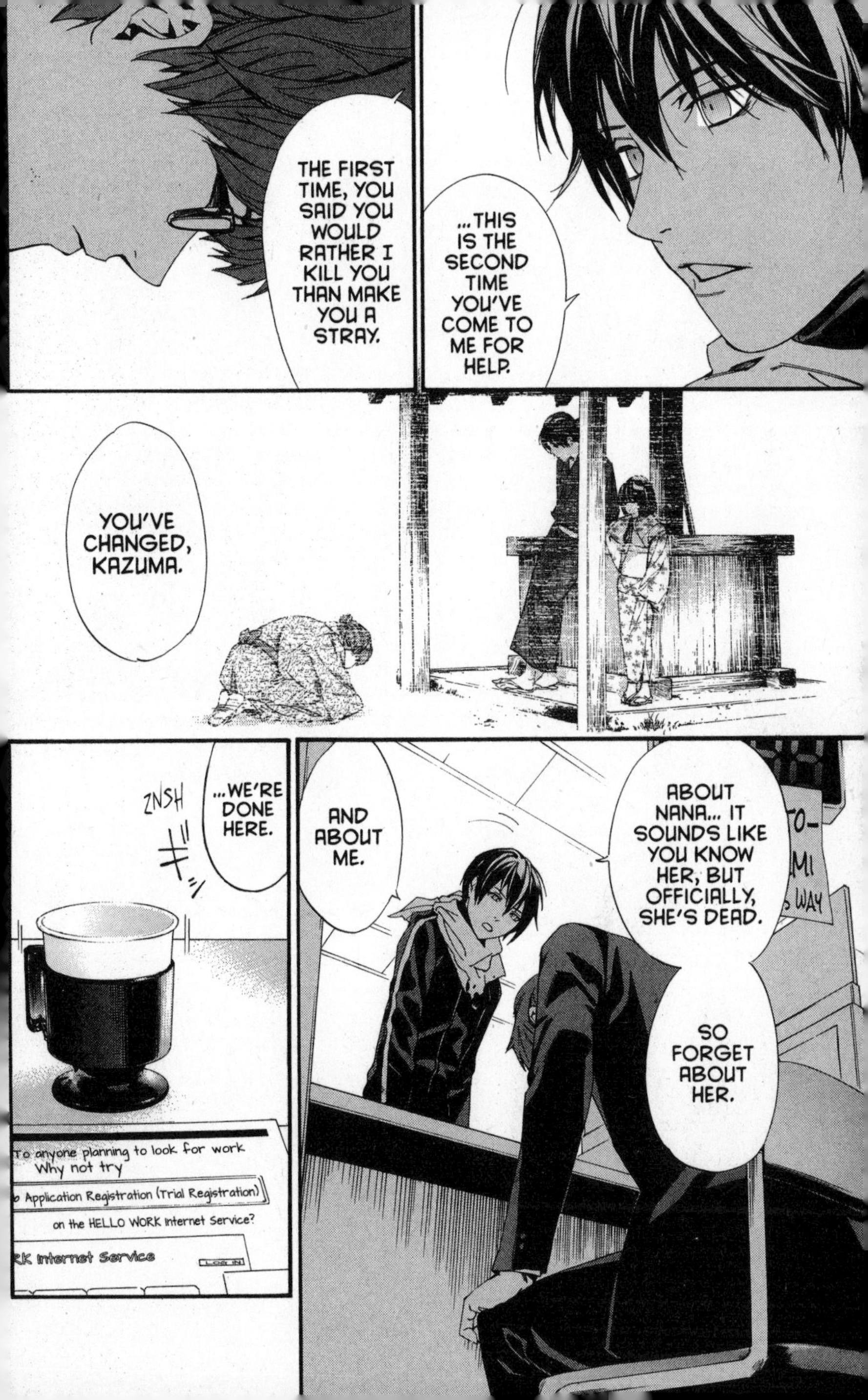
...THIS IS THE SECOND TIME YOU'VE COME TO ME FOR HELP.
THE FIRST TIME, YOU SAID YOU WOULD RATHER I KILL YOU THAN MAKE YOU A STRAY.
YOU'VE CHANGED, KAZUMA.
ABOUT NANA... IT SOUNDS LIKE YOU KNOW HER, BUT OFFICIALLY, SHE'S DEAD.
SO FORGET ABOUT HER.
AND ABOUT ME.
...WE'RE DONE HERE.
ZNSH
To anyone planning to look for work
Why not try
Application Registration (Trial Registration)
on the HELLO WORK Internet Service?
RK Internet Service
LOG IN

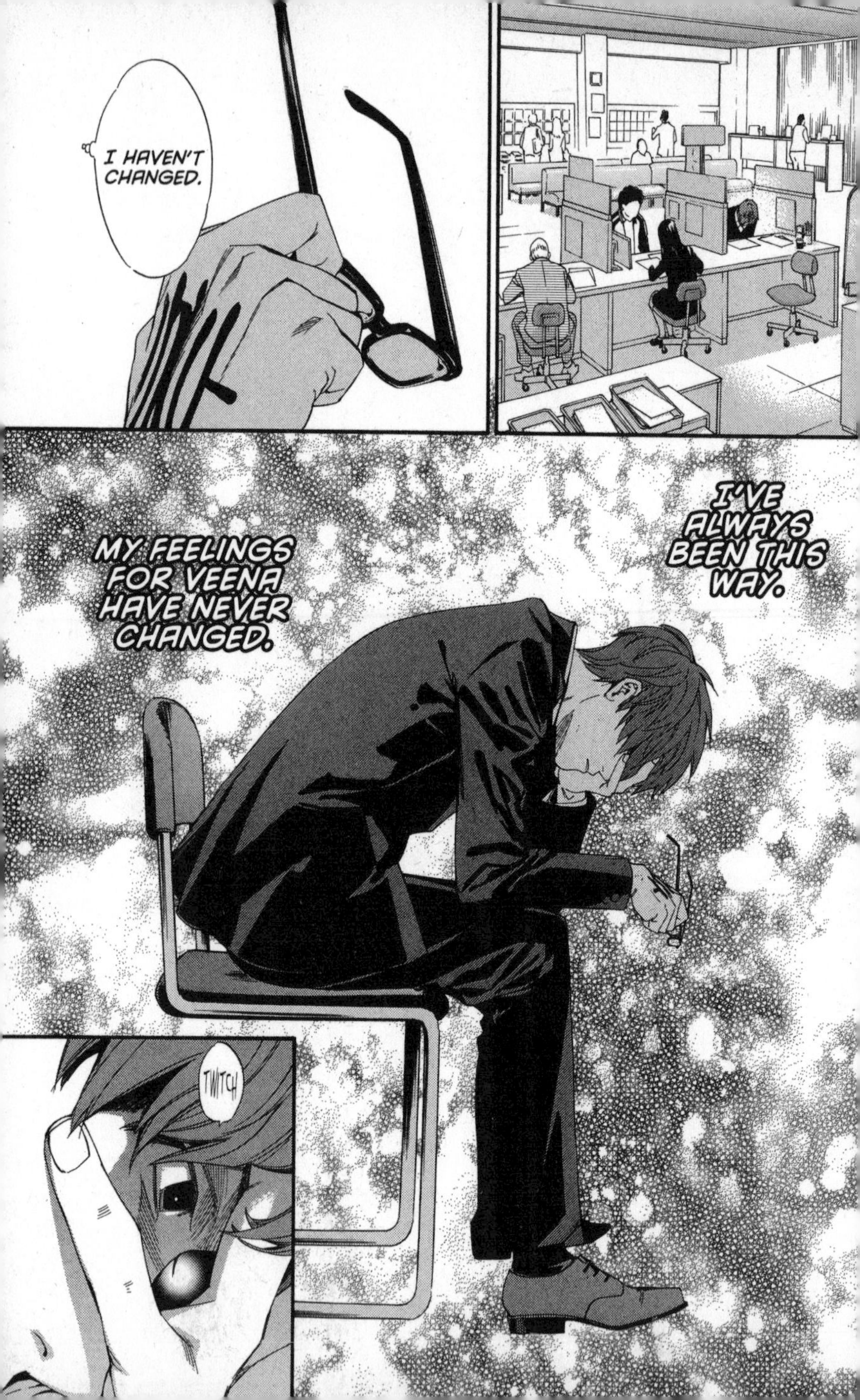
I HAVEN'T CHANGED.
I'VE ALWAYS BEEN THIS WAY.
MY FEELINGS FOR VEENA HAVE NEVER CHANGED.
TWITCH

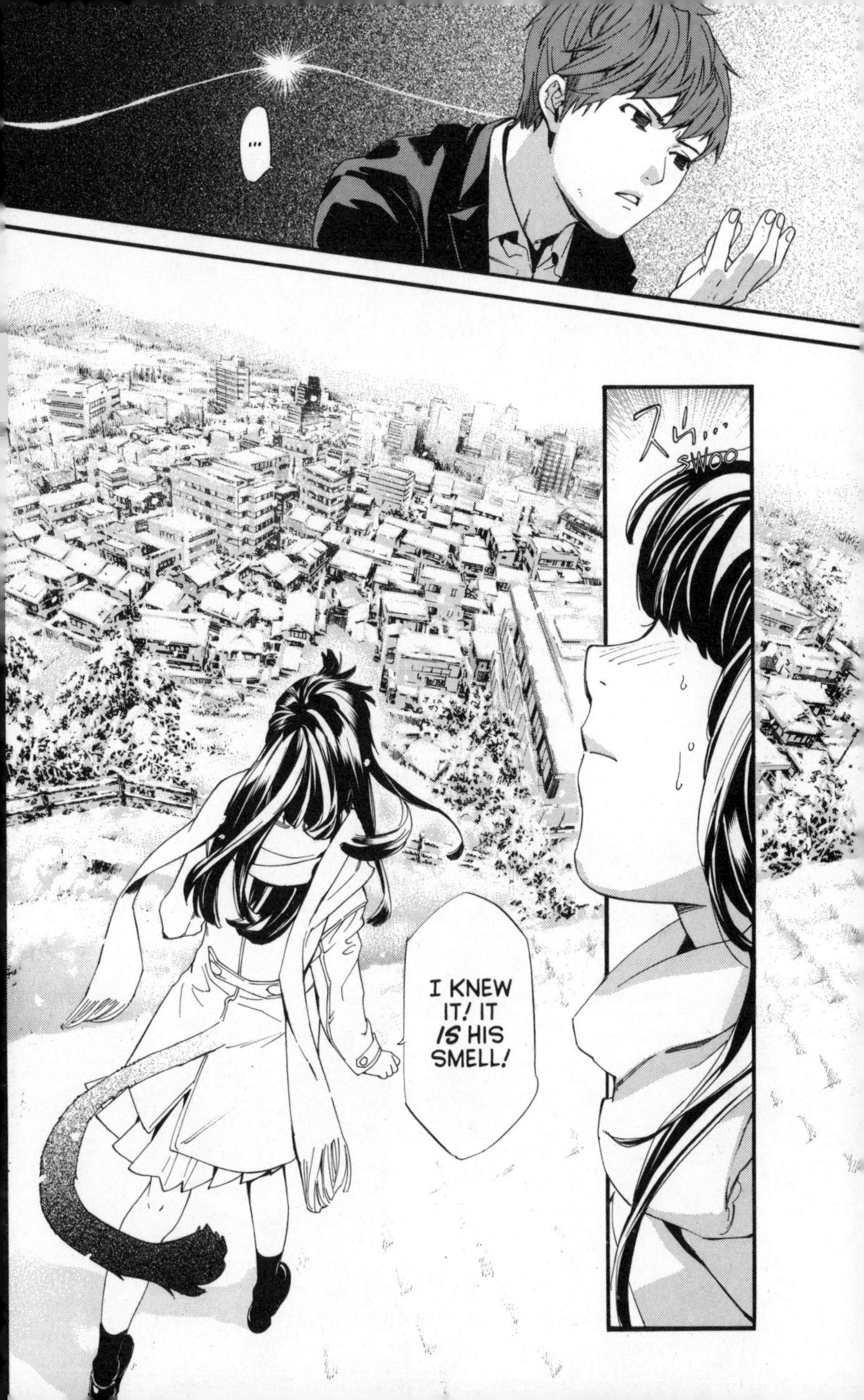
...
スん...
SWOO
I KNEW IT! IT *IS* HIS SMELL!

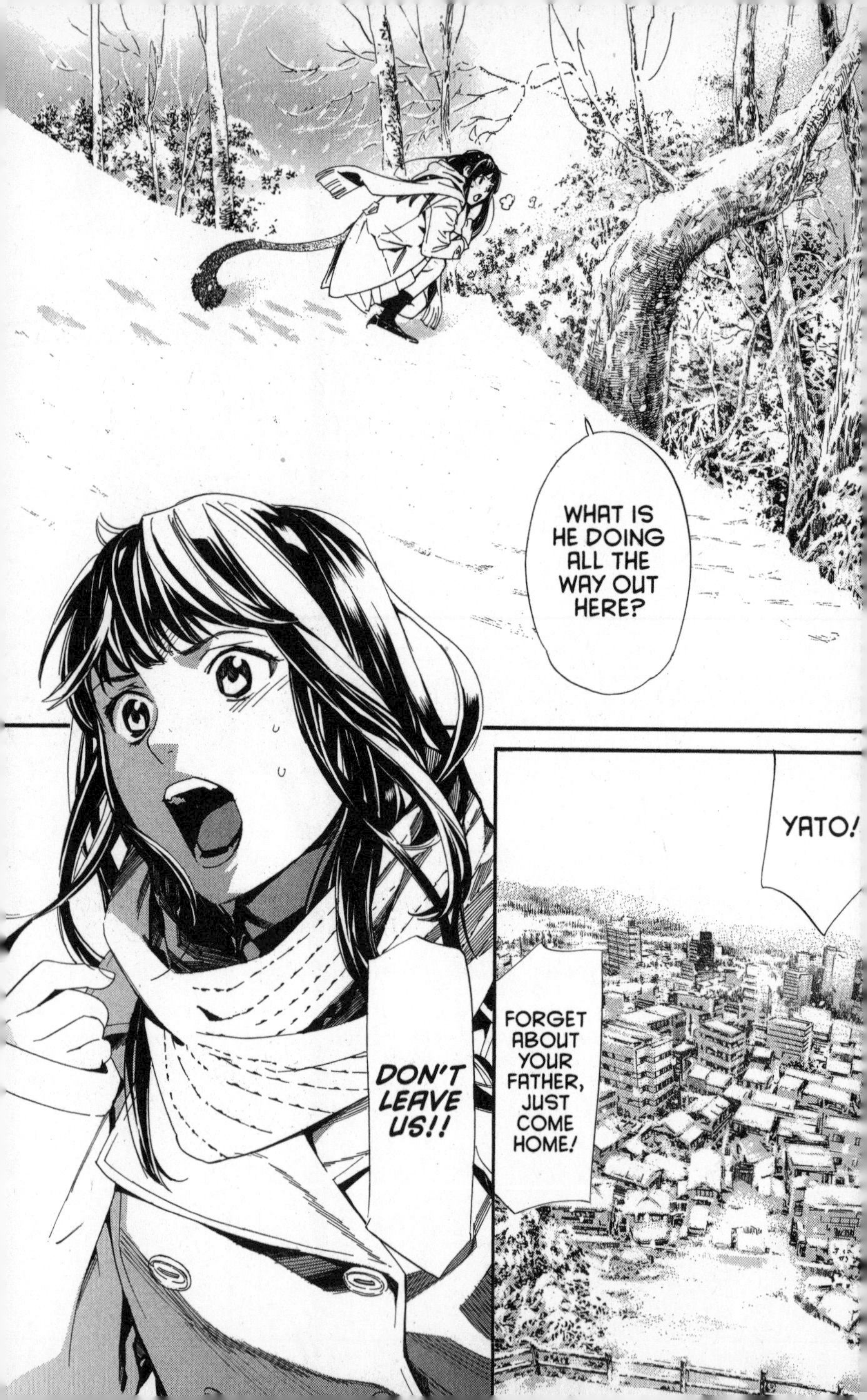
WHAT IS HE DOING ALL THE WAY OUT HERE?
YATO!
FORGET ABOUT YOUR FATHER, JUST COME HOME!
DON'T LEAVE US!!

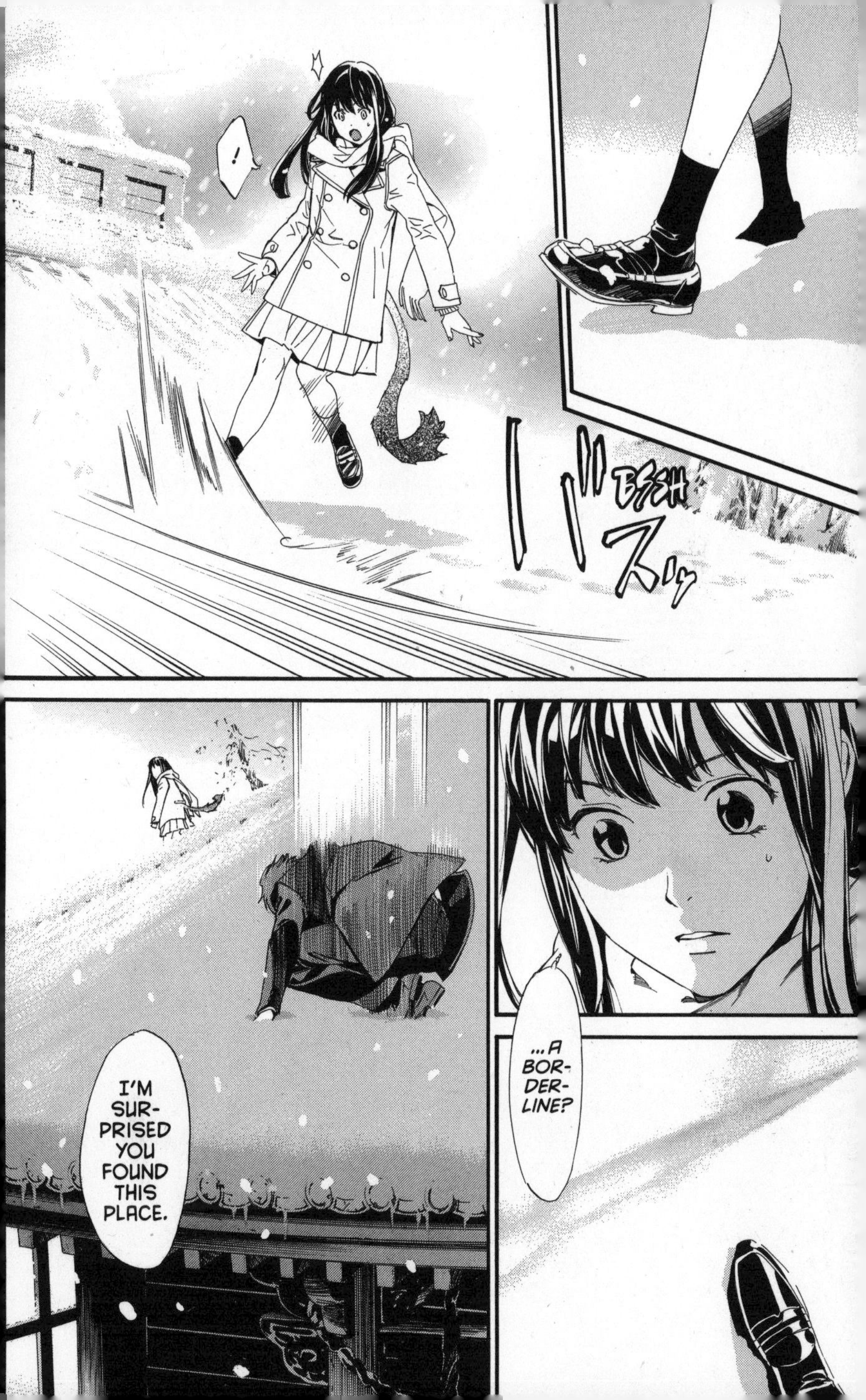
BSSH
ズッ
!
...A BORDER-LINE?
I'M SURPRISED YOU FOUND THIS PLACE.

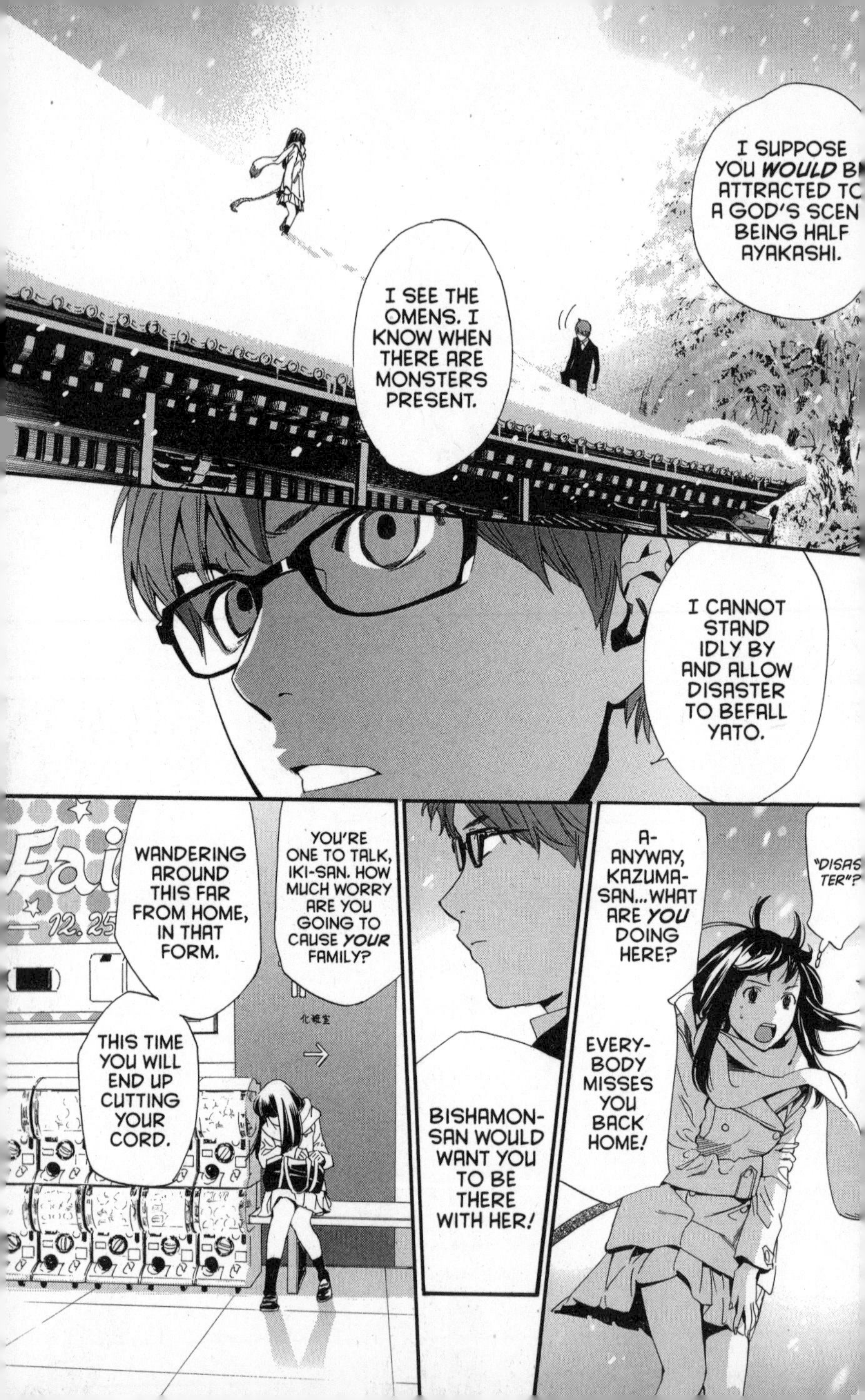
I SUPPOSE YOU *WOULD* B ATTRACTED TO A GOD'S SCEN BEING HALF AYAKASHI.
I SEE THE OMENS. I KNOW WHEN THERE ARE MONSTERS PRESENT.
I CANNOT STAND IDLY BY AND ALLOW DISASTER TO BEFALL YATO.
"DISASTER"?
A- ANYWAY, KAZUMA-SAN...WHAT ARE *YOU* DOING HERE?
EVERY-BODY MISSES YOU BACK HOME!
BISHAMON-SAN WOULD WANT YOU TO BE THERE WITH HER!
YOU'RE ONE TO TALK, IKI-SAN. HOW MUCH WORRY ARE YOU GOING TO CAUSE *YOUR* FAMILY?
WANDERING AROUND THIS FAR FROM HOME, IN THAT FORM.
THIS TIME YOU WILL END UP CUTTING YOUR CORD.
化粧室

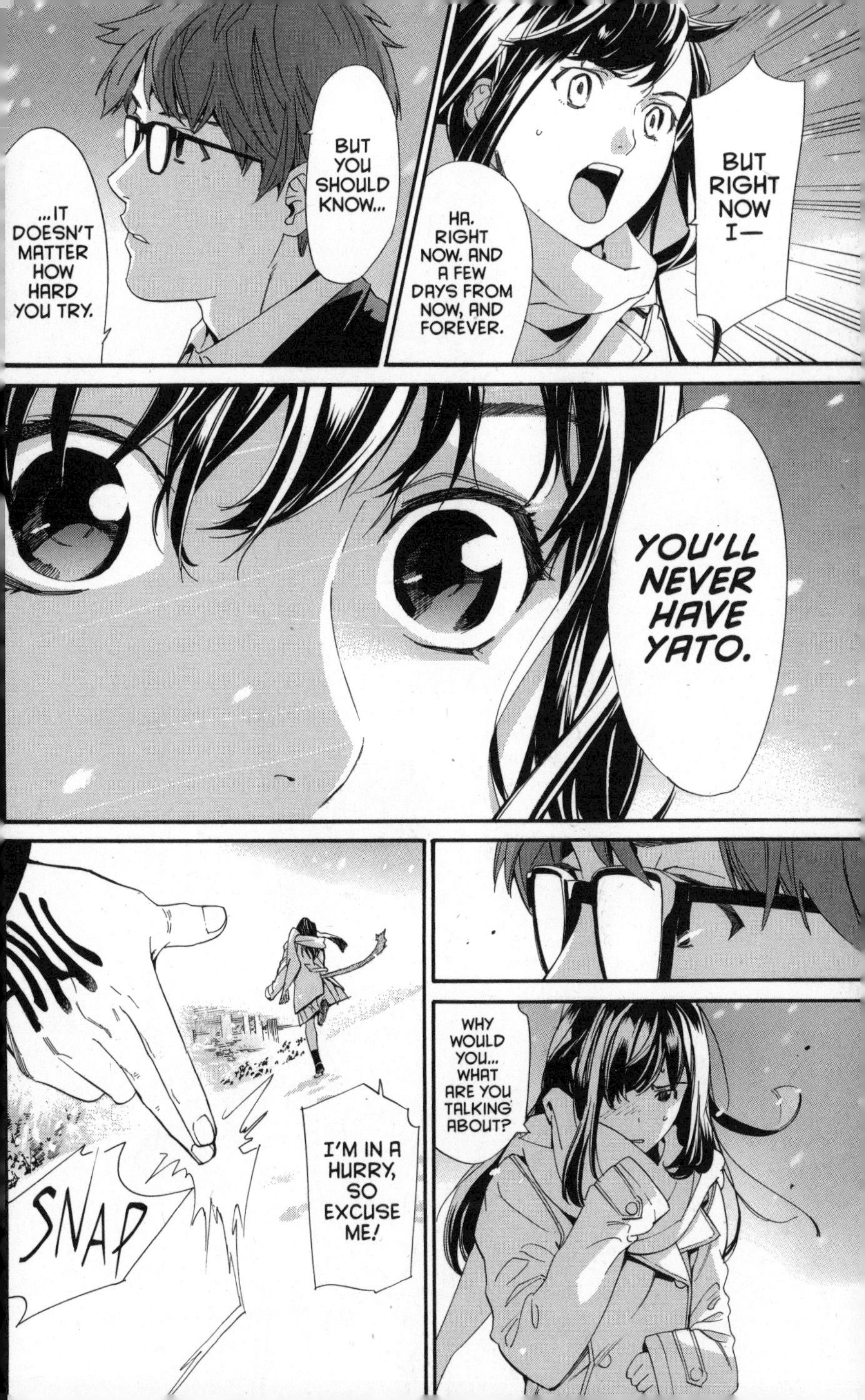
BUT RIGHT NOW I—
HA. RIGHT NOW. AND A FEW DAYS FROM NOW, AND FOREVER.
BUT YOU SHOULD KNOW...
...IT DOESN'T MATTER HOW HARD YOU TRY.
YOU'LL NEVER HAVE YATO.
WHY WOULD YOU... WHAT ARE YOU TALKING ABOUT?
I'M IN A HURRY, SO EXCUSE ME!
SNAP

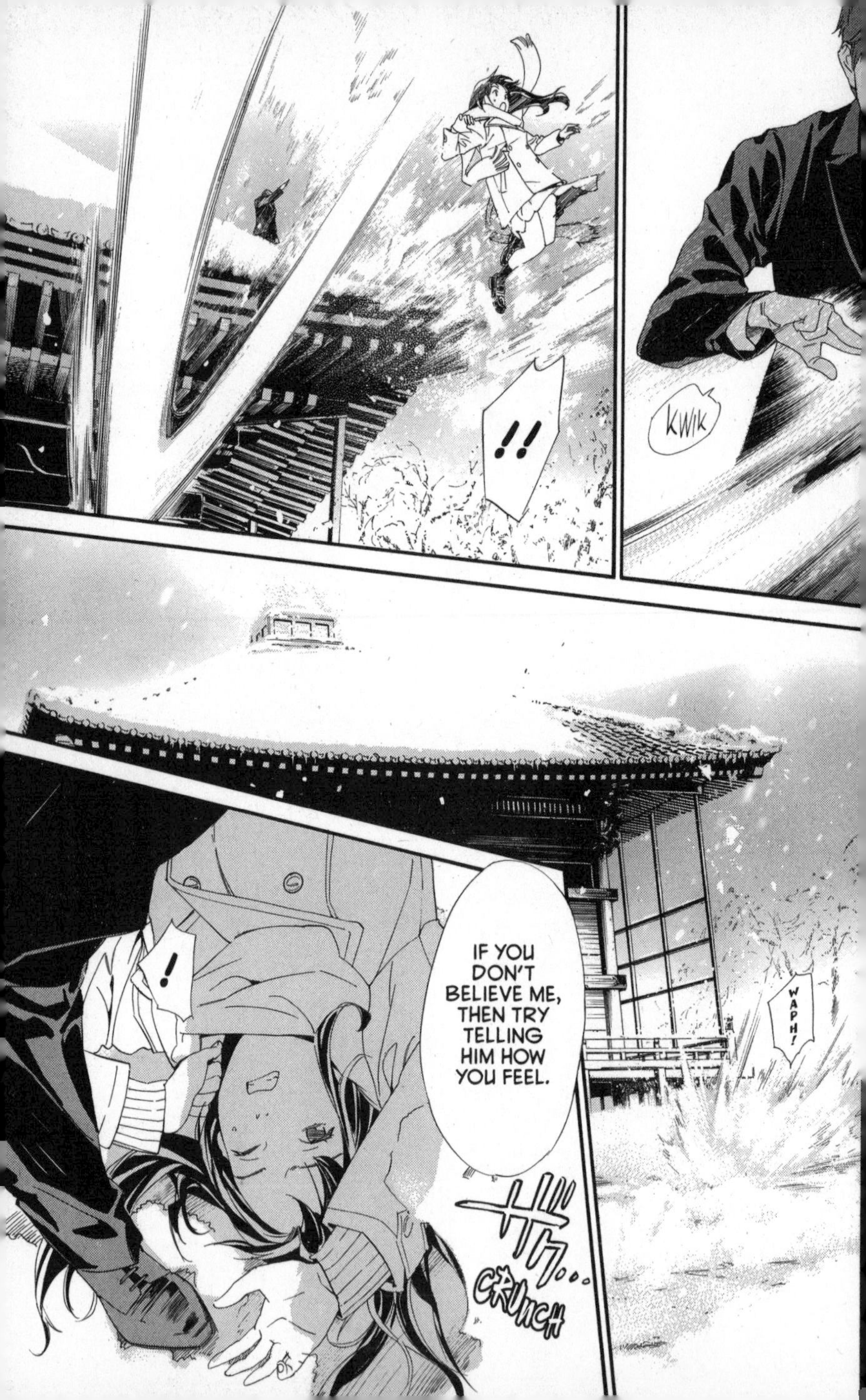
KWIK
!!
IF YOU DON'T BELIEVE ME, THEN TRY TELLING HIM HOW YOU FEEL.
WAPH!
!
CRUNCH

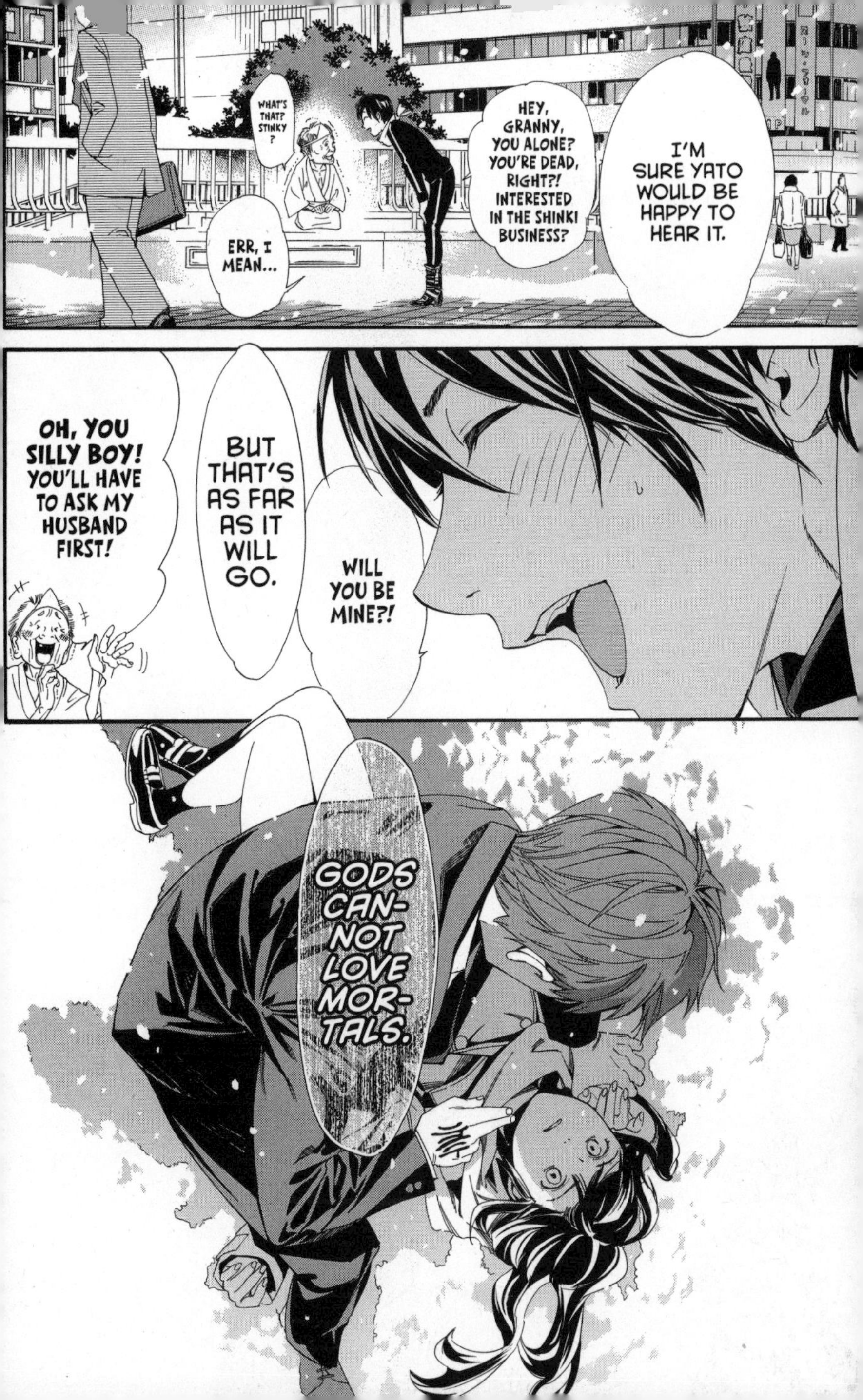
I'M SURE YATO WOULD BE HAPPY TO HEAR IT.
HEY, GRANNY, YOU ALONE? YOU'RE DEAD, RIGHT?! INTERESTED IN THE SHINKI BUSINESS?
WHAT'S THAT? STINKY?
ERR, I MEAN...
WILL YOU BE MINE?!
BUT THAT'S AS FAR AS IT WILL GO.
OH, YOU SILLY BOY! YOU'LL HAVE TO ASK MY HUSBAND FIRST!
GODS CAN-NOT LOVE MOR-TALS.

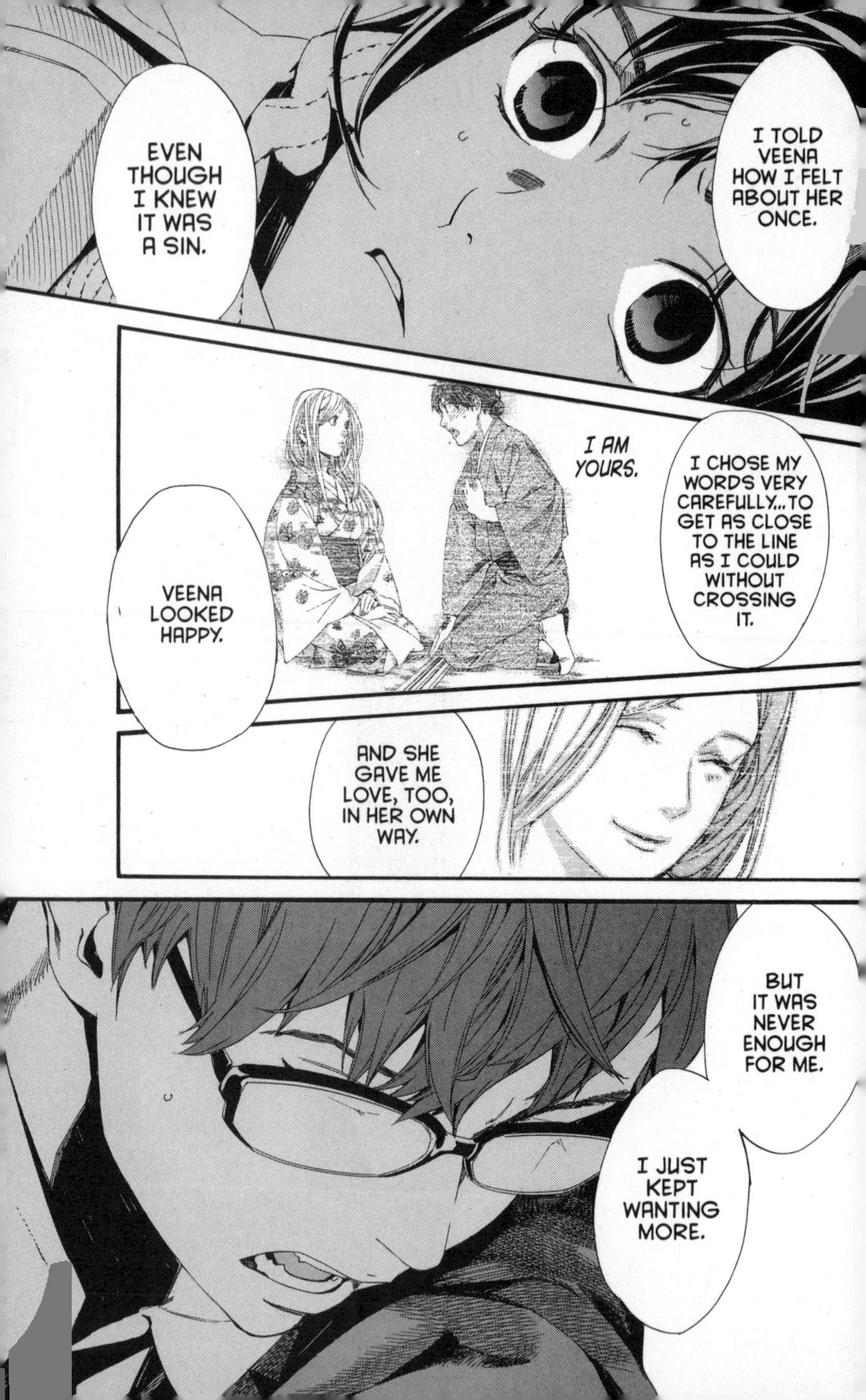
I TOLD VEENA HOW I FELT ABOUT HER ONCE.
EVEN THOUGH I KNEW IT WAS A SIN.
I CHOSE MY WORDS VERY CAREFULLY...TO GET AS CLOSE TO THE LINE AS I COULD WITHOUT CROSSING IT.
I AM YOURS.
VEENA LOOKED HAPPY.
AND SHE GAVE ME LOVE, TOO, IN HER OWN WAY.
BUT IT WAS NEVER ENOUGH FOR ME.
I JUST KEPT WANTING MORE.

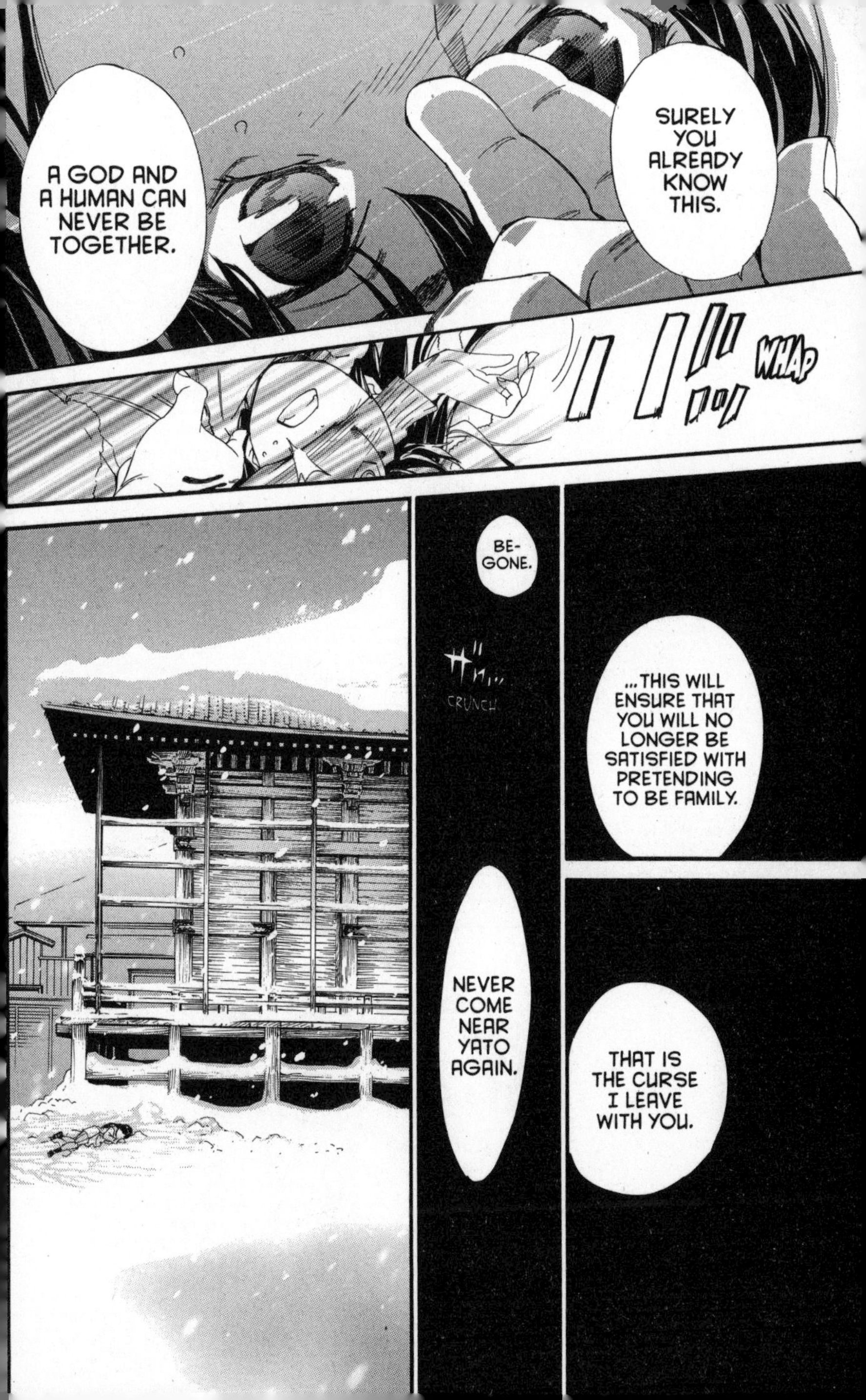
SURELY YOU ALREADY KNOW THIS.
A GOD AND A HUMAN CAN NEVER BE TOGETHER.
WHAP
...THIS WILL ENSURE THAT YOU WILL NO LONGER BE SATISFIED WITH PRETENDING TO BE FAMILY.
THAT IS THE CURSE I LEAVE WITH YOU.
BE-GONE.
CRUNCH
NEVER COME NEAR YATO AGAIN.

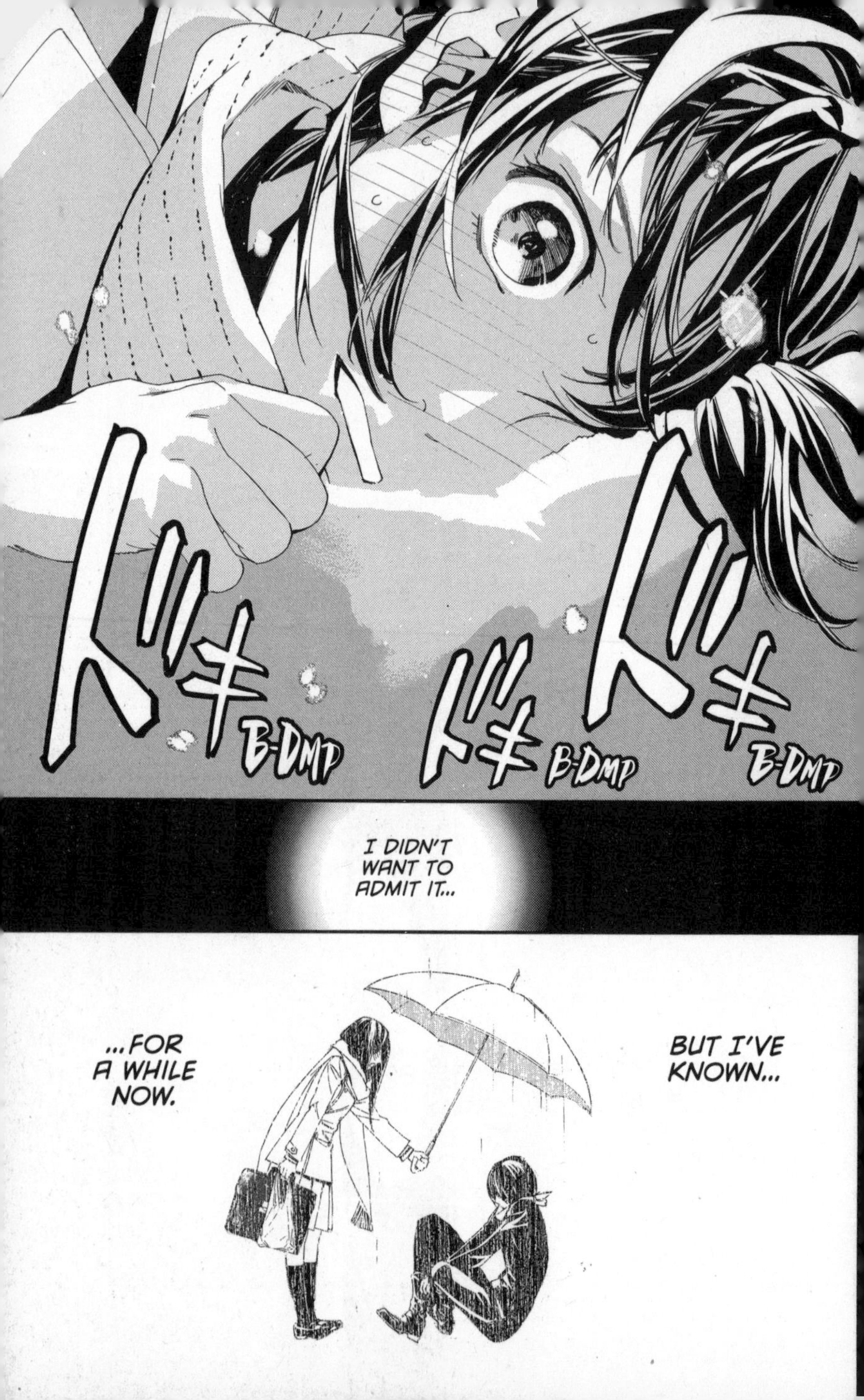
ドキ B-DMP
ドキ B-DMP
ドキ B-DMP
I DIDN'T WANT TO ADMIT IT...
BUT I'VE KNOWN...
...FOR A WHILE NOW.

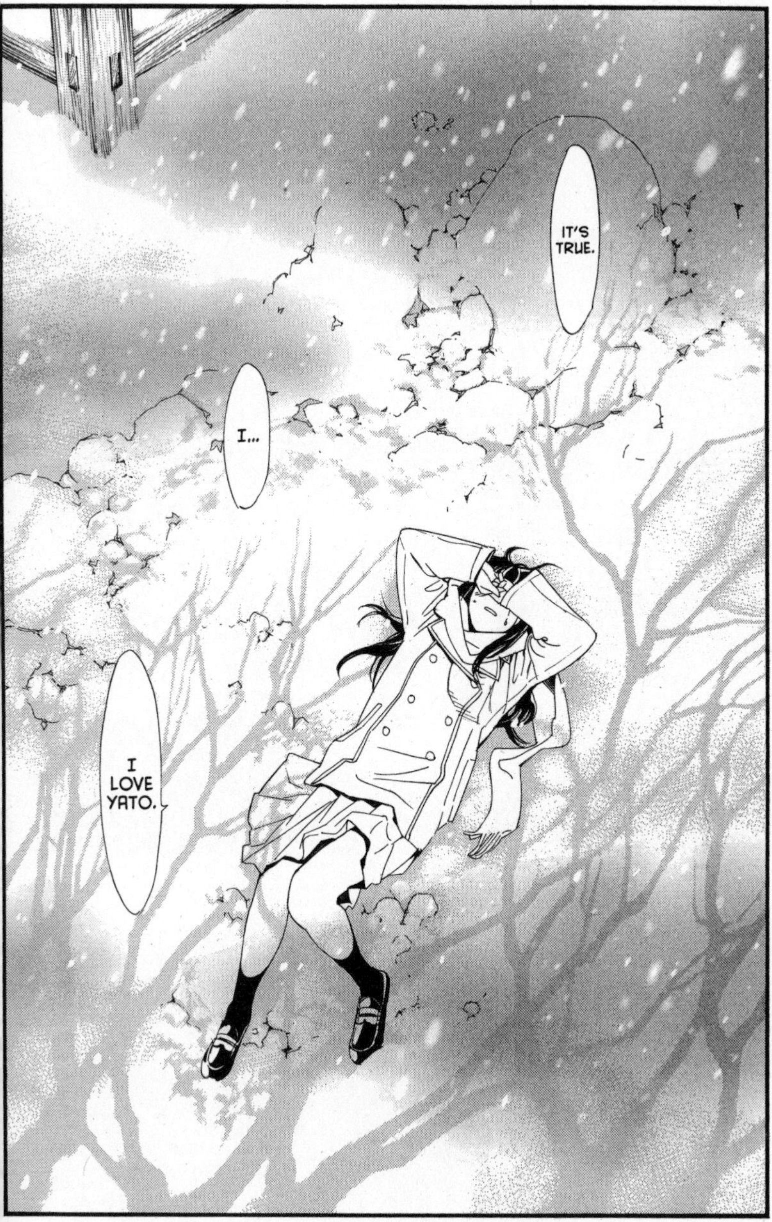
IT'S TRUE.
I...
I LOVE YATO.

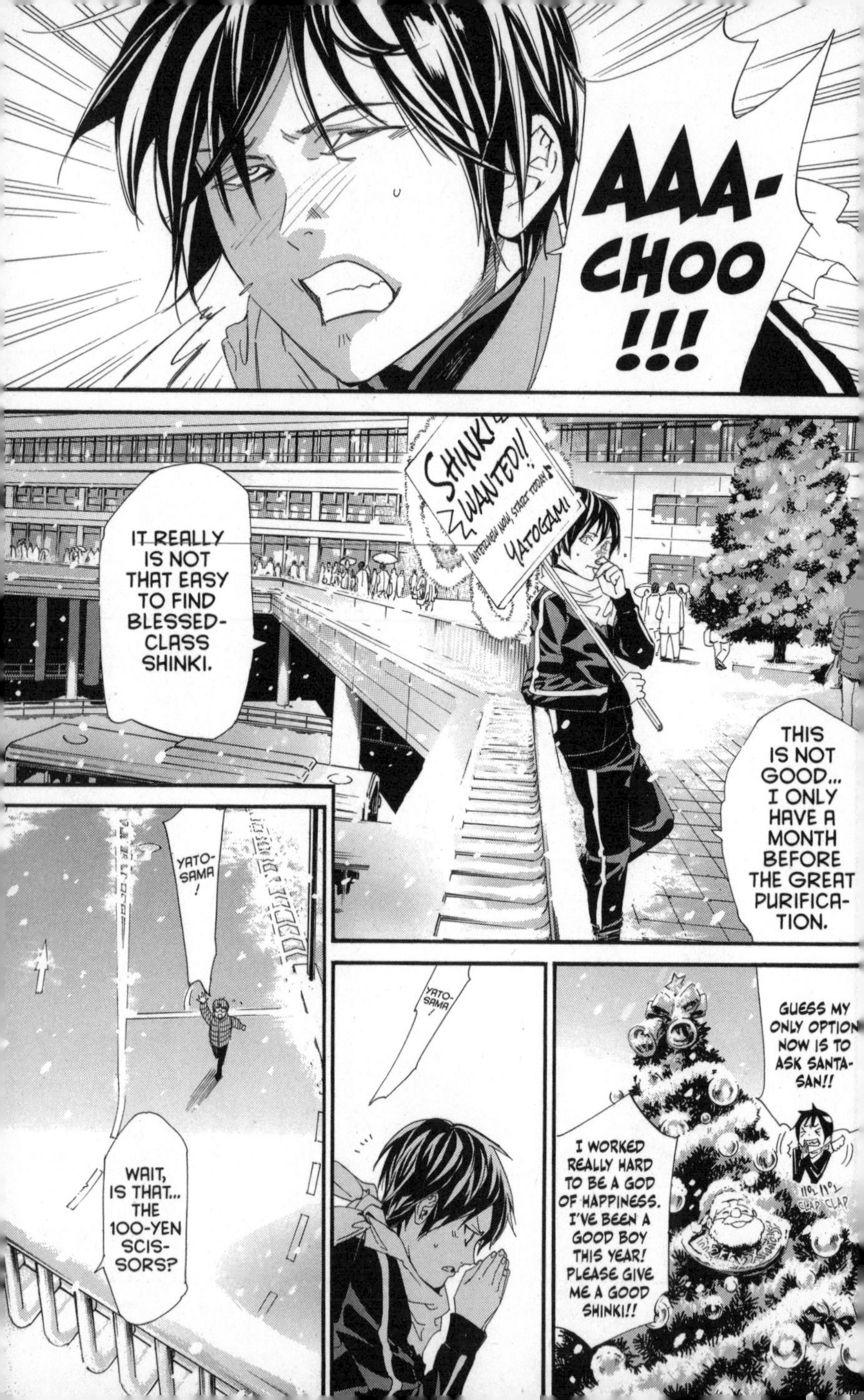
AAA-CHOO!!!
SHINKI WANTED!! INTERVIEW NOW, START TODAY! YATOGAMI
IT REALLY IS NOT THAT EASY TO FIND BLESSED-CLASS SHINKI.
THIS IS NOT GOOD... I ONLY HAVE A MONTH BEFORE THE GREAT PURIFICATION.
GUESS MY ONLY OPTION NOW IS TO ASK SANTA-SAN!!
CLAP CLAP
I WORKED REALLY HARD TO BE A GOD OF HAPPINESS. I'VE BEEN A GOOD BOY THIS YEAR! PLEASE GIVE ME A GOOD SHINKI!!
YATO-SAMA!
...
YATO-SAMA!
WAIT, IS THAT... THE 100-YEN SCISSORS?

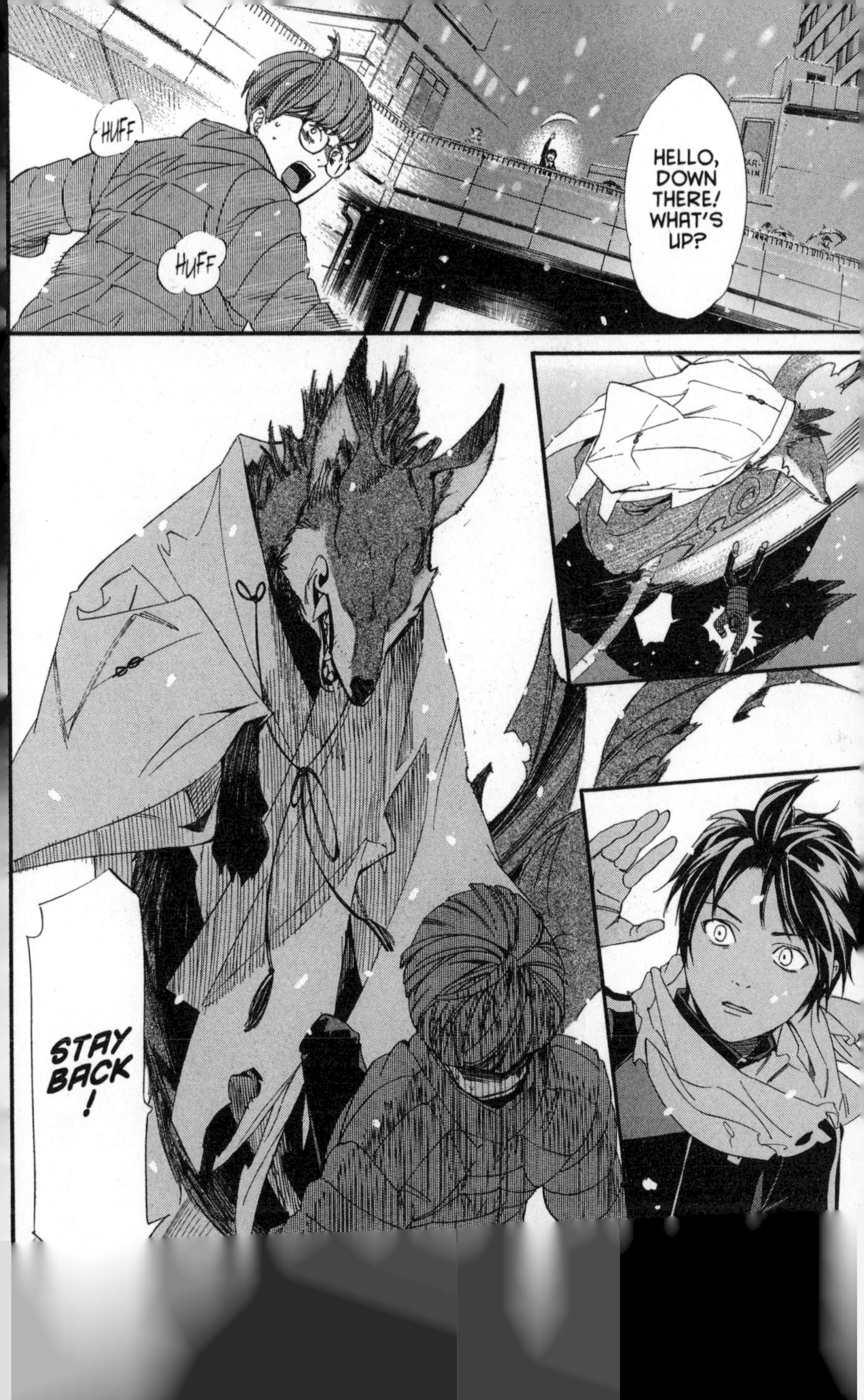
HELLO, DOWN THERE! WHAT'S UP?
HUFF
HUFF
STAY BACK!

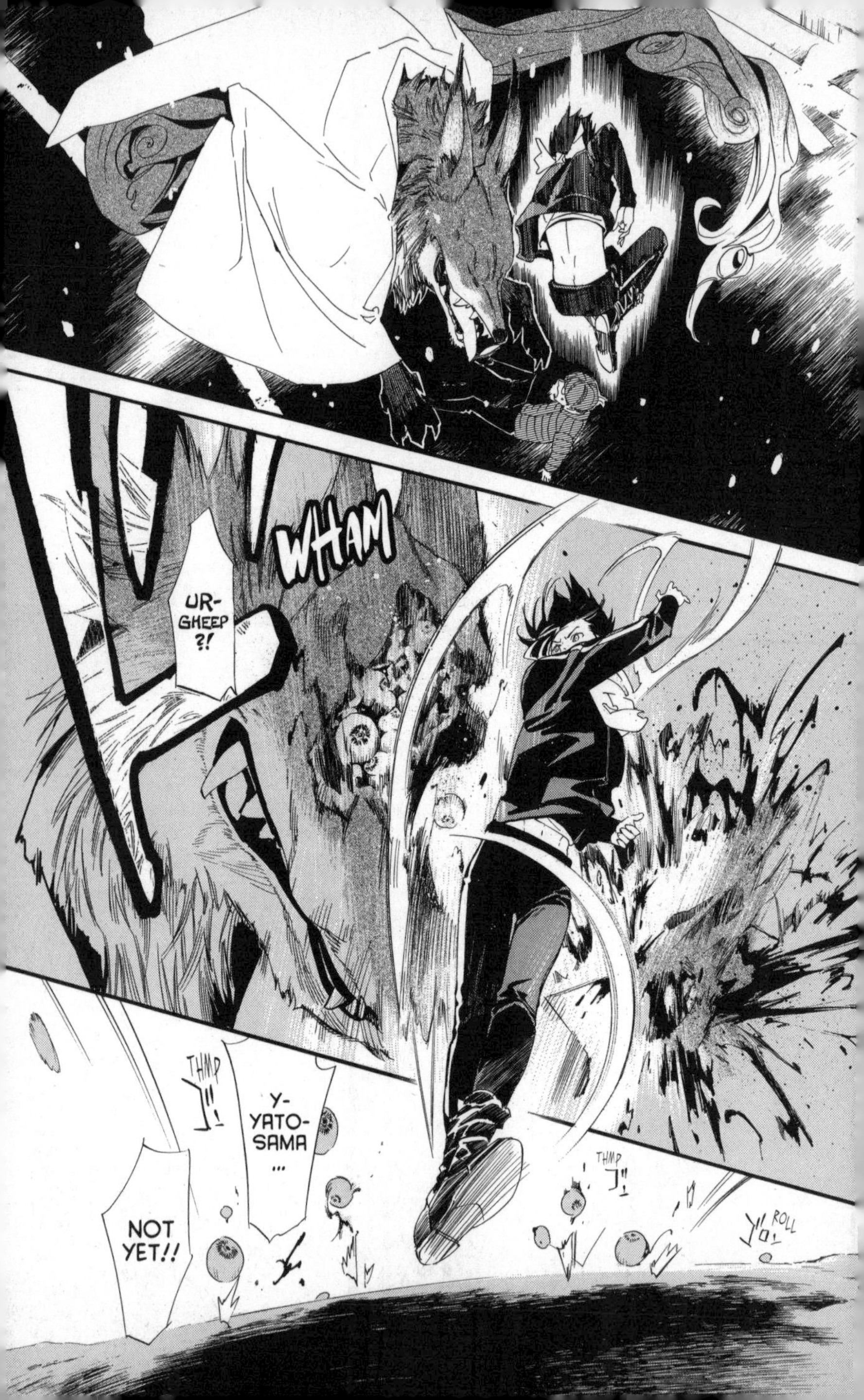
WHAM
UR-GHEEP ?!
THMP
Y-YATO-SAMA ...
NOT YET!!
THMP
ROLL

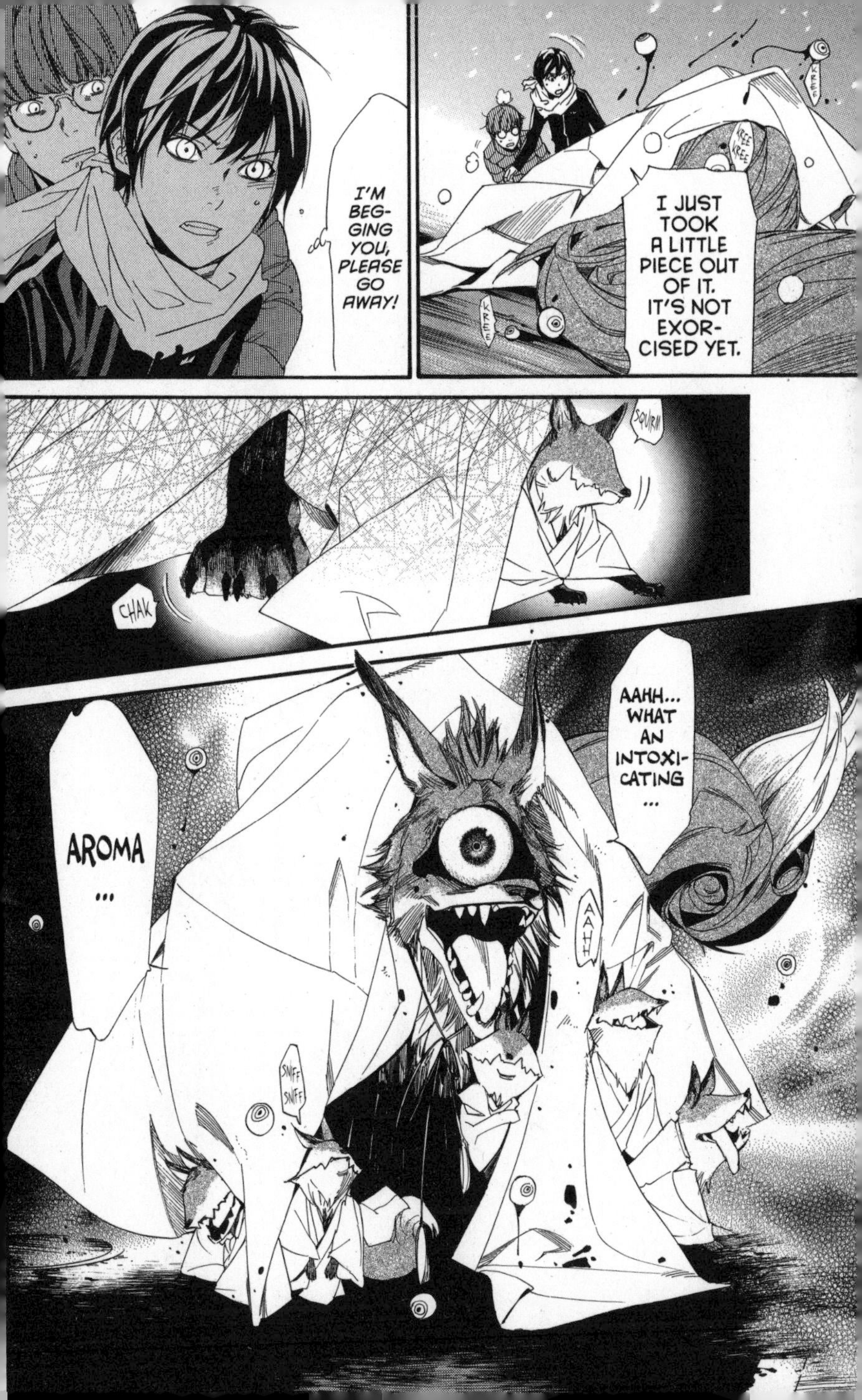
KREE
KREE KREE
I JUST TOOK A LITTLE PIECE OUT OF IT. IT'S NOT EXORCISED YET.
KREE
I'M BEGGING YOU, PLEASE GO AWAY!
SQUIRM
CHAK
AAHH... WHAT AN INTOXICATING...
AAHH
SNIFF SNIFF
AROMA...

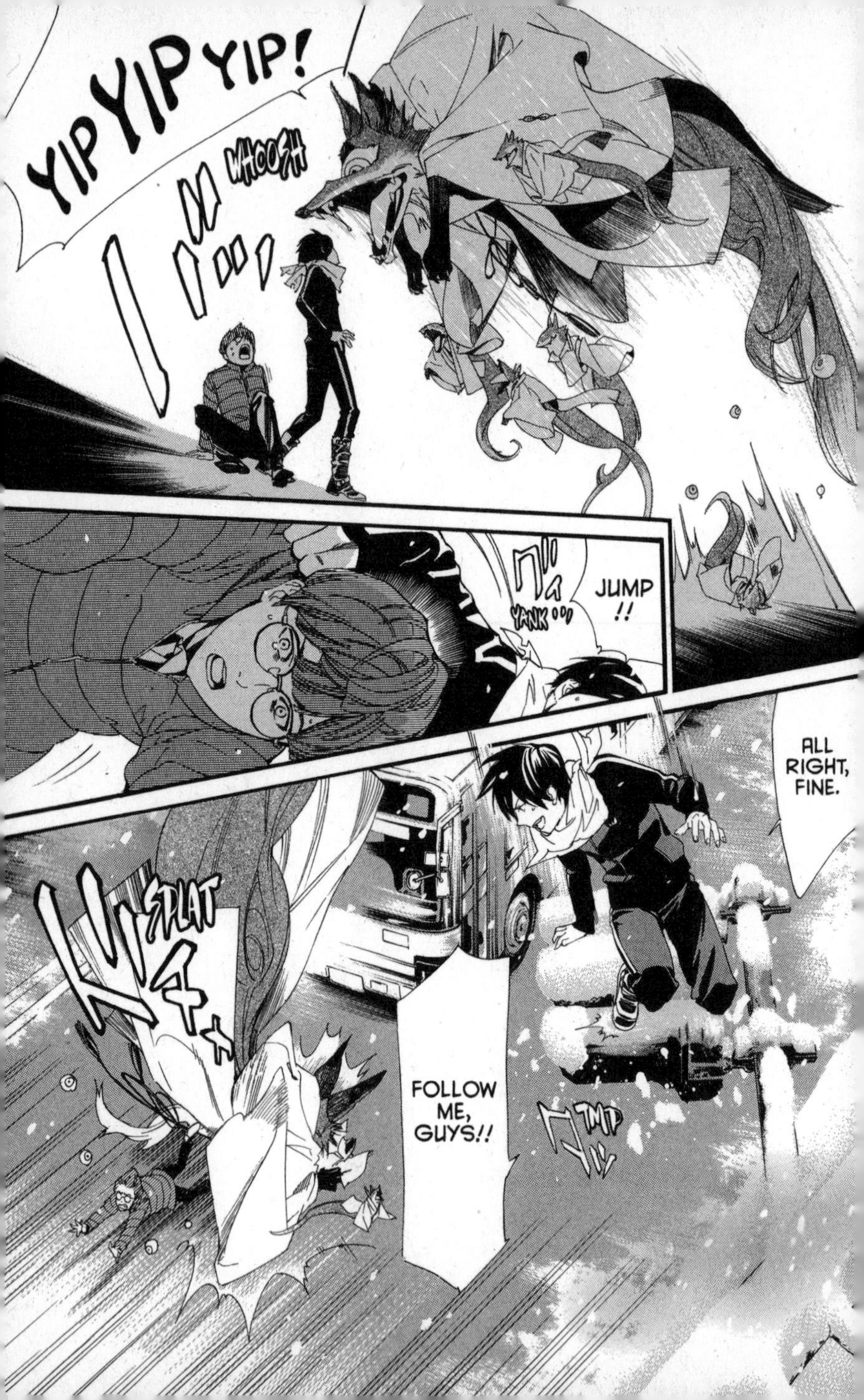
YIP YIP YIP!
WHOOSH
JUMP!!
YANK
ALL RIGHT, FINE.
FOLLOW ME, GUYS!!
TMP
SPLAT

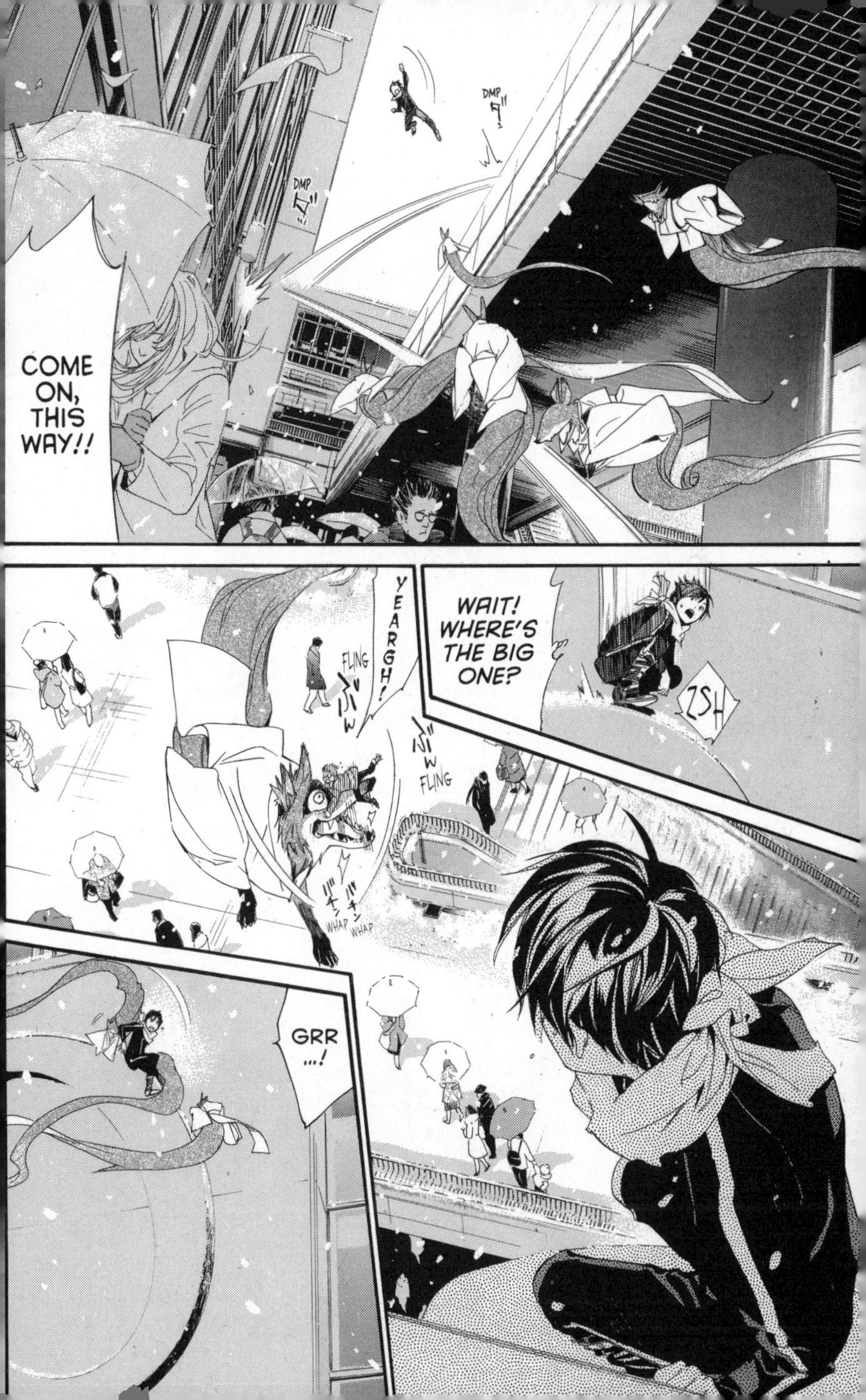
DMP ダッ
DMP ダッ
COME ON, THIS WAY!!
WAIT! WHERE'S THE BIG ONE?
ZSH
YEARGH!
FLING バッ
バッ FLING
バチン WHAP
バチン WHAP
GRR ...!

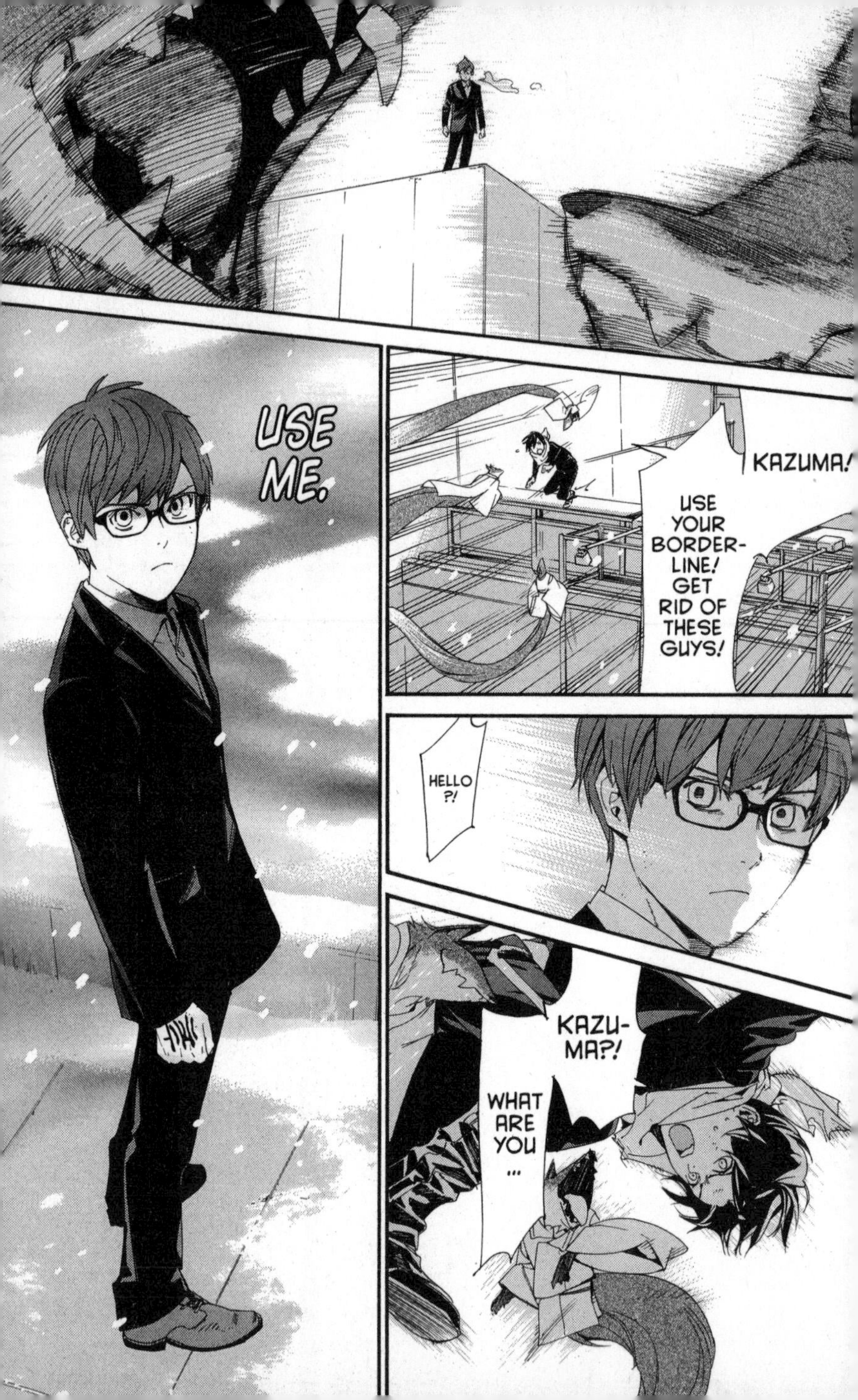
KAZUMA!
USE YOUR BORDER-LINE! GET RID OF THESE GUYS!
HELLO ?!
KAZU-MA?!
WHAT ARE YOU ...
USE ME.

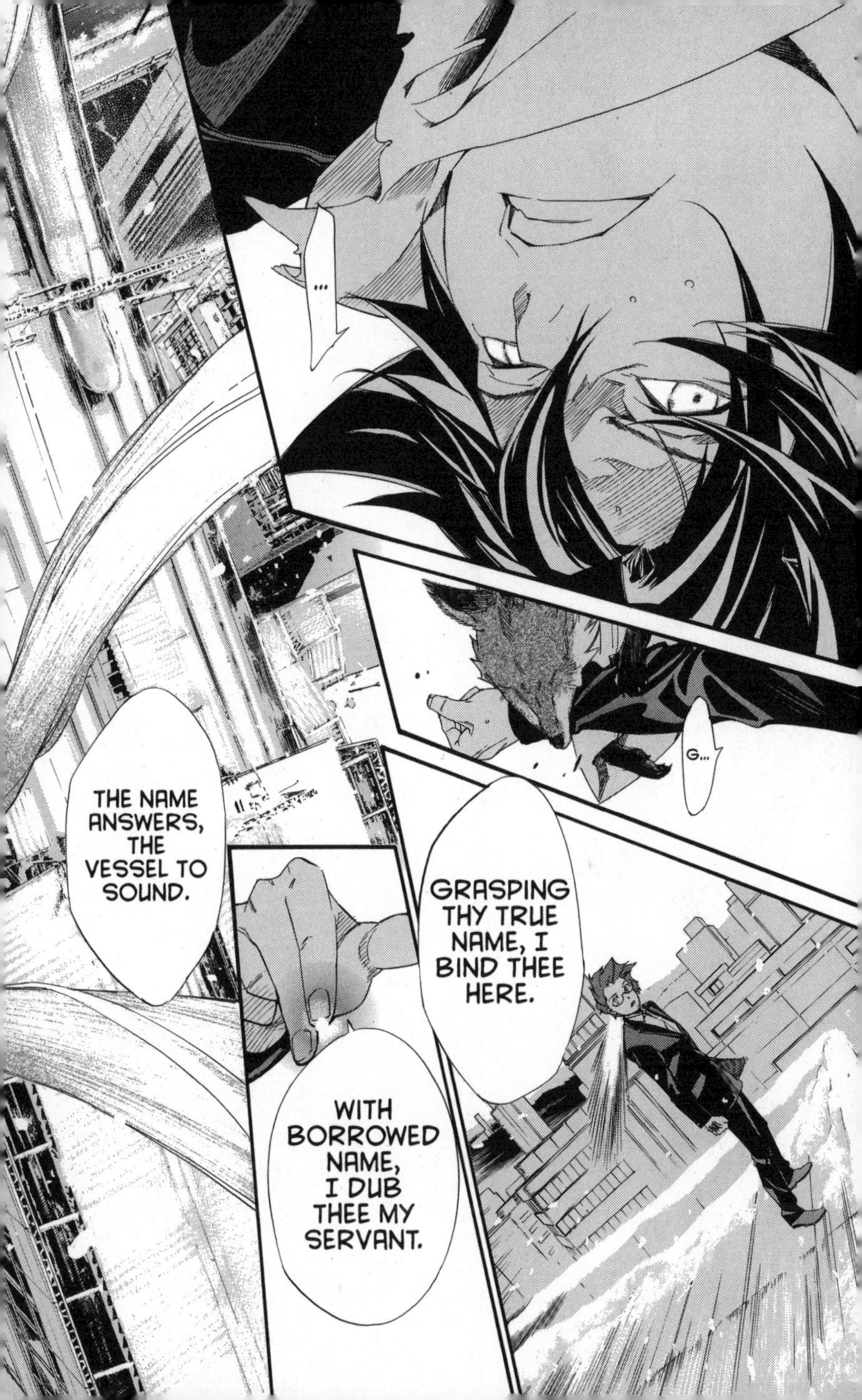
...
G...
GRASPING THY TRUE NAME, I BIND THEE HERE.
WITH BORROWED NAME, I DUB THEE MY SERVANT.
THE NAME ANSWERS, THE VESSEL TO SOUND.

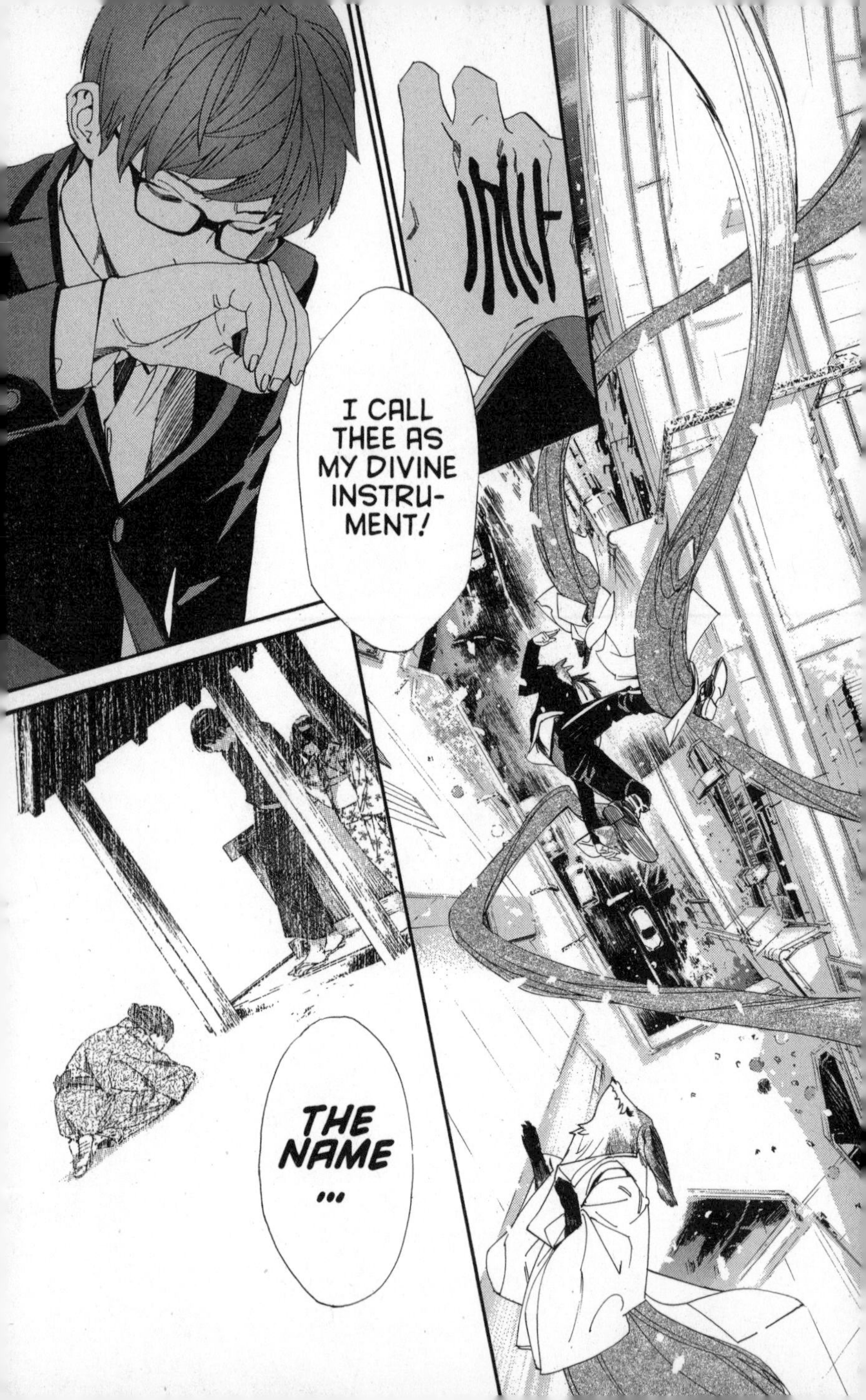
I CALL THEE AS MY DIVINE INSTRU-MENT!
THE NAME ...

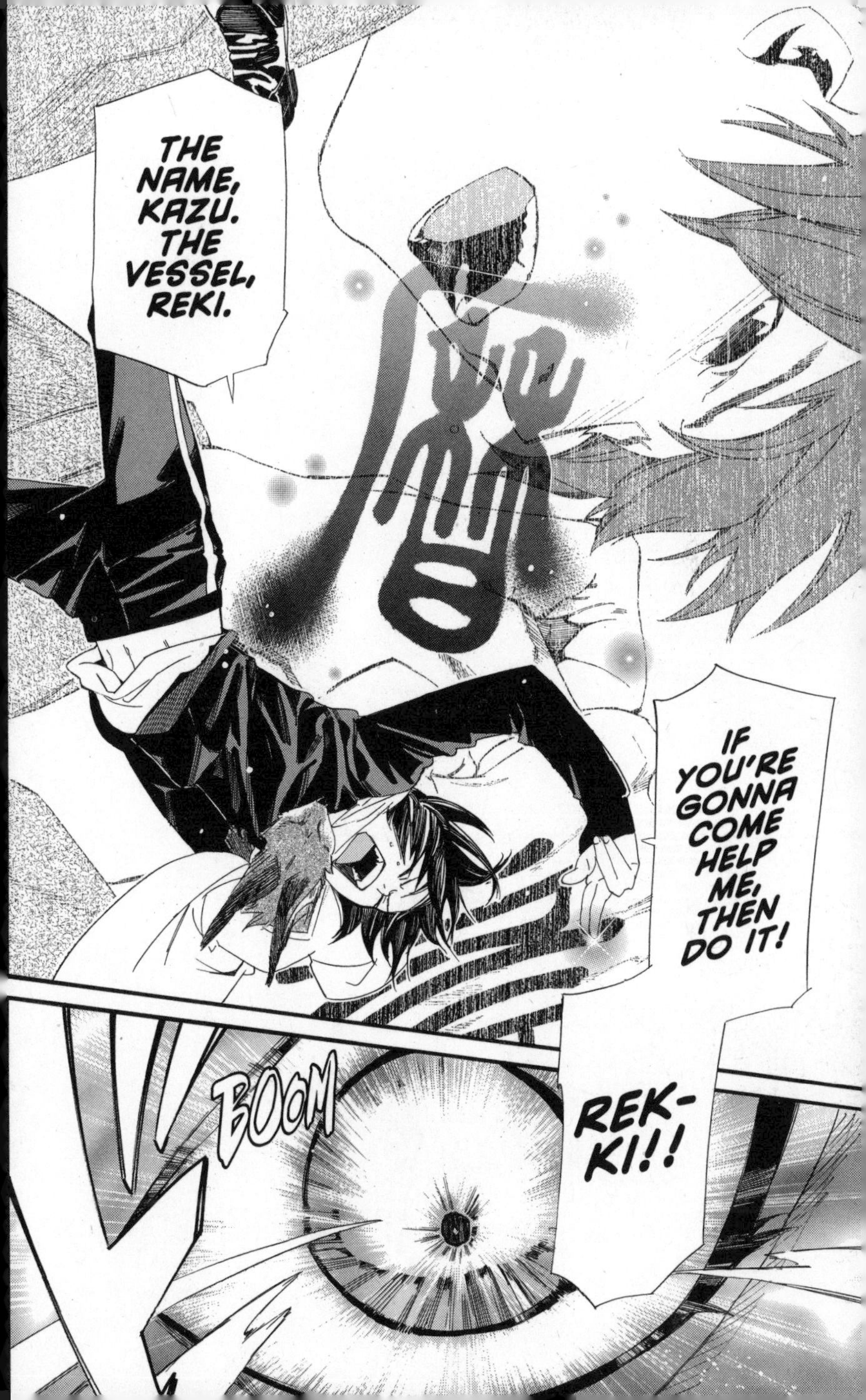
THE NAME, KAZU. THE VESSEL, REKI.
IF YOU'RE GONNA COME HELP ME, THEN DO IT!
REK-KI!!
BOOM

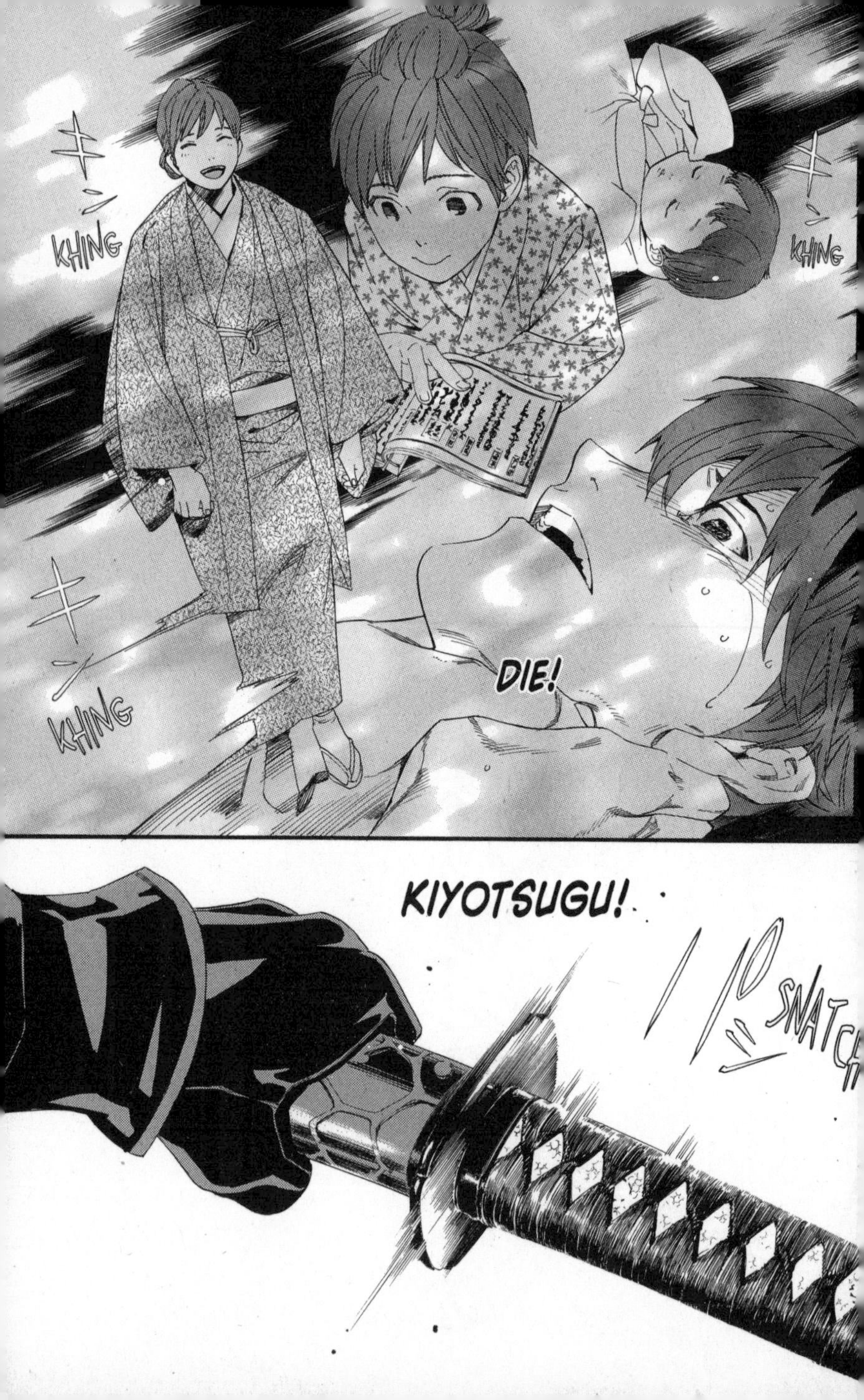
KHING
KHING
KHING
DIE!
KIYOTSUGU!
SNATCH

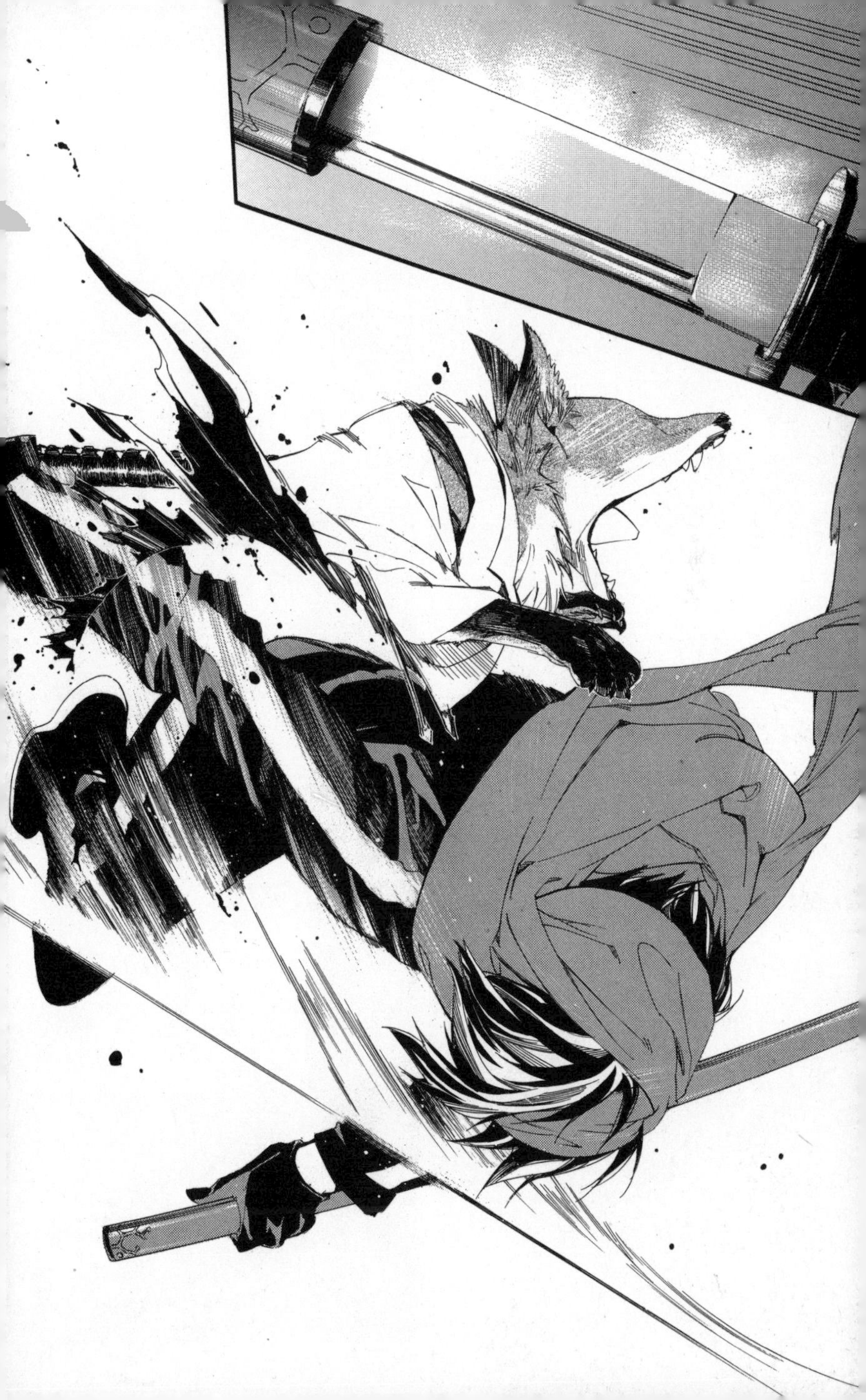

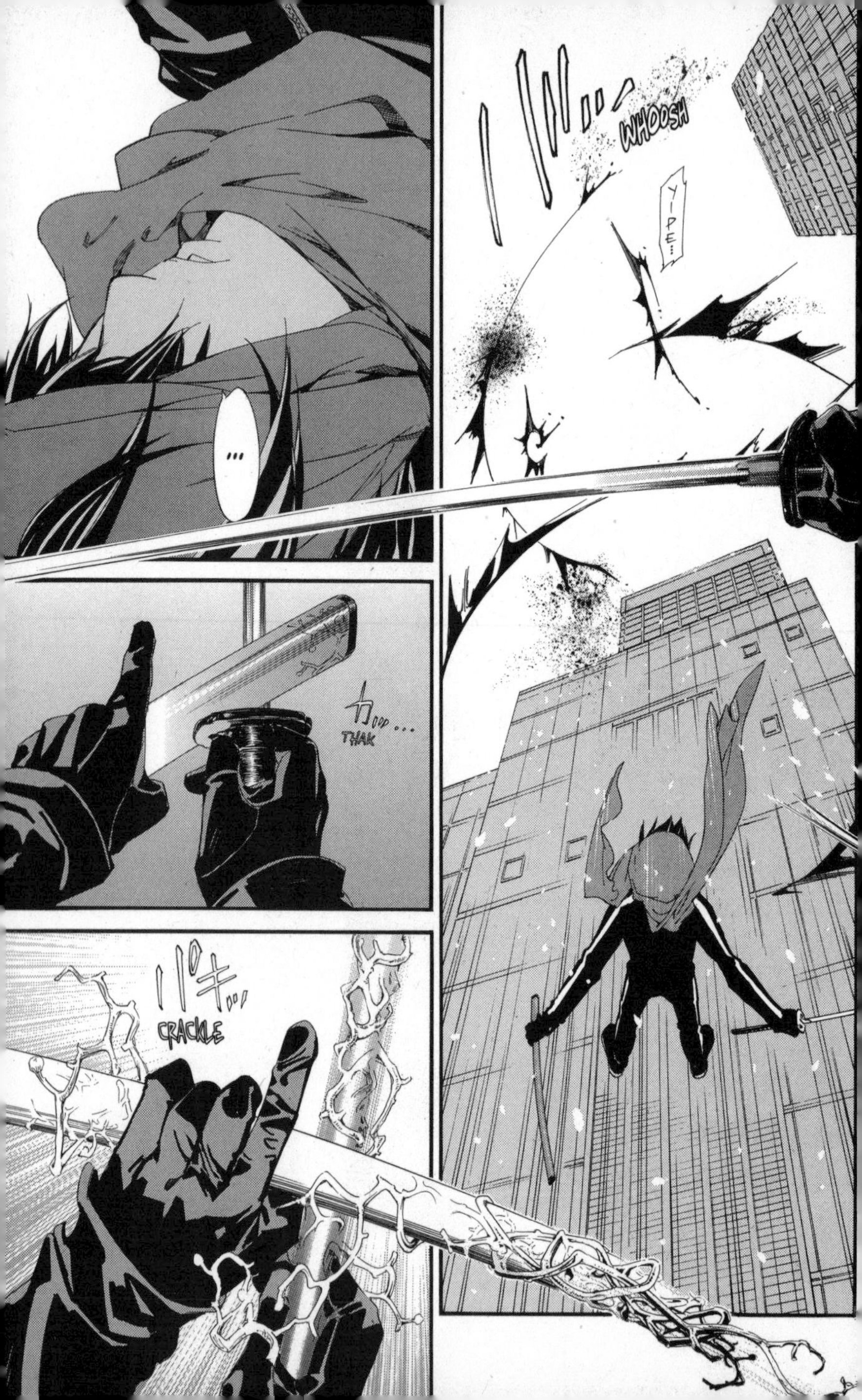
WHOOSH
YIPE...
...
THAK
CRACKLE

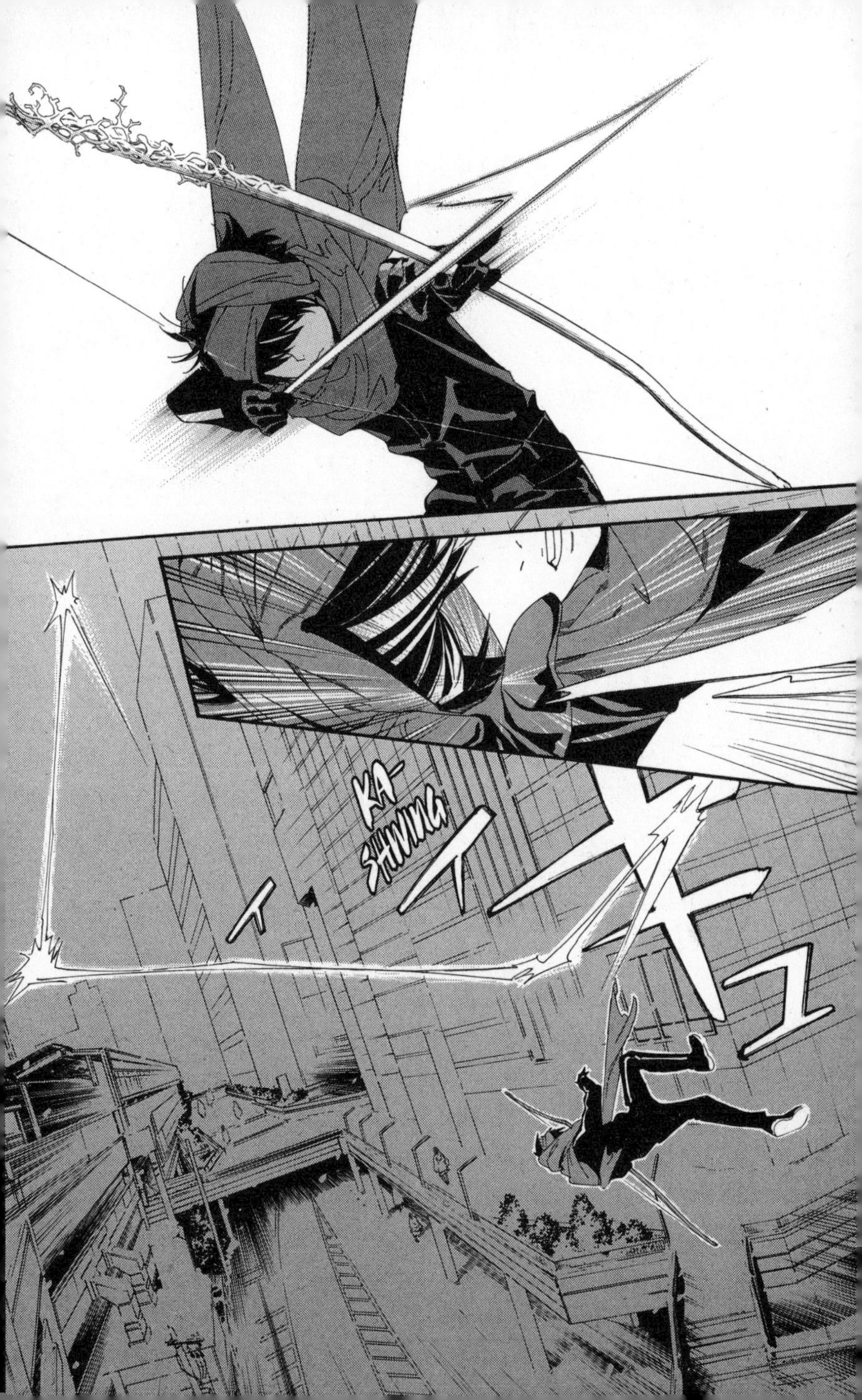
KA-SHWING

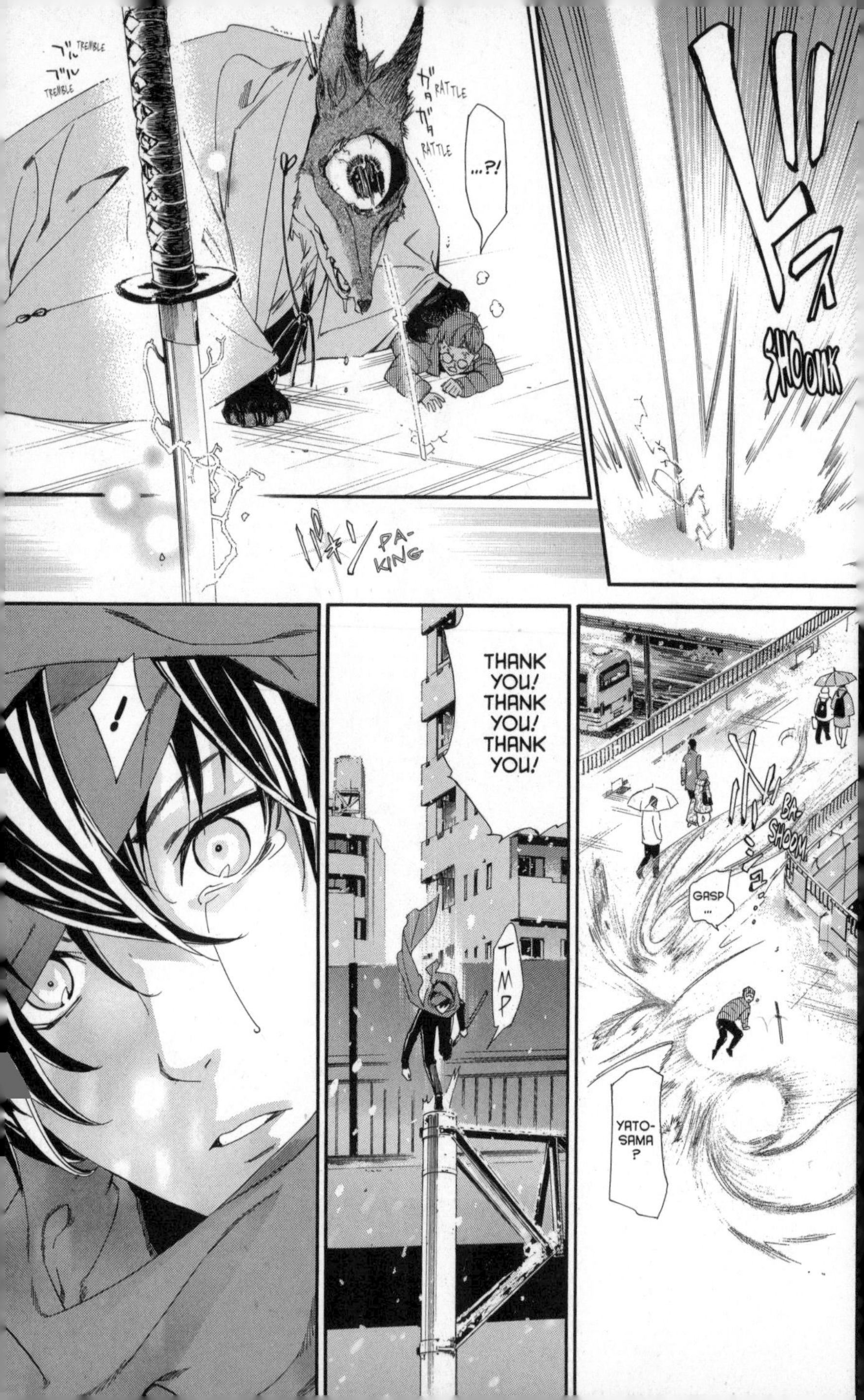
SHOOWK
TREMBLE
TREMBLE
RATTLE
RATTLE
...?!
PA-KING
BA-SHOOM
GASP...
YATO-SAMA?
THANK YOU! THANK YOU! THANK YOU!
TMP
!

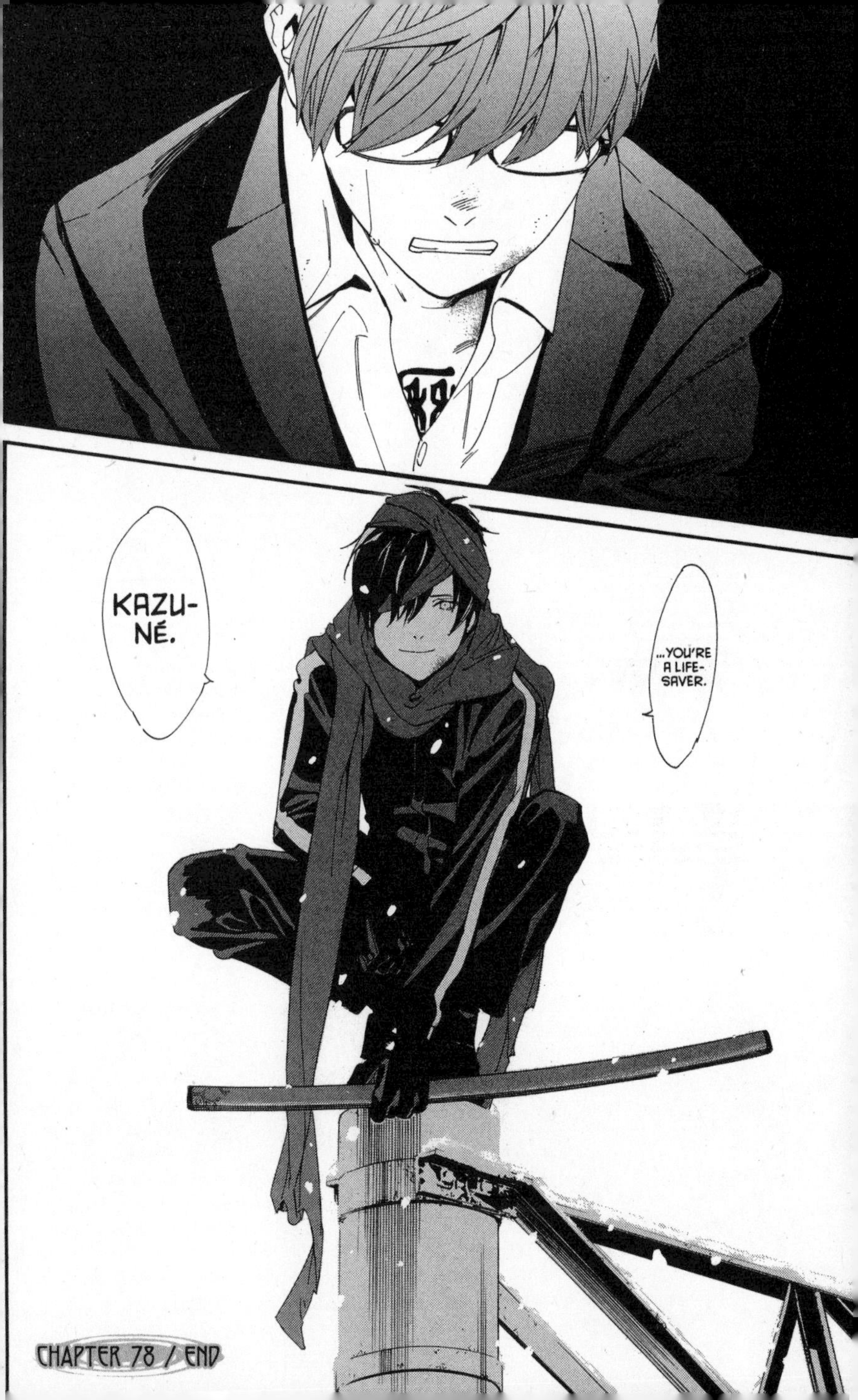
KAZUNÉ.
...YOU'RE A LIFE-SAVER.
CHAPTER 78 / END

野

異

神

[illegible]

[illegible]

師

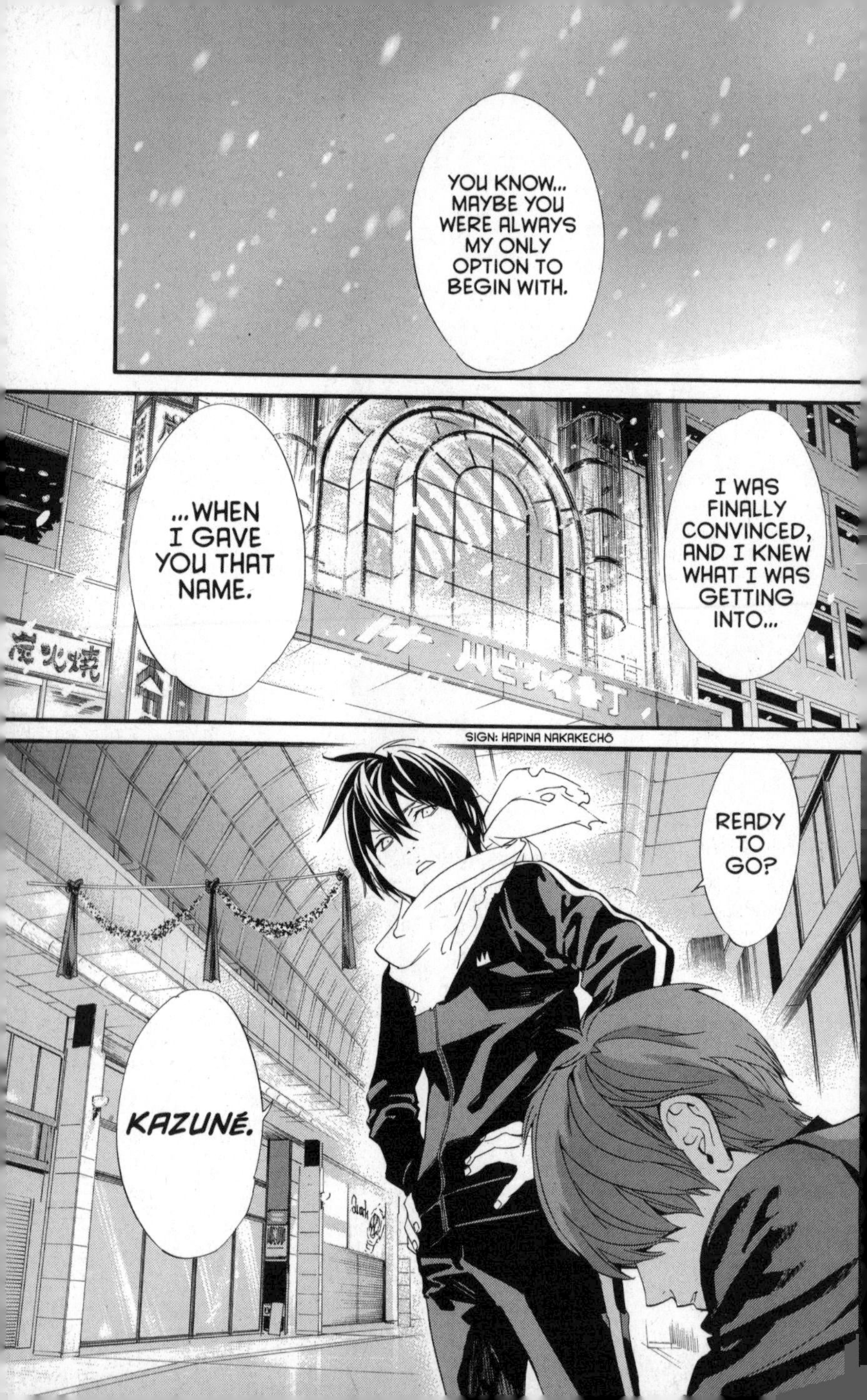
YOU KNOW... MAYBE YOU WERE ALWAYS MY ONLY OPTION TO BEGIN WITH.
I WAS FINALLY CONVINCED, AND I KNEW WHAT I WAS GETTING INTO...
...WHEN I GAVE YOU THAT NAME.
SIGN: HAPINA NAKAKECHŌ
READY TO GO?
KAZUNÉ.

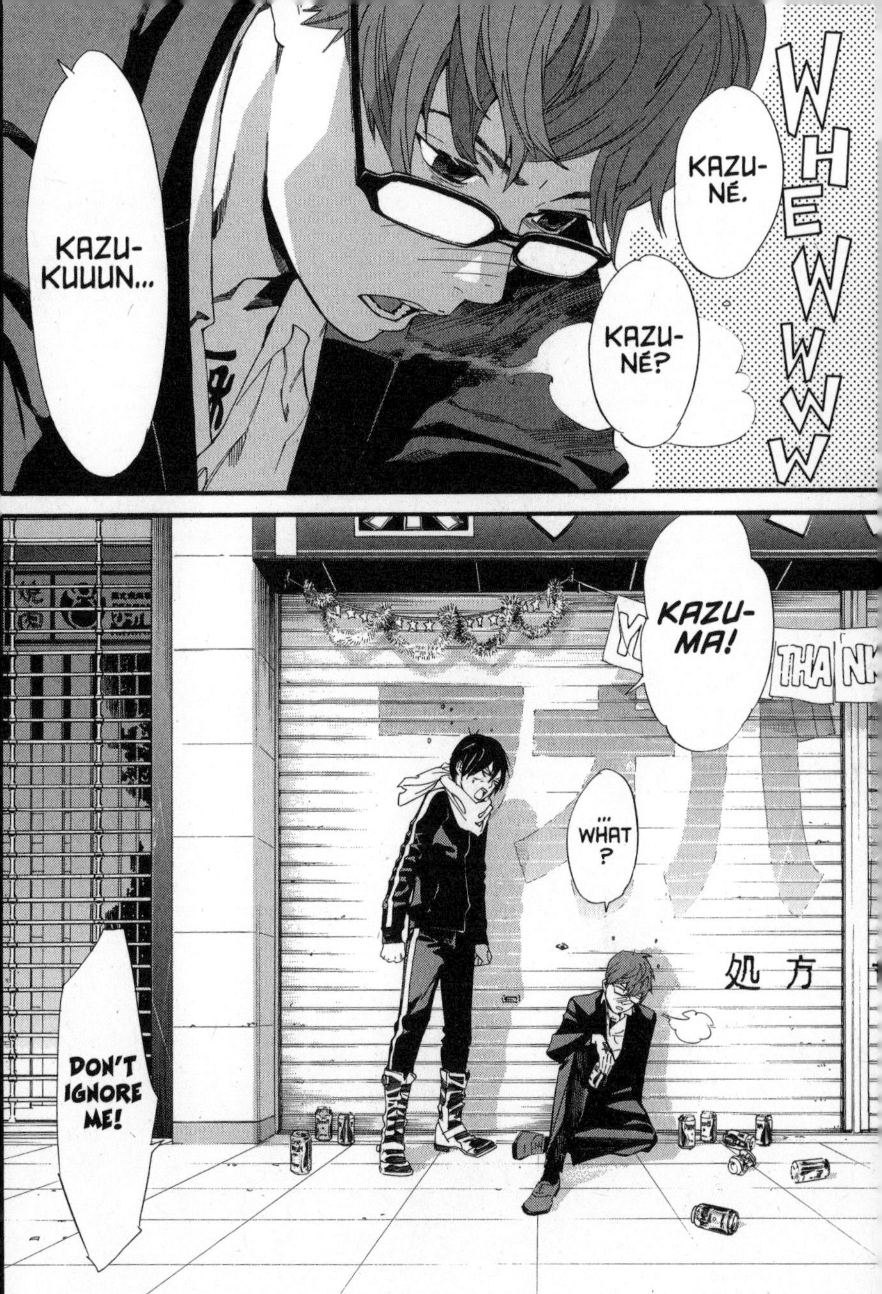
WHEWWWWW
KAZU-NÉ.
KAZU-NÉ?
KAZU-KUUUN...
KAZU-MA!
...WHAT?
DON'T IGNORE ME!
処方

CHAPTER 79: NEAR LOVE, FAR LOVE

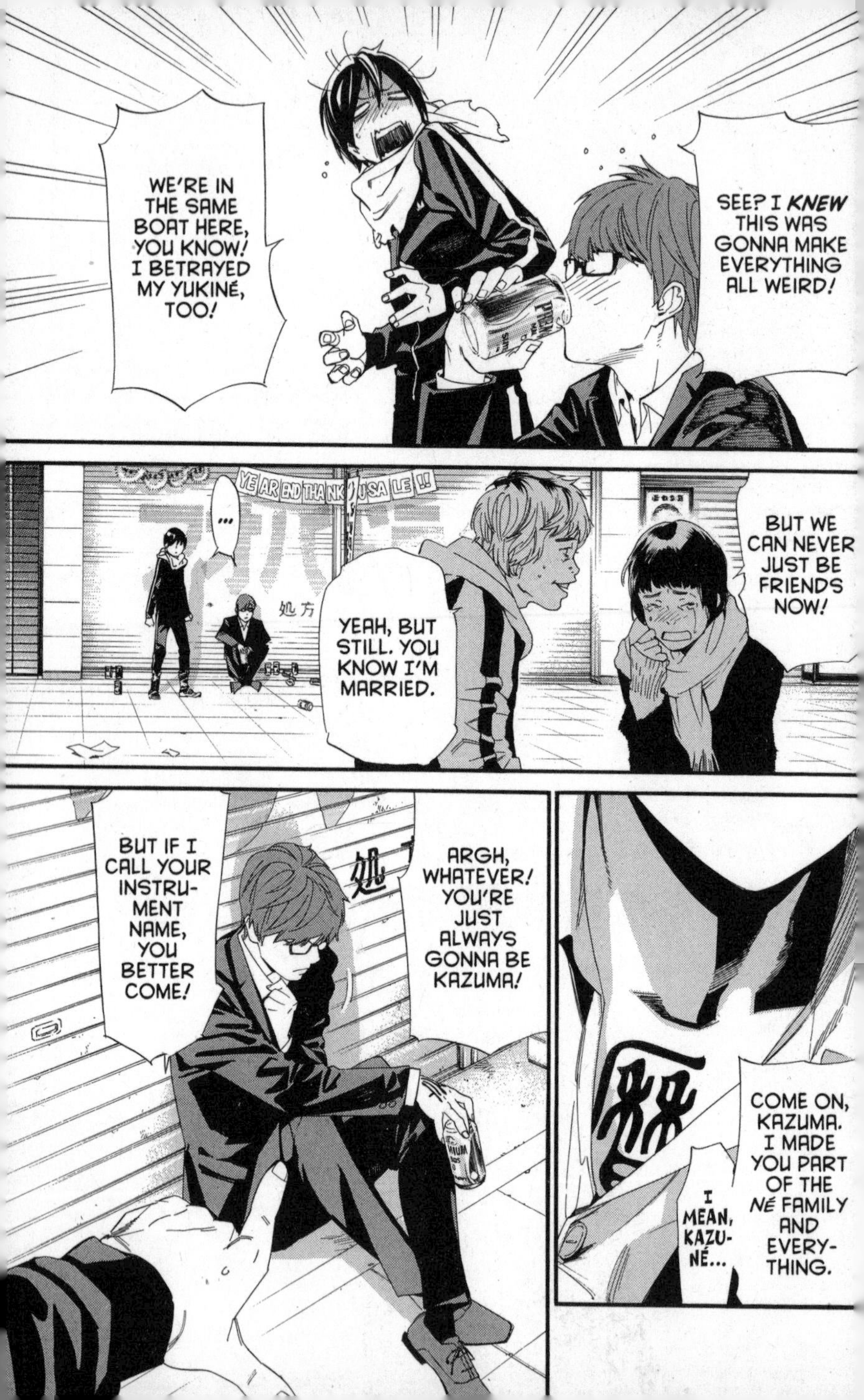
SEE? I *KNEW* THIS WAS GONNA MAKE EVERYTHING ALL WEIRD!
WE'RE IN THE SAME BOAT HERE, YOU KNOW! I BETRAYED MY YUKINÉ, TOO!
BUT WE CAN NEVER JUST BE FRIENDS NOW!
YEAH, BUT STILL. YOU KNOW I'M MARRIED.
YEAR END THANK U SALE!!
...
処方
COME ON, KAZUMA. I MADE YOU PART OF THE *NÉ* FAMILY AND EVERYTHING.
I MEAN, KAZU-NÉ...
ARGH, WHATEVER! YOU'RE JUST ALWAYS GONNA BE KAZUMA!
BUT IF I CALL YOUR INSTRUMENT NAME, YOU BETTER COME!

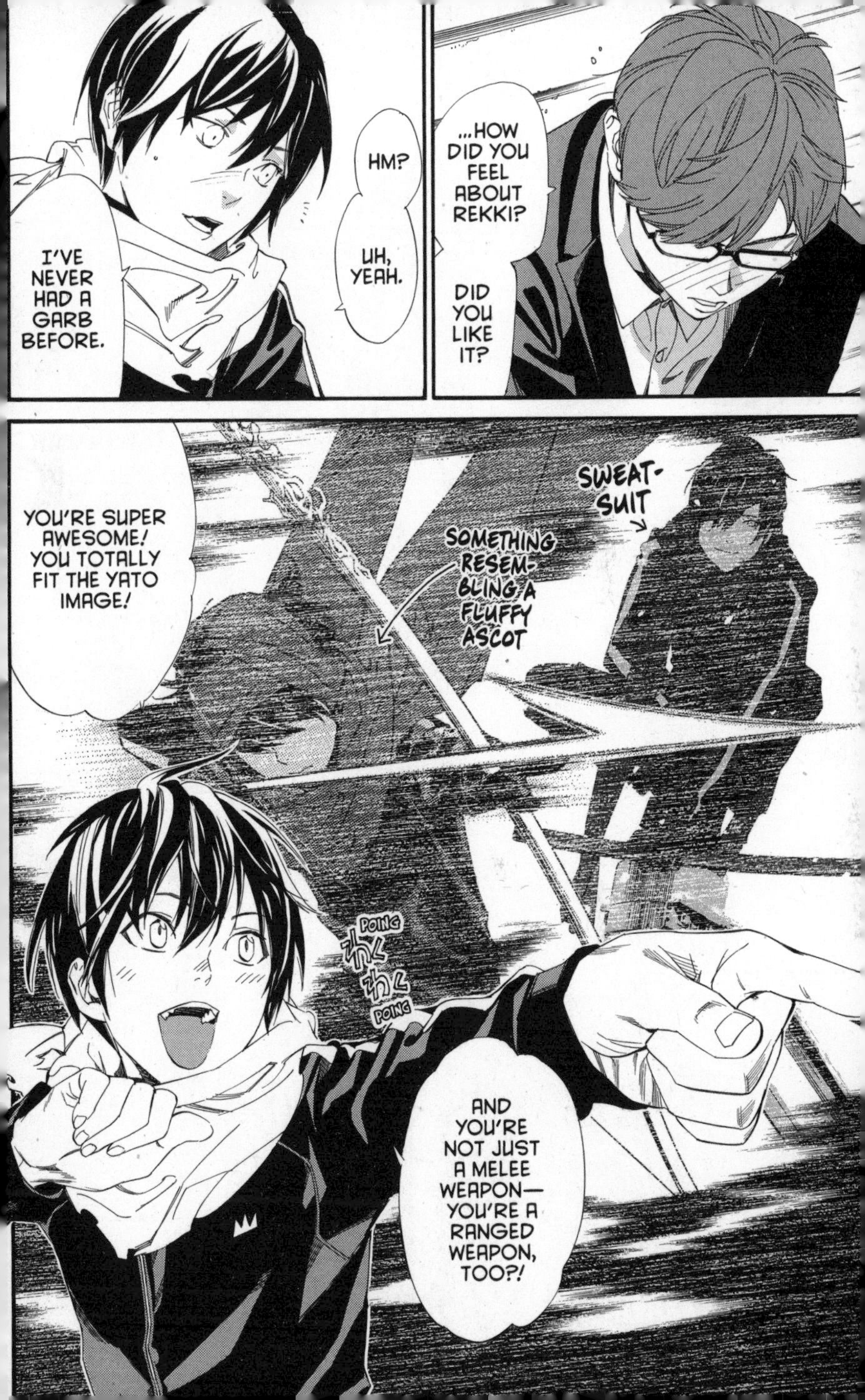
...HOW DID YOU FEEL ABOUT REKKI?
DID YOU LIKE IT?
HM?
UH, YEAH.
I'VE NEVER HAD A GARB BEFORE.
SWEAT-SUIT
SOMETHING RESEMBLING A FLUFFY ASCOT
YOU'RE SUPER AWESOME! YOU TOTALLY FIT THE YATO IMAGE!
POING
わく わく
POING
AND YOU'RE NOT JUST A MELEE WEAPON—YOU'RE A RANGED WEAPON, TOO?!

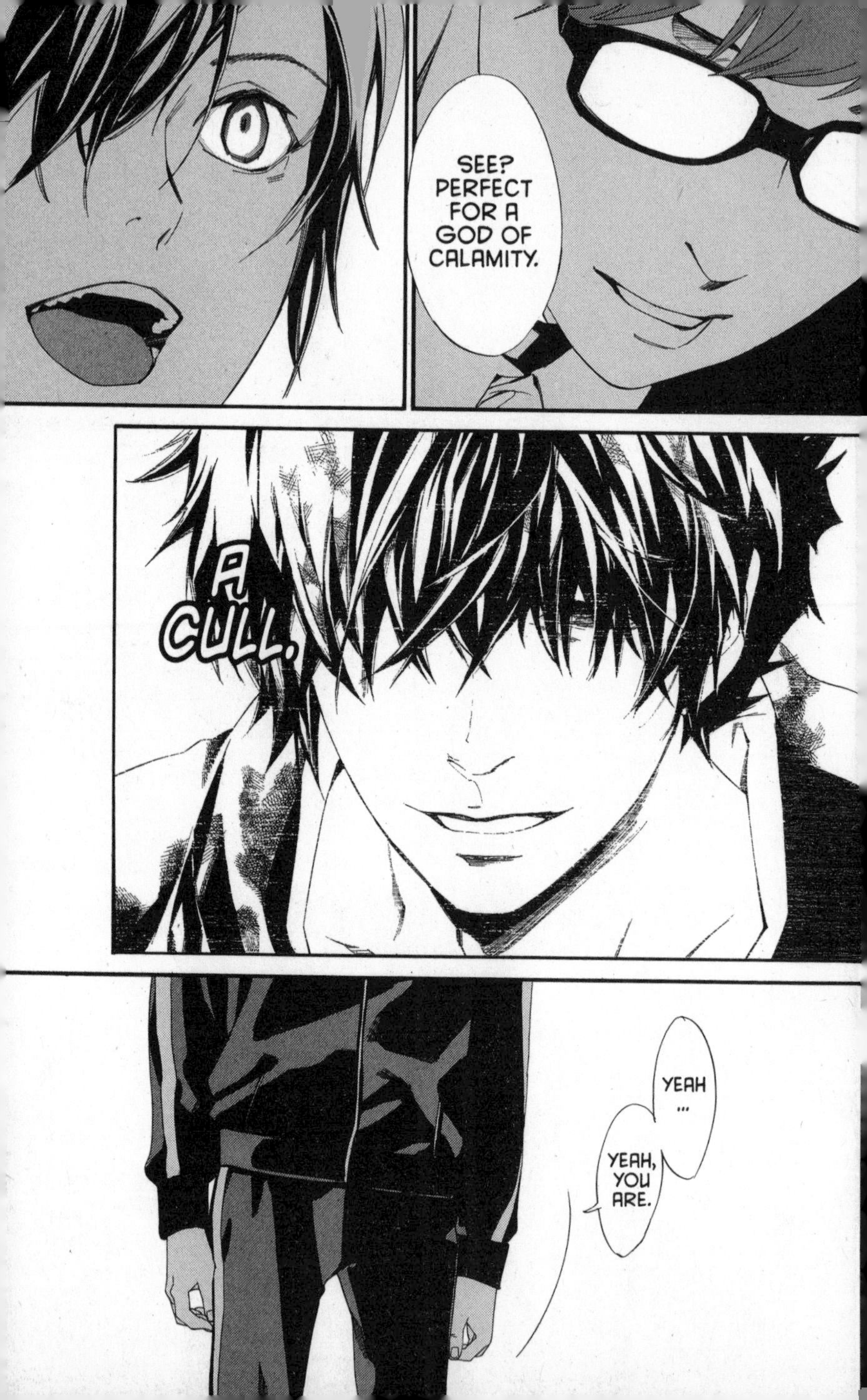
SEE? PERFECT FOR A GOD OF CALAMITY.
A CULL.
YEAH ...
YEAH, YOU ARE.

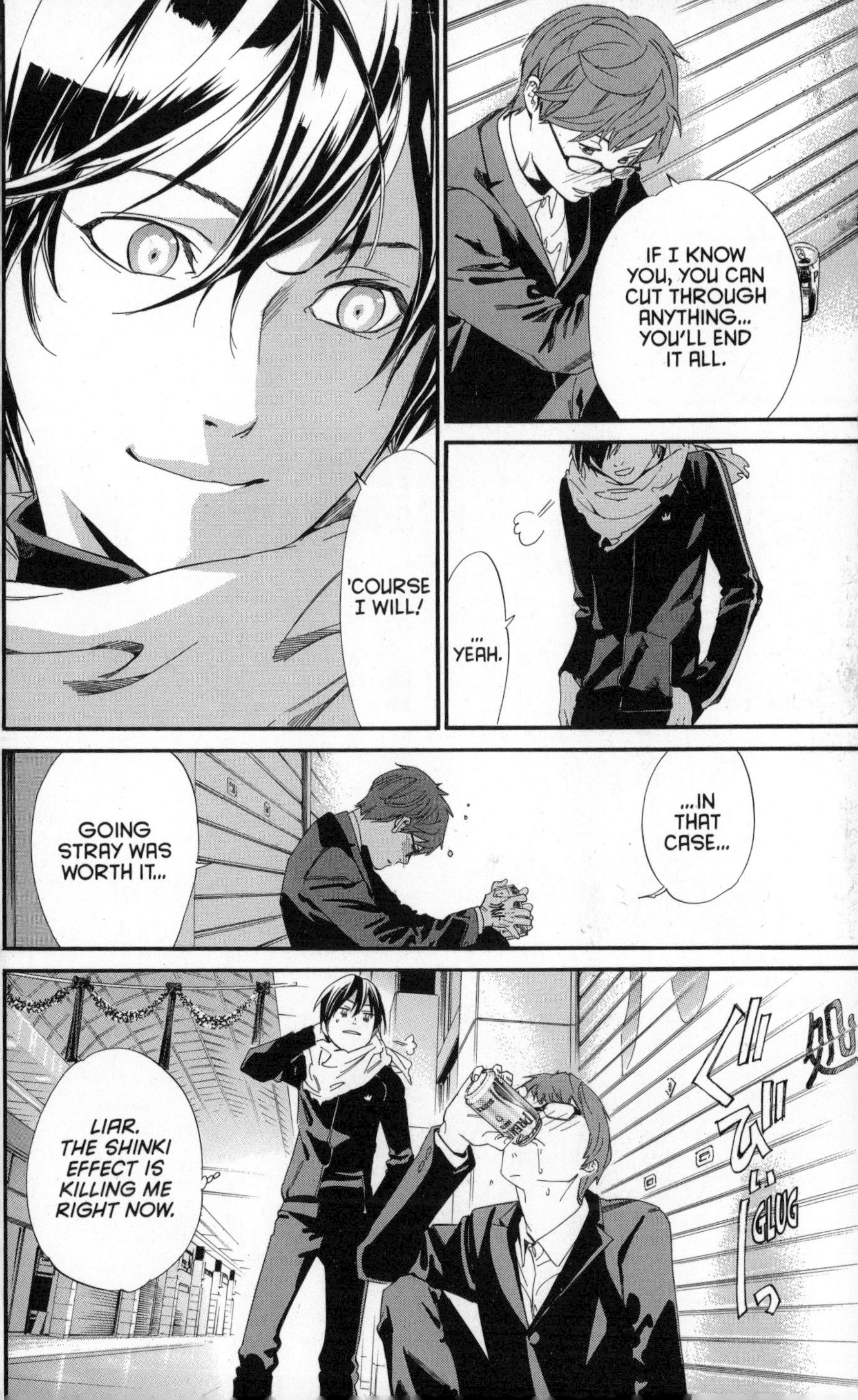
IF I KNOW YOU, YOU CAN CUT THROUGH ANYTHING... YOU'LL END IT ALL.
... YEAH.
'COURSE I WILL!
...IN THAT CASE...
GOING STRAY WAS WORTH IT...
GLUG
LIAR. THE SHINKI EFFECT IS KILLING ME RIGHT NOW.

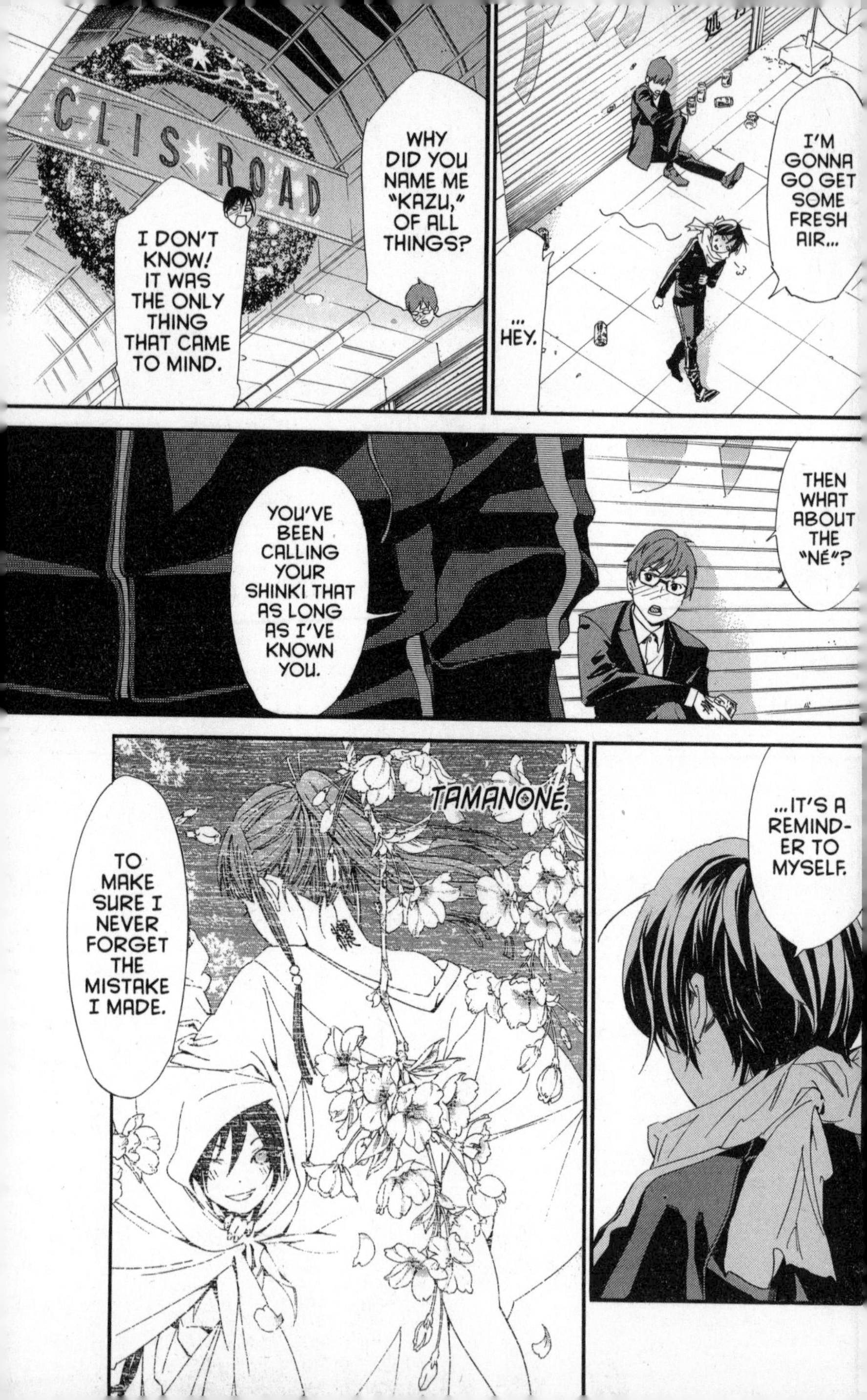
I'M GONNA GO GET SOME FRESH AIR...
...HEY.
CLIS ROAD
WHY DID YOU NAME ME "KAZU," OF ALL THINGS?
I DON'T KNOW! IT WAS THE ONLY THING THAT CAME TO MIND.
THEN WHAT ABOUT THE "NÉ"?
YOU'VE BEEN CALLING YOUR SHINKI THAT AS LONG AS I'VE KNOWN YOU.
...IT'S A REMINDER TO MYSELF.
TAMANONÉ.
TO MAKE SURE I NEVER FORGET THE MISTAKE I MADE.

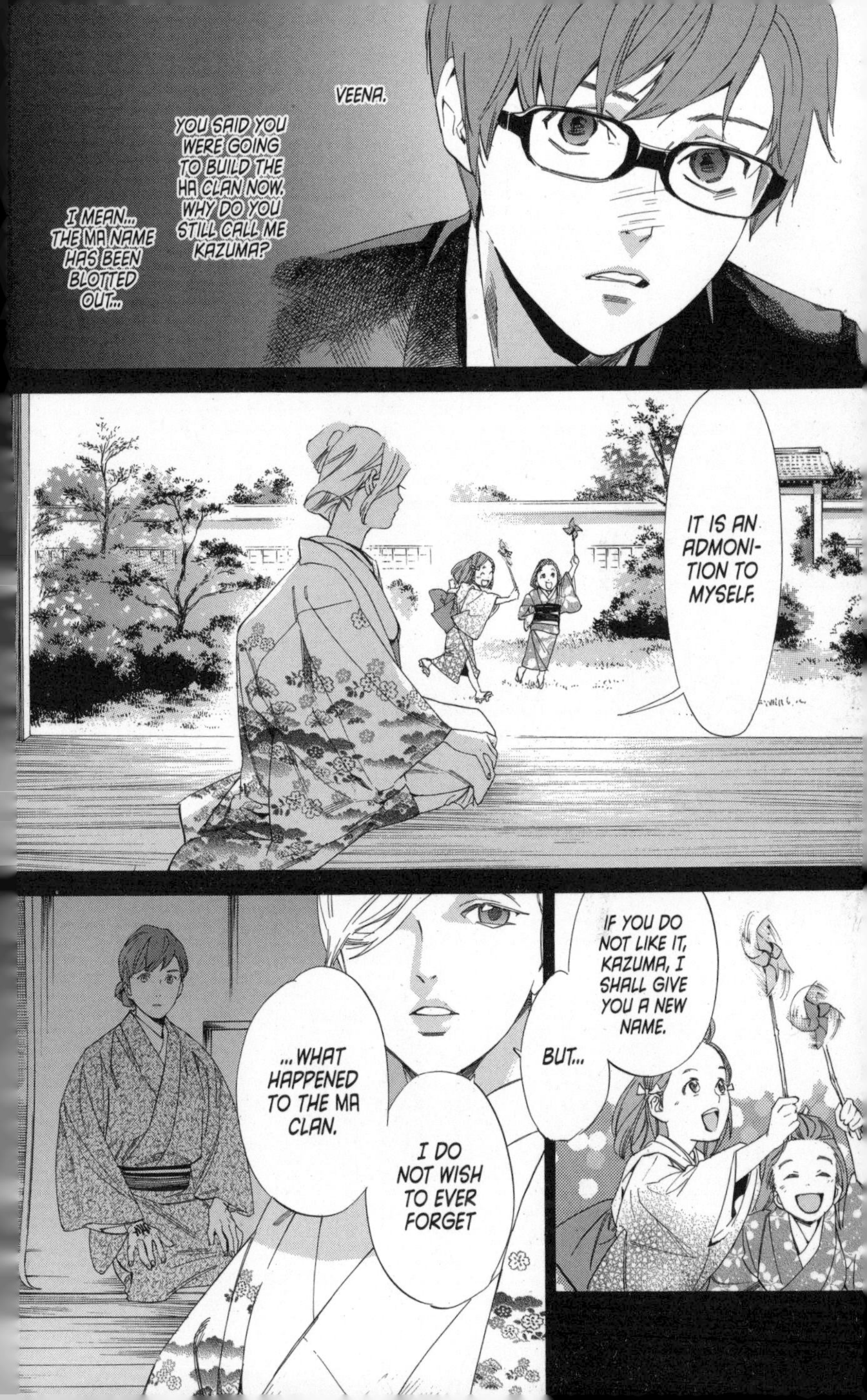
VEENA.
YOU SAID YOU WERE GOING TO BUILD THE HA CLAN NOW. WHY DO YOU STILL CALL ME KAZUMA?
I MEAN... THE MA NAME HAS BEEN BLOTTED OUT...
IT IS AN ADMONITION TO MYSELF.
IF YOU DO NOT LIKE IT, KAZUMA, I SHALL GIVE YOU A NEW NAME.
BUT...
I DO NOT WISH TO EVER FORGET
...WHAT HAPPENED TO THE MA CLAN.

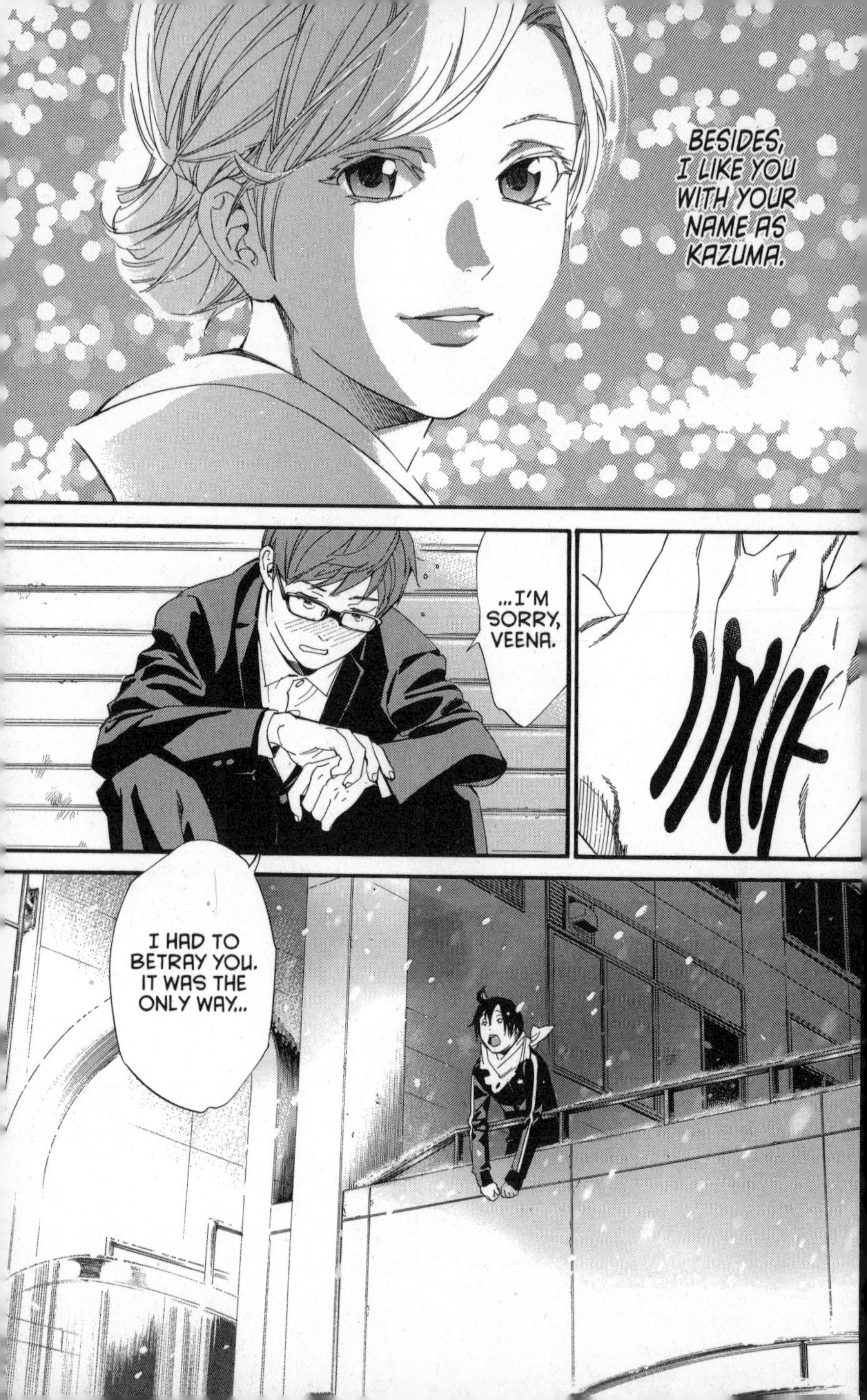
BESIDES, I LIKE YOU WITH YOUR NAME AS KAZUMA.
...I'M SORRY, VEENA.
I HAD TO BETRAY YOU. IT WAS THE ONLY WAY...

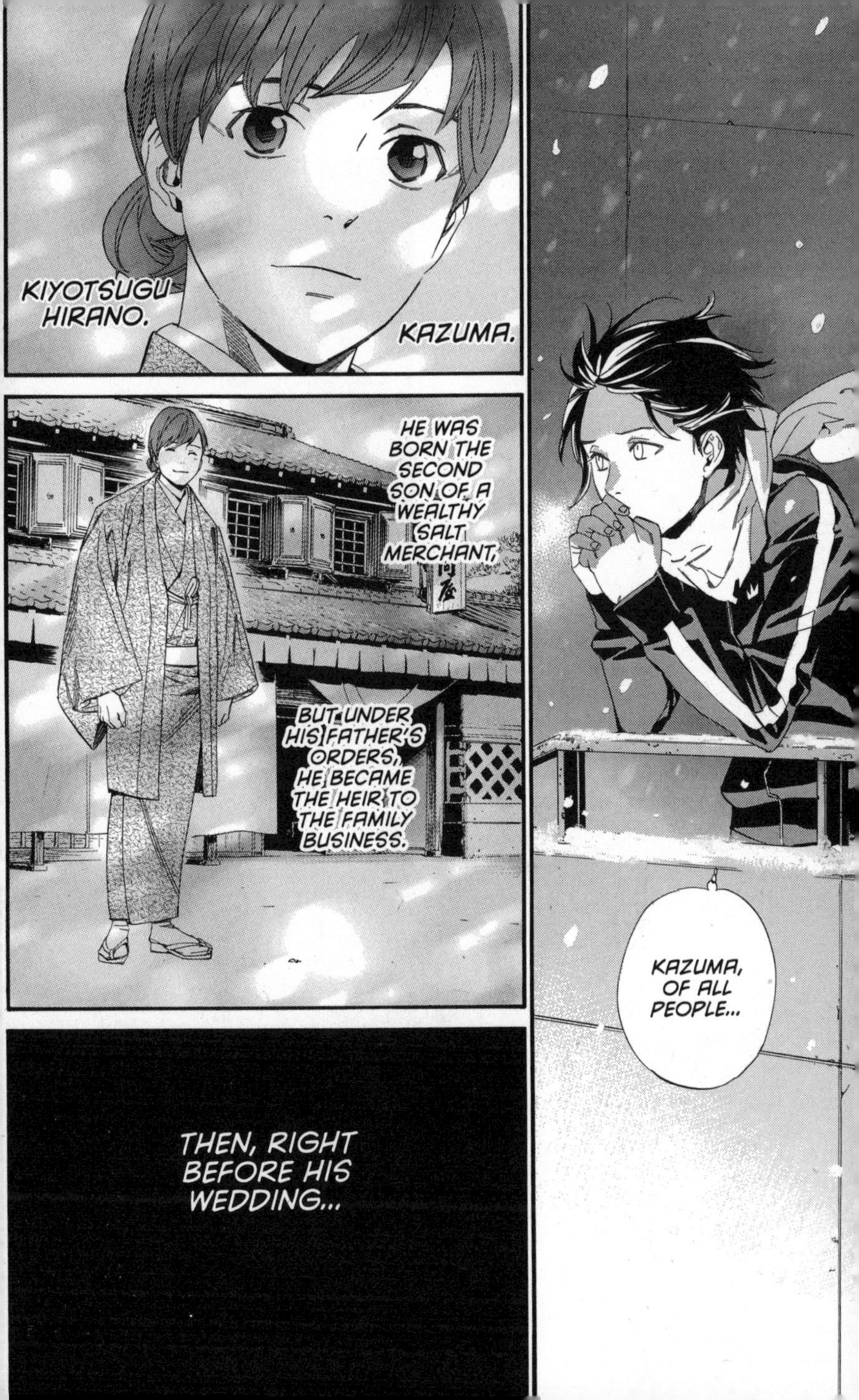
KAZUMA, OF ALL PEOPLE...
KAZUMA.
KIYOTSUGU HIRANO.
HE WAS BORN THE SECOND SON OF A WEALTHY SALT MERCHANT,
BUT UNDER HIS FATHER'S ORDERS, HE BECAME THE HEIR TO THE FAMILY BUSINESS.
THEN, RIGHT BEFORE HIS WEDDING...

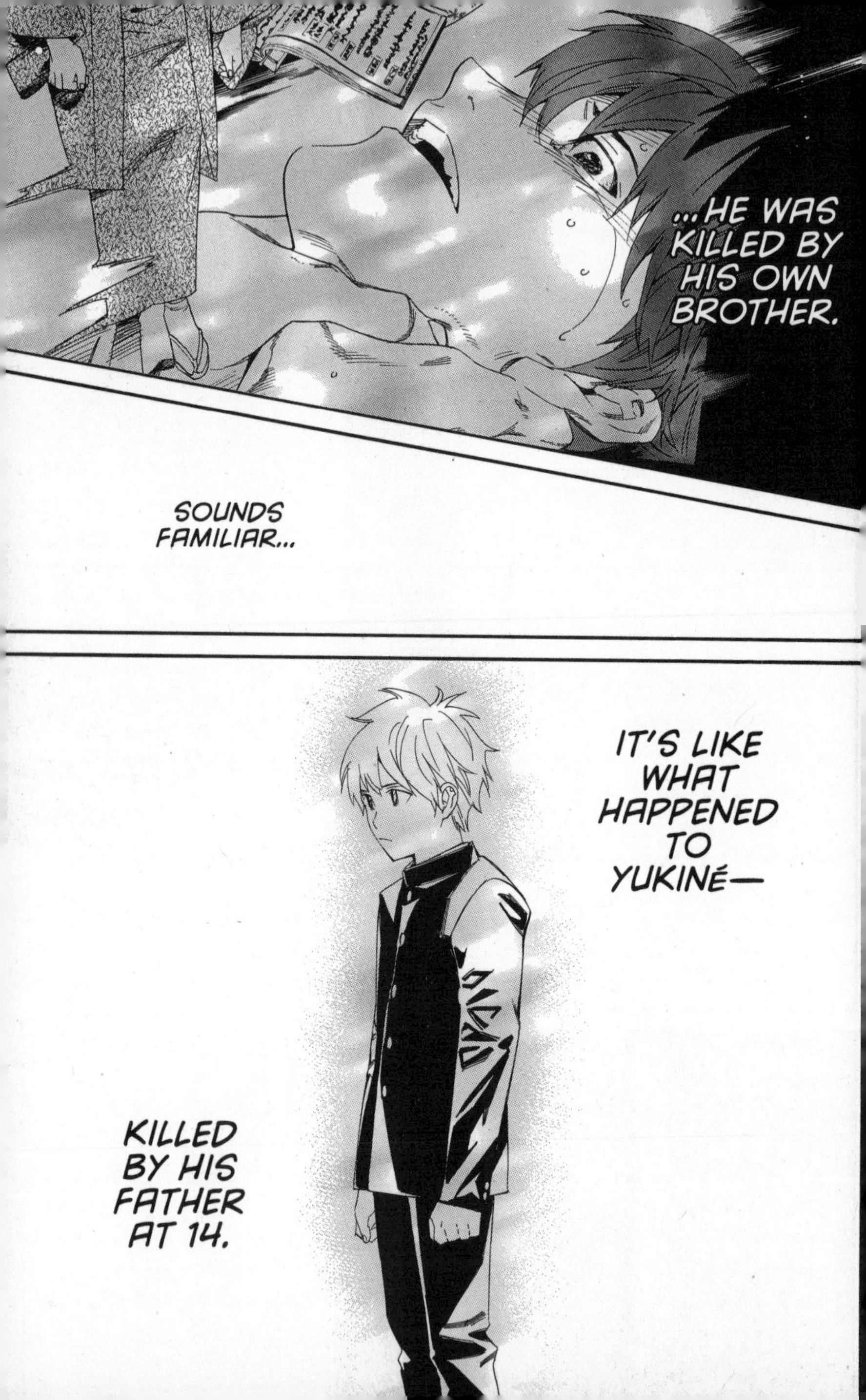
...HE WAS KILLED BY HIS OWN BROTHER.
SOUNDS FAMILIAR...
IT'S LIKE WHAT HAPPENED TO YUKINÉ—
KILLED BY HIS FATHER AT 14.

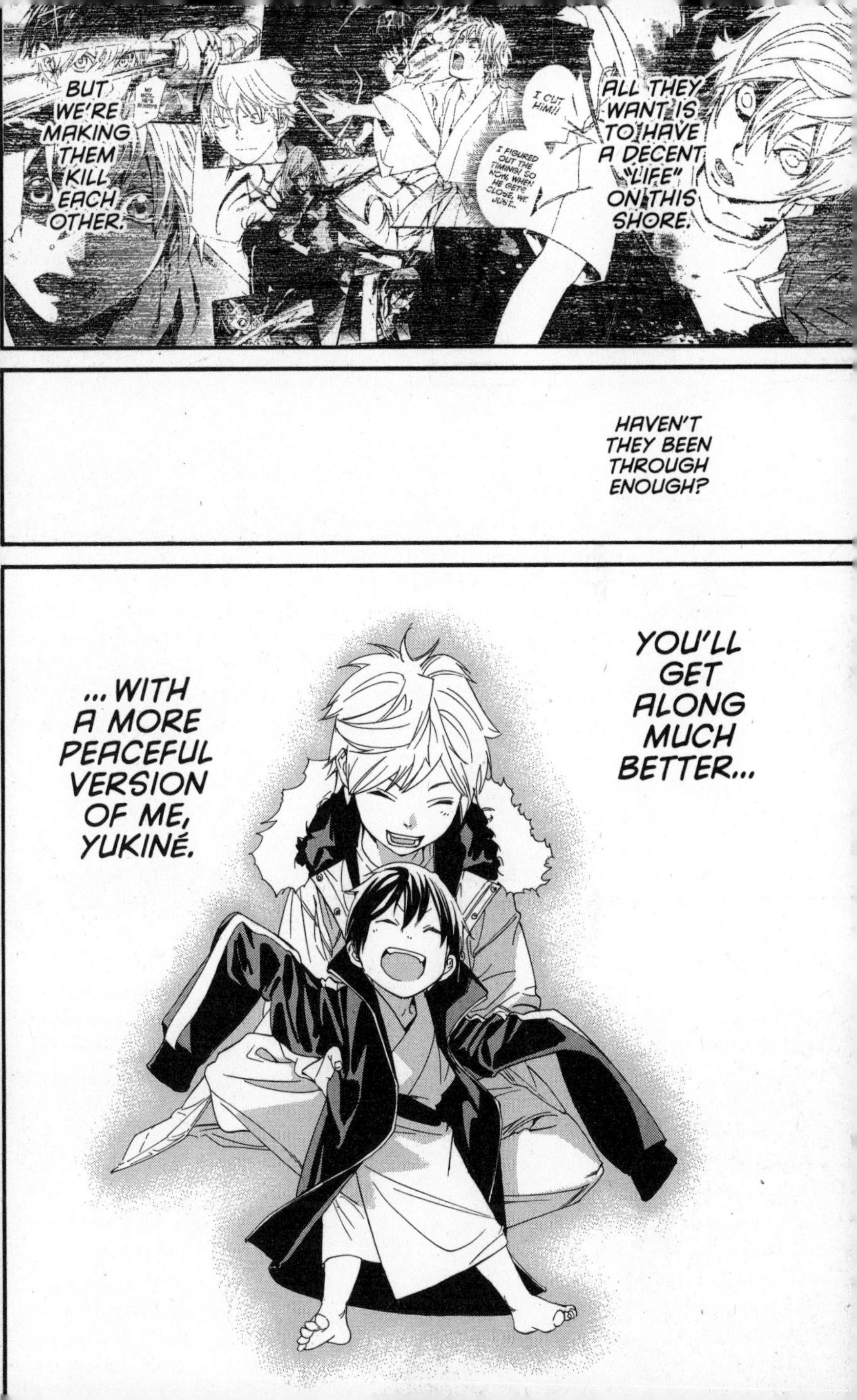
ALL THEY WANT IS TO HAVE A DECENT "LIFE" ON THIS SHORE.
I CUT HIM!!
I FIGURED OUT THE TIMING! SO NOW, WHEN HE GETS CLOSE, WE JUST...
BUT WE'RE MAKING THEM KILL EACH OTHER.
HAVEN'T THEY BEEN THROUGH ENOUGH?
YOU'LL GET ALONG MUCH BETTER...
...WITH A MORE PEACEFUL VERSION OF ME, YUKINÉ.

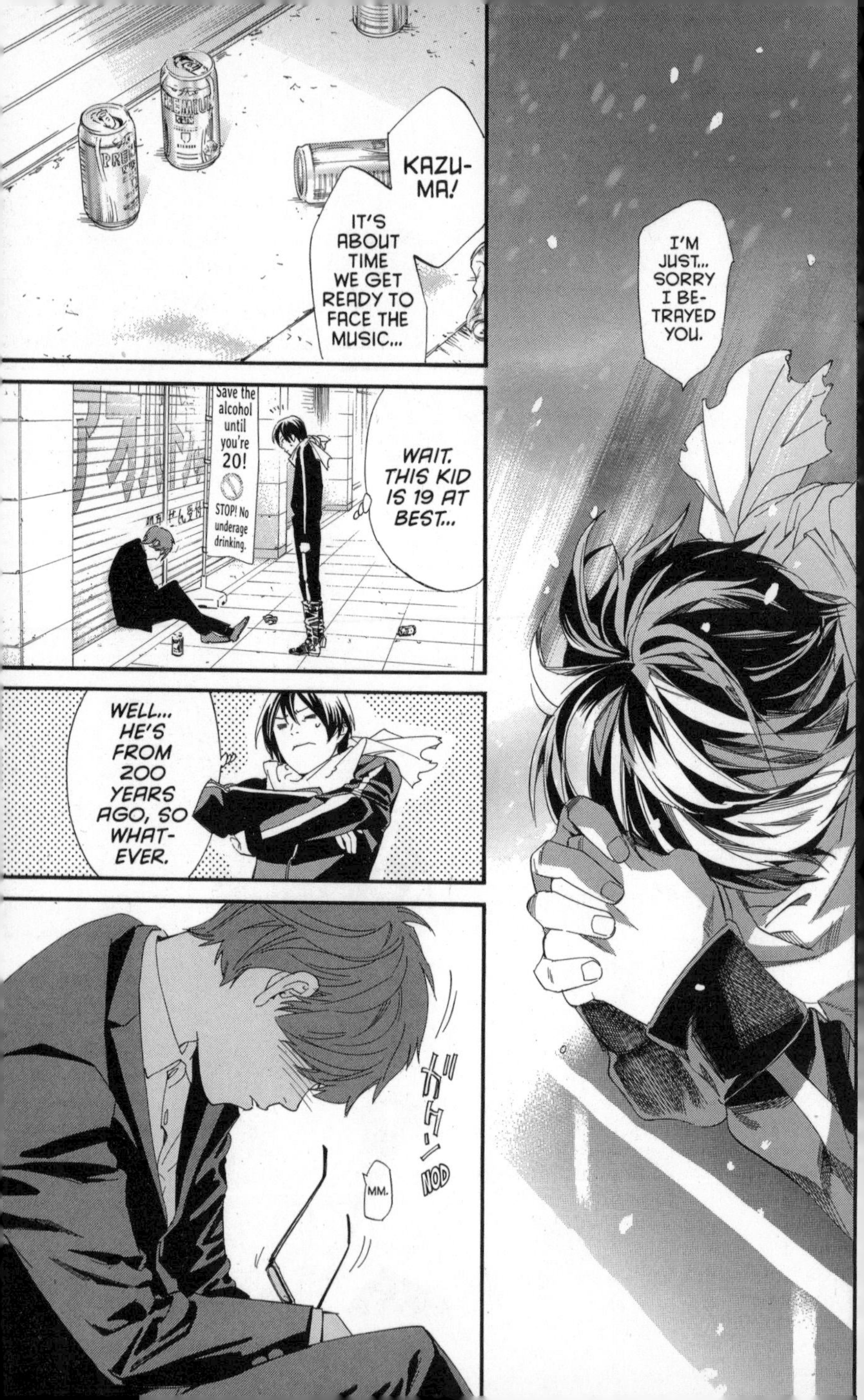
I'M JUST... SORRY I BE-TRAYED YOU.
KAZU-MA!
IT'S ABOUT TIME WE GET READY TO FACE THE MUSIC...
Save the alcohol until you're 20!
STOP! No underage drinking.
WAIT. THIS KID IS 19 AT BEST...
WELL... HE'S FROM 200 YEARS AGO, SO WHAT-EVER.
MM.
NOD

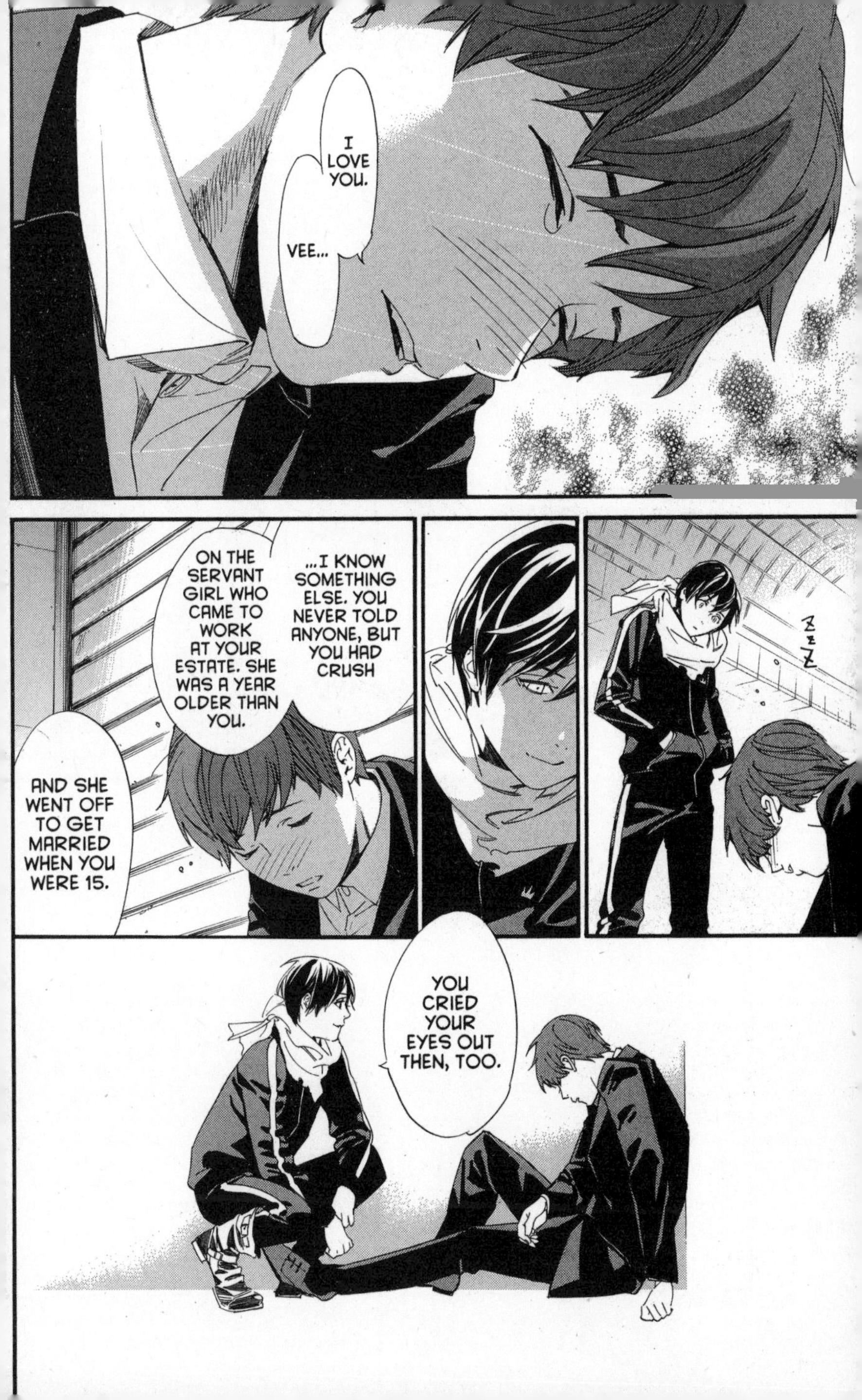
I LOVE YOU.
VEE...
...I KNOW SOMETHING ELSE. YOU NEVER TOLD ANYONE, BUT YOU HAD CRUSH
ON THE SERVANT GIRL WHO CAME TO WORK AT YOUR ESTATE. SHE WAS A YEAR OLDER THAN YOU.
AND SHE WENT OFF TO GET MARRIED WHEN YOU WERE 15.
YOU CRIED YOUR EYES OUT THEN, TOO.

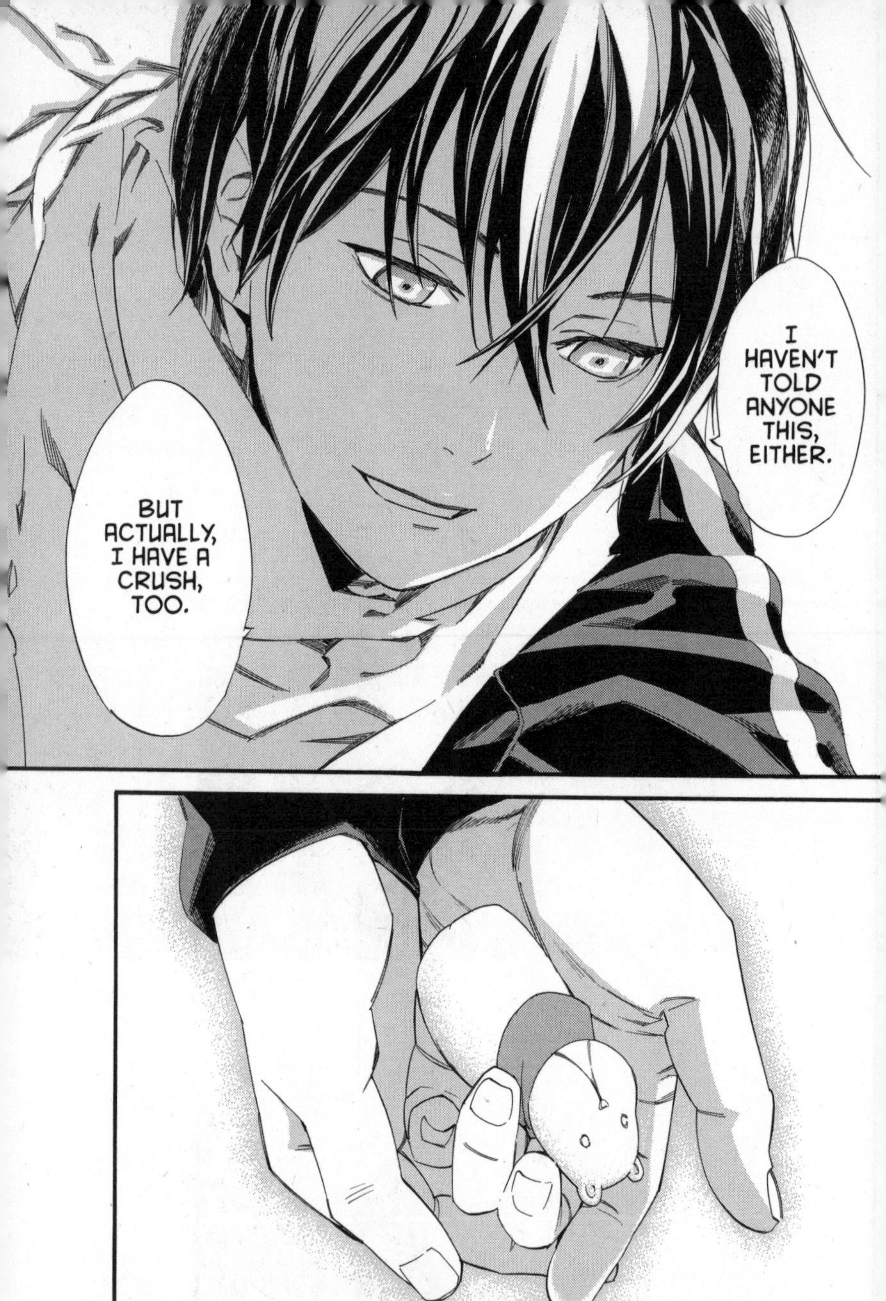
I HAVEN'T TOLD ANYONE THIS, EITHER.
BUT ACTUALLY, I HAVE A CRUSH, TOO.

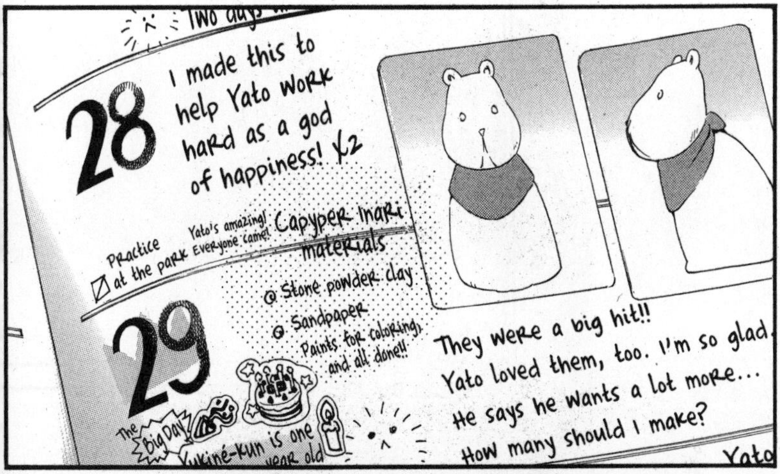
28
I made this to help Yato work hard as a god of happiness! X2
Practice
at the park
Yato's amazing! Everyone came!
Capyper Inari materials
Stone powder clay
Sandpaper
Paints for coloring, and all done!!
29
The Big Day
Yukiné-kun is one year old
They were a big hit!! Yato loved them, too. I'm so glad. He says he wants a lot more... How many should I make?
Yato
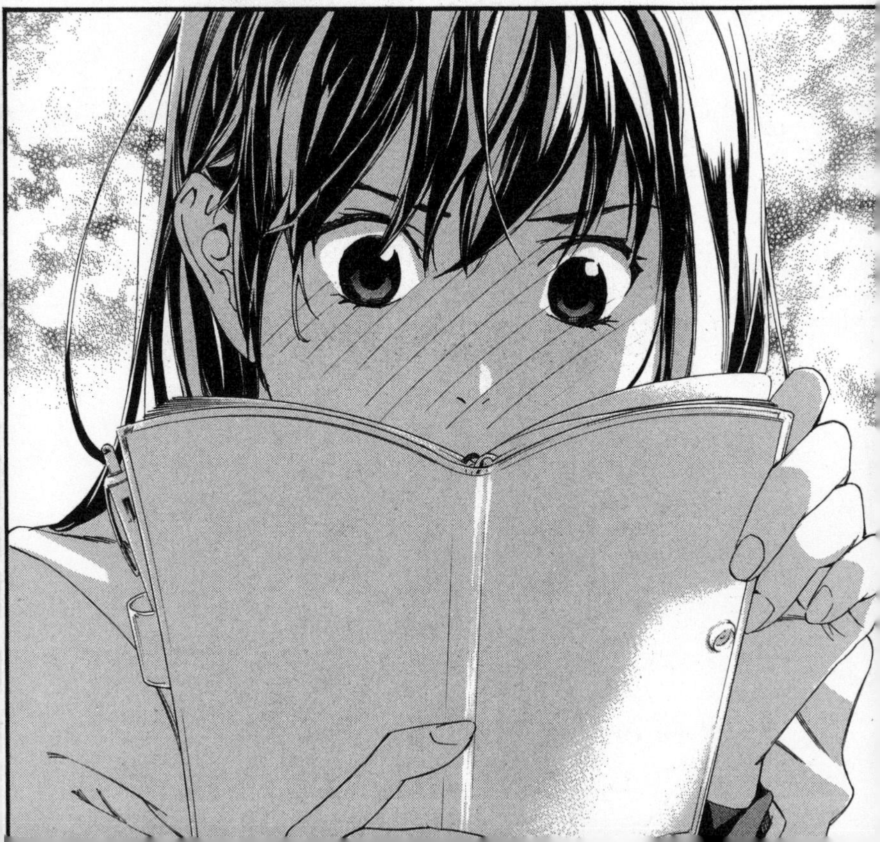

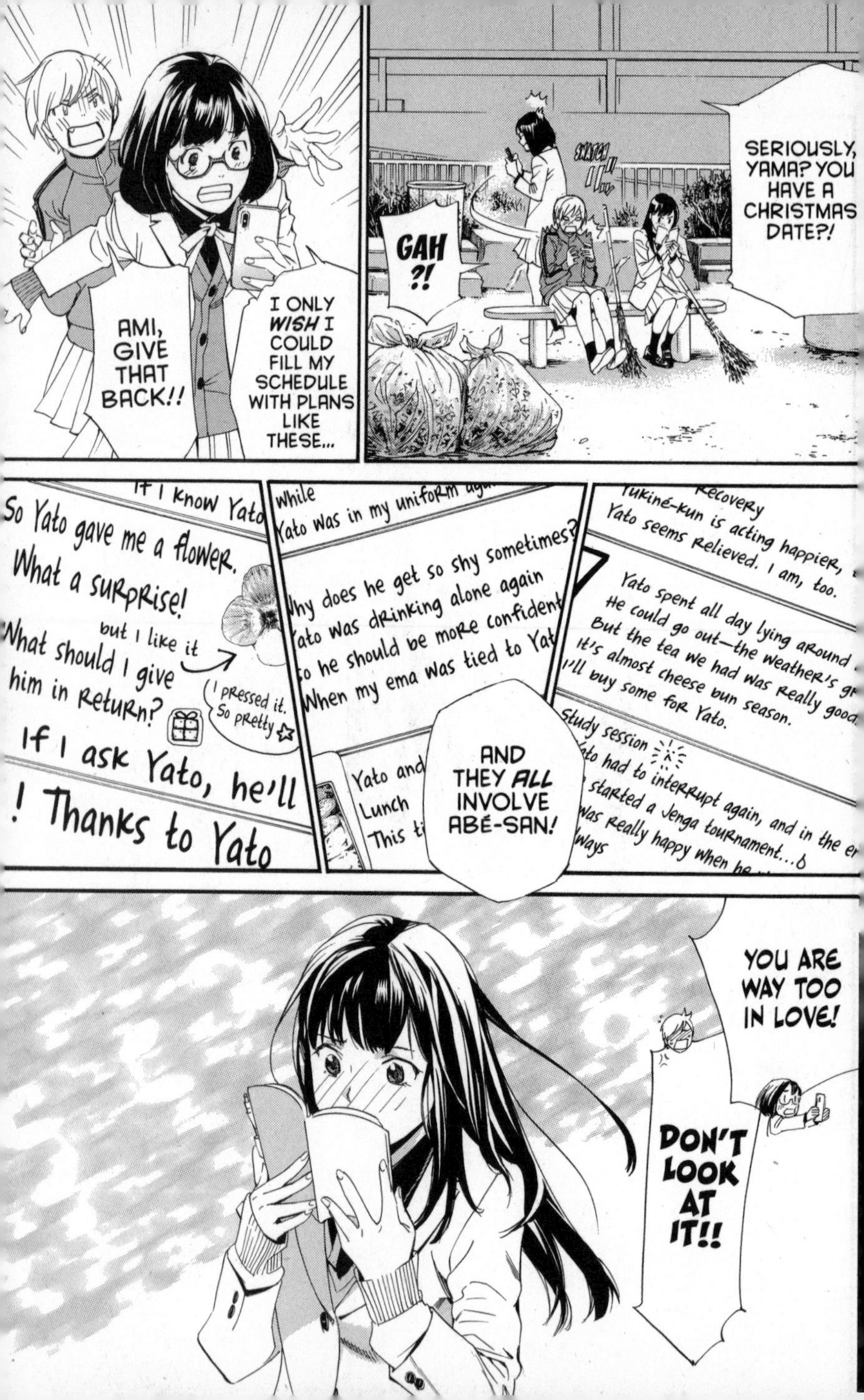
SERIOUSLY, YAMA? YOU HAVE A CHRISTMAS DATE?!
SNATCH
GAH ?!
I ONLY WISH I COULD FILL MY SCHEDULE WITH PLANS LIKE THESE...
AMI, GIVE THAT BACK!!
Recovery
Yukiné-kun is acting happier,
Yato seems relieved. I am, too.
Yato spent all day lying around
He could go out—the weather's gr
But the tea we had was really good
It's almost cheese bun season.
I'll buy some for Yato.
Study session
had to interrupt again, and in the e
started a Jenga tournament...
was really happy when
ways
AND THEY ALL INVOLVE ABÉ-SAN!
while
Yato was in my uniform
Why does he get so shy sometimes?
Yato was drinking alone again
So he should be more confident
When my ema was tied to Yat
Yato and
Lunch
This ti
If I know Yato
So Yato gave me a flower.
What a surprise!
but I like it
What should I give him in return?
I pressed it. So pretty
If I ask Yato, he'll
! Thanks to Yato
YOU ARE WAY TOO IN LOVE!
DON'T LOOK AT IT!!

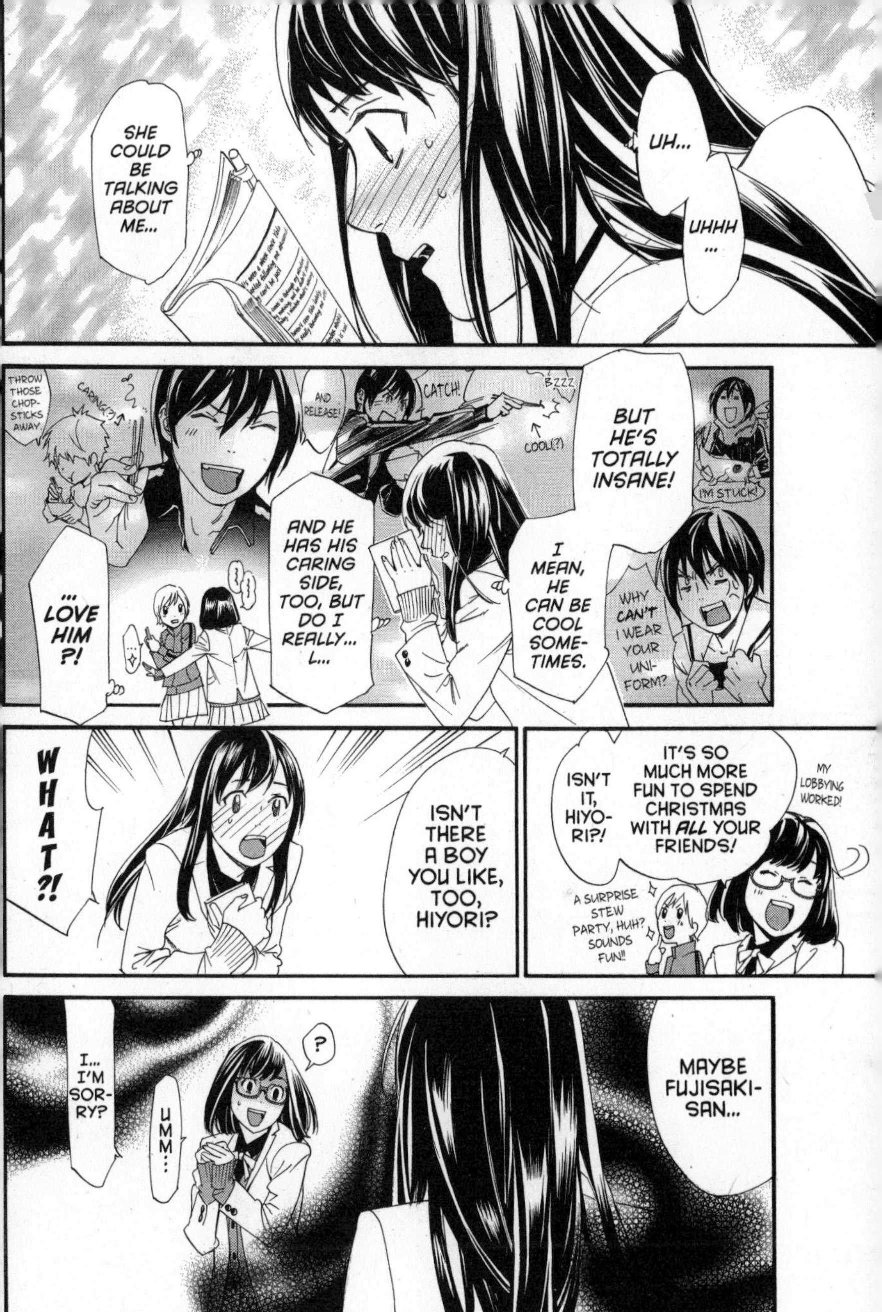
UH...
UHHH...
SHE COULD BE TALKING ABOUT ME...
BUT HE'S TOTALLY INSANE!
BZZZ
COOL(?)
I'M STUCK!
I MEAN, HE CAN BE COOL SOMETIMES.
WHY CAN'T I WEAR YOUR UNIFORM?
CATCH!
AND RELEASE!
AND HE HAS HIS CARING SIDE, TOO, BUT DO I REALLY... L...
CARING(?)
THROW THOSE CHOPSTICKS AWAY.
...LOVE HIM?!
IT'S SO MUCH MORE FUN TO SPEND CHRISTMAS WITH ALL YOUR FRIENDS!
MY LOBBYING WORKED!
ISN'T IT, HIYORI?!
A SURPRISE STEW PARTY, HUH? SOUNDS FUN!!
ISN'T THERE A BOY YOU LIKE, TOO, HIYORI?
WHAT?!
MAYBE FUJISAKI-SAN...
?
UMM...
I... I'M SORRY?

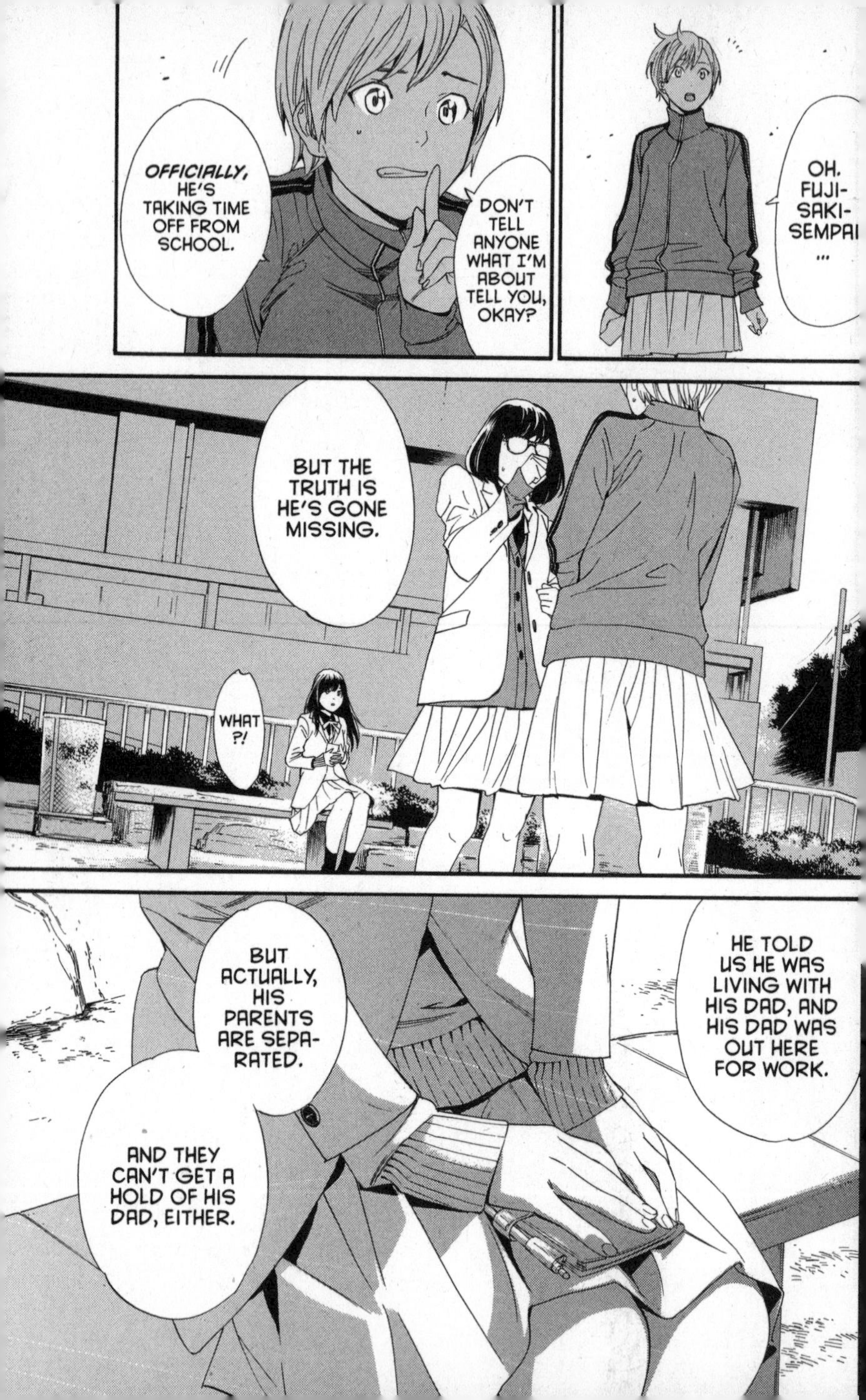
OH. FUJI-SAKI-SEMPAI ...
DON'T TELL ANYONE WHAT I'M ABOUT TELL YOU, OKAY?
OFFICIALLY, HE'S TAKING TIME OFF FROM SCHOOL.
BUT THE TRUTH IS HE'S GONE MISSING.
WHAT ?!
HE TOLD US HE WAS LIVING WITH HIS DAD, AND HIS DAD WAS OUT HERE FOR WORK.
BUT ACTUALLY, HIS PARENTS ARE SEPA-RATED.
AND THEY CAN'T GET A HOLD OF HIS DAD, EITHER.

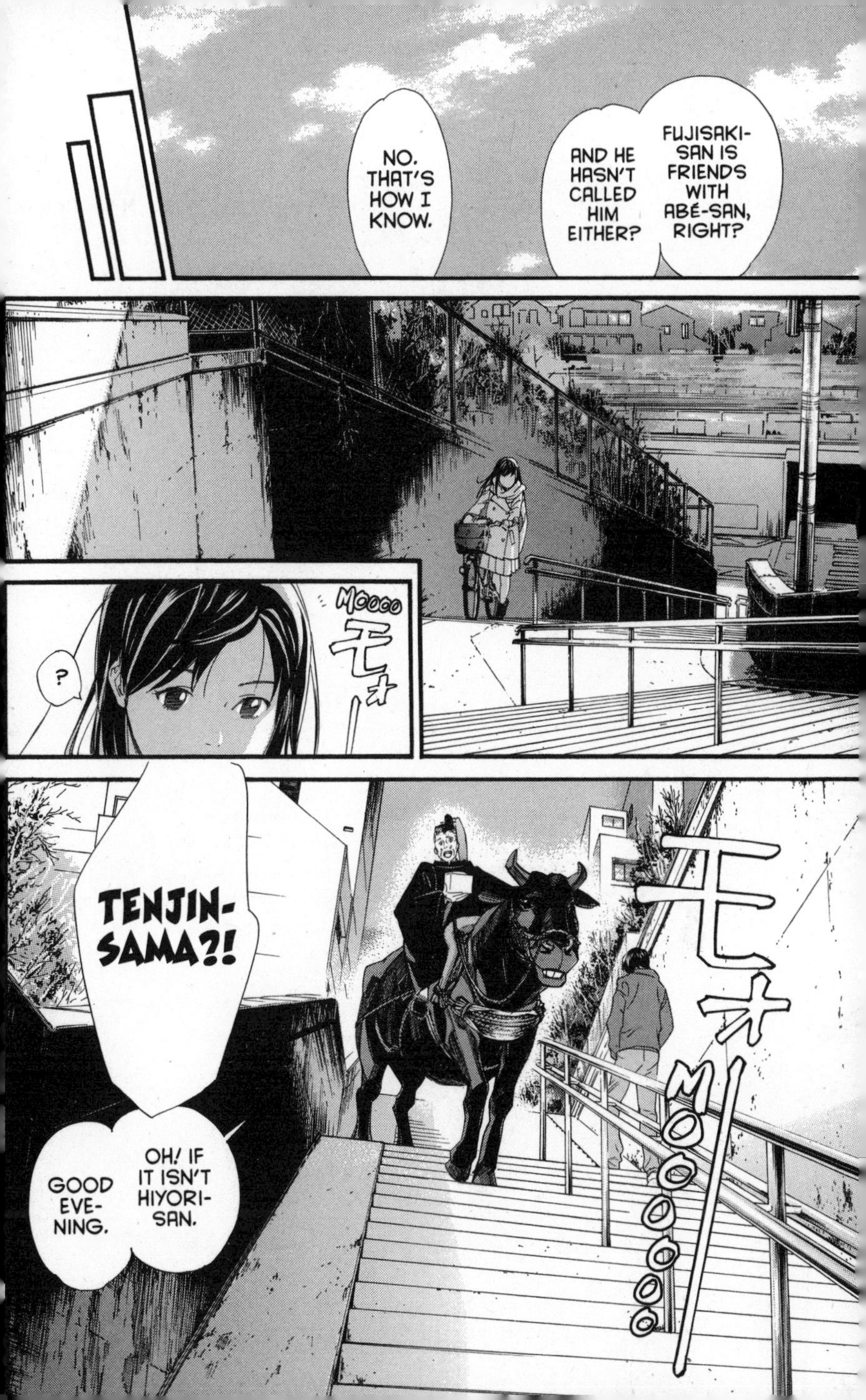
FUJISAKI-SAN IS FRIENDS WITH ABÉ-SAN, RIGHT?
AND HE HASN'T CALLED HIM EITHER?
NO. THAT'S HOW I KNOW.
MOOOO
モォ
?
モォ
MOOOOOOOOO
TENJIN-SAMA?!
OH! IF IT ISN'T HIYORI-SAN.
GOOD EVE-NING.

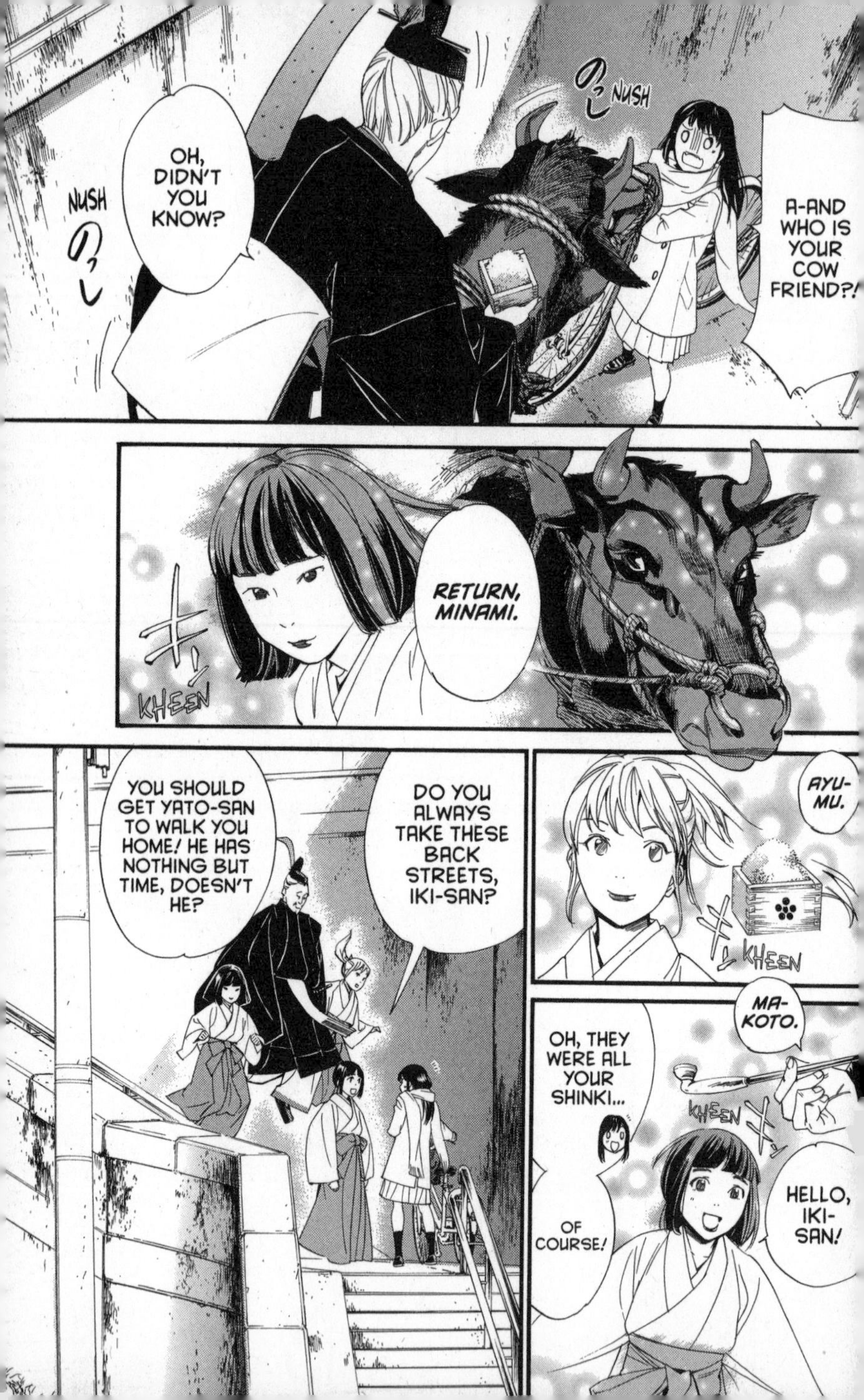
NUSH
A-AND WHO IS YOUR COW FRIEND?!
OH, DIDN'T YOU KNOW?
NUSH
RETURN, MINAMI.
KHEEN
AYU-MU.
KHEEN
MA-KOTO.
HELLO, IKI-SAN!
KHEEN
OH, THEY WERE ALL YOUR SHINKI...
OF COURSE!
DO YOU ALWAYS TAKE THESE BACK STREETS, IKI-SAN?
YOU SHOULD GET YATO-SAN TO WALK YOU HOME! HE HAS NOTHING BUT TIME, DOESN'T HE?

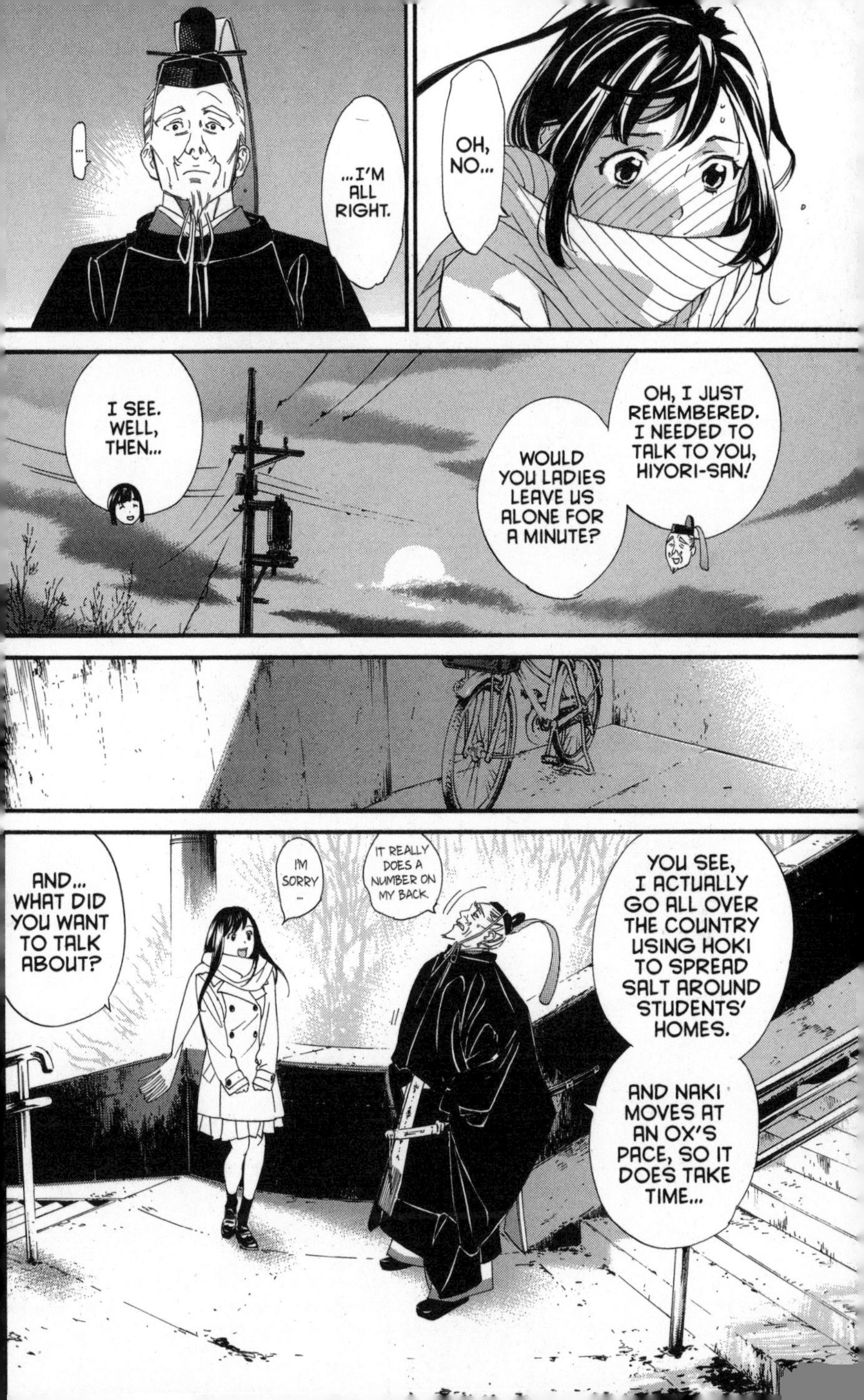
OH, NO...
...I'M ALL RIGHT.
...
OH, I JUST REMEMBERED. I NEEDED TO TALK TO YOU, HIYORI-SAN!
WOULD YOU LADIES LEAVE US ALONE FOR A MINUTE?
I SEE. WELL, THEN...
YOU SEE, I ACTUALLY GO ALL OVER THE COUNTRY USING HOKI TO SPREAD SALT AROUND STUDENTS' HOMES.
AND NAKI MOVES AT AN OX'S PACE, SO IT DOES TAKE TIME...
IT REALLY DOES A NUMBER ON MY BACK.
I'M SORRY ...
AND... WHAT DID YOU WANT TO TALK ABOUT?

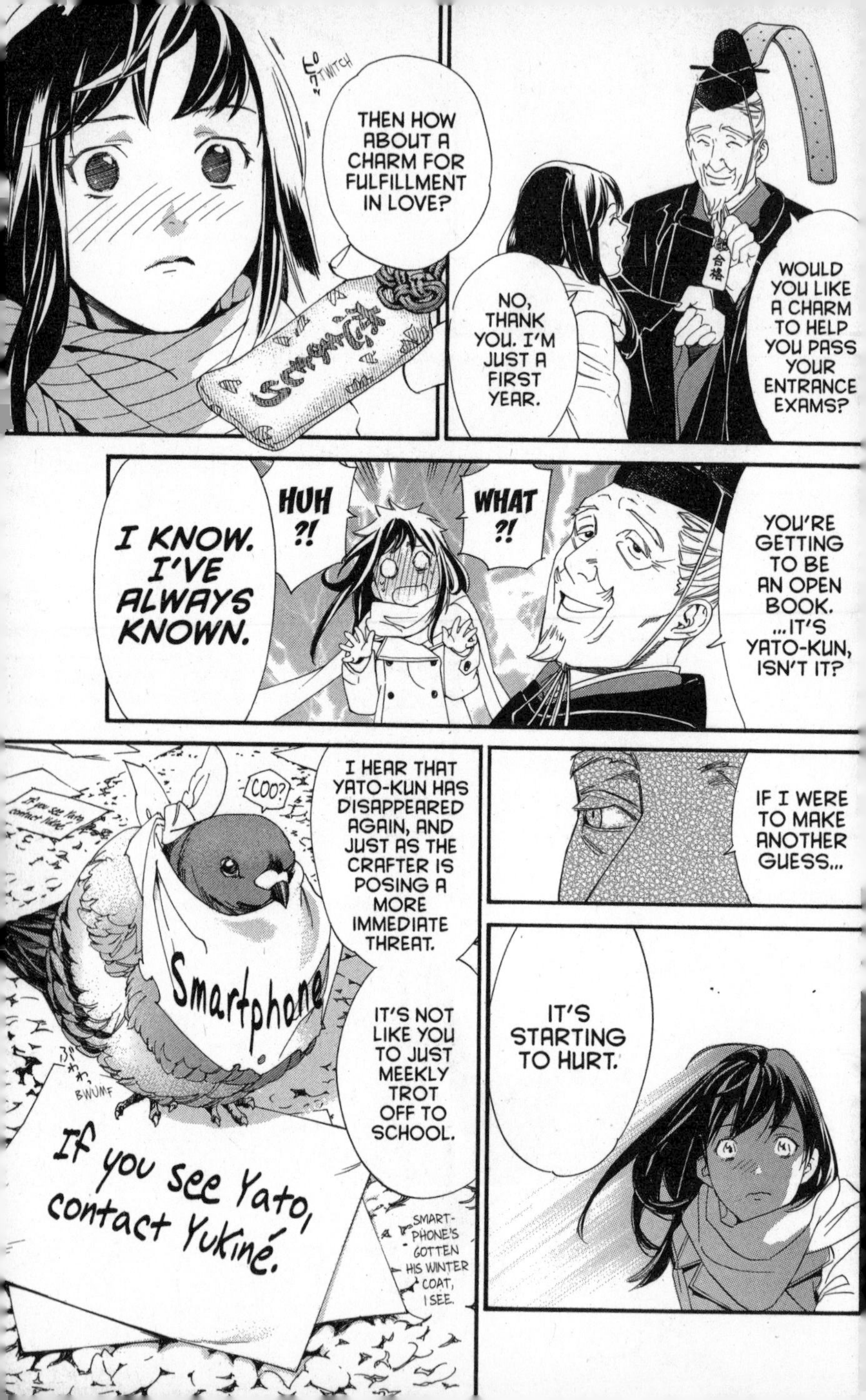

合格
WOULD YOU LIKE A CHARM TO HELP YOU PASS YOUR ENTRANCE EXAMS?
NO, THANK YOU. I'M JUST A FIRST YEAR.
TWITCH
THEN HOW ABOUT A CHARM FOR FULFILLMENT IN LOVE?
YOU'RE GETTING TO BE AN OPEN BOOK. ...IT'S YATO-KUN, ISN'T IT?
WHAT ?!
HUH ?!
I KNOW. I'VE ALWAYS KNOWN.
IF I WERE TO MAKE ANOTHER GUESS...
IT'S STARTING TO HURT.
I HEAR THAT YATO-KUN HAS DISAPPEARED AGAIN, AND JUST AS THE CRAFTER IS POSING A MORE IMMEDIATE THREAT.
IT'S NOT LIKE YOU TO JUST MEEKLY TROT OFF TO SCHOOL.
COO?
Smartphone
BWUMF
If you see Yato, contact Yukiné.
SMART-PHONE'S GOTTEN HIS WINTER COAT, I SEE.

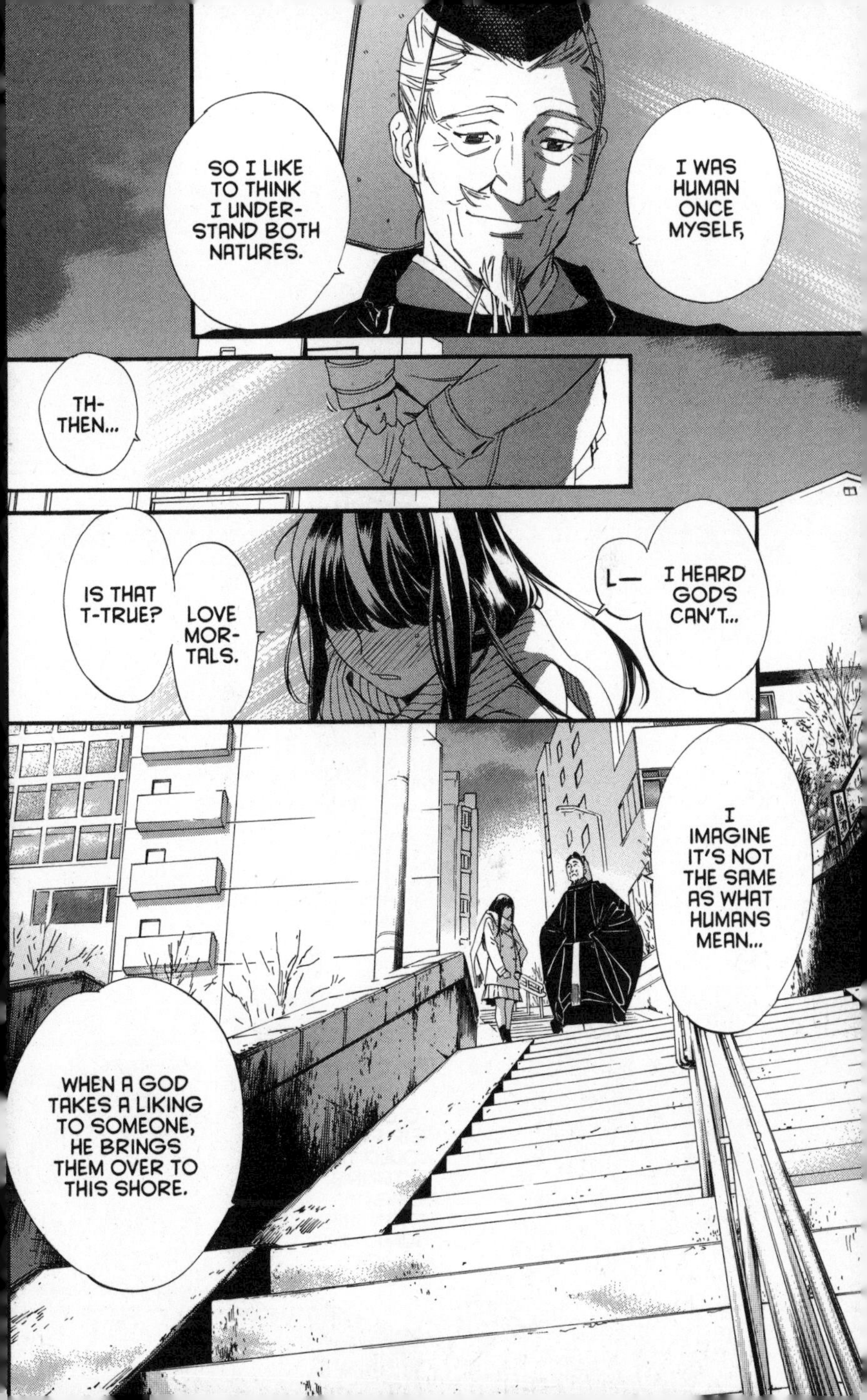
I WAS HUMAN ONCE MYSELF,
SO I LIKE TO THINK I UNDER-STAND BOTH NATURES.
TH- THEN...
I HEARD GODS CAN'T...
L—
LOVE MOR-TALS.
IS THAT T-TRUE?
I IMAGINE IT'S NOT THE SAME AS WHAT HUMANS MEAN...
WHEN A GOD TAKES A LIKING TO SOMEONE, HE BRINGS THEM OVER TO THIS SHORE.

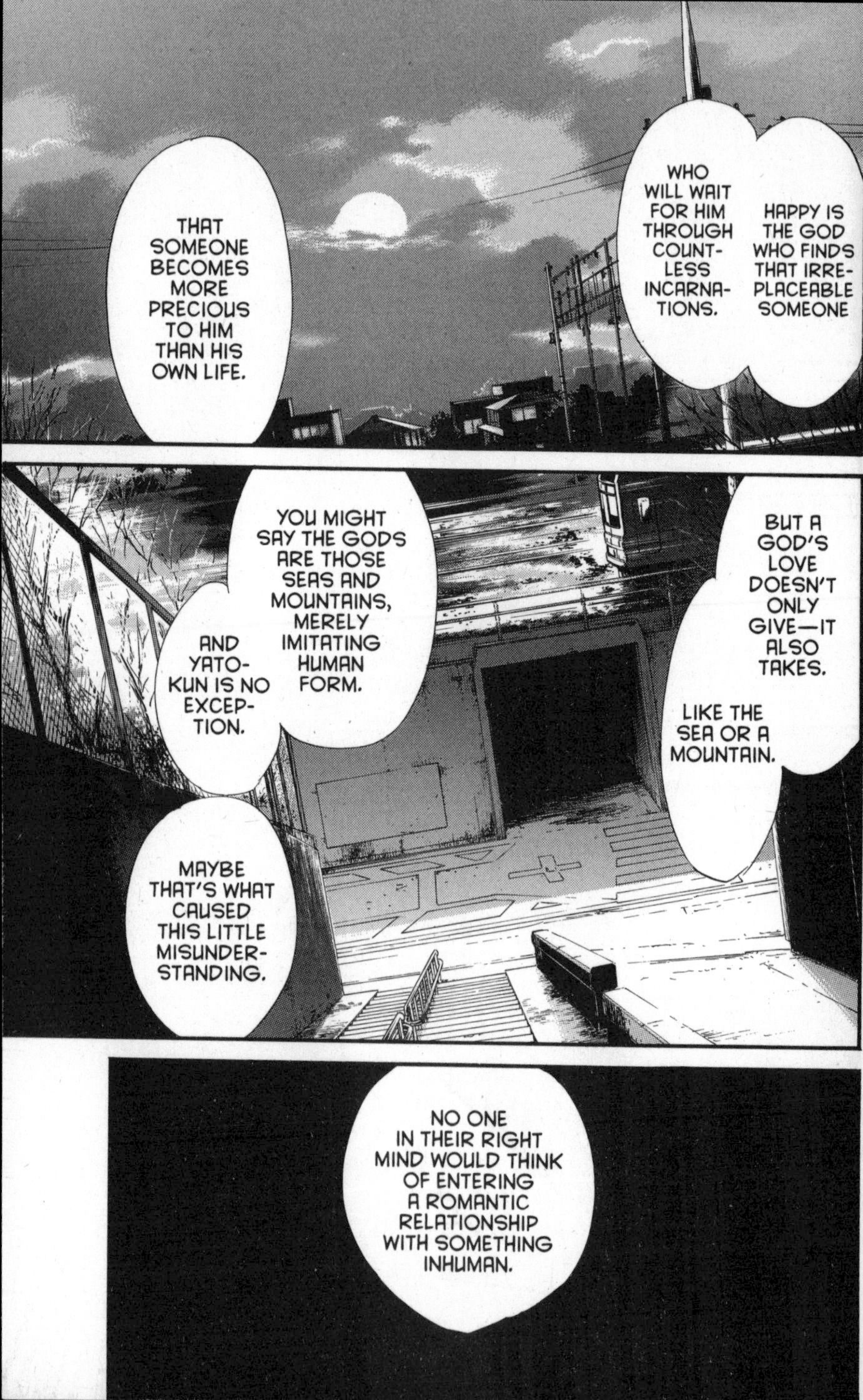
HAPPY IS THE GOD WHO FINDS THAT IRRE-PLACEABLE SOMEONE
WHO WILL WAIT FOR HIM THROUGH COUNT-LESS INCARNA-TIONS.
THAT SOMEONE BECOMES MORE PRECIOUS TO HIM THAN HIS OWN LIFE.
BUT A GOD'S LOVE DOESN'T ONLY GIVE—IT ALSO TAKES.
LIKE THE SEA OR A MOUNTAIN.
YOU MIGHT SAY THE GODS ARE THOSE SEAS AND MOUNTAINS, MERELY IMITATING HUMAN FORM.
AND YATO-KUN IS NO EXCEP-TION.
MAYBE THAT'S WHAT CAUSED THIS LITTLE MISUNDER-STANDING.
NO ONE IN THEIR RIGHT MIND WOULD THINK OF ENTERING A ROMANTIC RELATIONSHIP WITH SOMETHING INHUMAN.

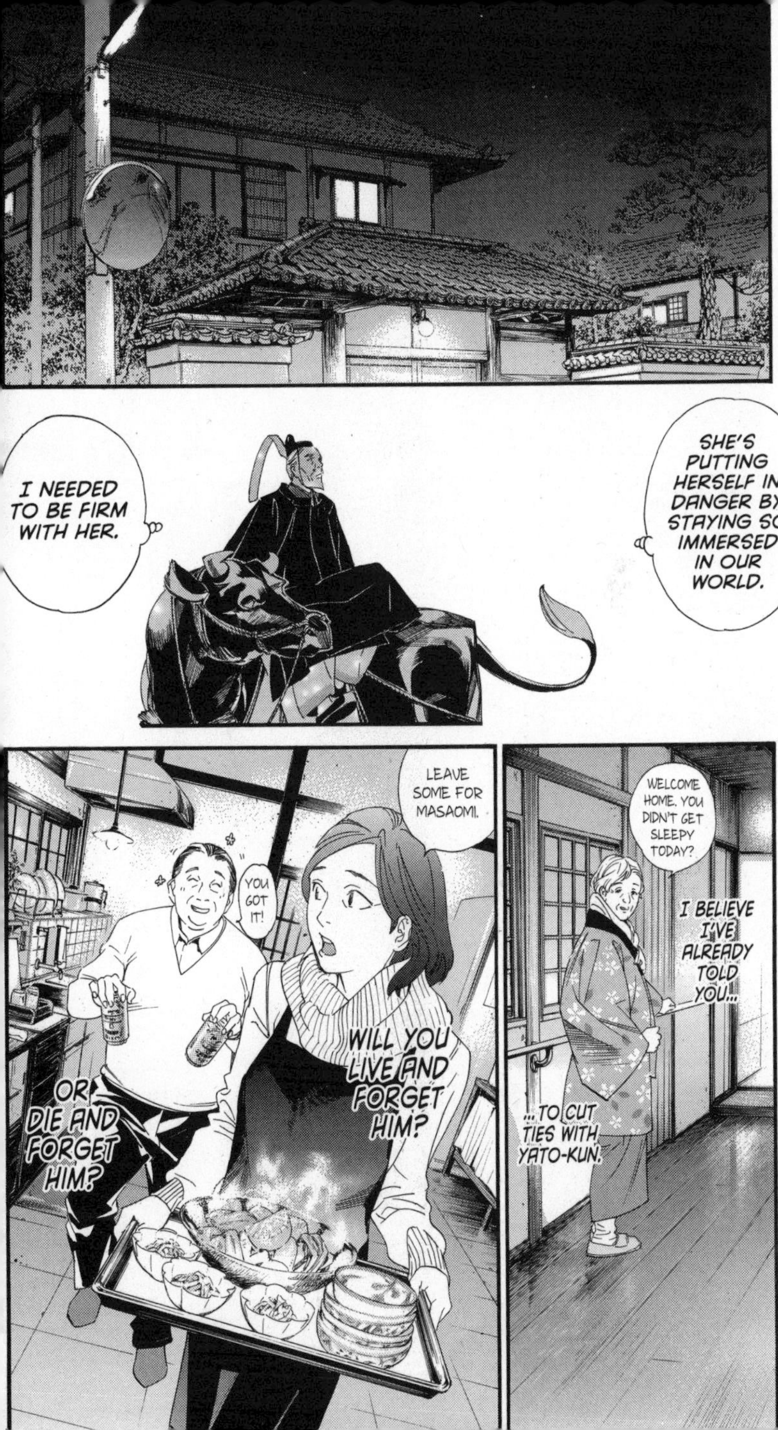
SHE'S PUTTING HERSELF IN DANGER BY STAYING SO IMMERSED IN OUR WORLD.
I NEEDED TO BE FIRM WITH HER.
WELCOME HOME. YOU DIDN'T GET SLEEPY TODAY?
I BELIEVE I'VE ALREADY TOLD YOU...
...TO CUT TIES WITH YATO-KUN.
LEAVE SOME FOR MASAOMI.
YOU GOT IT!
WILL YOU LIVE AND FORGET HIM?
OR DIE AND FORGET HIM?

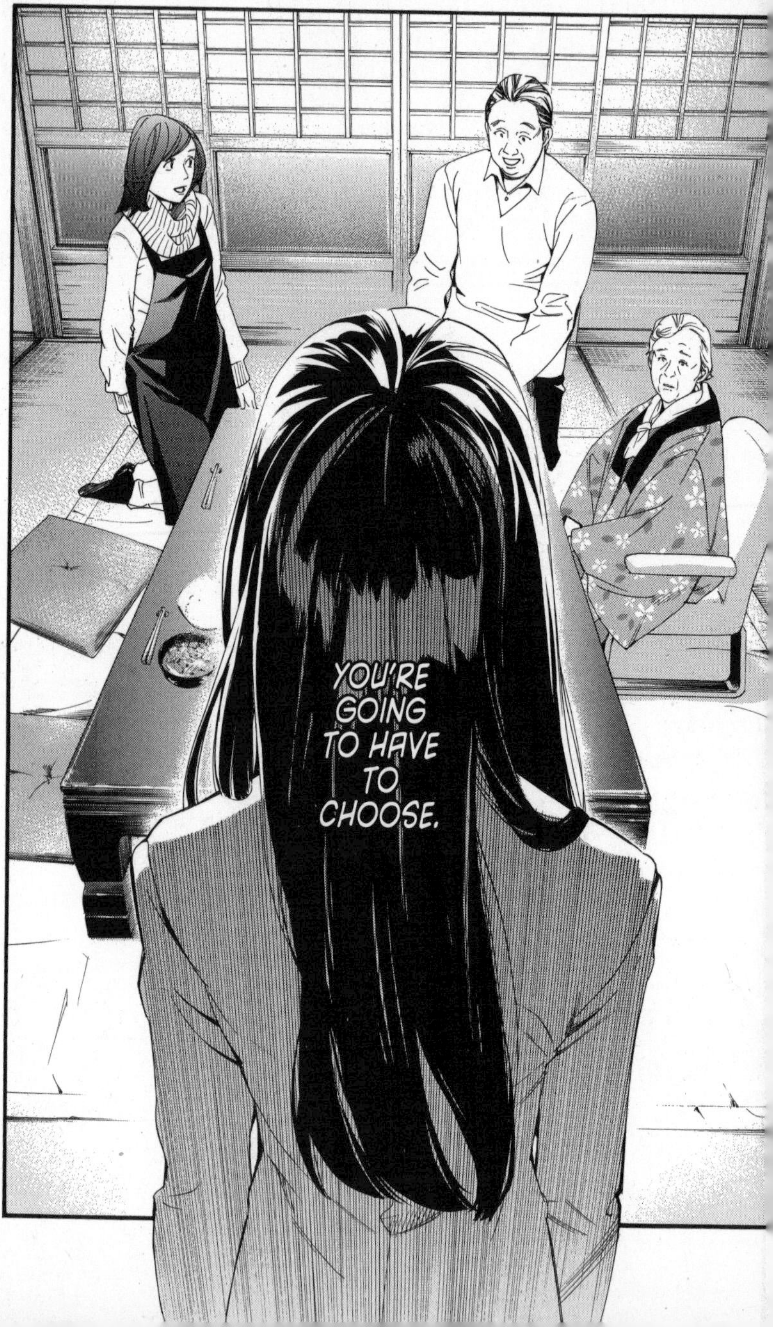
YOU'RE GOING TO HAVE TO CHOOSE.

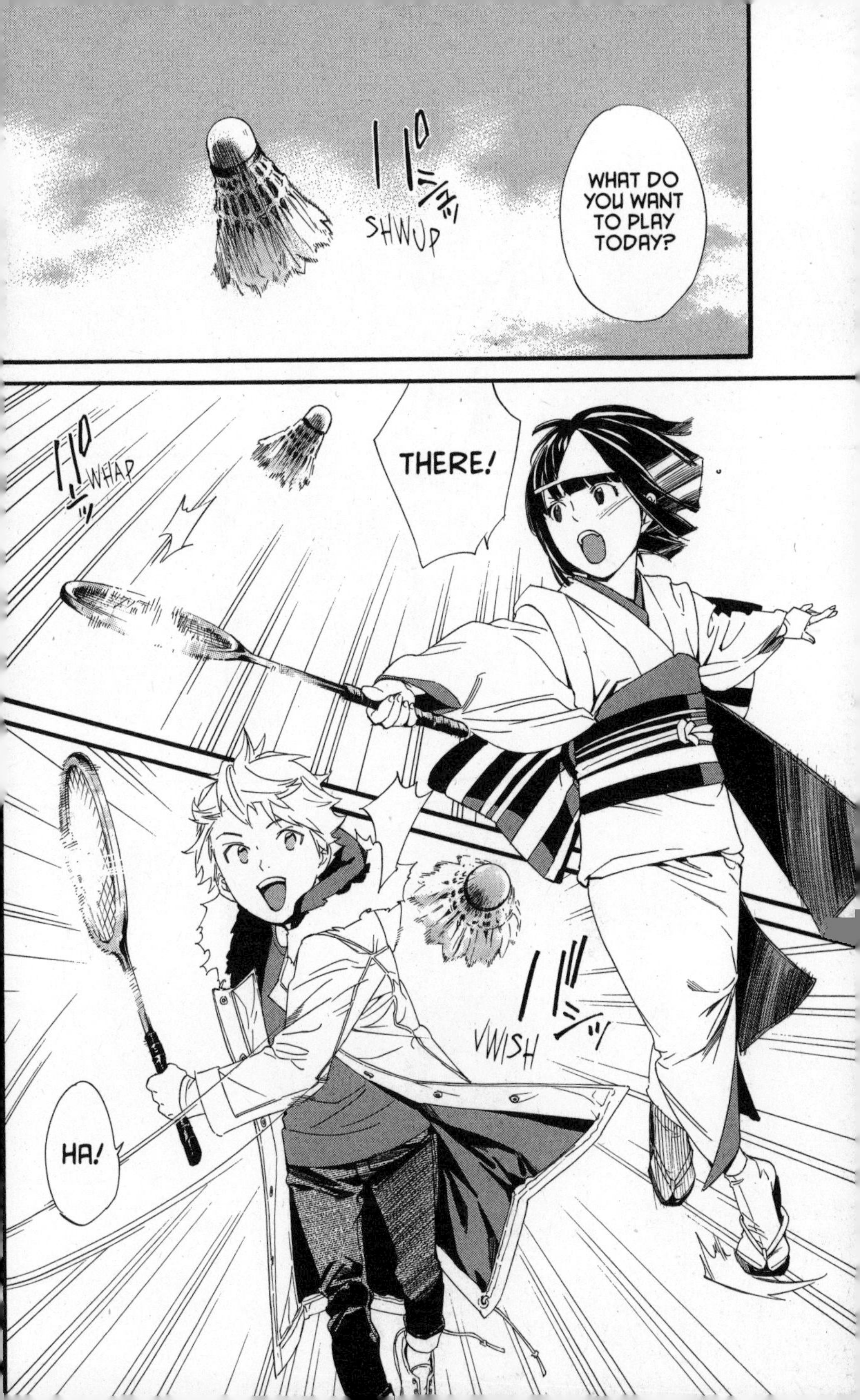
WHAT DO YOU WANT TO PLAY TODAY?
SHWUP
THERE!
WHAP
VWISH
HA!

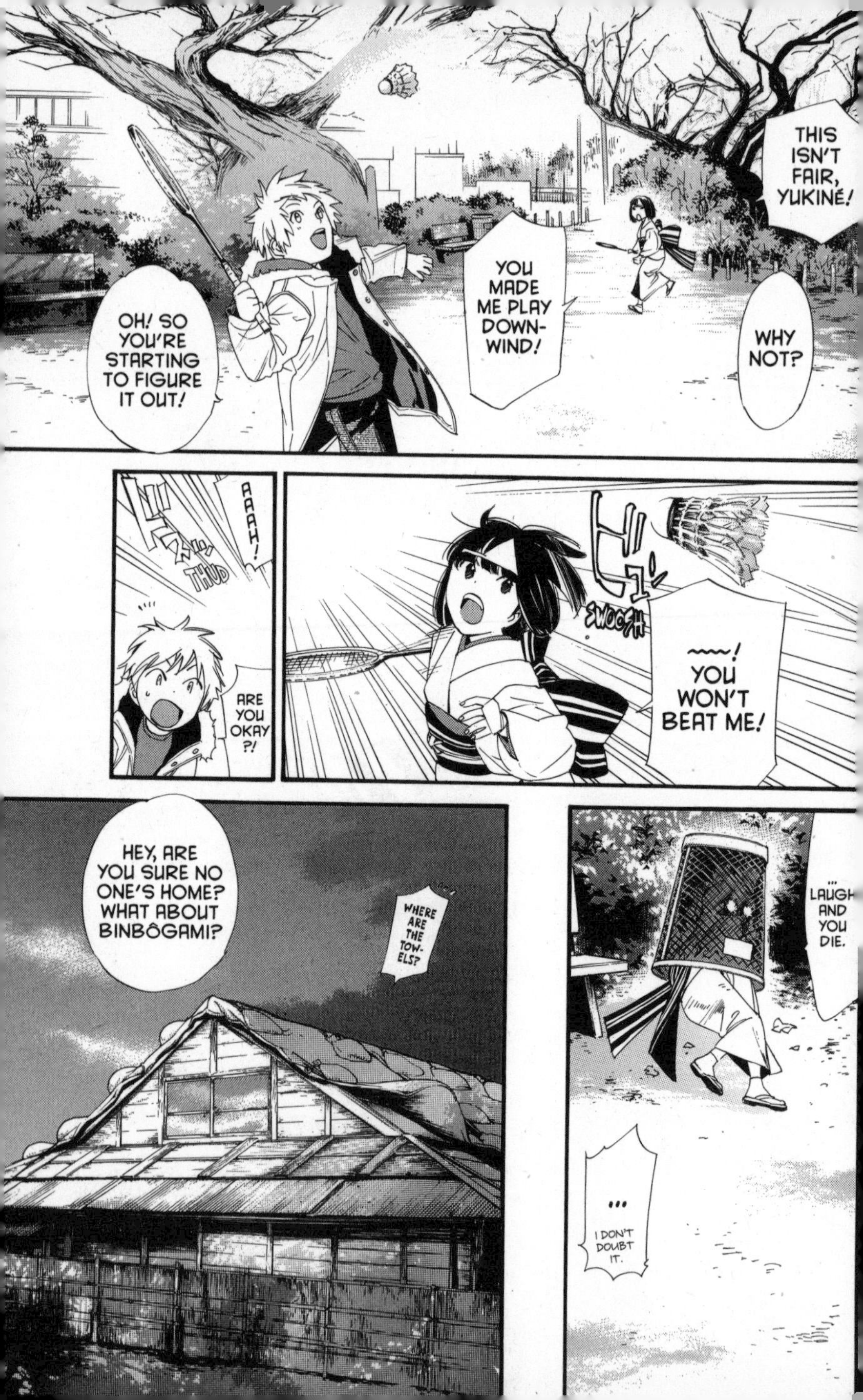
THIS ISN'T FAIR, YUKINÉ!
WHY NOT?
YOU MADE ME PLAY DOWN-WIND!
OH! SO YOU'RE STARTING TO FIGURE IT OUT!
SWOOSH
~~~! YOU WON'T BEAT ME!
AAAH!
THUD
ARE YOU OKAY?!
...LAUGH AND YOU DIE.
...
I DON'T DOUBT IT.
HEY, ARE YOU SURE NO ONE'S HOME? WHAT ABOUT BINBÔGAMI?
WHERE ARE THE TOWELS?
~~~

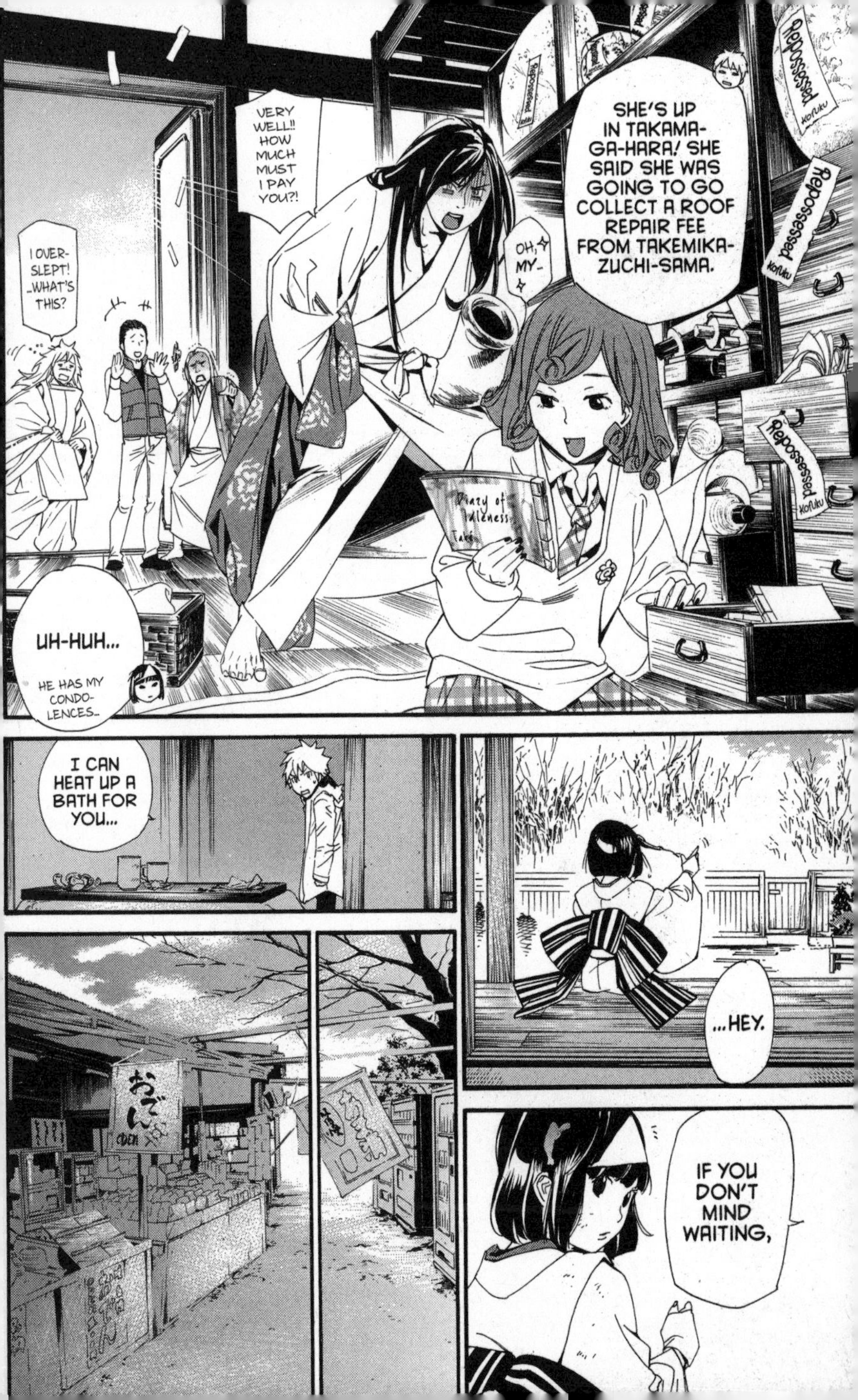
Repossessed
Koifuku
SHE'S UP IN TAKAMA-GA-HARA! SHE SAID SHE WAS GOING TO GO COLLECT A ROOF REPAIR FEE FROM TAKEMIKA-ZUCHI-SAMA.
OH, MY...
VERY WELL!! HOW MUCH MUST I PAY YOU?!
Diary of Idleness
I OVER-SLEPT! ...WHAT'S THIS?
UH-HUH...
HE HAS MY CONDO-LENCES...
...HEY.
I CAN HEAT UP A BATH FOR YOU...
IF YOU DON'T MIND WAITING,
おでん
ODEN

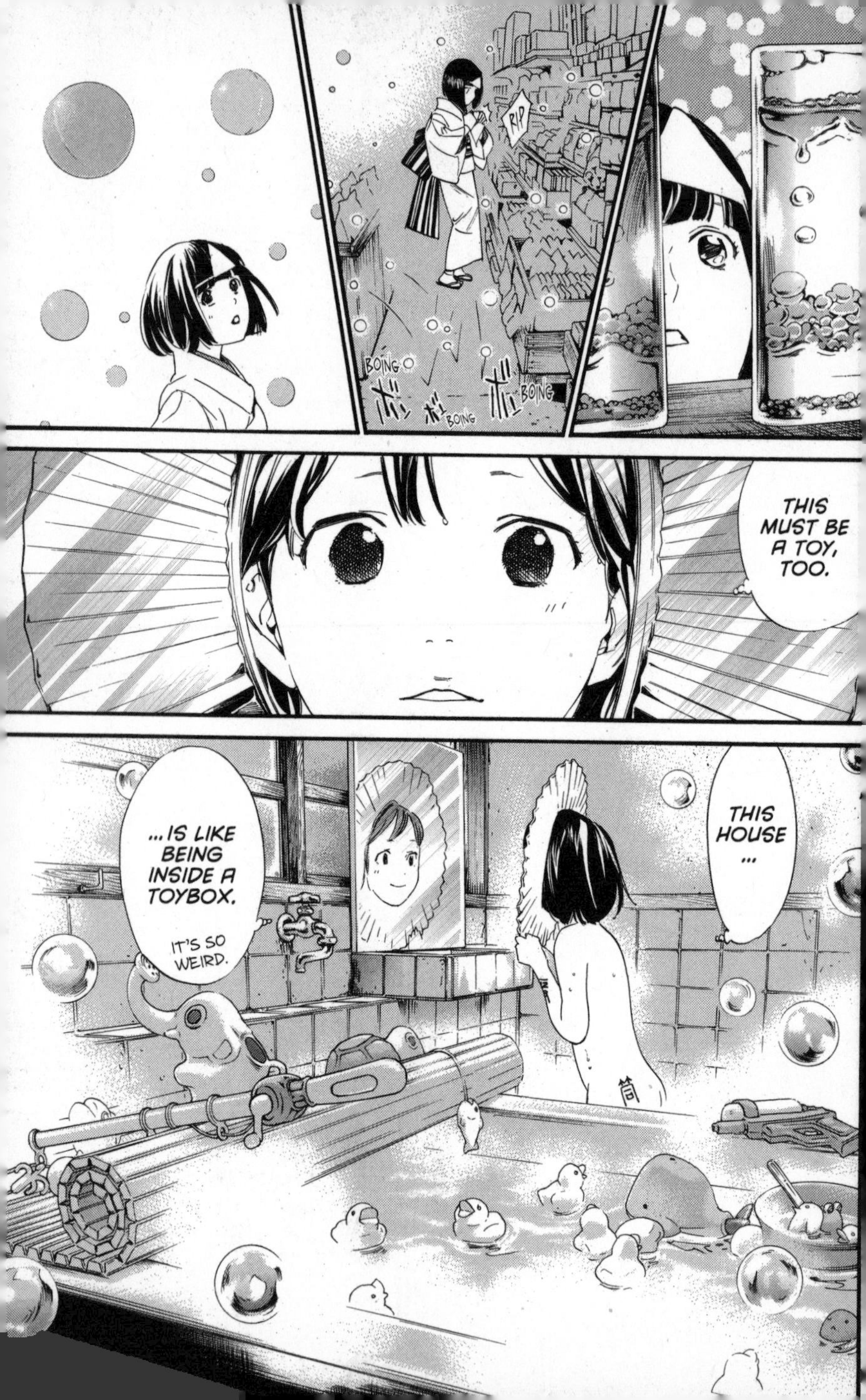
RIP
BOING
BOING
BOING
THIS MUST BE A TOY, TOO.
THIS HOUSE ...
...IS LIKE BEING INSIDE A TOYBOX.
IT'S SO WEIRD.

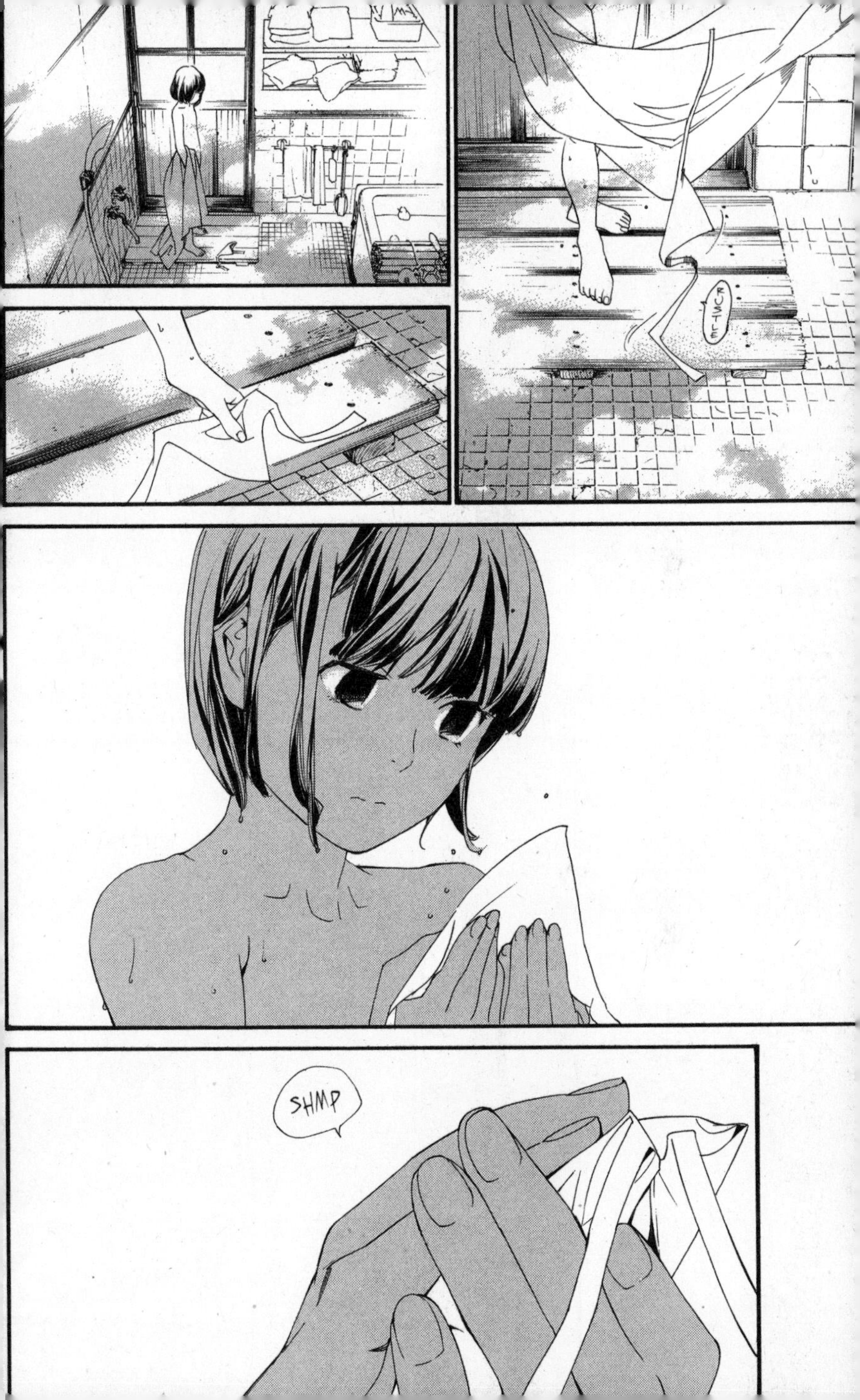
RUSTLE
SHMP

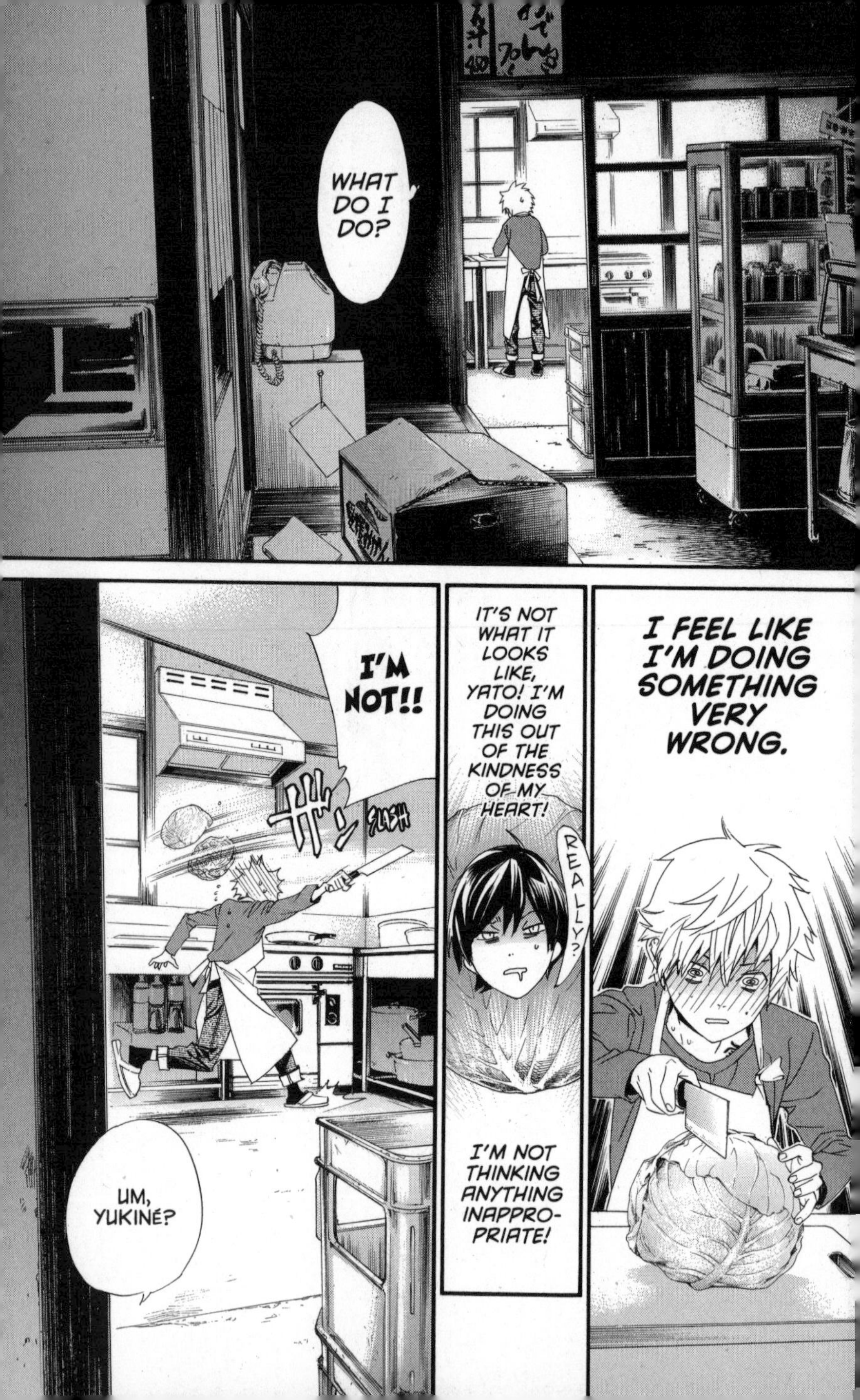
WHAT DO I DO?
I FEEL LIKE I'M DOING SOMETHING VERY WRONG.
IT'S NOT WHAT IT LOOKS LIKE, YATO! I'M DOING THIS OUT OF THE KINDNESS OF MY HEART!
REALLY?
I'M NOT THINKING ANYTHING INAPPRO-PRIATE!
I'M NOT!!
SLASH
UM, YUKINÉ?

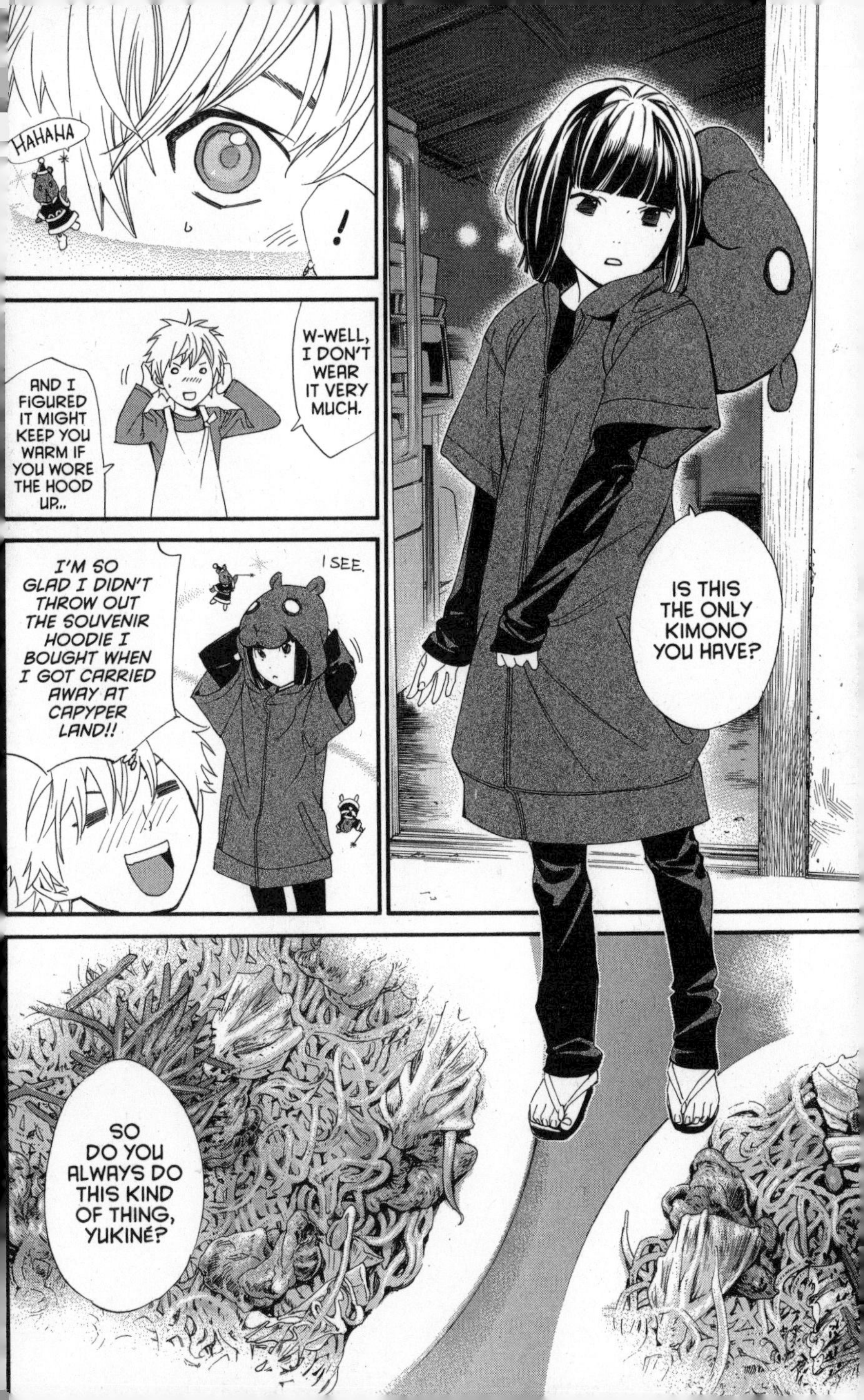
IS THIS THE ONLY KIMONO YOU HAVE?
HAHAHA
!
W-WELL, I DON'T WEAR IT VERY MUCH.
AND I FIGURED IT MIGHT KEEP YOU WARM IF YOU WORE THE HOOD UP...
I SEE.
I'M SO GLAD I DIDN'T THROW OUT THE SOUVENIR HOODIE I BOUGHT WHEN I GOT CARRIED AWAY AT CAPYPER LAND!!
SO DO YOU ALWAYS DO THIS KIND OF THING, YUKINÉ?

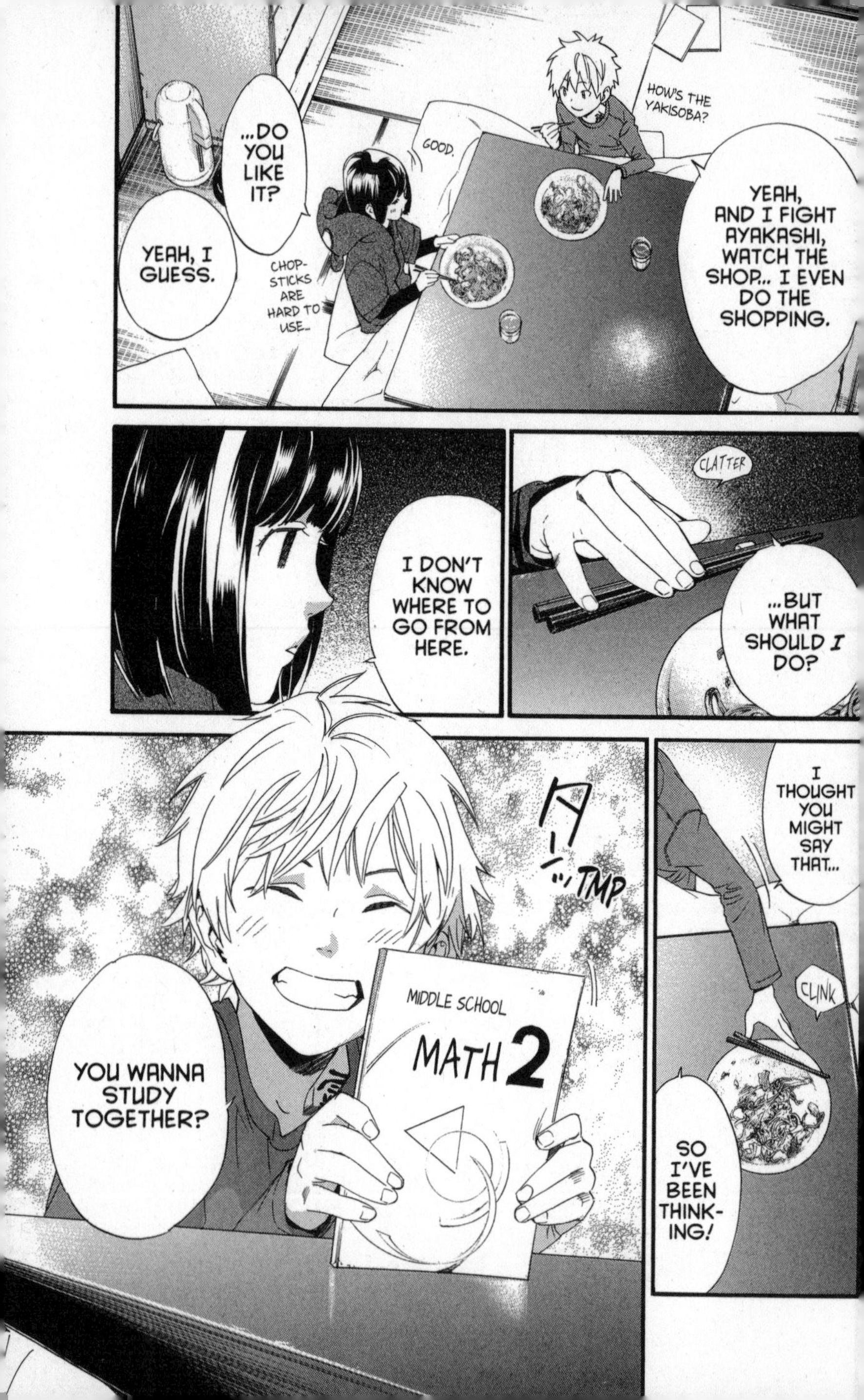
HOW'S THE YAKISOBA?
YEAH, AND I FIGHT AYAKASHI, WATCH THE SHOP... I EVEN DO THE SHOPPING.
GOOD.
...DO YOU LIKE IT?
YEAH, I GUESS.
CHOP-STICKS ARE HARD TO USE...
CLATTER
...BUT WHAT SHOULD *I* DO?
I DON'T KNOW WHERE TO GO FROM HERE.
I THOUGHT YOU MIGHT SAY THAT...
CLINK
SO I'VE BEEN THINK-ING!
TMP
MIDDLE SCHOOL
MATH 2
YOU WANNA STUDY TOGETHER?

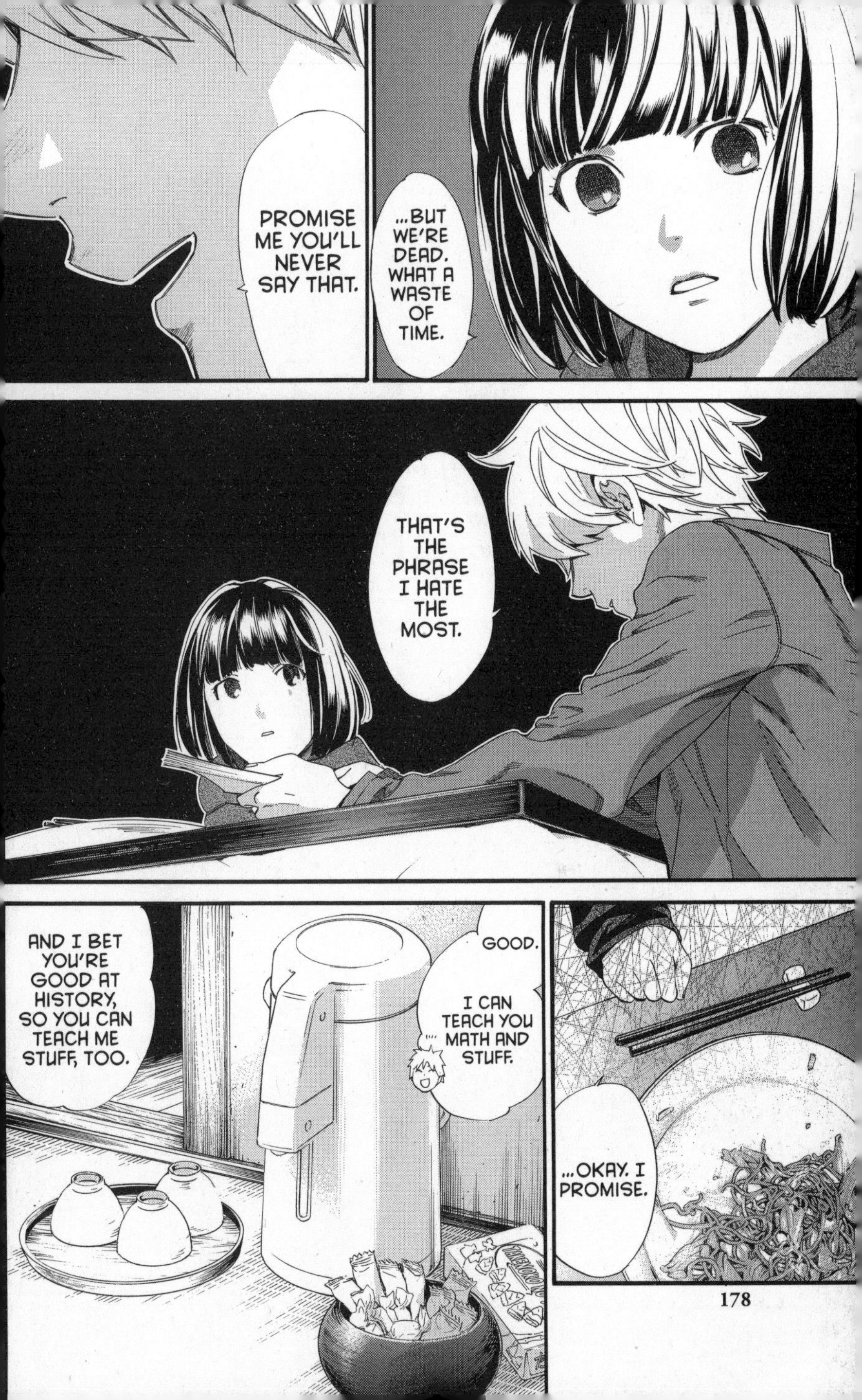
...BUT WE'RE DEAD. WHAT A WASTE OF TIME.
PROMISE ME YOU'LL NEVER SAY THAT.
THAT'S THE PHRASE I HATE THE MOST.
...OKAY. I PROMISE.
GOOD.
I CAN TEACH YOU MATH AND STUFF.
AND I BET YOU'RE GOOD AT HISTORY, SO YOU CAN TEACH ME STUFF, TOO.

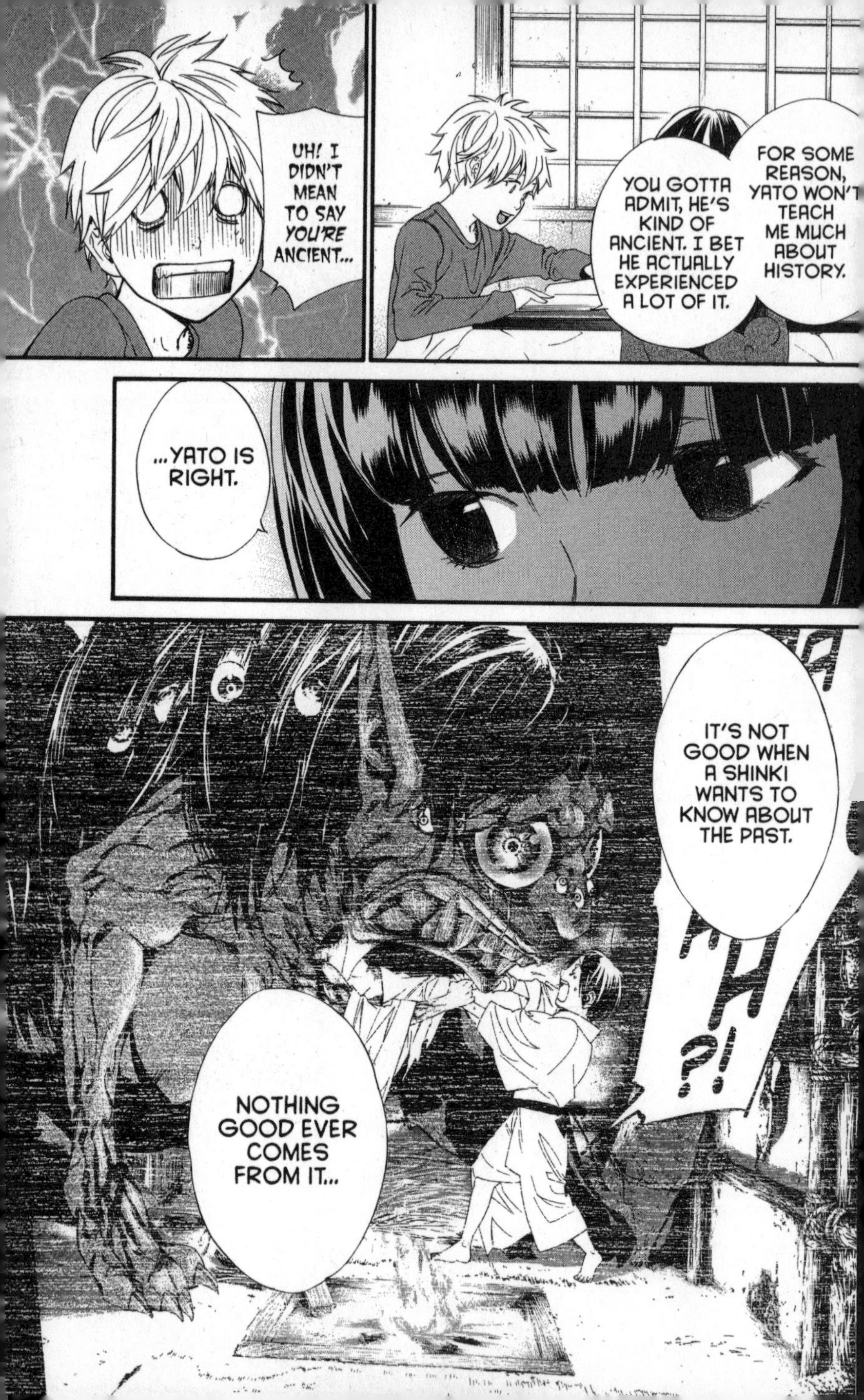
FOR SOME REASON, YATO WON'T TEACH ME MUCH ABOUT HISTORY.
YOU GOTTA ADMIT, HE'S KIND OF ANCIENT. I BET HE ACTUALLY EXPERIENCED A LOT OF IT.
UH! I DIDN'T MEAN TO SAY *YOU'RE* ANCIENT...
...YATO IS RIGHT.
IT'S NOT GOOD WHEN A SHINKI WANTS TO KNOW ABOUT THE PAST.
?!
NOTHING GOOD EVER COMES FROM IT...

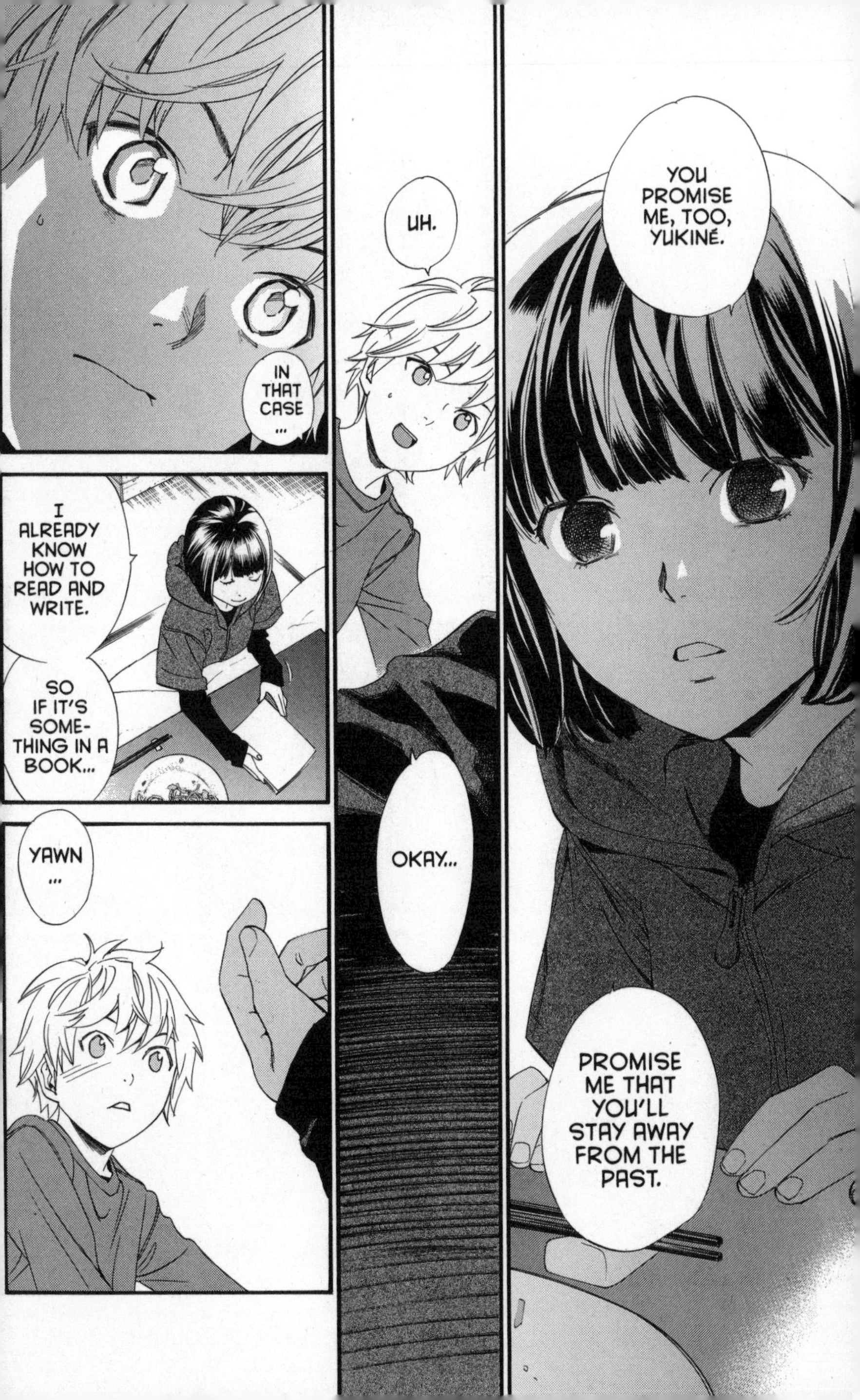
YOU PROMISE ME, TOO, YUKINÉ.
PROMISE ME THAT YOU'LL STAY AWAY FROM THE PAST.
UH.
OKAY...
IN THAT CASE...
I ALREADY KNOW HOW TO READ AND WRITE.
SO IF IT'S SOME-THING IN A BOOK...
YAWN...

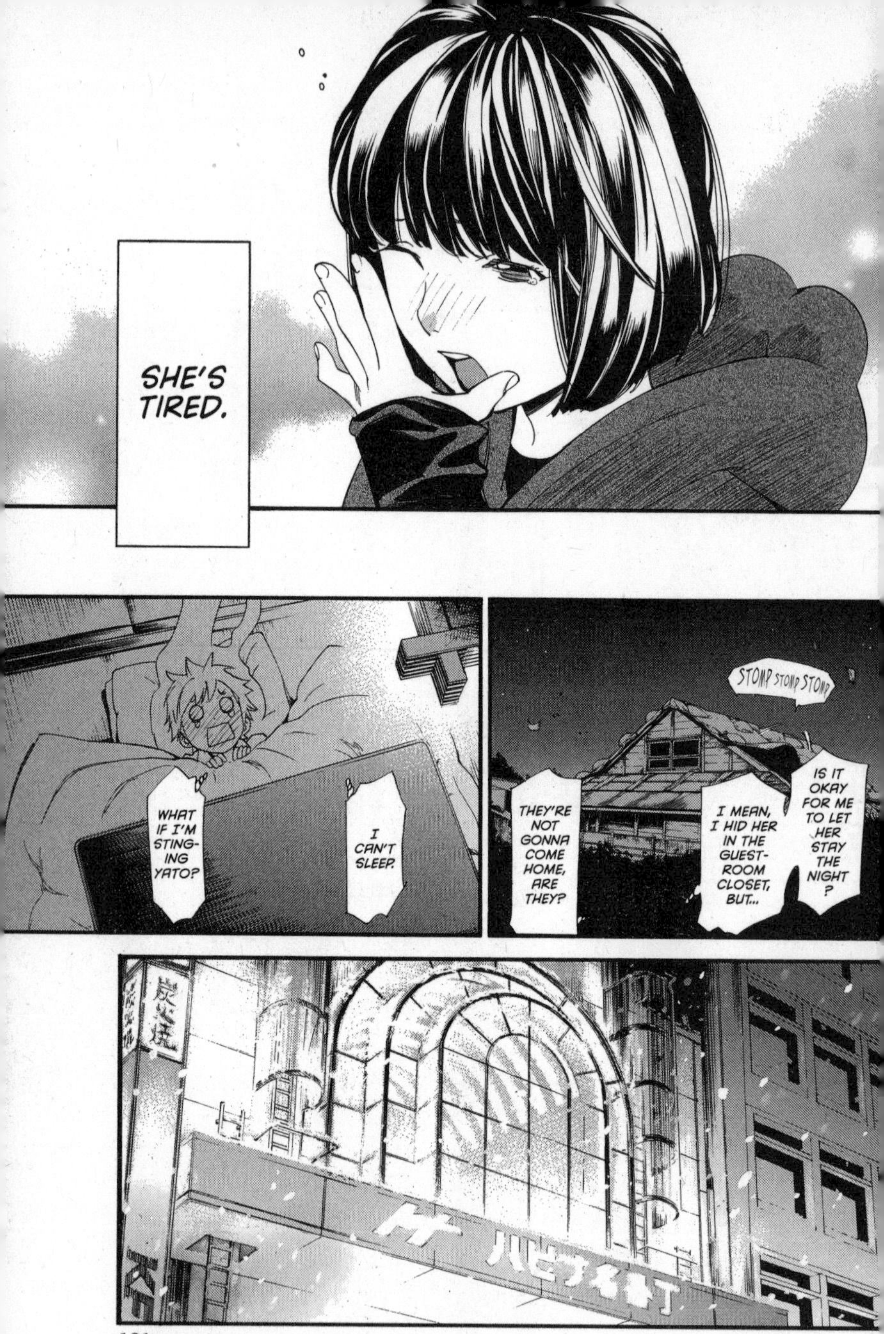
SHE'S TIRED.
STOMP STOMP STOMP
IS IT OKAY FOR ME TO LET HER STAY THE NIGHT?
I MEAN, I HID HER IN THE GUEST-ROOM CLOSET, BUT...
THEY'RE NOT GONNA COME HOME, ARE THEY?
I CAN'T SLEEP.
WHAT IF I'M STINGING YATO?

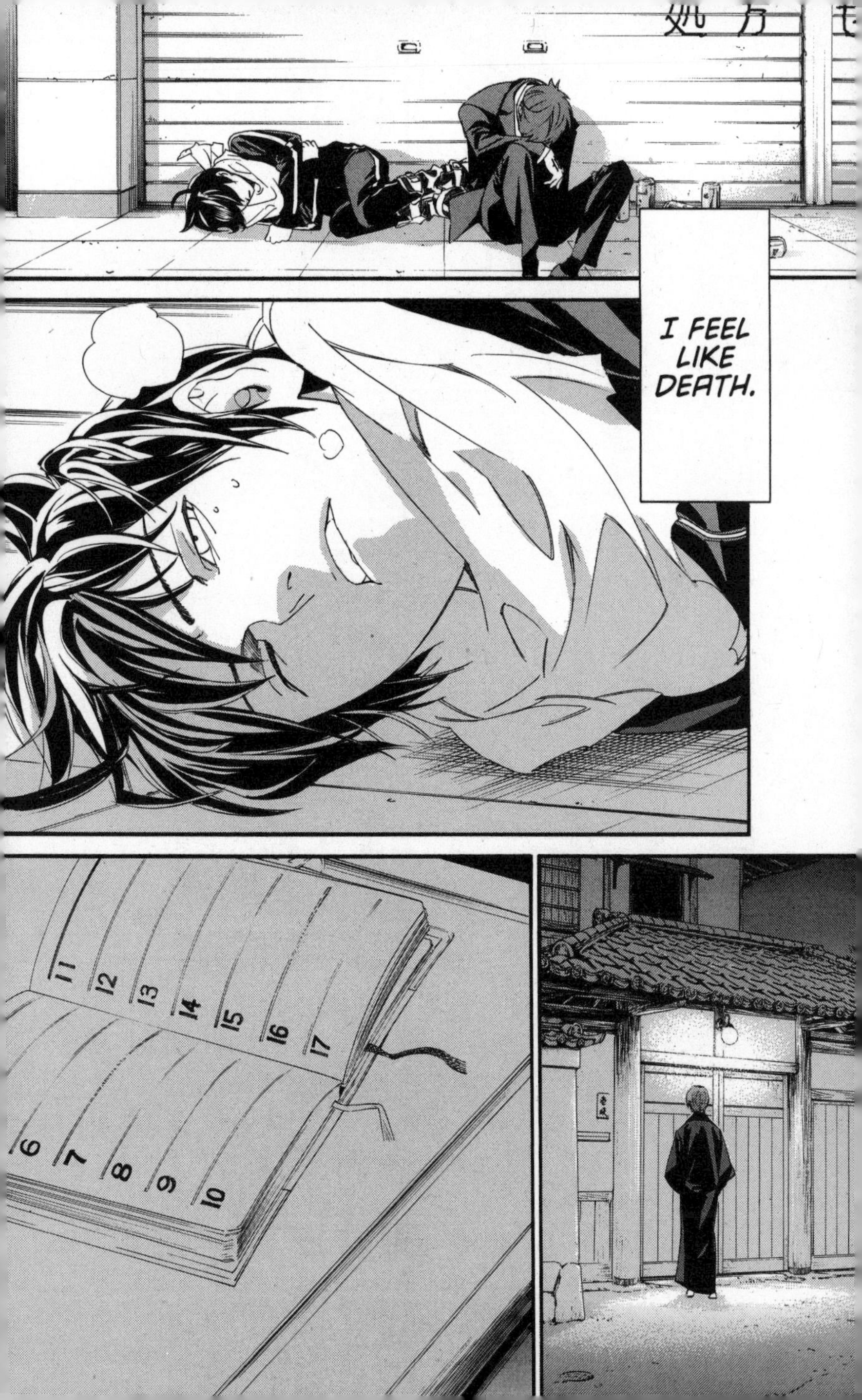
I FEEL LIKE DEATH.

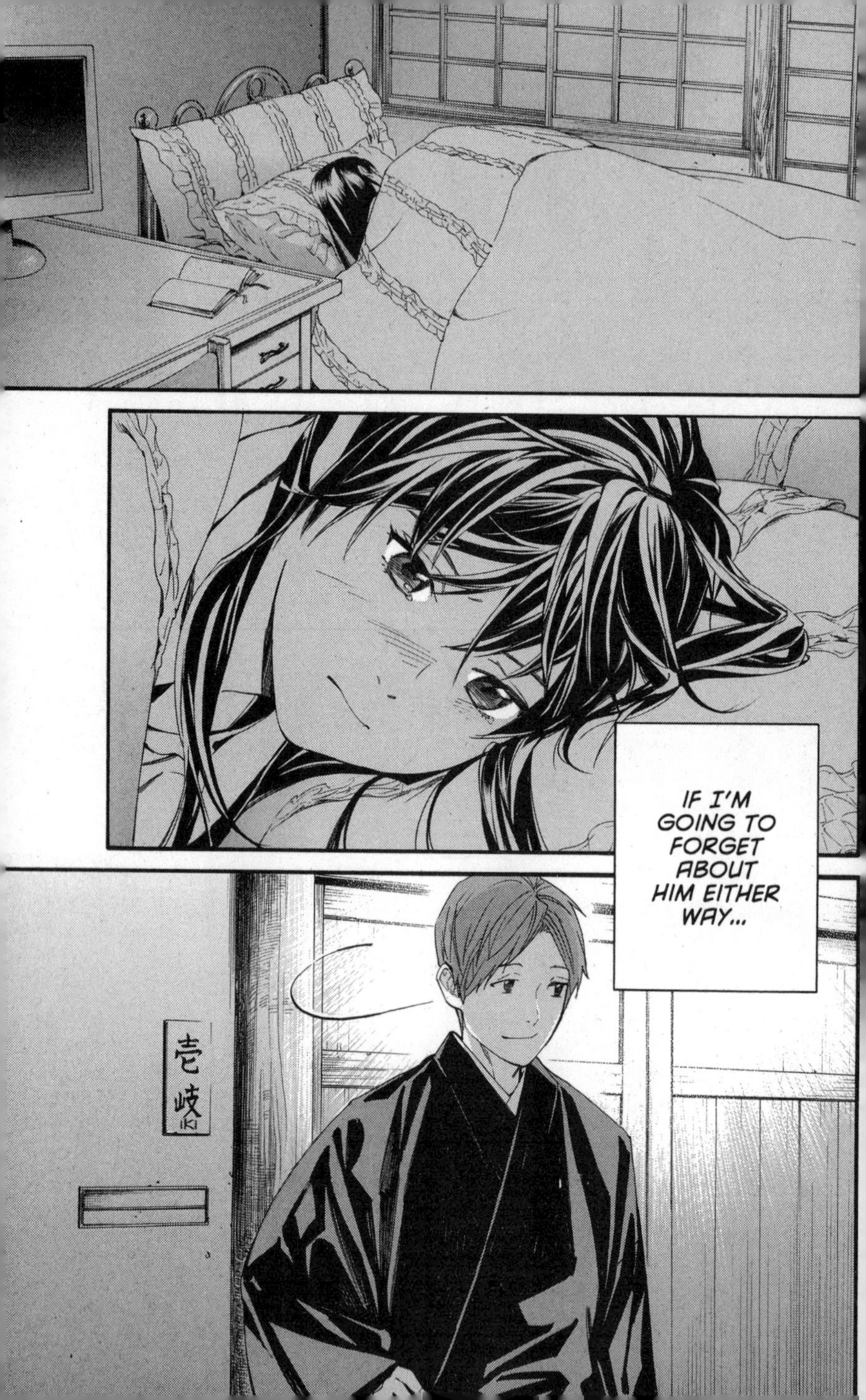
IF I'M GOING TO FORGET ABOUT HIM EITHER WAY...
壱岐

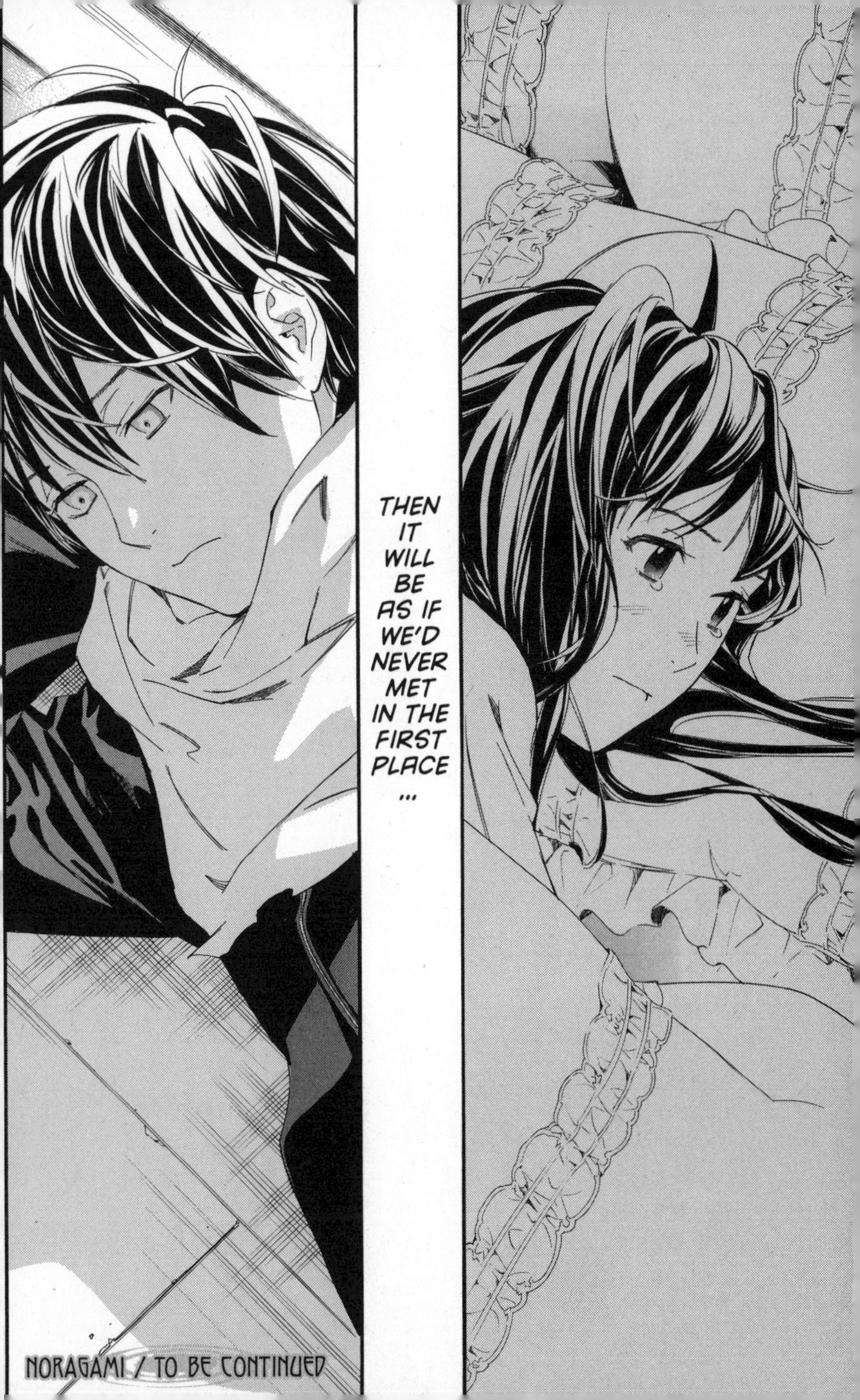
THEN IT WILL BE AS IF WE'D NEVER MET IN THE FIRST PLACE ...
NORAGAMI / TO BE CONTINUED

野

良

神

ATROCIOUS MANGA

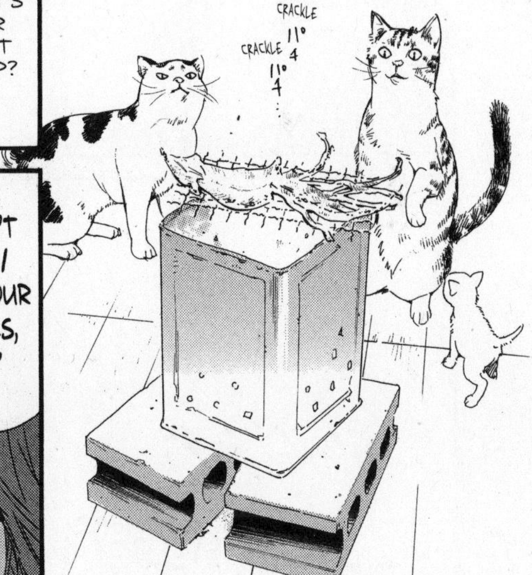
CRACKLE
CRACKLE

A DUO IS BORN

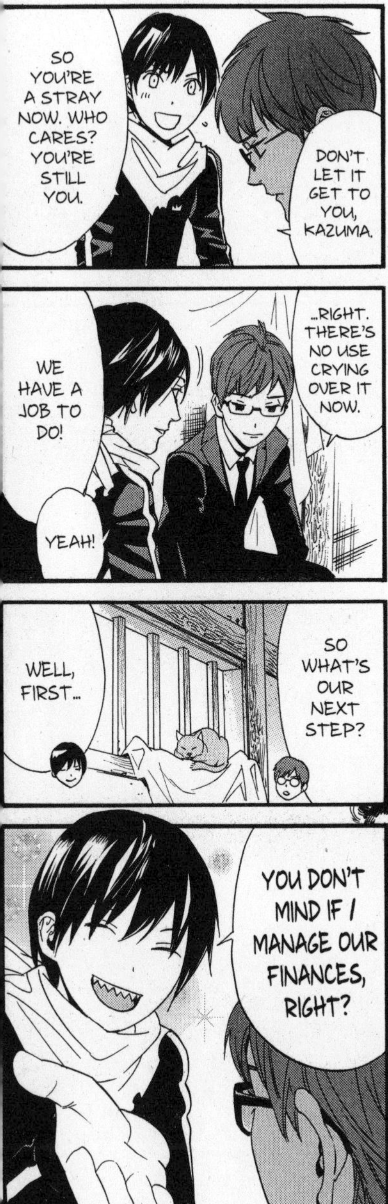
DON'T LET IT GET TO YOU, KAZUMA.
SO YOU'RE A STRAY NOW. WHO CARES? YOU'RE STILL YOU.
...RIGHT. THERE'S NO USE CRYING OVER IT NOW.
WE HAVE A JOB TO DO!
YEAH!
SO WHAT'S OUR NEXT STEP?
WELL, FIRST...
YOU DON'T MIND IF I MANAGE OUR FINANCES, RIGHT?

GETTING OFF ON THE RIGHT FOOT

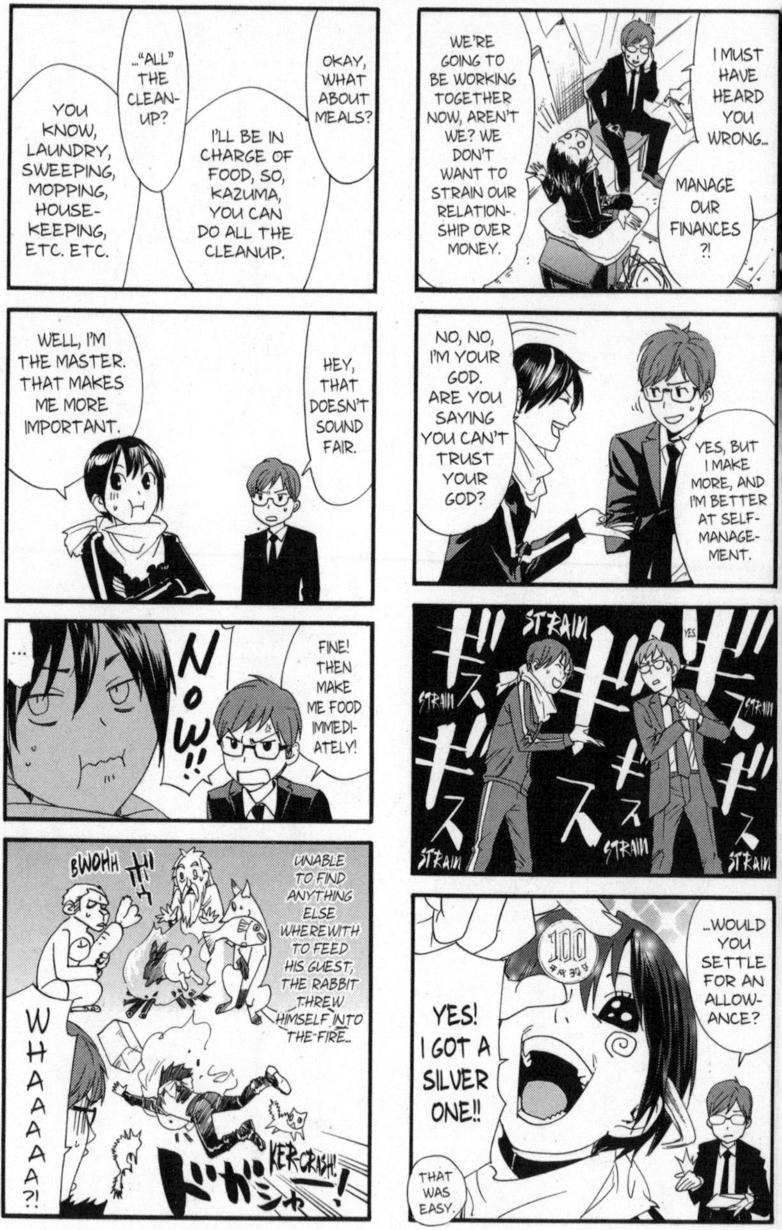
I MUST HAVE HEARD YOU WRONG...
WE'RE GOING TO BE WORKING TOGETHER NOW, AREN'T WE? WE DON'T WANT TO STRAIN OUR RELATIONSHIP OVER MONEY.
MANAGE OUR FINANCES?!
YES, BUT I MAKE MORE, AND I'M BETTER AT SELF-MANAGEMENT.
NO, NO, I'M YOUR GOD. ARE YOU SAYING YOU CAN'T TRUST YOUR GOD?
YES.
STRAIN
STRAIN
STRAIN
STRAIN
STRAIN
STRAIN
...WOULD YOU SETTLE FOR AN ALLOWANCE?
YES! I GOT A SILVER ONE!!
THAT WAS EASY.
OKAY, WHAT ABOUT MEALS?
I'LL BE IN CHARGE OF FOOD, SO, KAZUMA, YOU CAN DO ALL THE CLEANUP.
..."ALL" THE CLEAN-UP?
YOU KNOW, LAUNDRY, SWEEPING, MOPPING, HOUSEKEEPING, ETC. ETC.
HEY, THAT DOESN'T SOUND FAIR.
WELL, I'M THE MASTER. THAT MAKES ME MORE IMPORTANT.
FINE! THEN MAKE ME FOOD IMMEDIATELY!
NOW!!
...
UNABLE TO FIND ANYTHING ELSE WHEREWITH TO FEED HIS GUEST, THE RABBIT THREW HIMSELF INTO THE FIRE...
BWOHH
KER-CRASH!
WHAAAAAA?!

MASTER

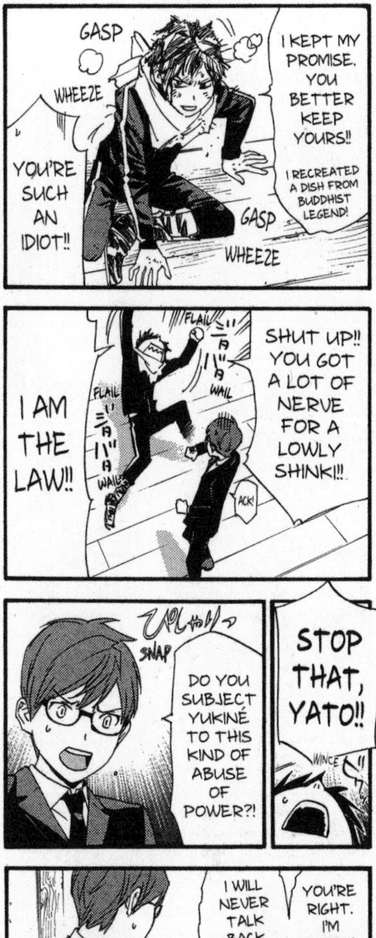
I KEPT MY PROMISE. YOU BETTER KEEP YOURS!!
I RECREATED A DISH FROM BUDDHIST LEGEND!
GASP
WHEEZE
YOU'RE SUCH AN IDIOT!!
GASP
WHEEZE
SHUT UP!! YOU GOT A LOT OF NERVE FOR A LOWLY SHINKI!!
FLAIL
WAIL
FLAIL
WAIL
ACK!
I AM THE LAW!!
STOP THAT, YATO!!
WINCE
SNAP
DO YOU SUBJECT YUKINÉ TO THIS KIND OF ABUSE OF POWER?!
YOU'RE RIGHT. I'M SORRY. PLEASE FORGIVE ME.
I WILL NEVER TALK BACK TO YOU AGAIN.
WRITTEN APOLOGY
SO YUKINÉ IS THE MASTER IN THAT RELATIONSHIP.
(AND A POWERFUL ONE AT THAT.)

"NÉ"

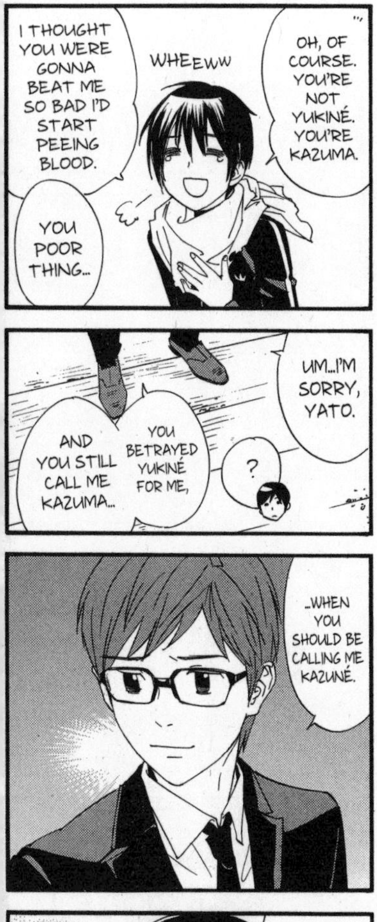
OH, OF COURSE. YOU'RE NOT YUKINÉ. YOU'RE KAZUMA.
WHEEWW
I THOUGHT YOU WERE GONNA BEAT ME SO BAD I'D START PEEING BLOOD.
YOU POOR THING...
UM...I'M SORRY, YATO.
?
YOU BETRAYED YUKINÉ FOR ME,
AND YOU STILL CALL ME KAZUMA...
...WHEN YOU SHOULD BE CALLING ME KAZUNÉ.
MEGANÉ* WOULD HAVE BEEN FUNNIER.
HEH HEH.
ONLY TO YOU.

*JAPANESE FOR "GLASSES" OR "FOUR-EYES"

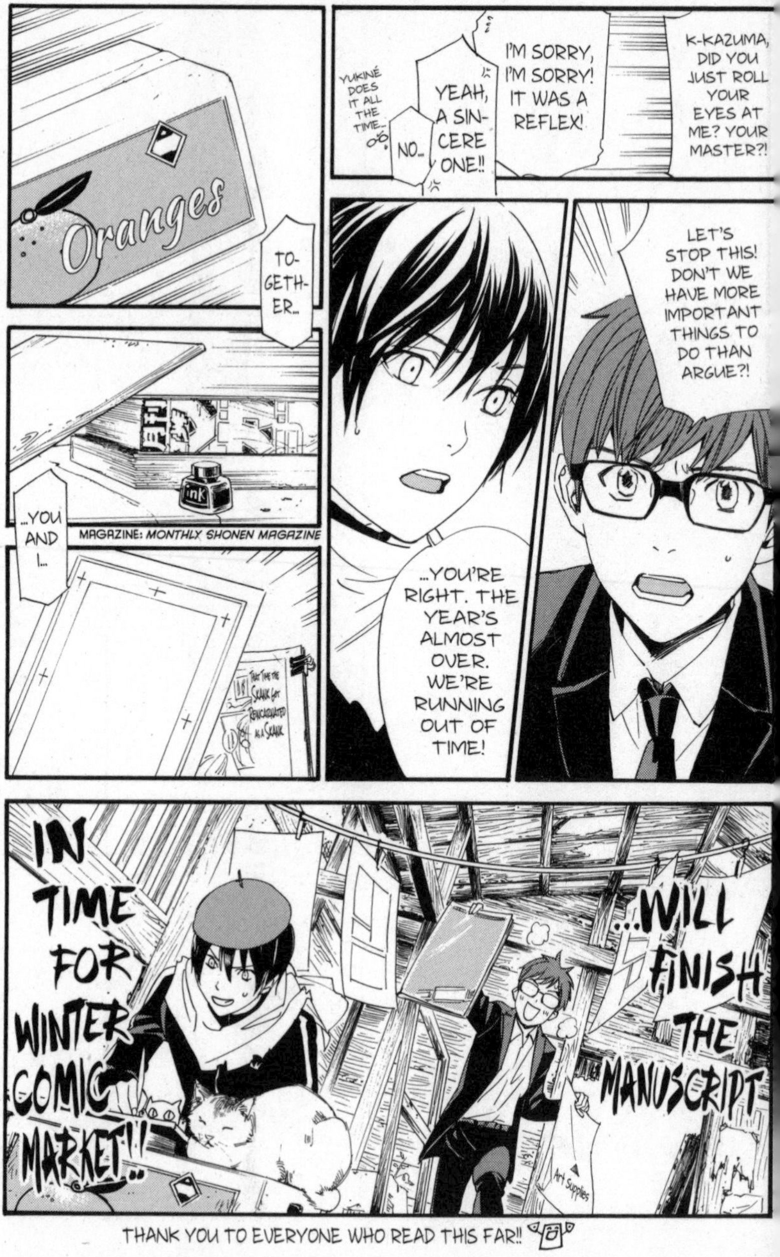
K-KAZUMA, DID YOU JUST ROLL YOUR EYES AT ME? YOUR MASTER?!
I'M SORRY, I'M SORRY! IT WAS A REFLEX!
YEAH, A SIN-CERE ONE!!
NO...
YUKINÉ DOES IT ALL THE TIME...
LET'S STOP THIS! DON'T WE HAVE MORE IMPORTANT THINGS TO DO THAN ARGUE?!
...YOU'RE RIGHT. THE YEAR'S ALMOST OVER. WE'RE RUNNING OUT OF TIME!
Oranges
TO-GETH-ER...
...YOU AND I...
ink
MAGAZINE: MONTHLY SHONEN MAGAZINE
That Time the Skank Got Reincarnated as a Skank
...WILL FINISH THE MANUSCRIPT
IN TIME FOR WINTER COMIC MARKET!!
Art Supplies

THANK YOU TO EVERYONE WHO READ THIS FAR!!

TRANSLATION NOTES

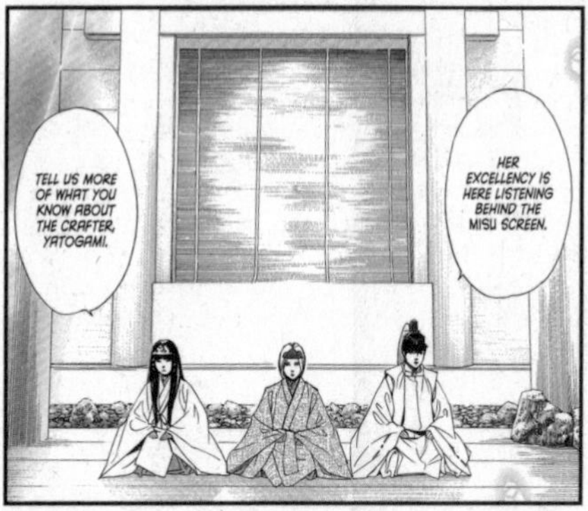
HER EXCELLENCY IS HERE LISTENING BEHIND THE MISU SCREEN.
TELL US MORE OF WHAT YOU KNOW ABOUT THE CRAFTER, YATOGAMI.

***Misu* screen, page 9**

The *misu* screen is the screen behind the Three Sacred Treasures. It is a type of *sudare*, or bamboo screen, that has been used in Japan for centuries to create shade, keep bugs away, block the wind, etc. The word *misu* is particularly used for a type of *sudare* that is used in palaces and shrines. People of high status kept their faces hidden from the view of others by staying behind these screens while speaking with visitors. Women in particular were known to follow this practice, as did men of high status. These screens are also used at shrines to shield the enshrined deity from public view. They marked a borderline between the more elevated individual and the "less worthy."

Gods of creation, page 14

"Creation" here is a translation of the Shinto term *musuhi*, which refers to the spiritual workings that lead to the creation of all things. More literally, Amaterasu describes the gods' role by saying that they tie together and create human beings, where the word for "tie" or "bind" is *musubi*, which is not only another pronunciation of *musuhi*, but is also used in the word for the matchmaking the gods were performing at the Divine Council. The creating (also *musuhi*) may be something the gods do personally, or something they did indirectly by putting two humans together who could make more humans.

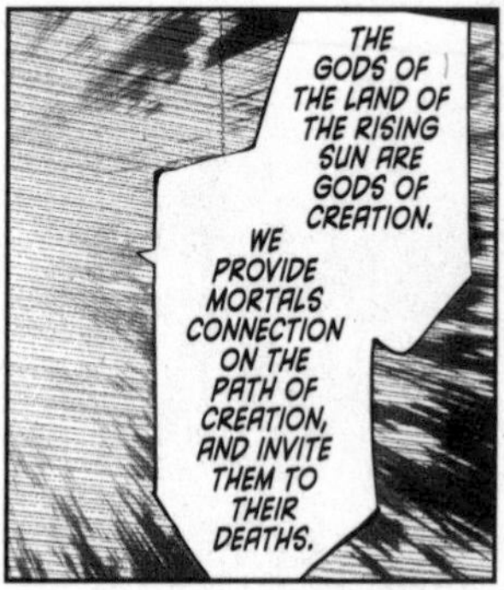
THE GODS OF THE LAND OF THE RISING SUN ARE GODS OF CREATION. WE PROVIDE MORTALS CONNECTION ON THE PATH OF CREATION, AND INVITE THEM TO THEIR DEATHS.

The Great Purification, page 17

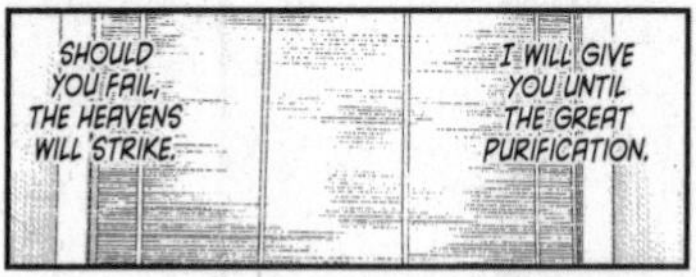
I WILL GIVE YOU UNTIL THE GREAT PURIFICATION.
SHOULD YOU FAIL, THE HEAVENS WILL STRIKE.

While Japanese temples and shrines perform purification rites on a daily basis, twice a year, a Great Purification is performed to cleanse the entire nation of its sins, disasters, and defilements. These Great Purification rituals are performed on June 30 and December 31. Naturally the ruler of the Heavens would want to resolve any potential disaster before this purification is to take place.

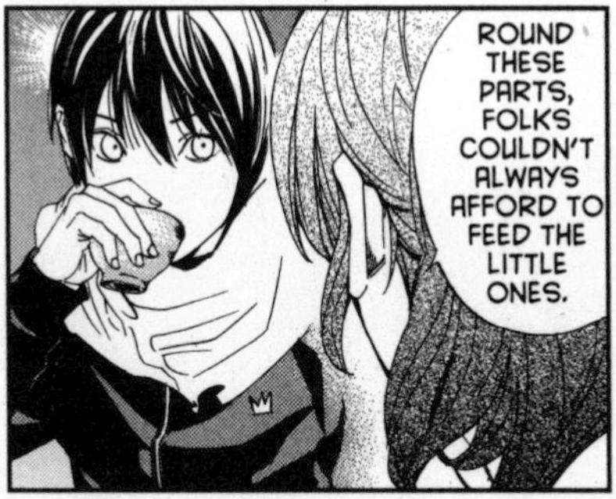
ROUND THESE PARTS, FOLKS COULDN'T ALWAYS AFFORD TO FEED THE LITTLE ONES.

Couldn't afford to feed the little ones, page 23

Here Arahabaki is referring to a sad practice called *kuchi-berashi*, meaning "to reduce the number of mouths (to feed)". In many cases, this involved sending young children off to be apprentices, so their employer could take on the burden of feeding them, but judging by the fact that these particular children are now "living" with Arahabaki, it is likely that they were simply left to die.

Better pack it in, page 39

When Nana says, "Better pack it in," the Japanese line was, "*Tsunda na*," meaning roughly, "It's really piled up." But in his current train of thought, Yato hears the phrase and immediately thinks of an alternate meaning, which is basically, "It's game over, dude." He then realizes that she was actually talking about the snow.

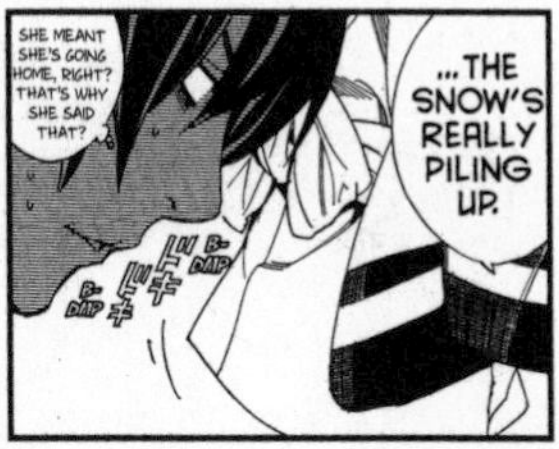
...THE SNOW'S REALLY PILING UP.
SHE MEANT SHE'S GOING HOME, RIGHT? THAT'S WHY SHE SAID THAT?

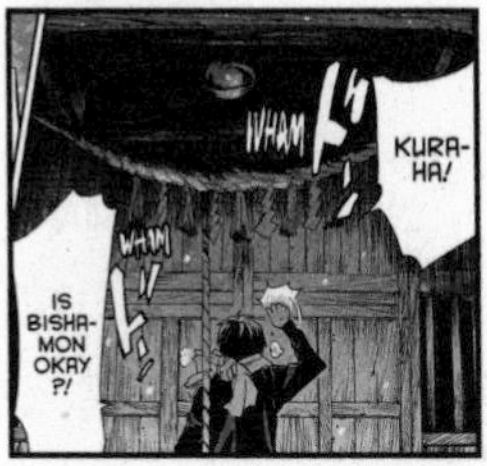
KURA-HA!
WHAM
WHAM
IS BISHA-MON OKAY ?!

Bishamon shrine, page 45

To get to Bishamon as soon as possible, Yato went to her closest shrine, near Arahabaki's home.

Kazuma's dark side, page 62

More literally, Yato says that Kazuma is about to "fall," using the same word for "fall" that has been used throughout the series to indicate a god or shinki becoming so corrupt that they perish or turn into an ayakashi. Because the English word "fall" wouldn't have come across that way without more context, the translators borrowed from another ominous phrase in this series, *ma ga sasu*, which they have translated in the past as "let his dark side get the better of him."

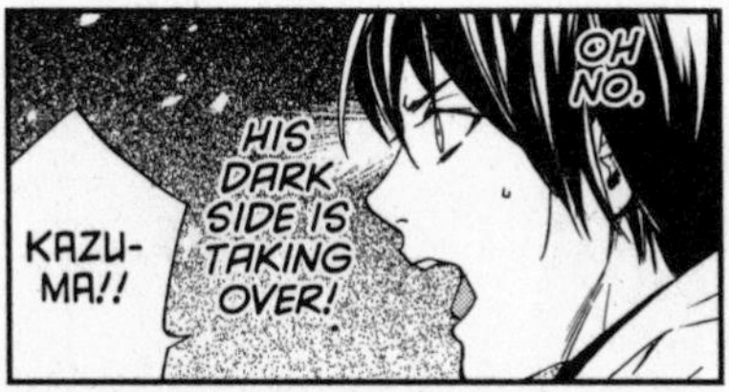
OH NO.
HIS DARK SIDE IS TAKING OVER!
KAZU-MA!!

THE FEMALE IS WITH THE STRAY, THIS ONE IS THE MALE.

THE TWO SNAKES WANT TO EAT EACH OTHER, SO THEY'LL GET AGITATED WHEN THEIR OPPOSITE IS NEARBY.

IT'S SOME-THING LIKE THE HEAVENS' BELLS.

Minonawa, page 79

Because this spell was invented before the use of written language, and the Japanese language has evolved much since then, it is difficult to ascertain the exact meaning of the spell. One meaning we can be sure of, however, is "snake rope," where the "rope (*nawa*)" is specifically used to capture and bind criminals.

Russian-roulette-style onigiri!

I THOUGHT I'D PUT A LITTLE EXTRA EFFORT INTO IT!?

OH... YOU SHOULDN'T HAVE...

Russian-roulette-style onigiri, page 95

Also known as rice balls, onigiri are snacks made of rice packed into a triangular shape and wrapped in seaweed. Often these rice balls have fillings such as pickled ume plums, salmon, etc. But there are no rules on what you can put inside a rice ball, and because the filling is surrounded in rice, unless you made the onigiri yourself, you never know what you're going to get. That being the case, it's easy to prank your friends by putting all kinds of unusual fillings inside.

Russian-roulette-style means that some of the fillings will be good, and some of the fillings will be...not good.

IT'S STUPID TO PRETEND WE'RE ALIVE.

It's stupid to pretend we're alive, page 99

The stray has been holding true to this policy for as long as we've known her. The reader may have noticed that when she wears her kimono, she wears it with the right side on top, and although this is normal for most feminine clothing in the West, in Japan, kimonos are worn with the left side on top regardless of the wearer's gender. ...At least, that's how living people wear their kimonos. In the land of the dead, people do things the opposite way, so dead people wear their kimono with the right side on top.

The headband the stray wears is another outward expression of the fact that she is dead. The readers may remember that this particular piece of the stray's ensemble has been referred to as a "ghostly crown." This triangle headband is called a *tenkan* (meaning "crown"), and is wrapped around the forehead of the deceased to prepare their body to go to their final resting place. The prevailing theory for the reason behind this practice is that, according to Buddhist beliefs, the next stop after death is to see Enma, the king of hell. It is very rude not to wear a crown in Enma's presence, and the king of hell is not someone you would want to offend, especially not when he controls your destiny in the afterlife.

Yato was my sidekick, page 100

To be precise, the stray describes young Yato as her *otôto-bun*, or "little brother part," meaning he took on the role of her little brother, but less in a familial capacity and more in an organizational one. For example, a low-level leader in the yakuza may have a gang of men at his command that all call him *aniki*, or "older brother," and they would be his *otôto-bun*.

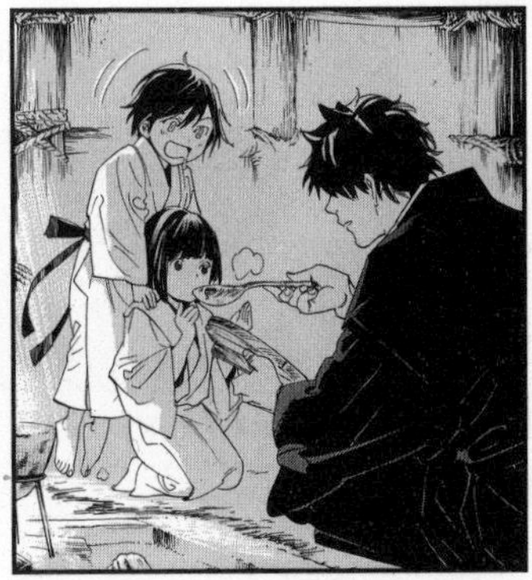

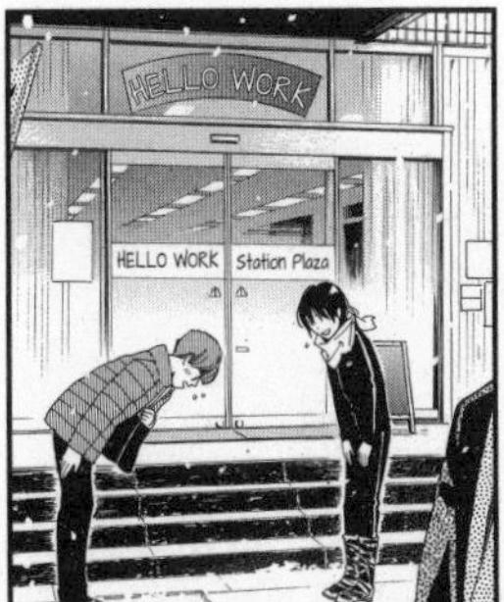
HELLO WORK
HELLO WORK
Station Plaza

Hello Work, page 108

Hello Work is the more common name for the Japanese government's Employment Service Center, a place people can go to find jobs and otherwise get help in getting hired. What better place for a god in need of a shinki to find a shinki in need of a job?

Stinky shinki, page 120

As the reader may have guessed, in the original Japanese text, this woman did not mistake the word shinki for "stinky." Instead, she heard the word sunki, short for *sunki-zuke*, or pickled turnip.

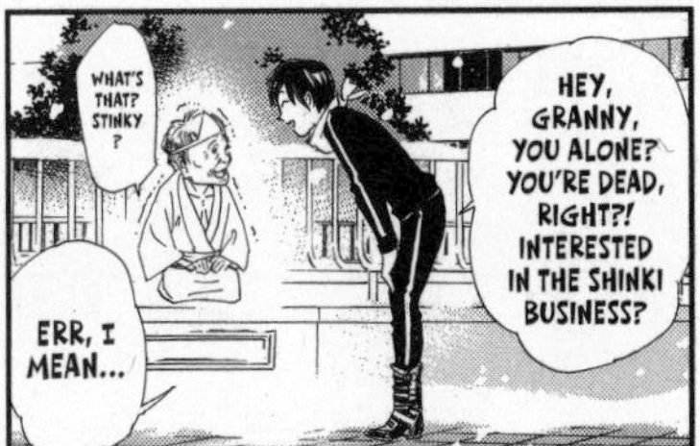
HEY, GRANNY, YOU ALONE? YOU'RE DEAD, RIGHT?! INTERESTED IN THE SHINKI BUSINESS?
WHAT'S THAT? STINKY?
ERR, I MEAN...

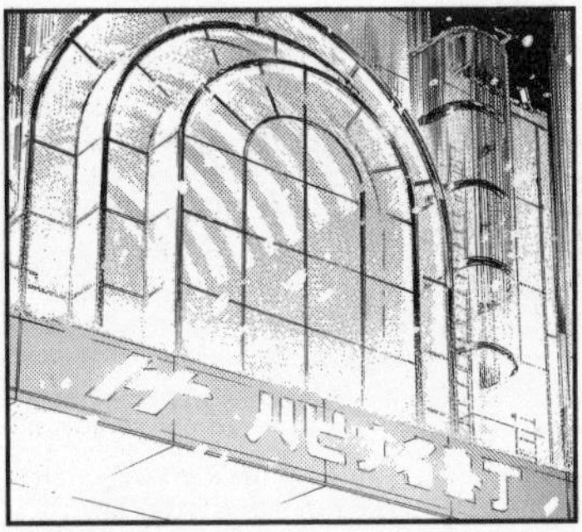

Hapina Nakakechô, page 143

Hapina Nakakechô is a shopping arcade right by Sendai station. From this we know that Yato has not yet left Japan's frozen north.

Why Kazu, page 149
The Japanese character for *kazu* used here is not the same *kazu* as in Kazuma—Kazuma's *kazu means* "omen." Kazuné's *kazu*, on the other hand, means "calendar," and can refer to the system of breaking down the flow of time into days, months, years, etc., or it can refer to a physical object that records these units of time. It may also be worth noting that the kanji character for Kazuné's *kazu* (暦) is made up of several parts, including most of the character for the *ma* (麻) that can be found in Kazuma.

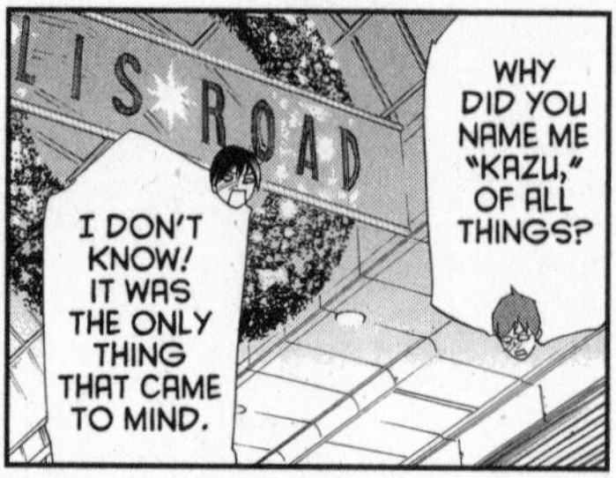

WHY DID YOU NAME ME "KAZU," OF ALL THINGS?
I DON'T KNOW! IT WAS THE ONLY THING THAT CAME TO MIND.

A wealthy salt merchant, page 152
During the Edo Period in which Kiyotsugu was born, the producers of salt were not allowed to sell their product directly to the public, so any and all salt sales went through a salt merchant, who naturally took his own cut of the profits. Because salt and salt-based seasonings were in high demand during this period, the phrase "wealthy salt merchant" is almost redundant.
Salt was also used traditionally for purification, which may be why the salt merchant included *kiyo* (pure) in his son's name. The *tsugu* means "subsequent," and is fitting either for a second son or a successor to the family fortune.

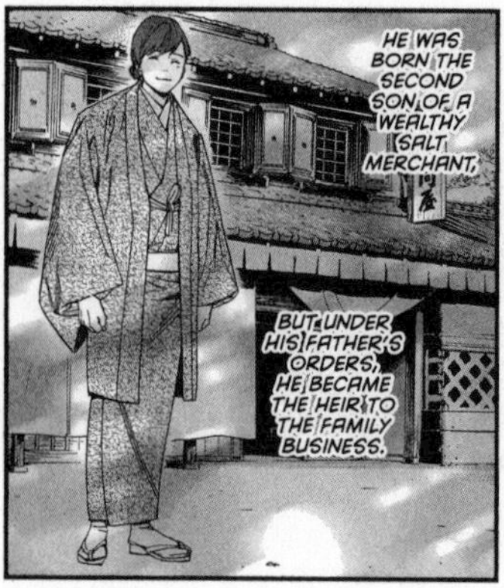

HE WAS BORN THE SECOND SON OF A WEALTHY SALT MERCHANT,
BUT UNDER HIS FATHER'S ORDERS, HE BECAME THE HEIR TO THE FAMILY BUSINESS.

19 at best, page 155
Specifically, Yato says that the kid is 19 by his *kazoe* age. *Kazoe* is an age-reckoning system in which everyone is said to be one year old at birth. In other words, he would be 18 by the normal reckoning, and 19 if we're charitable enough to give him an extra year. Either way, the age of majority (and the legal drinking age) in Japan is 20.

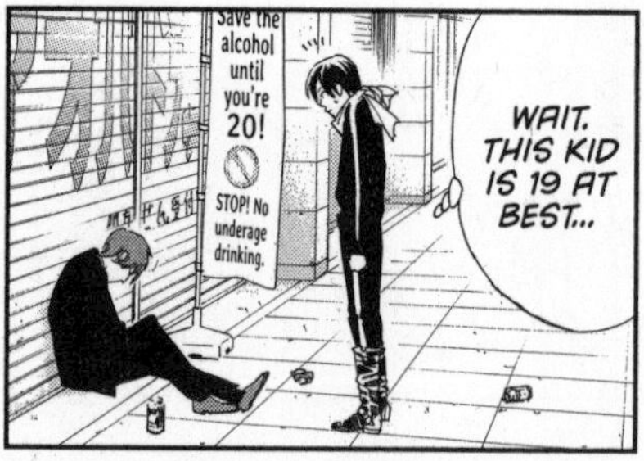

WAIT. THIS KID IS 19 AT BEST...
Save the alcohol until you're 20!
STOP! No underage drinking.

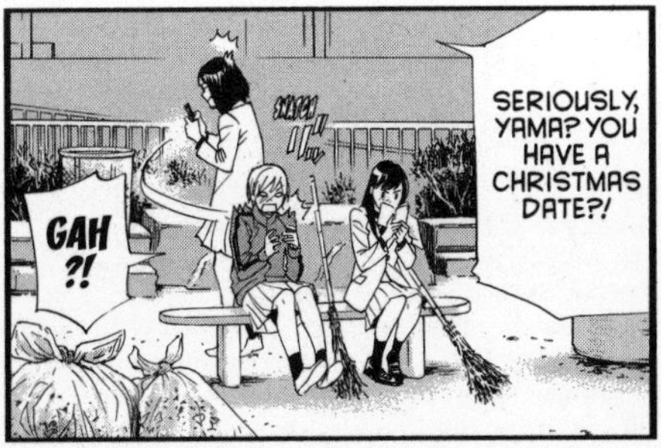
SERIOUSLY, YAMA? YOU HAVE A CHRISTMAS DATE?!
GAH ?!

Christmas date, page 159

While in many homes in the United States, Christmas is a time for families to come together, that had already been a New Year's tradition in Japan by the time Christmas was adopted as a holiday there. So while Christmas is still a fun time for kids to get presents from Santa, in general, the holiday is more of a time to get together with friends, or it's a time to get together with your significant other. In fact, Christmas is often treated in Japan the way Valentine's Day is treated in the U.S.

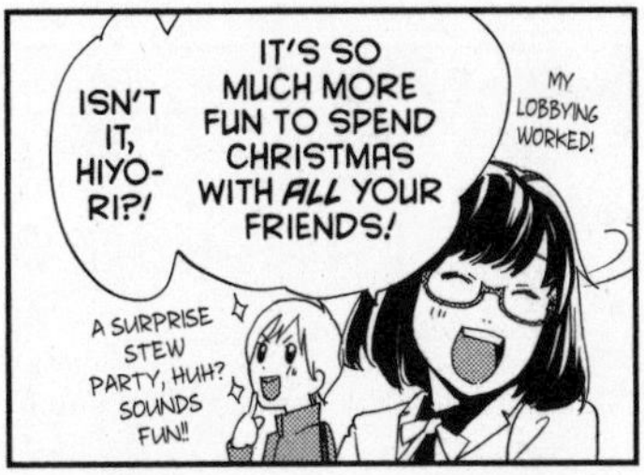
MY LOBBYING WORKED!
IT'S SO MUCH MORE FUN TO SPEND CHRISTMAS WITH ALL YOUR FRIENDS!
ISN'T IT, HIYO-RI?!
A SURPRISE STEW PARTY, HUH? SOUNDS FUN!!

Surprise stew, page 160

Yami nabe, literally "dark pot," is a potluck in the truest sense. People bring ingredients to include in a hot pot stew, without telling anyone else what they have brought. The resulting hot pot dish is sure to have surprising results.

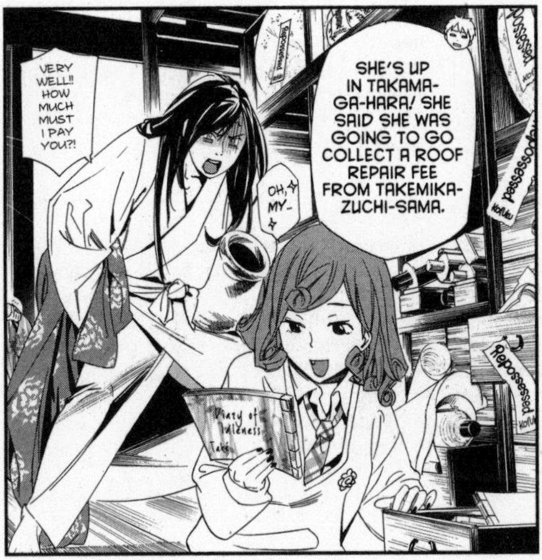
SHE'S UP IN TAKAMA-GA-HARA! SHE SAID SHE WAS GOING TO GO COLLECT A ROOF REPAIR FEE FROM TAKEMIKA-ZUCHI-SAMA.
VERY WELL!! HOW MUCH MUST I PAY YOU?!
OH, MY...
Diary of Idleness

Diary of Idleness, page 172

The title of Takemikazuchi's diary (*Tsurezure Nikki* in Japanese) may or may not have been inspired by *Essays in Idleness (Tsurezure-Gusa)*, a series of essays written by the monk Yoshida Kenkô in the fourteenth century. Much like a diary, Kenkô writes about anything from Buddhist truths such as the impermanence of life, to the beauty of nature, to amusing stories from his life.

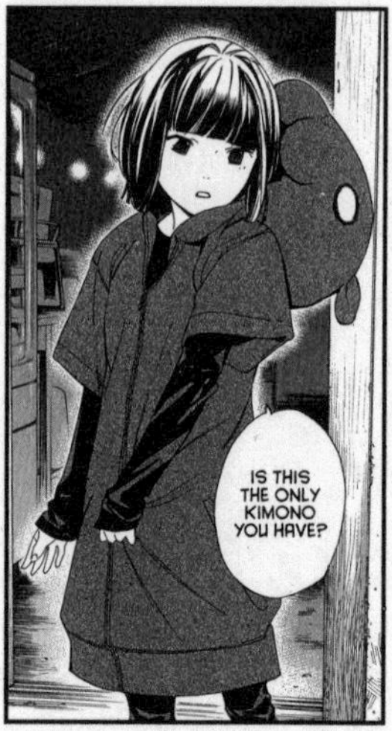
IS THIS THE ONLY KIMONO YOU HAVE?

The only kimono you have?, page 176
Even in Japan, the word *kimono* is mostly used to refer to traditional Japanese clothing, but it literally means "thing to wear." The line could have been translated as, "Is this the only thing to wear?", but because the stray has generally only worn traditional Japanese clothing, it makes sense that that would be her default term for clothes.

The rabbit threw himself into the fire, page 187
Yato is reenacting a scene from one of the lives of Buddha. When Buddha was reincarnated as a rabbit, he and his friends lived in a forest where the custom was to make food offerings to anyone who passed through. The rabbit realized he had no food to offer guests, and determined to offer his own flesh as meat instead. The first traveler to come to the forest after the decision was made turned out to be Sakra, the ruler of Heaven, and when the rabbit followed through on his offering without hesitation, Sakra was so touched by his virtue, that he drew an image of the rabbit on the moon for all to see.

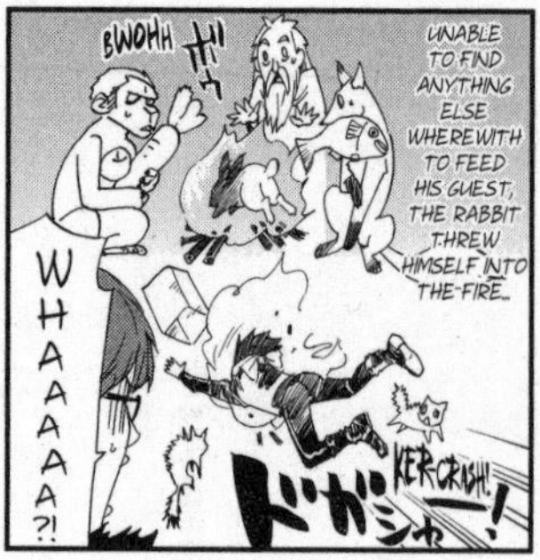
UNABLE TO FIND ANYTHING ELSE WHEREWITH TO FEED HIS GUEST, THE RABBIT THREW HIMSELF INTO THE FIRE...
BWOHH
WHAAAAA?!
KER-CRASH!
ドガシャー!

Did you roll your eyes at me?, page 189

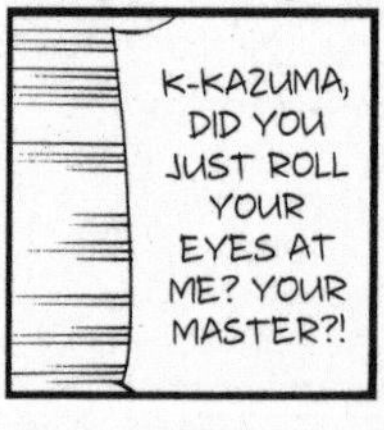
K-KAZUMA, DID YOU JUST ROLL YOUR EYES AT ME? YOUR MASTER?!

In the original Japanese, Yato suggests a joke to Kazuma, and Kazuma says it would only be funny to "you," using the second-person pronoun *omae*. Not only is it more polite to use someone's name rather than a pronoun when addressing someone in Japanese, but *omae* is one of the less respectful ways to say "you." On the next page, Yato calls him out on it, pointing out that that is no way to speak to his master, and Kazuma can't help but think about the unfairness of this lecture, as Yukiné often addresses Yato with the impolite *omae*.

野 N O R A 良 G A M I 神

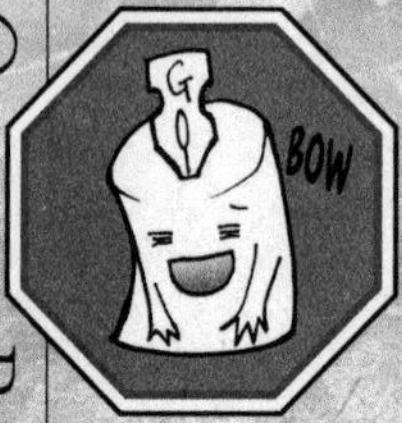
BOW

After 10 years here,
I finally realized that
I can see Mt. Fuji
from where I live.
I was sure it was the
roof of some building
a few houses down.

Adachitoka

‹ KAMOME ›
SHIRAHAMA

Witch Hat Atelier

A magical manga
adventure for
fans of Disney
and Studio
Ghibli!

The magical adventure that took Japan by storm is finally here, from acclaimed DC and Marvel cover artist Kamome Shirahama!

In a world where everyone takes wonders like magic spells
and dragons for granted, Coco is a girl with a simple dream:
She wants to be a witch. But everybody knows magicians
are born, not made, and Coco was not born with a gift for
magic. Resigned to her un-magical life, Coco is about to
give up on her dream to become a witch...until the day
she meets Qifrey, a mysterious, traveling magician. After
secretly seeing Qifrey perform magic in a way she's never
seen before, Coco soon learns what everybody "knows"
might not be the truth, and discovers that her magical
dream may not be as far away as it may seem...

KC
KODANSHA
COMICS

Magus of the Library

Mitsu Izumi

MITSU IZUMI'S STUNNING ARTWORK BRINGS A FANTASTICAL LITERARY ADVENTURE TO LUSH, THRILLING LIFE!

Young Theo adores books, but the prejudice and hatred of his village keeps them ever out of his reach. Then one day, he chances to meet Sedona, a traveling librarian who works for the great library of Aftzaak, City of Books, and his life changes forever...

Acclaimed screenwriter and director Mari Okada (*Maquia, anohana*) teams up with manga artist Nao Emoto (*Forget Me Not*) in this moving, funny, so-true-it's-embarrassing coming-of-age series!

When Kazusa enters high school, she joins the Literature Club, and leaps from reading innocent fiction to diving into the literary classics. But these novels are a bit more... *adult* than she was prepared for. Between euphemisms like fresh dewy grass and pork stew, crushing on the boy next door, and knowing you want to do that *one thing* before you die—discovering your budding sexuality is no easy feat! As if puberty wasn't awkward enough, the club consists of a brooding writer, the prettiest girl in school, an agreeable comrade, and an outspoken prude. Fumbling over their own discomforts, these five teens get thrown into chaos over three little letters: S...E...X...!

Anime coming soon!

O Maidens in your Savage Season

Mari Okada   Nao Emoto

EDENS ZERO
エデンズゼロ

HIRO MASHIMA IS BACK! JOIN THE CREATOR OF *FAIRY TAIL* AS HE TAKES TO THE STARS FOR ANOTHER THRILLING SAGA!

A high-flying space adventure! All the steadfast friendship and wild fighting you've been waiting for...IN SPACE!

At Granbell Kingdom, an abandoned amusement park, Shiki has lived his entire life among machines. But one day, Rebecca and her cat companion Happy appear at the park's front gates. Little do these newcomers know that this is the first human contact Granbell has had in a hundred years! As Shiki stumbles his way into making new friends, his former neighbors stir at an opportunity for a robo-rebellion... And when his old homeland becomes too dangerous, Shiki must join Rebecca and Happy on their spaceship and escape into the boundless cosmos.

A dark and sexy body-horror action manga perfect for fans of *Prison Scho* and *High School of the Dead*!

Shuichi Kagaya is a smart kid, and most smart kids his age would be thinking about college. Shuichi is also a monster, and he's smart enough to know that monsters don't go to college. But after he uses his monstrous form to save his classmate Claire Aoki, it doesn't matter what his plans for the future were, because he's not the one making the decisions anymore. Now that the seductive, sadistic Claire knows Shuichi's secret, she's got her own ideas about what a monster is good for—because he's not the first monster she's met...

GLEIPNIR

"You and me together...we would be unstoppable."

I'M STANDING ON A MILLION LIVES

By
Akinari Nao

Original Story by
Naoki Yamakawa

Yusuke Yotsuya doesn't care about getting into high school—he just wants to get back home to his game and away from other people. But when he suddenly finds himself in a real-life fantasy game alongside his two gorgeous classmates, he discovers a new world of possibility and excitement. Despite a rough start, Yusuke and his friend fight to level up and clear the challenges set before them by a mysterious figure from the future, but before long, they find that they're not just battling for their own lives, but for the lives of millions.